AUTO DICTIONARY

AUTO DICTIONARY

By John Edwards
Edited by John Lawlor

HPBooks
a division of
PRICE STERN SLOAN
Los Angeles

Library of Congress Cataloging-in-Publication Data

Edwards, John 1948-
Automotive dictionary : a complete glossary of terms for automotive enthusiasts, racers & engineers / by John Edwards; edited by John Lawlor.
p. cm.
Includes bibliographical references.
ISBN 1-55788-067-0 (Hardcover)
ISBN 1-55788-056-5 (Pbk.)
1. Automobiles—Dictionaries. 2. Automobiles, Racing—-Dictionaries. I. Lawlor, John, 1932- . II. Title.
TL9.E33 1993
629.2'03—dc20 92-23954
CIP

Published by HPBooks
a division of Price Stern Sloan, Inc.
11150 Olympic Boulevard
Los Angeles, California 90064

10 9 8 7 6 5 4 3 2

Interior photos and illustrations by Michael Lutfy, Dave Emanuel, Tom Monroe, Larry Shepard, Fred Puhn, David Vizard and Ron Fournier

NOTICE: The information in this book is true and complete to the best of our knowledge. All recommendations on parts and procedures are made without any guarantees on the part of the author or Price Stern Sloan. Tampering with or altering any emissions-control device, or modifying an emissions-controlled vehicle is in violation of federal regulations. Author and publisher disclaim all liability incurred in connection with the use of this information.
This book is printed on acid-free paper.

ABOUT THE AUTHOR

JOHN EDWARDS

John Edwards became a professional automotive mechanic while attending college. As a mechanic he worked primarily on Italian cars. In 1971, he became the service manager of Tom Hubert Imports, a Fiat dealership in the Los Angeles area.

During the 1970s he developed a keen interest in SCCA production race cars and began designing and building his own pistons, headers, oil pans, intake manifolds and various other racing products. John also spent a period of time at Keith Black Racing Engines working as a fabricator and machinist. In 1976 he moved to Ventura, California and worked several years as an automotive and diesel engine machinist. In 1979 he opened JO/EL Engineering, an engine machine shop, in Santa Paula, California.

John started his teaching career in 1984 and is currently teaching Automotive Engine Rebuilding and Machine Tool Technology classes for the Ventura County Superintendent of Schools, Regional Occupational Program in Oxnard, California. In his spare time, John enjoys keeping his hands in the racing business. He still continues to build Fiat racing parts and he also writes technical articles for a variety of automotive publications. John Edwards lives in Ventura, California with his wife, Elaine.

ABOUT THE EDITOR

Photo by Chan Bush

JOHN LAWLOR

John Lawlor has been an automobile enthusiast since boyhood. He started writing about cars while still in college with a weekly motoring column in the campus newspaper at Loyola Marymount University in Los Angeles, California.

He became a professional journalist in the late 1950s, when he went to work for Petersen Publishing, where he became the senior editor of *Motor Trend* and later, an editor in the firm's book division.

During the 1960s, he moved to Bond Publishing Company, where he was an assistant editor of *Car Life* and a contributor to the parent magazine, *Road & Track*. He has also served as the managing editor of *Popular Hot Rodding* and *Speed Age* magazines.

In 1967, he served as public relations director for the Inaugural Mexican 1000, the first off-road race down Mexico's Baja California peninsula. His efforts resulted in more event coverage by motor enthusiasts' magazines than any previous motorsport event of any kind. As a result, in 1979 Lawlor became the first, and as of this writing, only journalist or publicist elected to the Off-Road Hall of Fame, sponsored by the Specialty Equipment Market Association (SEMA). In 1989, he was similarly honored as one of the first ten inductees into the *Dune Buggies* and *Hot VWs Magazine* Hall of Fame.

He is the author of three books: *How to Talk Car*, a dictionary of automotive terms and slang, published by Topaz/Felsen Books; *Inside Full-Time Four-Wheel Drive*, a guide to the New Process 203 system published by Chrysler in the mid-70s; and the *Auto Math Handbook,* a basic explanation of the mathematical theories, equations and formulas for automotive enthusiasts, published by HPBooks.

After a tenure as an editor for *Trailer Life* and *MotorHome* magazines, John is currently a full-time freelance automotive writer and is working on another HPBook. He lives in Studio City, California.

INTRODUCTION

A dictionary of any type is supposed to be the "definitive" resource on the subject it pertains to. When John Edwards first approached me with the idea to do an automotive dictionary, I realized that we had the opportunity to do just that on the subject of all things automotive. John first began developing the idea while teaching classes to automotive students, most of whom were ESL (English as a Second Language), and had trouble enough understanding plain English, let alone complex engineering terms. John would therefore assign a list of 8 words per day to his students, requiring that they compile them in a notebook. After several years, he realized he had the basis for a dictionary, which brought him to HPBooks.

Of course, this has been done before, but perhaps never quite with the same result you now have in your hands. Many of the previous dictionaries or published glossaries have focused on a single aspect, say engineering or a particular form of motorsports; but our goal was to cover as much ground as possible, from engineering to motorsport to hot rodding—and all the areas in between. To achieve this goal, I enlisted the help of John Lawlor, who once wrote a popular dictionary entitled *How to Talk Car*. In addition, John's 35 years experience as an automotive journalist, and his ability to translate complex terms into simple definitions (as illustrated in his HPBooks', *Auto Math Handbook*) made him uniquely qualified to carry out this daunting task.

And so began a year-long quest for the racing jargon, hot rodding nomenclature, street slang and hard-core engineering terms that are used in various parts of the automotive industry on a daily basis. Top automotive writers, editors, technicians, enthusiasts and racers were polled, and volumes of books and magazines were studied, until we had doubled the size of the original manuscript. After a while, we realized we couldn't make the *Auto Dictionary* all things to all people. Given the vast diversity of the automotive world, it became obvious that we would not be able to include every word ever uttered by every enthusiast or invented by every engineer. Many terms are regionally, not universally, understood; what gets a nod of recognition from a California hot rodder will draw a blank stare from one in the Midwest or South, and vice versa. So what we decided to do early on, was include terms that are universally understood, accepted and recognized, ones that have survived throughout the years to become a permanent entry in the automotive lexicon.

You'll also realize we had to add a few more restrictions. For instance, you won't find specific model names (Camaro, or Mustang) or personalities or historical automotive figures, unless they are used within the context of another definition. Nicknames, such as "the Snake" (Don Prudhomme), "Big Daddy"

ACKNOWLEDGEMENTS

Although the *Auto Dictionary* started out as a small list of words I compiled for my students, it has grown to become much more than that, thanks in large part to the following people:

Jerry Rothman and Peter Vack, an author in his own right, provided encouragement and advice as the project began to grow. My mentor, John Van Zant, was always there with words of encouragement.

Dean Batchelor, a former Bonneville competitor and *Road & Track* editor; Chris Hemer, an automotive author and editor for Argus Publishers; Spence Murray, a former editor of *Rod & Custom*; Carl Weir, a 30-year veteran professional mechanic; and Dick Wells, a former NHRA and SEMA executive—all of them provided detailed technical term analyses in the preparation of this book. Noted technical writer and fellow HP author Dave Emanuel, was kind enough to supply about two dozen of his photos for use in this book.

John Lawlor handled the enormous task of editing the original materials with superb acumen. Without John's numerous contributions, this book would not be as extensive as it is. Thank you, mother hen!

All the people at Price Stern Sloan have been wonderful to work with since day one. Michael Lutfy, the Automotive Editorial Director of HPBooks, has made my dream a reality. His vision and guidance through this project have been first class. Many of the photographs in this book were taken by Michael.

Finally, I want to thank my wife, Elaine, for her support and patience throughout this, and so many other projects in my life. She definitely keeps my act together.

John Edwards

(Don Garlits), or "King Richard" (Richard Petty) and "Ironhead" (Dale Earnhardt) won't be listed in this edition, nor will bios on Alfred P. Sloan, William C. Durant, Bunkie Knudsen, Henry Ford, Harley Earl, Bill Mitchell, Zora Duntov or Lee Iacocca, to name but a few. The MIT engineering grad student may not find what he needs for his thesis, but that's what the tomes published by the SAE are for. However, that's not to say that some of these items won't appear in future editions as we continue to add refinements and updates. I'd appreciate your thoughts on this.

What you will find is a comprehensive alphabetical listing of engineering terms (*volumetric efficiency, torque, brake specific fuel consumption*); automotive components (*throttle body, camshaft, pintle, open chamber heads, dog clutch*); racing jargon (*holeshot, slingshot, shut the door, trailered, gilhooey, dice, draft, late apex*); hot rodding slang (*tubbed, slammed, bumpin', huffer, bumpstick, Tijuana chrome*); suspension geometry (*camber, lateral weight transfer, toe-in, roll center*); and brief histories of major automotive manufacturers. There's much more, of course, and I heartily challenge you to think of a term and see if it is missing. We played this game, and more often than not, we found the entry.

To be sure, there will be readers of this book disappointed to find that their favorite term is not included in the following pages—in spite of the aforementioned caveats—and I expect to hear from them. If you are one such reader, send us your entry. If we agree it should be in the book, then it will appear in a future edition. In the meantime, I hope that you'll find the *Auto Dictionary* to be a most valuable asset to your automotive library.

Michael Lutfy
Automotive Editorial Director
HPBooks

A

A
Model A Ford, built from 1928 through 1931, or any hot rod based on either stock or repro Model A chassis and/or body components.

AACA
Antique Automobile Club of America, 501 West Governor Road, Hershey, PA 17033; (717) 534-1910.

A&P mechanic
Airframe and power mechanic, one who is certified to maintain and repair aircraft.

AARA
Antique Auto Racing Association, P.O. Box 486, Fairview, NC 28730; (704) 628-3425.

A-arm
Triangular-shaped suspension control device, with two points connected to the chassis and one to the wheel spindle. Also referred to as *A-frame*.

ABS
1. See *antilock braking system.*
2. Acrilonitrile butadiene styrene, a tough but lightweight plastic used for some auto parts.

ABDC
After bottom dead center. When a piston starts upward in a cylinder on either the compression or exhaust stroke.

AC
See *alternating current*.

A/C
Air conditioning.

A.C.
British sports car. The A.C. name derives from the "Autocarrier," a three-wheeled car built from 1911 through 1913. A.C. Cars Ltd. is best known in the United States for supplying the chassis and body of the Shelby Cobra during the mid 1960s. The company was acquired by Ford Motor Company in the late 1980s.

A cam
Pattern used to grind pistons in an oval or cam shape with a 0.005-inch difference between the thrust face and the pinhole side.

accelerator
The foot pedal which controls the rate of flow of air/fuel mixture into the engine. Also called *throttle*.

accelerator pump
A device within a carburetor that enriches the air/fuel mixture when the accelerator pedal is depressed suddenly. It prevents hesitation or a *flat spot* when the idle fuel circuit changes to the main fuel metering circuit.

accelerometer
Instrument which measures a vehicle's rate of acceleration, either linear or lateral, usually in *g* force or feet per second per second.

accessible area
In auto bodywork, an area behind a body panel that allows access for repairs.

ACCUS
Automobile Competition Committee for the United States, 1500 Skokie Boulevard, Suite 101, Northbrook, IL 60062; (312) 272-0900. American affiliate of FISA, coordinating major U.S. auto racing events with the international calendar; ACCUS includes representatives from NASCAR, NHRA, SCCA, IMSA and USAC.

acetic acid
Activator used in RTV/silicone sealants to make them more rubber-like in composition.

acetone
$(CH_3)_2CO$, highly flammable liquid sometimes used as a racing fuel additive; acetone helps prevent other chemicals in a fuel mixture from separating. Also used as a solvent to clean parts.

acetylene
C_2H_2, highly flammable gas used for metal cutting and welding.

acid dip
1. To immerse racing stock car body panels in acid in order to reduce sheet metal thickness and, with it, vehicle weight; same as *chem mill*.

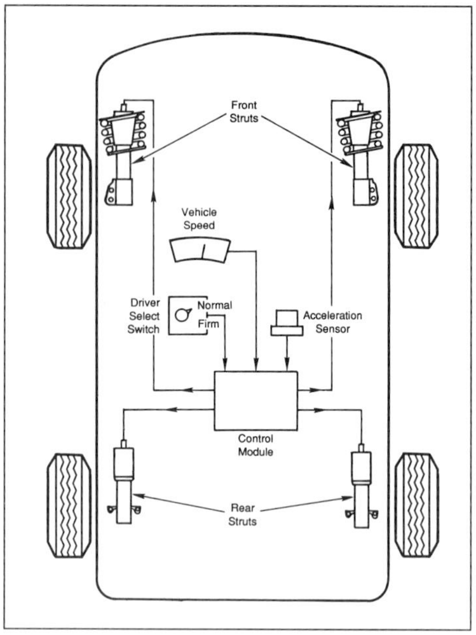

active suspension (Oldsmobile)

2. In paint and bodywork, a method of paint stripping; a car can be dipped to remove all traces of old paint and to remove chemical impurities from the metal.

Ackermann steering
Linkage which allows the front wheel on the inside of a turn to follow a tighter circle than the front wheel on the outside of the turn without scrubbing the tire treads on the road surface.

ACRL
American City Racing League, P.O. Box 3420, Sunnyvale, CA 94088; (408) 752-8650. SCCA-sanctioned racing series for three-car teams representing specific cities, running Sports 2000 *spec cars* with 2.0-liter Ford engines.

acrylic
$C_nH_{2n-2}O_2$, an artificial resin sometimes added to paint to provide a harder finished surface.

ACT
Air charge temperature, i.e., the temperature of incoming air in a fuel injection system. An ACT *sensor* measures such temperatures.

active restraint
A passenger restraint, such as a lap safety belt, which must be attached or connected by the person using it, as opposed to a *passive restraint*, which attaches or connects automatically.

active suspension
Electronic system with sensors which anticipate changes in road surface or condition and adjust wheel position and damper resistance accordingly.

adapter, adaptor
Device to connect an engine and transmission not originally designed to be used together; an adapter would be needed, for example, to attach a big-block Chevy or Chrysler Hemi engine to a Ford *top loader* transmission.

adhesion
1. Property of oil causing it to cling to metal surfaces, such as bearings.
2. Ability of a tire to remain in contact with a road surface.

adhesive bonding
Technique for bonding metals and/or plastics together during the assembly of vehicle panels and bodies. The Pontiac Fiero and Chevrolet's Lumina APV passenger van utilized this procedure. Also a process used to attach aftermarket body kits, such as rocker panels and spoilers.

adiabatic engine
Powerplant in which heat loss is kept at a minimum. The combustion chambers are insulated with high-temperature materials that retain heat rather than allowing it to be dissipated through the cooling and exhaust systems. As a result, a higher proportion of thermal energy is converted to useful power.

adjustable shock
Shock absorber which can be stiffened or softened in *jounce* and *rebound* to deal with differences in vehicle load and/or road conditions.

adjusting shim
Metal shim available in various thicknesses to change valve clearance on some overhead cam engines.

adjusting sleeve
Device on steering linkage to change *toe-in* or *toe-out.*

advance
To adjust the timing of the ignition or valve operation so that the spark or valve opening occurs earlier in the engine's operating cycle.

AERA
Automobile Engine Rebuilders Association, 1430 Broadway, New York, NY 10018; (212) 354-3300. Professional organization that provides technical assistance to the engine rebuilding industry.

aerobic sealer
Substance used to hold parts together that requires the presence of oxygen, such as RTV, or *room temperature vulcanizing*, a silicone rubber sealing compound. Opposite of *anaerobic sealer.*

aerodynamic drag, aerodynamic resistance
Resistance of air against an object, such as an automobile or airplane, trying to pass through it; aerodynamic drag is a product of four major factors, C_d or coefficient of drag, frontal area, vehicle speed and air density. Also referred to as *air drag* and *air resistance*.

AFB
Stands for aluminum four-barrel carburetor. Used by Carter carburetors to describe their four-barrel carburetor, introduced in 1957. It is called the Carter AFB.

AFC
Air Flow Controlled. Early Bosch pulsed fuel injection systems, particularly those with L-Jetronic air mass sensors are examples of air flow controlled systems.

AFR
Air/fuel ratio. See *air/fuel mixture*, *air/fuel ratio*.

A-frame
See *A-arm*.

adjusting sleeve

aftermarket
Accessories or equipment added to a car after the vehicle has been purchased; many aftermarket items are produced by independent manufacturers, but some are also available from *OEM* suppliers.

A/Gas
Under NHRA drag rules, one of four classes for non-supercharged coupes and sedans which weigh from 6.50 to 8.49 pounds per cubic inch of engine displacement.

AHRA
American Hot Rod Association, one-time drag race sanctioning body no longer in business.

AIA
Automobile Importers of America, 1725 Jefferson Davis Highway, Suite 1002, Arlington, VA 22202; (703) 979-5550. Professional organization of firms importing cars and trucks into the United States.

air bag
1. Passive restraint with an inflatable bag hidden in the steering wheel in front of the driver or in the dash ahead of the right front seat passenger. In a front-end collision, a sensor at the front of the vehicle will immediately cause the air bag to inflate and prevent the driver or passenger from being thrown forward into the steering wheel, dashboard or windshield.
2. Inflatable bladder used in place of a spring in air suspension. See also *Air Lift*.

air box
Enclosed chamber to duct air into a carburetor or intake manifold.

air brake
1. Braking system on some heavy-duty trucks which uses compressed air to expand the brake shoes by cam or wedge against the brake drums.
2. Movable aerodynamic spoiler which can be raised against the wind to slow a high-speed vehicle.

air cleaner
Device mounted on an engine containing a porous paper or wire mesh filter that prevents dirt particles in the air from entering the induction system. Also called *air filter*.

air-cooled engine
Powerplant cooled by the passage of air around external fins on the cylinders rather than by the passage of a liquid coolant through internal waterjackets. The engine in the Volkswagen Beetle is a familiar example of an air-cooled unit.

air dam
Panel across the bottom of a race car's front end, designed to reduce air pressure beneath the vehicle for a better ground effect.

air drag
See *aerodynamic drag*.

air filter
See *air cleaner*.

airflow sensor
Instrument for measuring airflow in an electronic fuel injection system. This information is processed by the electronic control module, along with other sensory data, to calibrate the air/fuel mixture.

air cleaner

air jack

air foil
Inverted wing on a race car, designed to increase downward aerodynamic force and, with it, vehicle traction.

air/fuel mixture, air/fuel ratio
Proportion of air to fuel provided by a carburetion or fuel injection system; an ideal mixture would be *stoichiometric*, the chemically ideal ratio (14.7:1) that would achieve complete combustion, with the end products consisting primarily of water and carbon dioxide.

air horn
1. Audible warning device in which sound is produced by a blast of compressed air through a reed or resonator.
2. In a carburetor, the upper part of the carburetor barrel, or an external carburetor barrel such as a velocity stack.

air injection system
Exhaust emissions control device which directs fresh air into the exhaust manifold for additional combustion of unburned hydrocarbons and conversion of carbon monoxide to carbon dioxide.

air jack
Device which uses compressed air to lift a vehicle. On some race cars, such as Indy cars and sports GT cars, the jacks are built into the car's chassis, so the whole car can be raised instantly, enabling the pit crew to change all four tires at once.

Air Lift
Tradename of a pneumatic helper spring with an ordinary tire valve that simplifies increasing or decreasing air pressure to compensate for changes in load.

airless blasting
Method of surface-cleaning parts using propelled shot.

air lock
Pocket of air that blocks the normal flow of a liquid. An air lock can occur in such places as a hydraulic brake line or the cooling system.

air-over hydraulic brakes
System used on some heavy trucks in which hydraulic brakes are actuated by a pneumatic master cylinder.

air resistance
See *aerodynamic drag.*

air scoop
Opening at the front or along the side of a vehicle's bodywork, ducting cool air from the outside to the radiator, induction system, oil cooler or brakes.

air shock
Suspension damper which uses compressed air to raise the load carrying capacity of the vehicle.

air springing, air suspension
Suspension system which uses bladders of compressed air, rather than metal springs, to support the vehicle. See also *air bag,* def. 2.

air-to-air intercooler
On a turbocharged engine, a heat exchanger using ambient air to cool air coming from the turbo to the intake manifold.

air-to-water intercooler
On a turbocharged engine, a heat exchanger using liquid coolant from the radiator to cool air coming from the turbo to the intake manifold.

AK steel
See *aluminum killed steel.*

ALCL
Assembly line communications link, an electrical connector used to check a vehicle's operating systems while it is still on the assembly line.

Alfa Romeo
Italian sports car. The "Alfa" in Alfa Romeo stands for "Anonima Lombardo Fabbrica Automobili," or Lombardy Automobile Manufacturing Company, which was founded in 1910. The "Romeo" is for industrialist Nicola Romeo who took over the firm in 1915. Today, Alfa Romeo is a part of Fiat.

align bore
Machine operation to correct an engine's out-of-round and warped main bearing housings. May be done with either stationary or portable equipment. See also *align hone*, below.

align hone
Machine operation to correct an engine's out-of-round and warped main bearing housings using a special honing mandrel. Must be done with stationary equipment. See also *align bore*, above.

alignment gap
Distance between two adjacent auto body panels. When an alignment gap varies much, it's a sign of poor assembly quality.

alignment pin, alignment stud
Pin or stud used to align one part with another, such as the pins used to align a cylinder head on an engine block.

align ream
Machine or hand process to enlarge the inside diameter of bushings to the proper size.

alky
Alcohol, usually methanol, used as a racing fuel.

Allison
Aircraft engine built by General Motors. Allisons were once used in both drag and lakes cars but with limited success; though tremendously powerful, they're too big and heavy for high-performance use.

alloys
Light-weight aluminum or magnesium alloy wheels. See also *mags.*

Allstate
Badge-engineered version of the Kaiser Henry J, sold by Sears Roebuck in the early 1950s.

all-terrain vehicle
Small, light-weight vehicle with high-flotation tires, designed primarily for off-highway use.

all-wheel drive
Vehicle drivetrain with every wheel under power. On a four-wheeled vehicle, all-wheel drive is generally understood as a full-time four-wheel drive system with a center differential. Abbreviated AWD. Not the same as 4WD.

altered
Drag racing vehicle with stock-looking coupe, sedan or roadster bodywork but without normal street equipment; in the altered, designated by the letter "A," both the engine and cockpit may be moved rearward for better weight distribution.

alternating current
Electrical current which regularly reverses the direction of its flow in a circuit. The reversal occurs between 60 and 120 times a second and is expressed in cycles per second or CPS. Abbreviated AC. See also *direct current.*

alternator
Electricity generating device, which converts mechanical energy from a drive belt into electrical energy in the form of alternating current. A rectifier then converts the alternating current to the direct current needed to operate a vehicle's electrical system. Even with the need for this conversion, the AC alternator is more efficient, especially at lower engine speeds, than the DC generator once used in most motor vehicles.

aluminized coating
Metal spray process used to coat engine components which are subject to high temperatures for long periods, in order to increase heat dissipation to the atmosphere.

aluminum killed steel
Steel alloy which has been "killed" with aluminum in the molten stage to refine its grain structure. Killing is a process of stopping molten steel from bubbling and combining with oxygen after it is poured into ingots. Generally, finer grain steels are tougher and more ductile than coarser grain steels. See also *silicon killed steel.*

amber lens
The color lens used for the turn signals and flashers on modern motor vehicles.

AMC
See *American Motors Corporation.*

altered

American Austin
Small American car based on the Austin Seven, produced from 1930 to 1934 under license from the Austin Motor Company Ltd. of Great Britain. In 1937, the American Austin was redesigned and renamed the *Bantam*; the new version continued in production until 1941.

American Motors Corporation
American Motors Corporation, the fourth largest automaker in the United States from 1954, when it was formed by a merger of Nash Motor Company and Hudson Motor Car Company, until 1988, when it was absorbed by Chrysler Corporation. AMC's better known products are the Pacer, Gremlin, Javelin and Jeep vehicles.

ammeter
Instrument showing the amount of amperage in an electrical circuit.

amperage
Strength of an electrical current in amperes.

ampere
Standard unit for measuring the strength of an electrical current.

amp/hour
Amperes per hour, standard unit for measuring a rate of electrical current flow.

anaerobic sealer
Substance used to hold screws and bolts in place that does not require the presence of oxygen. The product *Loctite* is an anaerobic. Opposite of *aerobic sealer.*

analog instrument
Display which shows some physical quantity, such as mph, rpm, voltage, or fuel supply, with a movable needle on a dial. Most expert drivers feel that the variable position of the needle makes an analog instrument easier to read at a quick glance than a digital instrument. Consequently, analog instruments are much more common on race cars than their digital counterparts, although most present-day Indy and Formula One race cars use digital instruments.

anaroid tube
In a fuel injection system, thermomechanical device which regulates the amount of fuel being injected according to differences in temperature and pressure in the intake manifold.

anchor
1. Mounting point on a vehicle structure for a non-structural but stressed component, such as a seat or seat belt.
2. In plural form, a slang expression for brakes.

anchor end
End of a brake shoe attached or positioned to a fixed point on the backing plate.

angle block
Cylinder block that does not have a deck at 90 degrees to the cylinders.

angle mill
A machining operation to mill the deck surface at a shallow angle on the exhaust side, in order to decrease combustion chamber volume and thereby increase compression ratio.

angle plug head
Cylinder head with spark plugs angled toward the exhaust valves. See illustration next page.

anneal
1. With aluminum, to soften the metal to make it more ductile by heating it to 640 degrees F. (338 C.) and then cooling it to 450 degrees F. (323 C.) until recrystalization occurs.
2. With steel, a heating and cooling of the metal in the solid state, usually requiring gradual cooling.

annulus
Any type of ring gear, including the ring part of the ring and pinion in the rear end, and the gears in the planetary gearset of an automatic transmission.

anode
In an electrolytic cell, the positively charged electrode toward which current flows. Opposite of *cathode.*

anodize
To apply a protective oxide coating to a metal surface by using the metal as the anode in an electrical cell and allowing an electrolyte to act on it.

ANSI
American National Standards Institute, 1430 Broadway, New York, NY 10018; (212) 354-3300. Privately funded organization that promotes uniform standards in such areas as measurement.

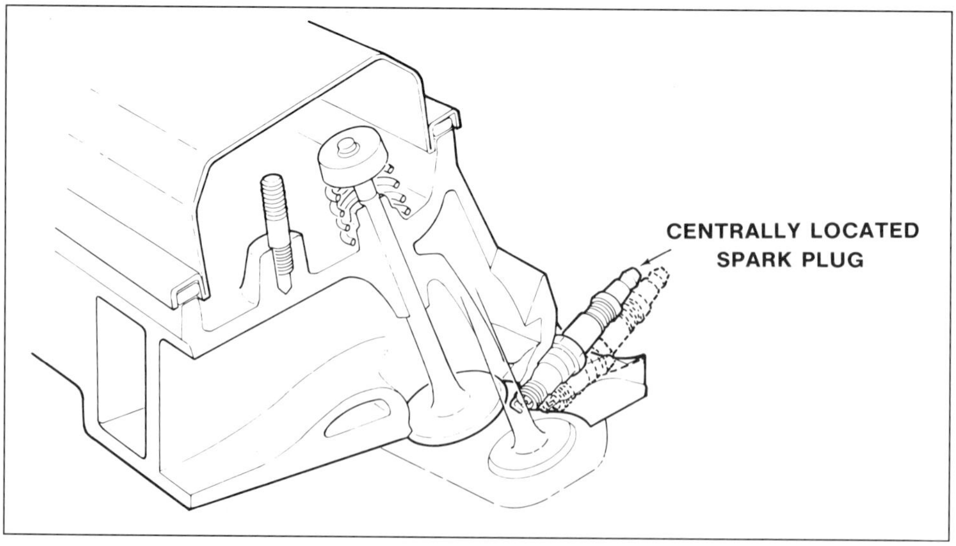

angle plug head (Chevrolet)

anti-dive
Suspension geometry that resists a vehicle's tendency to drop or dive on the front springs when braking.

anti-foam agent
Oil additive that reduces foaming caused by the churning action of the crankshaft in the oil in the crankcase.

anti-fouler
In an engine that burns excessive oil, a device installed on a spark plug to retract the tip from the combustion chamber and thereby reduce the possibility that the electrode will be fouled by the oil.

antifreeze
Chemical such as ethylene glycol added to the water in a vehicle's cooling system to lower the freezing point of the mixture for winter operation.

anti-knock additive
Compound added to gasoline that increases octane and thereby decreases *knock.*

anti-knock index
Measure of a particular fuel's anti-knock characteristics, i.e., its ability to resist premature ignition from compression or any other source of heat before the spark plug fires. The anti-knock index is the average of the motor octane number or MON and the research octane number or RON. See also *octane* and *octane number.*

anti-lock braking system
System which, under hard braking, senses when a tile is about to lose traction and automatically decreases the braking force at that wheel to keep the brake from locking, preventing an uncontrollable skid. Abbreviated ABS.

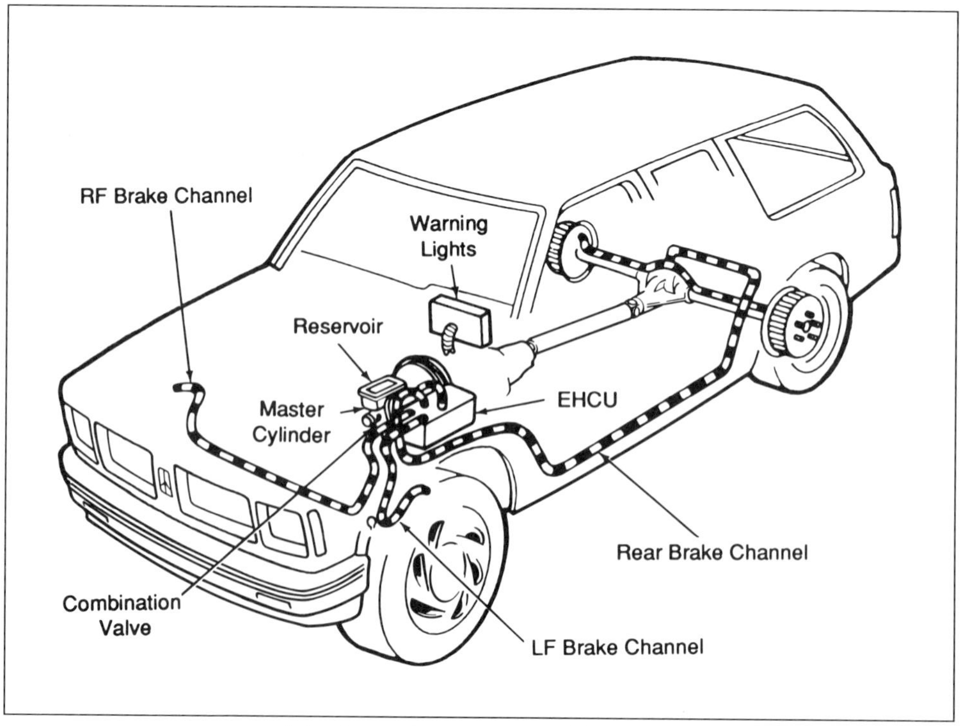

anti-lock brake system (Oldsmobile)

anti-pump-up lifter
Hydraulic valve lifter designed to resist excessive pressure build-up during high rpm operation and thereby reduce the risk of a valve remaining open and causing piston or valve damage during the compression stroke.

antique
According to the Antique Automobile Club of America, an automobile built before 1930.

anti-roll bar
Suspension component to prevent body roll in turns; should not be confused with either *roll bar* or *anti-sway bar.*

anti-seize compound
Coating that reduces the risk of seizing on screws and bolts that are subject to high heat.

anti-smog device
Vehicle part or combination of parts designed to reduce exhaust emissions.

Anti-Spin
Oldsmobile limited-slip differential.

anti-squat
Suspension geometry that resists a vehicle's tendency to drop or squat on the rear springs when accelerating.

anti-sway bar
Suspension component to prevent side-to-side body movement in relation to the axles and wheels, but does not prevent body roll; sometimes called simply *sway bar*. Should not be confused with *anti-roll bar*.

APAA
Automotive Parts and Accessories Association, 4600 East-West Highway, Suite 300, Bethesda, MD 20814-3415; (301) 654-6664. Professional trade organization serving the automotive aftermarket industry.

apex
The innermost point of a turn or corner on a roadway or race course.

apex seal
Seal used to retain combustion pressure at all three tips of the rotor in a rotary engine.

API
American Petroleum Institute, 1220 L Street, N.W., Washington, DC 20005; (202) 682-8000. Professional organization which sets standards for petroleum products.

API gravity
Scale of the gravity or density of liquid petroleum products, expressed in API degrees; the higher the API degrees, the lighter the product.

A-pillar, A-post
Structural support on either side of a car's windshield, just ahead of the front door. See photo p. 18.

API ring
Printed ring on the top or side of an oil or lubricant container, stating the API specifications and ratings of the contents.

appearance money
Payment to popular drivers to compete in a race, so that their participation can be advertised ahead of time in hopes of attracting a larger crowd.

application cable
Line which engages a vehicle's emergency brake.

approach angle
Maximum angle in degrees of a line running forward and upward from the front tire contact point to the lowest obstruction under the front of the vehicle; see also *departure angle*.

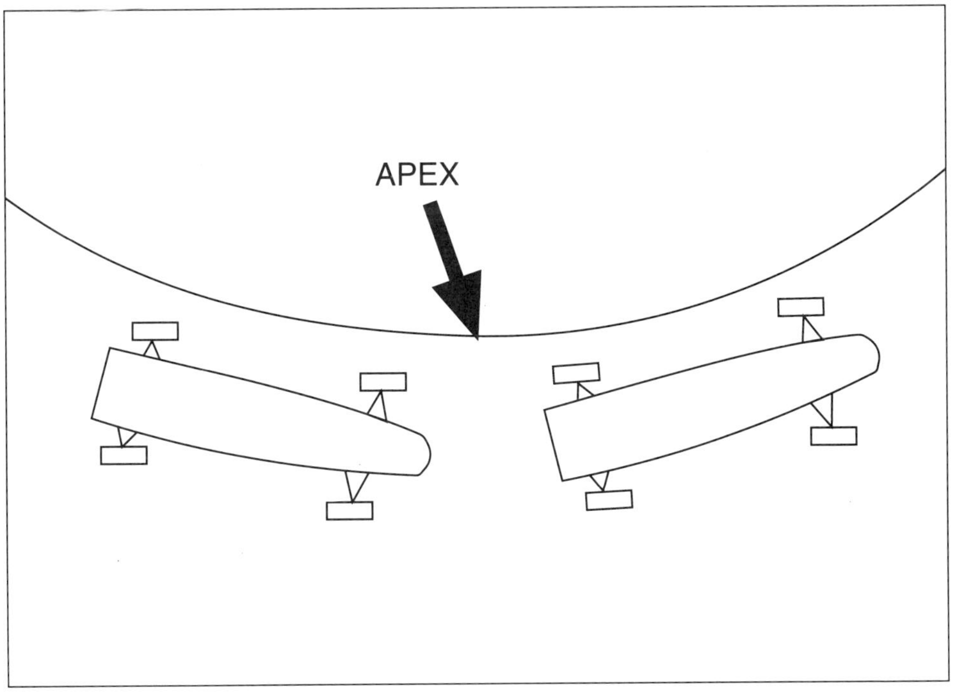

apex

apron
The inner edge of an oval track.

aquaplaning
What happens on wet pavement when a tire is unable to displace enough water to stay in contact with the ground and, instead, rides on the water itself; same as *hydroplaning* or simply *planing*.

arbor
Tapered metal shaft used to secure a cutting tool or a part being turned on a lathe.

arbor press
Mechanical press that uses an arbor to force parts together or apart, such as bearings in or out of housings, or on or off shafts.

arc
1. Discharge of electrical current across a gap between two electrodes.
2. To run *flat-out* on an oval track.

arc welding
Welding process that fuses metal by heating it with an electric arc and simultaneously depositing the electrode in the molten puddle.

arm
Crankshaft throw. See also *long arm* and *short arm*.

Armco
Tradename for a particular type of guard rail or barrier used on both auto race courses and public roadways.

armored ring groove
Metal ring groove cast into a piston during manufacture to increase resistance to wear.

Arnold gauge
Instrument to align the centers of crankshaft journals and the centers of a crankshaft grinder.

articulated vehicle
Large truck or bus with two or more separate wheeled units, consisting of a tow vehicle or tractor with a fifth-wheel hitch and one or more trailers. An articulated layout makes it easier for an exceptionally long vehicle to go around corners. See also *semi* and *semi trailer*.

ASE
National Institute for Automotive Service Excellence, 1920 Association Drive,

Reston, VA 22091; (703) 648-3838. Presents awards to auto mechanics who are successful in tests of their automotive knowledge and skill.

A shim
Valve spring adjuster/insert with a thickness of 0.060 inch, used to balance spring pressure and to correct installed height.

ASIA
Automotive Service Industry Association, 25 Northwest Point Blvd., Elk Grove Village, IL 60007-1035; (708) 228-1310. Professional trade organization serving the automotive service industry.

ASME
American Society of Mechanical Engineers, 345 East 47th Street, New York, NY 10017; (212) 705-7727. Professional organization for mechanical engineers.

ASTE
American Society of Test Engineers, 3030 Harbor Lane, Suite 100, Minneapolis, MN 55447; (612) 553-7714.

Aston Martin
British luxury sports car. The "Aston" derives from Aston Clinton, site of a hill climb, and the "Martin" is for Lionel Martin, one of the developers of the first Aston Martin prototype in 1914. Aston Martin Ltd. acquired Lagonda Motors Ltd. in 1958, and the combined companies became Aston Martin Lagonda Ltd. That firm, in turn, became part of Ford Motor Company in the late 1980s. See also *Lagonda.*

aspect ratio
1. On a tire, the relationship of section height to section width. See *Section Width Section Height.*
2. On an airfoil or wing, the relationship of width, or *wingspan*, to length, or *chord.*

asphalt eater
Top-performing drag car.

assembly lube
Special lubricant used to coat parts that rub or rotate against each other during initial assembly. Examples are *Moly Lube*, *X-All* and *Lubriplate.*

ASTM
American Society for Testing and Materials, 1916 Race Street, Philadelphia, PA 19103; (215) 299-5400. Professional organization which develops and promotes standards for testing materials, products, systems and services.

asymmetrical cam
Camshaft with different profiles for the intake and exhaust lobes.

ATA
American Trucking Associations, 2200 Mill Road, Alexandria, VA 22315. National federation of independent and autonomous commercial trucking associations.

Atari dashboard
Digital instrument panel, so called because of its resemblance to an Atari video game.

ATC
Honda tradename for a three-wheeled, all-terrain cycle.

ATDC
After top dead center, when a piston starts downward in a cylinder on either the intake or combustion stroke.

ATF
Automatic transmission fluid.

ATV
Generic term for *all-terrain vehicle*, usually four-wheeled.

atmo
Racing engine running on atmospheric pressure, i.e., without the forced induction of supercharging or turbocharging.

Auburn
American classic car. The Auburn Automobile Company was formed in 1900 and took its name from its location in Auburn, Indiana. The company was acquired by E.L. Cord in 1924 and later produced both Cord and Auburn automobiles until Cord's entire operation, which also included the Duesenberg Corporation in Indianapolis, went out of business in 1937. One of the most remarkable Auburn designs was a boat-tail speedster of the mid-1930s that later became the basis for several replicars in the 1970s and 1980s.

Audi
German luxury car. The Audi Automobile Works was founded by August Horch in 1910, after he left a company bearing his own name which he had started 10 years earlier. "Audi" is simply a Latinized form of the name "Horch." In 1932, Audi and Horch joined two other German automakers, DKW and Wanderer, to form *Auto Union.* Today, Audi is the only one of the four original Auto Union nameplates still in use, and it is owned by Volkswagen. See *Auto Union.*

Austin
Major British automaker, founded by Herbert Austin in 1906. The most memorable product of the Austin Motor Company Ltd. was the Austin Seven, introduced in 1922. It was one of the most successful small cars of all time and was produced under license by American Austin in the United States, BMW in Germany and Rosengart in France. (The early 1930s Datsun in Japan is also sometimes described as an Austin Seven built under license, but that was not the case.) In recent years, Austin was absorbed by the Rover Group and the nameplate is no longer in use.

autocross
Form of automotive competition held on a tight, closed course, emphasizing vehicle handling and agility rather than flat-out speed. See also *gymkhana* and *slalom.*

auto ignition
Short for *automatic ignition*, a condition when a spark ignition engine continues to run after the ignition system has been switched off, usually as the result of hot spots such as carbon deposits in the combustion chambers. See also *dieseling* and *running on.*

automatic levelling control
Device in the suspension system of a vehicle, particularly at the rear, which maintains proper ride height even when the vehicle is heavily loaded.

automatic steering effect
Tendency of a vehicle to travel straight out of a turn when the steering wheel is released. See also *self-centering.*

Auto Union
Combine formed in 1932 by four German automakers: Audi, Horch, DKW and Wanderer. During the mid-and-late 1930s, Auto Union not only manufactured passenger cars but also fielded a team of mid-engined Grand Prix cars designed by Ferdinand Porsche. After World War II, the Horch and Wanderer were never

revived but a new DKW was built from 1950 to 1966, while the Audi reappeared in 1965 when Volkswagen acquired a controlling interest. Today, the DKW is gone and the Audi is the only one of the four makes still being produced.

aux
Auxiliary item of equipment, such as an *aux battery* or *aux fuel tank.*

auxiliary air valve
Device which allows air to bypass a closed throttle during engine start and warm-up.

auxiliary shaft
In an overhead cam engine, a separate shaft that drives such devices as the fuel pump, oil pump and distributor.

auxiliary springs
1. Added springs on a vehicle, particularly at the rear, to support heavy loads.
2. Second or third valve spring designed with different natural resonant frequencies to cancel out unwanted harmonic vibrations, which can limit engine speed. A *dual valve spring* with a damper is generally favored by high performance engine builders.

auxiliary venturi
In a carburetor, small venturi mounted within main venturi to provide increased air velocity. Same as *booster venturi* and *secondary venturi.*

Avanti
Avanti is Italian for "forward" and was the name of a personal luxury coupe designed for Studebaker by Raymond Loewy and introduced in 1962. When Studebaker went out of business in the mid 1960s, a group of private investors bought the rights to the Avanti and it has continued in production, although sometimes intermittently, to the present day.

A V-8
Ford Model A retrofit with a later model V-8 engine.

avgas
Aviation gasoline, which is generally higher in octane than automobile gasoline.

aviation snips
Hand tool for cutting sheet metal, particularly heat-treated aluminum alloy and stainless steel, originally developed for the aircraft industry but also widely used for automotive bodywork.

AWD
See *all-wheel drive.*

axle
1. Transverse beam or shaft connected to the wheels on either side of a vehicle. A *live axle* transmits power to the wheels, while a *dead axle* does not.
2. By extension, a pair of wheels at either end of a vehicle, even when the wheels are independently suspended and not actually connected by a beam or shaft. A brake shop may advertise the cost of repairs per axle, for example, or a local law may prohibit commercial vehicles with three or more axles from using some streets or roads.

axle bearing
Bearing which supports a rotating axle or half shaft in an axle housing.

axle boot
See *boot.*

axle flange
Flange to which a road wheel attaches at the end of an axle shaft.

axle housing
Non-rotating housing which contains a rotating axle or half shaft.

axle shafts
Individual rotating shafts on either side of the differential which deliver power from the final drive assembly to the drive wheels. Also called *half shafts.*

axle tramp, axle wind-up, axle hop
During hard acceleration, tendency of a live axle housing to rotate slightly with the wheels and then snap back. Once the action is underway, it may repeat several times, creating a loss of traction, until the driver releases the accelerator.

B

B
Model B Ford, a four-cylinder car built in 1932; in other words, a *four-banger deuce.*

babbit
Soft alloy of tin, lead, copper and antimony in varying amounts, used in engines for rod and main bearings. Babbit was popular in early engines because it could be melted and poured in place and then align-bored to proper size. It is still used today with hard chromed crankshafts. It was named for its 19th century inventor, metallurgist Isaac Babbit.

baby Moons
Small chrome-plated, hemispherically shaped wheel covers. Although the name does describe their shape, it actually comes from the name of the pioneering hot rodder who developed them, the late Dean Moon. See also *Moon discs.*

backbone frame
Chassis structure with a single, boxed member running down the center; it usually divides into two parallel members at the front and rear to support the powertrain and suspension.

back cut
Machine process used to cut an angle less than the face angle on valves. This process flattens out the underhead area of the valve and reduces its thickness.

backfire
Uncontrolled explosion of unburned or partially burned fuel in either the intake or exhaust system; usually the result of a flame from the combustion escaping past an intake or exhaust valve.

back flush
To use a reverse flow of water to clean out the cooling system of a vehicle.

backing plate
In a drum braking system, round plates used to position the brake shoe in the drums.

backlash
Excessive clearance or movement between two interconnected parts, such as a pair of gears.

backlight
Rear window on a vehicle, regardless of body type.

back motor
Mid- or rear-mounted engine.

back pressure
1. Resistance to free flow of gasses in the exhaust system.
2. Excessive build-up of pressure in an engine's crankcase; same as *crankcase pressure.*

backstaging
Placing a vehicle at the start of a drag race behind the usual staging position; same as *shallow staging* and opposite of *deep staging* and *overstaging.*

backyard mechanic
Amateur mechanic, usually one who has little or no technical schooling. Same as *shade tree mechanic.*

bad
Good.

badge engineering
Producing the same car under more than one name; some Dodges and Plymouths and even Mitsubishis are badge-engineered versions of each other, as are some Fords and Mercurys and even Mazdas. Another example is the Geo line of vehicles distributed by Chevrolet, which are made by a variety of other manufacturers.

baffle
1. Barrier designed to prevent liquids from sloshing or surging in the radiator, oil pan or fuel tank.
2. Barrier to reduce noise in the exhaust system.

Baja
Spanish for "lower"; in motorsport, the term refers specifically to Mexico's Baja California peninsula, a rugged desert region that has been the setting for some of the world's toughest off-road races. Baja is not a place in the State of California and is not written "Baja, California" with a comma.

Baja Bug

Baja Bug
Volkswagen Beetle modified for off-road use, particularly with a bobbed nose and tail to improve approach and departure angles over rough terrain. The Baja Bug was developed in the late 1960s by Drino Miller.

balance
In engine building, to balance all rotating and reciprocating parts, both statically and dynamically, for the smoothest possible operation.

balance pipe, balance tube
1. Pipe or tube connecting the exhaust pipes in a dual exhaust system to equalize pressure between them.
2. Pipe or tube connecting the venturis of dual carburetors.

balance shaft
In an engine, rotating shaft incorporating a harmonic balancer or vibration damper, designed to counteract the natural vibration of other rotating parts, especially the crankshaft. Balance shafts are used primarily in I-4 or V-6 engines, which tend to run roughly without them. Two counter-rotating shafts are used in an I-4, while only one is needed in a V-6.

balance tube
See *balance pipe.*

balancer
Crankshaft pulley, usually made of heavy material, which contributes to overall crankshaft balance as it rotates.

balk ring
In a manual transmission, a rotating device that prevents, or balks, premature engagement of gears during shifts up or down.

ballast
Material added to a racing chassis to alter weight distribution and/or bring overall vehicle weight up to a minimum class requirement.

ball bearing
Bearing which has small metal balls in two races.

ball joint
In an independent front suspension, ball and socket assembly that connects the A-arm to the wheel spindle.

balloon foot
Derogatory term used to describe a slow driver, one who tends to lift off the throttle early and back-off, refusing to keep his *foot in it.*

banjo housing
On a live axle, a banjo-shaped final drive case.

Bantam
Small American car derived from the American Austin and produced from 1937 to 1941. Because of the small size and light weight, Bantam coupe and roadster bodies were once popular for hot rodding and are still seen occasionally in repro form.

BAR
In California, Bureau of Automotive Repair, a state agency that regulates the auto service and repair industry.

bare out
To strip a car body to its basic shell; usually one of the first steps when completely rebuilding or restoring a vehicle; similar to *body in white.*

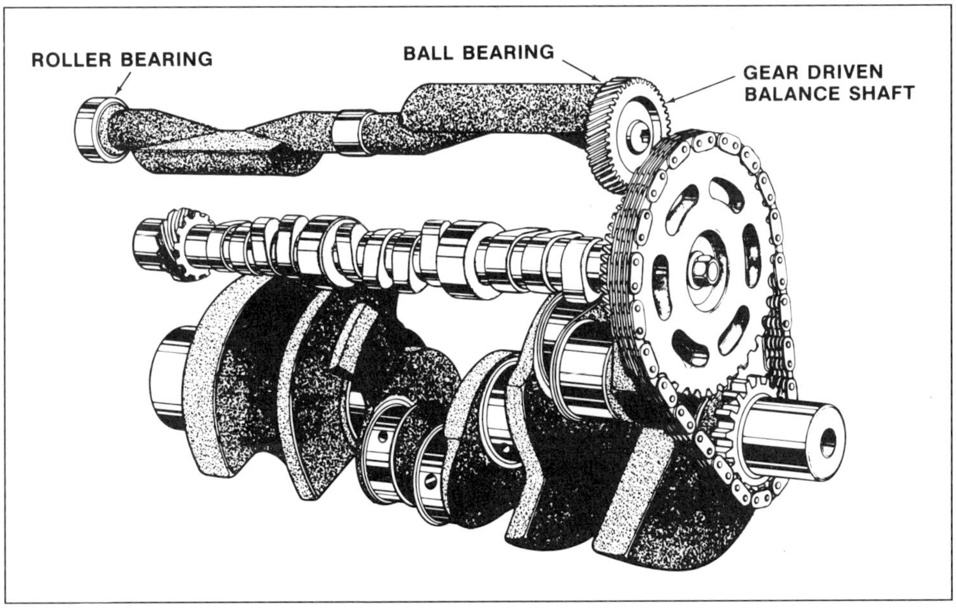

balance shaft assembly (Chevy V-6)

baloneys
Oversized tires.

banger
Collision involving two or more vehicles.

bang shift
Rapid, forced shift of a manual transmission without releasing the clutch or accelerator; see also *Muroc shift.*

barf
To damage or destroy, especially in a way that leaves parts scattered.

barrel
1. Cylinder.
2. Carburetor venturi, as in *four-barrel,* which means the carburetor has four venturis.

basket of snakes

barrel-faced ring
Compression piston ring with a rounded contact face.

barrel finish
Rounded surface on a piston skirt.

barrel roll
Vehicle rollover sideways, as opposed to an *endo*, which would be end-over-end.

base circle
Round, portion of a camshaft lobe, concentric with the journal, where no lift is generated. Also called the *heel*. See *lobe*.

base coat
Initial layer of paint.

baseline
Initial reference point; in dyno testing, for example, the output figures for a box stock engine provide the baseline for interpreting the effects of any subsequent modifications.

base station
In metalworking, the bottom section of a station buck that serves as a reference point.

basic fuel metering
In a continuous flow fuel injection system, the amount of fuel delivered to the injectors, based on airflow sensor readings of engine load and rpm.

basic fuel quantity
In a pulsed fuel injection system, the amount of fuel delivered to the injectors, based on airflow sensor readings of engine load and rpm.

basket of snakes
Tuned exhaust system with individual, intertwined headers; same as *bunch of bananas*.

bathtub
1. In an overhead valve engine, combustion chamber with a quench area shaped like an inverted bathtub, with the valves seated at its base.
2. Auto body design that looks like an inverted bathtub, a style popular in the late 1940s and early 1950s which has enjoyed a revival in larger General Motors cars of the early 1990s.

battery capacity
The energy output of a battery, measured in amp/hours.

Baumé, Bé
Measure, using a hydrometer, of the specific gravity of a liquid. There are actually two Bé scales, one for liquids with greater densities than water, and the other for liquids with lesser densities than water. Named in honor of Antoine Baumé, an 18th century French chemist who devised the scales.

BBC
On a truck, horizontal distance from the front bumper to the back of the cab.

B cam
Pattern used to grind pistons in an oval or cam shape with a 0.006-inch difference between the thrust face and the pinhole side.

BBDC
Before bottom dead center. The position of the piston as it approaches the end of a downward intake or combustion stroke.

BDC
Bottom dead center. The position of a piston at the end of a downward stroke; see also *TDC*.

bead
1. The inner rim of a tire that seals against the wheel rim. The bead is usually reinforced with an embedded wire loop.
2. In welding, a narrow half-round pattern where metal has been joined by heating.
3. In metalworking, a decorative or structural half-round channel formed into the metal in a continuous line.

bead blaster
Device used to clean parts with air pressure and glass beads.

bead breaker
Tool used to break the seal between a tire bead and a wheel rim.

bead lock
On circle dirt-track race cars, a plate that clamps a tire bead to a wheel rim.

beam axle
See *dead axle*.

beans
Horsepower.

bearing back
Outside surface of a bearing that seats against the housing bore.

bearing bore
See *housing bore*.

bearing cap
That part of the lower engine assembly that holds the lower bearing half in place against the crankshaft.

bearing cap register
Cut-out portion of the block that keeps the bearing cap aligned to the housing bore.

bearing crush
Pressure exerted when two bearing halves are installed in the block and the bearing cap is bolted into place.

bearing i.d.
Inside diameter of a bearing installed in its housing.

bearing o.d.
Outside diameter of a bearing installed in its housing.

bearing scraper
Sharp, triangular hand tool used to scrape burrs from bearing; not for precision inserts.

bearing shell
One half of a single rod or main bearing set.

bearing spacer
Device used to position a bearing in the housing bore.

bearing upper
The half of a rod or main bearing that is positioned opposite the bearing cap.

beater
Car for everyday transportation, as opposed to a show vehicle or collectible rarely used on the street; same as *driver* or *grocery getter*.

beef
To strengthen or reinforce, especially for high-performance or heavy-duty use.

beehive spring
Spring in either the valvetrain or suspension that is wound in the shape of a beehive.

Beetle
The original Volkswagen sedan, so called because of its Beetle-like shape. It was designed by Ferdinand Porsche for Adolf Hitler, who reportedly told Dr. Porsche that he wanted a "people's car" able to cruise 60 mph, achieve 40 mpg, powered by an air-cooled engine, able to seat 5 people and sell for less than 1000 marks retail. The Beetle made its debut in February 1939, and is one of the most enduring automotive designs in history. As of 1992, it is still produced in Mexico.

bell
To turn down the edge of a hole in sheet metal with a smooth curve.

bell housing
Bell-shaped enclosure for the flywheel and clutch on a manual transmission or the flywheel and torque converter on an automatic transmission.

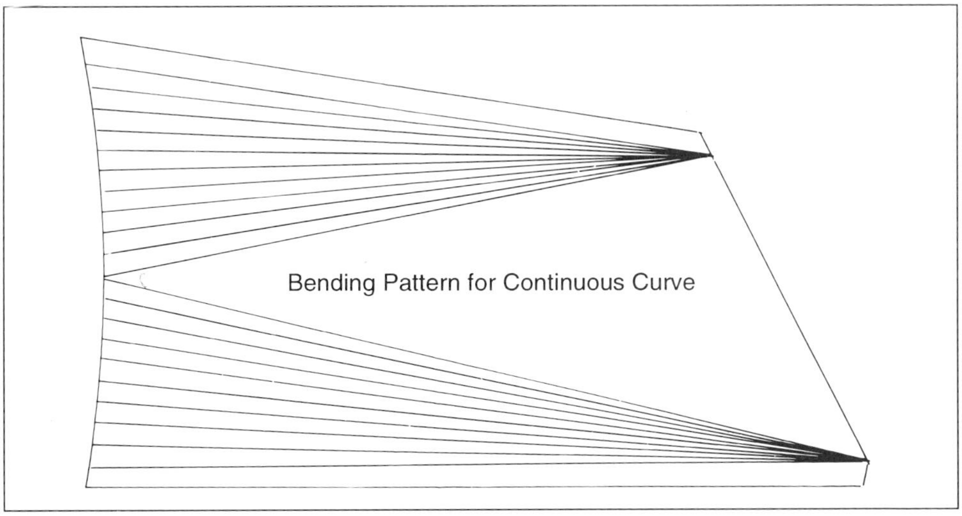

bending sequence

bell mouthing
Shape of a guide or bearing that is normal in the middle but tapered oversize at either end.

belly pan
Body panel or panels covering the bottom of a car's chassis and enclosing undercarriage components; used to reduce coefficient of drag, especially on lakes cars.

belly tank
Originally, a teardrop-shaped auxiliary fuel tank from a World War II aircraft; in the postwar years, the belly tank's size and aerodynamic design made it a natural for adaptation as a lakester.

belted-bias ply
See *bias-belted ply*.

beltline
Line down the side of a car defined by the top edge of the lower body and bottom edge of the *greenhouse*, or roof and window assembly.

bench race
To talk about racing, especially right after an event; the hot rodder's equivalent of Monday morning quarterbacking.

bench seat
Full-width seat in a car or truck that can accommodate two or three passengers.

bench test
Test of an engine or other major component with it removed from the vehicle for easier observation.

bend
1. To cause something to assume a curved or angular shape.
2. Something which has been bent; a curve or angle.

bending sequence
In metalworking, the order in which several different bends are formed so that each successive bend is not blocked by a previous bend. Also called a *bending pattern*.

Bendix drive
Starter drive with a pinion wheel carried on a coarse, helically grooved shaft. When the starter motor is turned on, it causes a sudden rotation of the shaft and, with it, the pinion. The pinion, in turn, rotates the ring gear around the edge of the flywheel and, with it, the crankshaft. When the engine

fires, the sudden jolt at the flywheel disengages the Bendix drive.

Bendix screw
The coarse, helically grooved shaft of a Bendix starter drive.

bent eight, bent six
V-8 or V-6 engine.

Bentley
British high-performance luxury car. Bentley Motors Limited was founded in 1920 by W.O. Bentley. From 1924 through 1930, Bentleys won the 24 Hours of Le Mans five times. In 1931, the company was acquired by Rolls-Royce Limited, which transformed the Bentley into a smaller, sportier car that complemented the Rolls line of large luxury vehicles. However, from the late 1940s until the early 1980s, the Bentley was little more than a badge-engineered Rolls. That's been changing in recent years with a renewed emphasis on high-speed handling and performance for the Bentley and on traditional silence and smoothness for the Rolls.

bent stovebolt
Chevrolet V-8. See also *stovebolt.*

Benz
Karl Benz built what is generally recognized as the first practical automobile with an internal combustion engine in Mannheim, Germany in 1885. It was a three-wheeled vehicle with two wheels at the rear driven by a horizontal, one-cylinder engine. However, it wasn't until 1893 that Benz began regular production of a four-wheeled car, the Benz Victoria. In 1926, Benz and Company merged with the Daimler Motor Company of Bad Cannstatt, builder of Mercedes cars. The combined companies became Daimler-Benz and their products were renamed Mercedes-Benz. See also *Daimler* and *Mercedes, Mercedes-Benz.*

benzene
C_6H_6. The simplest of the so-called aromatic hydrocarbons, a highly flammable liquid sometimes found in refined gasoline. Benzene is also highly toxic, and the concentration of it in gasoline is restricted by law to as little as 3.0 percent in some areas.

benzole
Mixture of aromatic hydrocarbons, with a high proportion of benzene, used as a fuel additive and a solvent.

berm
1. Curb-like buildup of dirt along the edges of an unpaved road.
2. Similar buildup on the outside of turns on a circle dirt track.

bezel
Trim ring or frame, either painted or chromed, usually surrounding lamps or openings such as gauges.

bhp
See *brake horsepower.*

bias-belted ply
Tire design with the same type of diagonal carcass plies as the bias ply, but with separate belts or plies directly under the tread as well, like those of a *radial ply.* See also *bias ply*, below, and *radial ply.*

bias-ply
Tire design with carcass plies arranged diagonally to the centerline of the tread; alternate plies are reversed to cross at angles of 30 or 40 degrees. The simple bias-ply tire does not have any belts or plies directly under the tread. See also *bias-belted ply*, above, and *radial ply.*

big arm
Throw on a crankshaft that's been stroked; by extension, big arm is sometimes used to mean an engine with a stroked crank.

big block, big bore
V-8 engine displacing more than 400 cubic inches, such as the typical muscle car powerplant.

big end
1. The larger end of a connecting rod which attaches to the crankshaft. See *little end.*
2. In drag racing, the far end of the quarter-mile, where competing vehicles reach their highest speeds before they shut off.

bigfoot lifter
Valve lifter with a foot that is larger than the main body. Same as *mushroom lifter.*

big red wrench
Slang for an oxyacetylene cutting rig.

bigs-and-littles
On a custom or hot rod, combination of large rear tires and small front ones.

Big Three
Three major American automakers: General Motors Corporation, Ford Motor Company, and Chrysler Corporation.

billet
Solid bar of metal, rectangular or cylindrical in shape. Parts machined from a single billet are generally stronger than those forged or cast.

billet camshaft
Camshaft machined from a single billet of steel.

billet crankshaft
Crankshaft machined from a single billet of steel. Generally stronger than cast or forged crankshafts; used primarily for racing applications.

bimetal engine
Powerplant with the head(s) and block made of different metals, such as one with aluminum heads and a cast-iron block.

bimetal spring
Carburetor choke spring made of a layer of copper and a layer of steel; a bimetal spring is sensitive to heat and cold because of the different expansion rates of the two metals.

binder
1. Main component of automotive paint. Lacquers, enamels and two-part enamels represent the major types of the binder. Lacquers can be *nitrocellulose* or *acrylic* (plastic) based. One-part enamels are *alkyd* or *acrylic*, and two-part enamels can be *epoxy* or *polyurethane* or *acrylic urethane*, among others. The binder is made of a *resin* (melamine is common in OEM paints), a drying oil (such as linseed oil in house paints) or a plastic (polyurethane or polyvinyl chloride, for example).
2. In plural form, another term for brakes. A driver who locks up his tires is said to be "hard on the binders."

binnacle
Console or self-contained stand for instruments, switches and controls, separate from the dashboard, and usually on or near the steering column. The word derives

birdcage, def. 2

from a nautical term for a similar stand housing a compass near the helm.

birdcage
1. Plate on an axle housing for attaching suspension components.
2. Chassis space frame with numerous small pieces of structural tubing instead of just a few large ones.

bite
Traction.

black box
Central control unit for a computerized system; the "black" refers not so much to the actual color of the device's housing as to the seemingly mysterious way in which it works.

black flag
In road or circle track racing, signal to a driver to come into the pits for consultation with race officials. Usually, a driver is black flagged because of a safety or driving violation, or because there appears to be a potentially dangerous malfunction or problem with the race car, such as leaking fuel.

black light
Ultraviolet radiation, used to detect fine cracks in metal parts.

black smoke
What the exhaust looks like when the air/fuel mixture is too rich.

black water
In an RV, sewage water, which must be stored in a tank aboard the vehicle until it can be disposed of at a *dump station.*

blacky carbon
Gasoline, a term used in derision by racers running on *fuel.*

blank
Solid, unformed piece of metal, similar to a *billet,* from which parts are made.

bleed
1. To drain fluid from a tube or line, such as an oil line or brake line, to remove an air bubble or air lock.
2. To draw air into a system, such as into a carburetor to lean the air/fuel mixture.

bleeder screw
Tool for bleeding air from a brake line.

bleeding
1. Small liquid leak.
2. In bodywork, when one paint color shows through another.

blinky
Timing light at the end of a quarter-mile drag strip.

blistering
1. Tread on a tire separating from the carcass because of excessive heat.
2. Bubbles or pimples appearing in the top coat film of paint, often months after application.
3. To go exceptionally fast, as in "He set a blistering pace."

blip
Quick punch of the throttle to rev an engine momentarily, such as when warming it up, or during downshifting by using the *heel-and-toe* method.

Block Check
Tradename of a device which detects oil or gasoline in the cooling system, because of a blown head gasket or other mishap. A special blue fluid is placed in a cylinder on a hose which is attached to the radiator. If there are hydrocarbons in the cooling system, the blue fluid turns yellow.

blow
1. To supercharge an engine.
2. To damage or destroy some internal part of an engine or transmission by overrevving the engine.

blowby
Leakage of air-fuel mixture or burned gasses from the combustion chamber into the crankcase, because of worn piston rings.

blower
Supercharger or turbocharger.

blower & blown engine, def. 2

blower belt

blower belt
Reinforced cover with retaining straps mandated for use by NHRA on supercharged engines that prevents parts from scattering should the supercharger explode.

blown engine
1. A seriously damaged engine, such as when a rod has kicked out through the block.
2. An engine that has a supercharger or turbocharger. See photo previous page.

blown head gasket
Broken gasket that leaks water and/or oil and reduces engine vacuum and compression.

blow off, blow the doors off
To defeat a competitor decisively, especially in a match race.

blow torch
Jet-powered car for drag or lakes competition.

blueprint
To rebuild an engine to its OEM design specs, remachining each component to the precise measurements shown for it on the factory blueprint.

blue smoke
What the exhaust looks like when the air/fuel mixture is contaminated with oil.

Blue Streak
Tradename of a Goodyear high-performance tire.

BMEP
See *brake mean effective pressure.*

BMW
German sports and luxury cars. "BMW" stands for "Bayerische Motoren-Werke," or Bavarian Motor Works. The firm was founded in 1916 in Munich to build aircraft engines. In 1923, BMW introduced its first motorcycle and, in 1928, it began production of its first car, the BMW Dixi, which was the British Austin Seven built under license.

bobbed
Trimmed or shortened, such as the front and rear ends of a Baja Bug.

bobtail
Vehicle body with a short rear overhang, whether by original design as on a Jeep or the tractor part of a tractor-trailer rig, or as a result of modification as on a fad car.

bob weight
Weight attached to a rod journal to simulate the reciprocating mass of the piston, rings, rod, bearings, pin and retainers when balancing a crankshaft.

body filler
Plastic, putty-like material used to fill and smooth imperfections in body panels.

body knocker
Person who does bodywork; same as *tin worker.*

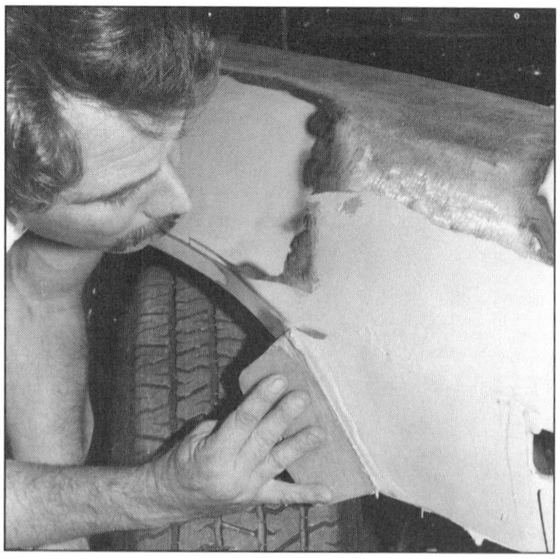

body knocker & body filler

body roll
Tendency of a vehicle chassis to roll toward the outside of a turn as a result of cornering forces. When the body rolls, the wheels roll with it, and the tires are no longer perpendicular to the road surface, which decreases their ability to pull the car around the corner.

body in white
Brand-new, unpainted and untrimmed auto body.

boiling the hides

bog
1. To lose power and falter momentarily while accelerating, as when coming *off the line* in a drag race.
2. In off-road driving, to slow or stall in soft dirt, sand or mud.
3. As a noun, mud hole.

bogey, bogie
On a heavy truck, a structural subassembly with its own frame, axle(s) and wheels. The bogie may be attached in such a way that it is not an integral part of the vehicle but is towed, which can increase its load-carrying capacity.

boggin'
Racing an off-road vehicle across a mud hole, usually from 100 to 200 feet long; because full-throttle handling in mud can be squirrelly, side-by-side match race boggin' could be dangerous, so the competitors are usually timed individually.

boiling the hides
Smoking the tires during a drag race. See photo previous page.

bolt circle diameter
On a wheel, diameter of an imaginary circle passing through the bolt hole centers.

bolt grade
Strength of a bolt, expressed in tensile strength and shear pressures.

bolt-on
Aftermarket accessory or item of equipment which can be installed on a vehicle without special modifications or major disassembly.

bolt stretch
1. Condition when a bolt is elongated, and the shank diameter and/or threads are smaller than spec.
2. Condition when a bolt is torqued to a specific setting and, as a result, is stretched a predetermined amount.

bonding
Process of connecting two or more materials using chemical, electrical or mechanical forces, singly or in combination.

Bondo
Tradename for a two-part, plastic body filler; sometimes used generically, albeit incorrectly, to describe all such fillers.

bone yard
Facility selling used parts for vehicles.

bonnet
1. Safety helmet.
2. British term for the hood of a vehicle.

Bonneville
Salt flats in northwestern Utah, one of the world's most famous courses for high-speed trials; scene of an annual week-long meet sponsored by the SCTA and also the setting for numerous land speed record (LSR) attempts.

off in the boonies

boondocks, boonies
Remote, undeveloped area, from "bundak," meaning mountain in the Tagalog language of the Phillipines. Same as *outback* or *tules.* A racing driver described as "off in the boonies" is one who has spun off course. See also *tules.*

boondockin'
Traveling in a remote, undeveloped area, usually in a 4x4 or other off-road vehicle.

boost
1. Increase in intake manifold pressure provided by a blower.
2. To start a car with booster or jumper cables. Same as *jump start.*

booster cables
See *jumper cables.*

booster venturi
In a carburetor, device which mixes fuel with incoming air.

boot
1. Flexible cover to retain grease and/or oil in a transmission or CV joint.
2. Slang for tire.
3. British term for the rear deck or trunk of a car.

Borden tube
See *anaroid tube;* not to be confused with *Bowden tube.*

bore
1. Diameter of a cylinder.
2. As a verb, to increase the diameter of a cylinder; see also *bored-and-stroked* and *overbore.*

bore align
To machine an engine's main bearing journals to assure they are in perfect alignment and that the crankshaft will be exactly perpendicular to the cylinder bores; to bore align or *centerline,* as it's also called, is one of the first and most crucial steps to blueprinting an engine.

bore centers
Center-to-center distance between two bores.

bored-and-stroked
Combination of enlarged cylinder bore and lengthened piston stroke to increase an

engine's displacement in hopes of also increasing its horsepower.

bore-to-the-water
To bore a cylinder out far enough to break through the wall into the water passage; a liner or *bore sleeve* is then installed in the cylinder to replace the wall.

boss
1. Reinforced extension on a part that holds a mounting pin, bolt or stud; the extensions within a piston that hold the piston pin provide an example.
2. As a slang term, outstanding, top quality; the Boss Mustangs of the late sixties and early seventies, for example, were as "boss" as their name suggested.

bounce back
Condition when particles of paint sprayed on a body panel bounce away from the surface.

bound
In a shock absorber, the inward travel of the piston rod. The opposite of *rebound.*

boundary layer
Thin layer of air along the inner wall of an intake port. Because of surface friction along the wall, the boundary layer usually moves slower than the central air mass.

Bousefield tool
Device for narrowing the top and bottom of a valve seat after the valve angle has been cut.

A, B & C pillars

box
1. Gearbox or transmission.
2. Computer, as in *black box.*

boxed
Strengthened with box-shaped reinforcements; a boxed frame, for example, has added channel iron, usually along the sides, for greater rigidity, and a boxed rod has a reinforced rib.

boxer
1. Horizontally opposed engine, such as the one in the Volkswagen Beetle.
2. With a capital "B," a Ferrari model with an opposed 12-cylinder engine.

box stock
Absolutely standard, conforming to OEM specs in every way. Same as *out of the box.*

B-pillar, B-post
Structural support just behind a car's front door. See also *A-pillar* and *C-pillar.*

bracket racing
In drag racing, a handicap system that allows two cars from different classes to race each other. A specific elapsed time (ET) index is assigned to each vehicle. The car with the slower index is allowed to start first, with the other car following at an interval corresponding to the difference in the indexes for the two; in theory, if both cars run right on their respective indexes, they should cross the finish line at the same time. If one car runs under its index, it is said to *breakout* and is disqualified, and the other car automatically wins. Otherwise, the car closest to its respective index wins.

bottom
When a car's chassis hits the lowest point allowed by its suspension system, it is said to bottom; in other words, the springs are fully compressed.

bottom end
Crankshaft, main bearing, and connecting rod bearing assembly in an engine; not the opposite of top end!

bottom out
In oval track racing, when a car settles down tightly on its springs as it travels through a banked turn; if the car is going fast enough and the bank is high enough, centrifugal force tends to push the vehicle downward toward the track surface, causing the chassis to *bottom.*

bowel
Pocket beneath the valve seat in the cylinder head.

Bowden cable
Mechanical control with a multi-strand wire cable encased in a flexible outer housing.

Bowden tube
Flexible housing for a *Bowden cable.*

bow tie
1. Chevrolet, after its bow tie-shaped emblem.
2. With initial capitals, Bow Tie is the tradename of a line of aftermarket performance equipment offered by Chevrolet.

brain bucket
Helmet.

brain fade
Mental lapse, sometimes used as an explanation when a driver loses control of a race car for no obvious physical or mechanical reason.

brake
1. Device to slow or stop a vehicle, or to prevent it from moving when it is parked.
2. British term for *station wagon.*
3. See also *prony brake.*

brake band
Round metal band with friction material on the inner diameter; used primarily on emergency brakes.

brake bias
Excessive braking force at one end of a vehicle, either front or rear, causing the brakes at that end to lock before the brakes at the other end. The resulting imbalance can lead to a loss of control.

brake cylinder
On drum brakes, a hydraulic cylinder that forces the brake shoes against the friction surface inside of the drum to slow or stop a vehicle.

brake drum
Hollow, cylindrical hub with a friction surface inside against which the brake shoes act.

brake fade
A loss of braking efficiency, usually because the friction surface has overheated from repeated hard use.

brake fluid
Specially formulated liquid used in hydraulic brake systems.

brake hop
Condition where the rear axle, in reaction to braking forces, raises the rear wheels off the ground; once the wheels are off the ground, the braking forces go to zero and the wheels return to the ground, then are raised again. This violent cycling produces brake hop. This is a common problem that occurs when the swing arm length of the rear suspension is too short.

brake horsepower, brake torque
Engine output at the flywheel as measured on a dynamometer. The term derives from the fact a dyno originally used a friction device called a *prony brake* to determine the torque; the brake horsepower was then calculated from the combination of torque and rpm. See also *indicated horsepower, indicated torque.*

brake lights
Red lamps at the rear of a vehicle that go on when the brakes are applied to warn vehicles following that this vehicle is slowing or stopping.

brake mean effective pressure
Average effective pressure within an engine's cylinders at a specific brake horsepower and rpm. Abbreviated BMEP. See also *indicated mean effective pressure.*

brake pad
On a disc brake, the pad of friction material applied by the caliper to the disc to slow or stop the vehicle.

brake shoe
Semicircular device that is pressed against the inside of the brake drum to slow or stop a vehicle.

brake specific fuel consumption
Measure of an engine's fuel efficiency during dyno testing; the brake specific, as it's called for short, is determined by dividing the fuel consumption in pounds per hour by the observed horsepower. Generally, the figure will be 0.50 or less. Abbreviated BSFC.

brake torque
See *brake horsepower, brake torque.*

break
To damage a car in any way; probably the most famous use of the term in this sense was by Craig Breedlove after he crashed his 500-mph "Spirit of America" jet car at Bonneville: "I broke my racer."

breaker
In a points and condenser ignition system, a spring-loaded switch in the distributor, actuated by a rotating cam, that opens and closes the circuit to each spark plug.

breaker points
In a points and condenser ignition system, the metal switch contacts the breaker touches to open a circuit. Also simply called *points.*

break-in
To run a new vehicle at steady, moderate speeds to assure even initial wear of all engine components.

breakout
In drag racing, when a car runs an ET quicker than its index. A breakout is usually grounds for disqualification.

breakover angle
See *ramp angle.*

break rule
Regulation in drag racing permitting a car which has been defeated in an elimination to return to competition if the vehicle which beat it is unable to come to the line for its next round.

breathing
Ability of an engine to draw air/fuel mixture in through its intake system and discharge burned gasses through its exhaust system. Much attention is given to improving breathing in racing engine development, because the better an engine breathes, the better it will perform.

Bricklin
American-financed and Canadian-built "Safety Sports Car," promoted by Malcolm Bricklin and introduced in 1974. Manufactured in St. John, New Brunswick, the Bricklin looked like a mid-engined car but was actually front-engined, with a 5.9-liter AMC V-8 in early models and a 5.7-liter Ford V-8 in later ones. Fewer than 3,000 Bricklins had been built when the company suspended operations at the end of 1975.

Brickyard
Indianapolis Motor Speedway, so called because the track was originally paved with bricks. Indy has long since been repaved with asphalt, but a yard-wide strip of the original bricks crossing the center of the front straight remains as the start-finish line.

Brinell test
Technique for testing the hardness of a metal. A small ball of hard material, such as chrome steel, is pressed under a heavy load into the surface of the metal under test. The Brinell hardness number is the quotient of the pressure applied divided by the spherical area of the depression the ball made. Named after J.A. Brinell, a 19th and 20th century Swedish engineer who developed a device to conduct the test.

brinelling
Condition when a steel shim gasket is torqued into place on a block. The embossed steel areas cause a slight indentation, or *brinelling*, on the deck surface of the head and block.

British Imperial System
System of measurement used in the United Kingdom. The United States Customary System of measurement is based largely on the British Imperial System but there are also some important differences, notably in the measurement of both liquid and dry capacity or volume. The British Imperial gallon, for example, is more than 20 percent larger than the U.S. gallon.

bug catcher

broach
1. Specifically, the Van Norman model 570 cylinder head resurfacing machine.
2. Generally, a tool for reshaping or resizing parts.
3. As a verb, to use such a tool.

brody
Controlled rear wheel skid, used for fast cornering on dirt tracks. See also *drift* and *power slide.*

bronze guide
Valve guide made of bronze alloy, usually with a high aluminum and/or silicon content, to increase wear resistance.

bronze guide liner
Thin bronze guide, with 0.015-inch wall thickness; easy and fast to install, but must be broached to stay in place.

bronze guide reamer
Reamer with a special right-hand spiral, used to ream bronze guides.

bronzewall
Type of valve guide repair using a special tap to cut threads into the guide and a special thread-like insert that screws into the threaded guide. The threaded liner must be reamed to size after installation.

brougham
1. Originally, a closed four-wheeled carriage with an outside driver's seat.
2. In the vintage and classic eras, a brougham was a formal four-door car with an open driver's compartment and an enclosed passenger compartment; same as *sedan de ville* or *town car.*
3. In modern times, several automakers have used brougham as a model designation for a luxury sedan, usually four-door, such as the *Cadillac Brougham.*

BSFC
See *brake specific fuel consumption.*

B shim
Valve spring adjuster/insert with a thickness of 0.030 inch, used to balance spring pressure and to correct installed height.

BTDC
Before top dead center, position of a piston as it approaches the end of an upward compression or exhaust stroke.

Btu
British thermal unit, the amount of heat required to raise the temperature of 1.0 pound of water 1.0 degree F.; equivalent to 251.9957636 calories.

bubble, bump spot
Slowest qualifying position for a race, such as 33rd for the Indy 500, or 16th in Top Fuel eliminations; a driver on the bubble or in the bump spot is vulnerable as long as qualifying runs continue, because anyone turning a better time will bump him from the field.

bubble top
Transparent roof on an automobile. Bullet-proof bubble tops are sometimes used on parade vehicles, such as presidential and royal limousines, because they allow the dignitaries riding in them to be seen without being exposed to the weather and sniper bullets.

buck
100 mph.

bucket
1. Individual driver or passenger seat.
2. Passenger compartment of a roadster body, especially on a Model T.
3. Overhead camshaft valve lifter.

bucks up, bucks down
To have and have not.

buff
Enthusiast.

buff book
Magazine for auto enthusiasts, such as *Car and Driver, Hot Rod* or *Road & Track.*

bug
1. Any minor flaw or malfunction, particularly in a vehicle of experimental design.
2. Volkswagen Beetle, because of its bug-like shape.
3. With a capital "B," *Bugatti,* see below.

Bugatti
Classic French racing, sports and luxury cars. Yes, French. Ettore Bugatti was as Italian as his name, but the company he started in 1909, Automobiles E. Bugatti, was in Molsheim in the French province of Alsace. Bugatti's cars were noteworthy for their lightness and agility, and his race cars were among the winningest vehicles of the 1920s and 1930s. At the other extreme, his Type 41 Royale of 1929 through 1933 was one of the biggest, heaviest passenger cars ever built. Production at Automobiles E. Bugatti was interrupted by the outbreak of World War II in 1939, and the company never really recovered from the shock. A

bumpin'

few cars, based on prewar designs, were assembled in the postwar years, but Bugatti himself died in 1947 and, by 1956, his family gave up any further pretense of building automobiles. Nonetheless, the Bugatti nameplate lives on. In 1991, a new Bugatti was announced that is faster than anything Ettore ever imagined and even more exotic and expensive than his legendary Royale. The name is being used with the family's permission on an extraordinary supercar being built in the land of Ettore Bugatti's birth, Italy.

bug catcher
Scoop-like intake on a fuel injection system or blower. Generally characterized by 3 circular ports with flapper valves that open as the throttle is depressed. See photo previous page.

buggy
Small, light-weight, off-road vehicle, based on standard passenger car components, with little or no bodywork; sometimes referred to as a *dune buggy* because of the vehicle's popularity for use on sand. The Volkswagen Beetle is by far the most popular basis for such conversions.

Buick
David Dunbar Buick, a successful plumber and inventor of Scottish ancestry, founded the Buick Motor Car Company in Detroit in 1903, but moved the company northward to Flint, Michigan in 1904 before he started building cars. The first production Buick, the 1904 Model B, had a two-cylinder engine with overhead valves, which would be a Buick feature long before it became standard industry practice. In late 1904, William Durant joined the Buick board of directors. Over the next four years, Durant gained control of the company and, in 1908, David Buick left and Durant absorbed the Buick Motor Car Company into his newly formed corporation, General Motors.

build
Beyond its obvious definition, to make or construct, build is used by hot rodders when they mean to prepare or to modify. For example, when a rodder prepares an engine for racing, he *builds* it; when he customizes a car, he *builds* it.

bulge
The high spot or crown of stretched metal.

bulletproof
Indestructible.

bullnose
On a custom car, the smooth nose of the hood when the hood ornament has been removed and the holes for it have been filled in.

bull ring
Dirt oval track, especially one-half mile or less in length.

bump
1. To be forced out of a racing lineup by a faster qualifier; see also *bubble*, *bump spot*.
2. To do auto bodywork.

bumpin'
Cruising in a lowered vehicle, such as a low rider. Such a vehicle bounces when driven over bumps or potholes because the body rides on the frame or bump stops, with little or no suspension travel. Some low riders feature hydraulically controlled suspensions which force the front or rear to bounce up and down.

bump shop
Auto bodywork facility.

bump steer
Change in steering direction as a result of sudden deflection of the suspension, as when a tire hits a bump. It is caused by the change in *toe* of the wheel through suspension travel.

bump stick
Camshaft.

bump stop
Block, usually rubber, used to limit the deflection of the suspension when a tire hits a bump.

bunch of bananas
Tuned exhaust system with individual, intertwined headers; same as *basket of snakes*.

Bunting Bronze
Tradename of a type of bronze used for bushings.

performing a burn-out in the burn-out box

burette
Cylindrical glass container used to measure amounts of liquid in cubic centimeters. A burette is used, for example, to measure how much liquid is poured into a combustion chamber when cc-ing a cylinder head to find an engine's compression ratio.

burn daylight
To waste valuable daytime, particularly in any form of racing that has both day and night running.

burn down
In drag racing, an attempt during staging to delay a race against a competitor whose vehicle doesn't have a radiator, in hopes its engine will overheat.

burn-out
Deliberate rear wheelspin, induced by quick spurts in first and reverse gears, to clean, scuff and heat the tire surfaces for better traction immediately before a drag elimination. For better cleaning, bleach or water is applied to the tires prior to the burn out. A burn-out is also performed by would-be street racers as a display of horsepower, much to the chagrin of the police.

burn-out box
In drag racing, area behind the starting line where driver's perform their *burn-out.*

burn time
Time, usually in milliseconds, needed for a given amount of air/fuel mixture to burn within the combustion chamber.

burn rubber
To accelerate fast enough that the drive tires leave black streaks of rubber on the pavement.

burr knife
Long triangular tool for scraping bearings or removing burrs from parts.

bus
1. Large, enclosed vehicle with room for many passengers, often driven over a regular route. The word derives from *omnibus.* 2. Slang for a family car, especially an older one.

bushing
Layer of metal, usually brass or bronze, used to separate two pieces of steel.

bushing driver
Tool used to install and remove bushings.

business coupe
Inexpensive two-door body type with no rear seat, popular in the 1930s and 1940s.

butane
C_4H_{10}, gaseous fuel that becomes liquid when compressed. Butane is similar to propane, but has the disadvantage of freezing at only 31 degrees F., making its use in cold climates impractical. Both butane and propane are forms of *liquified petroleum gas.*

butt gap
Distance between the ends of a piston ring, measured in thousandths of an inch. A rule of thumb is that the gap should be 0.005 inch per inch of bore.

butt-weld
Type of weld that fuses together the edges of two pieces of metal.

Butyl
Tradename of a synthetic rubber that is highly resistant to gasses and oxidation.

buzz box
Small car with a noisy engine.

bye
Solo run during drag eliminations. To equalize wear and tear, all cars may be required to make the same number of runs; if there's an uneven number of competitors, at least one round will occur where the odd car will have to run by itself.

bypass
Valve used to regulate pressure or control quantity of a liquid or gas. A bypass is used, for example, to regulate oil pressure in an engine and maintain it at an even level.

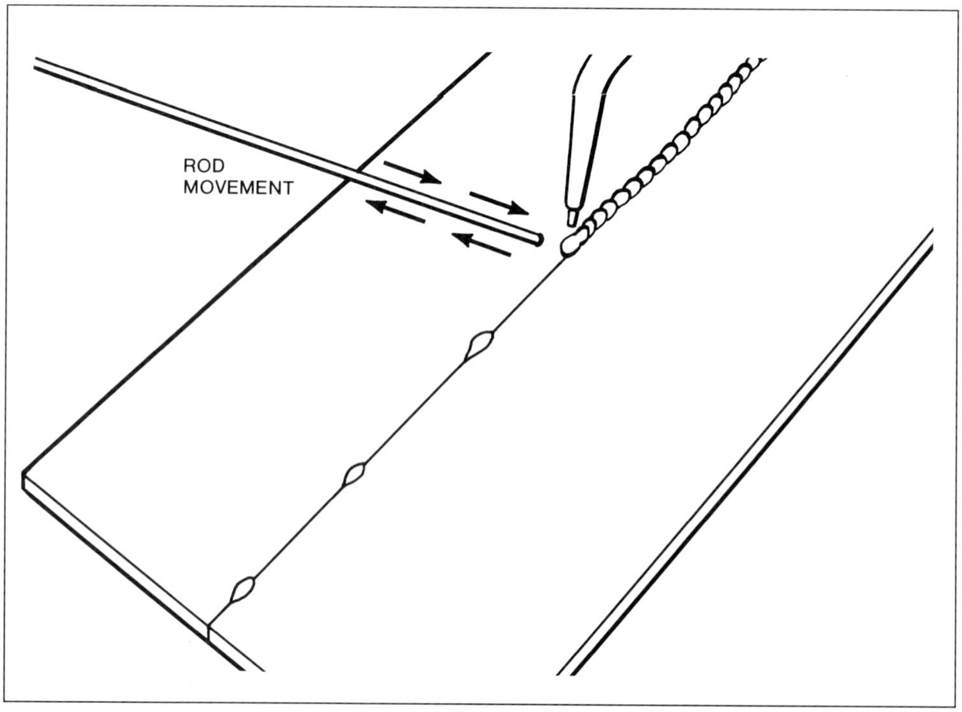

butt-weld

C
1. To raise the arch of a chassis frame for added clearance over the rear axle in order to lower the overall height of the frame side rails.
2. Symbol for the element carbon.
3. With a period after it, C. stands for Celsius, the Système Internationale des Unités (SI) measure of temperature.

CA
On a truck, horizontal distance from the back of the cab to a point directly above the centerline of the rear axle or, with tandem rear axles, above the centerline of the tandem assembly.

cab
1. Driver/passenger compartment of a truck.
2. Short for *taxicab*.

cab-behind engine
Type of truck with the cab behind the engine. Also referred to as a *conventional cab*.

cab-over engine
Type of truck with the cab above the engine, rather than behind it. The cab itself usually tilts forward for access to the powerplant. A cab-over engine tractor has better visibility and is shorter and thus more maneuverable than a cab-behind engine unit.

cabriolet
European term for convertible, particularly as distinguished from a traditional *roadster*.

Cad, Caddy
Cadillac.

Cadillac
The company that became Cadillac began as the Detroit Automobile Company in 1899. Two years later, it was reorganized as the Henry Ford Company, with Ford himself in charge. However, Ford left after only three weeks to pursue other interests. In 1903, the company was again reorganized as the Cadillac Automobile Company of Detroit. It was named after Antoine de la Mothe Cadillac, a French explorer who had founded the village of Detroit in 1701. Henry Martyn Leland, a 60-year-old machinist and engineer known as the "Master of Precision," directed the new company. In 1908, William Durant bought Cadillac and added it to General Motors' growing collection of automakers. Leland remained in charge of what was now the Cadillac Division of GM until 1917, when he left to start the Lincoln Motor Company.

CAFE
Corporate Average Fuel Economy, the gas mileage standard for each automaker's entire line of vehicles set annually by the Department of Transportation.

cage
1. In bearings, metal structure that separates balls or rollers.
2. Short for *roll cage*.

caliper
1. Instrument consisting of two curved legs attached at one end, used to measure diameter or thickness. For cylinders and tubes, there are both inside and outside calipers to measure inside and outside diameters, respectively.
2. In a disc brake, the part which applies friction material against the rotating disk to slow or stop it.

calorie
Amount of heat required to raise the temperature of 1.0 gram of water 1.0 degree C.

cam
1. Generally, any eccentric device which converts rotating to reciprocating movement.
2. Short for *camshaft*.

cam adjuster
For drum brakes, a tool to set shoe-to-drum clearance.

cam and kit
Specially ground camshaft sold with a complete set of compatible valvetrain components, including lifters and springs. When buying a high performance or racing camshaft, it is necessary to replace all other valvetrain components, so that all the parts involved are properly matched.

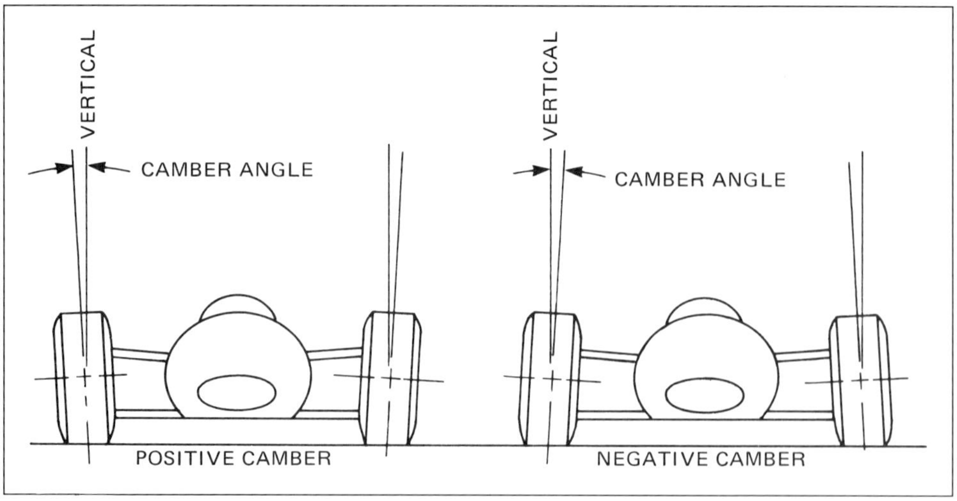

camber

cam angle
Amount in degrees that ignition points are opened or closed.

camber
1. Inward or outward tilt of the wheels on a vehicle, as viewed from the front or rear, measured in degrees. If the wheels tilt inward at the top, the camber is negative; if they tilt outward at the top, the camber is positive.
2. Convex curvature of a road surface, slightly higher in the middle than it is at the sides.

camber compensator
Device to maintain proper camber on the rear wheels of a vehicle equipped with swing axles.

cam button
In an engine, a device which keeps a camshaft properly positioned.

cam duration
Amount of time, expressed in crankshaft degrees, that a camshaft lobe holds an intake or exhaust valve open.

cam ground
Machined to a slightly out-of-round shape, as pistons are, to allow them to expand with engine heat without getting stuck against the cylinder walls.

camel hump heads
High-performance cylinder heads produced by Chevrolet, identified by two camel-like humps on the outside end of the casting. Also called *double hump* heads. The 492 castings are a popular example.

cam lift
Distance, expressed in thousandths of an inch, a cam lobe raises the valve lifter away from the base circle.

cammer
Any engine with an overhead camshaft, although the term is widely used to describe Ford's SOHC 427 big-block engine.

cam sensor
Camshaft-mounted sensor which signals TDC (top dead center) in cylinder number one.

camshaft
In an engine, a lobed shaft which is driven by chain, belt or gears from the crankshaft and which, in turn, opens the intake valves to admit air/fuel mixture and the exhaust valves to discharge burned gasses.

can
See *nitromethane.*

Can-Am
Canadian-American Challenge Cup, former annual series of SCCA road races for unlimited sports cars, with events in both Canada and the United States. The Can-Am was noteworthy for having no restriction on engine displacement. As a result, cars built for the series were among the most powerful closed-course racing vehicles ever seen.

Candy Apple Red
Tradename for a clear-coated metallic red paint job, popular for custom paint jobs. The process involves spraying a base coat of gold paint upon the vehicle surface and then applying several coats of translucent red paint. This effect creates the "candied apple" appearance.

SOHC 427 cammer

canister
Metal can filled with charcoal, used to filter fuel vapors before they are admitted to the atmosphere.

canister purge solenoid
Solenoid that directs fuel vapors to a charcoal canister for processing before they are released to the atmosphere.

canted valves
Cylinder head layout with the intake valves at one angle and the exhaust valves at another, such as in the Chevrolet big-block V-8. Referred to informally as a *porcupine head.*

cantilever tire
Tire with the tread wider than the rim.

cap
1. Part of the distributor used to direct the sequence and the route of the electrical energy used to fire the spark plugs.
2. Small metal part used to act as an interface between the valve stem end and rocker arm, usually made of a hardened steel.
3. Half-round removable part of the connecting rod or main bearing.

cape top
On a true coupe de ville, the fixed enclosure over the rear seat.

cap grinder
Machine to grind flat the surface of a rod or main cap.

CAR
Carcinogenic effects.

carb
1. See *carburetor.*
2. In capital letters, CARB is an acronym for California Air Resources Board, the agency which sets exhaust emissions standards for all cars and trucks registered in the state.

carbide
1. Compound of a solid element, usually a metal, with carbon.
2. Very hard mixture of carbides of various metals, especially tungsten carbide; used for tool bits and cutting edges.

carbide seat cutter
Valve seat counterbore tool made with carbide cutter blades; used to cut through induction hardened and special alloy valve seats.

carbide valve guide reamer
Tool made from a solid piece of carbide, used to ream bronze valve guides to size.

carbolic acid
Active ingredient used in cold dip tanks; very toxic, handle with extreme care.

carbon
Apart from being a natural element, carbon can be a byproduct of combustion and collect in deposits within an engine's combustion chambers. See also *carbonize.*

carbon arc welder
Welder that uses carbon rods and electricity to cut or weld metal together.

carbon fiber
A very strong, lightweight fiber made by *pyrolyzing* (change chemically with heat) synthetic fibers, such as rayon. Used frequently in race car construction, such as Formula One, Indy cars and sports prototypes because of its lightweight, high-strength properties.

carbon monoxide
CO, an extremely poisonous, colorless, odorless gas that is the byproduct of the incomplete combustion of gasoline.

carbon pile tester
Device to test the condition of a lead cell storage battery.

carbon tracks
Condition when there is carbon build-up in a crack on a distributor cap, running from one post to another and causing shorting and misfiring.

carbonize
To form carbon deposits as a byproduct of combustion within an engine.

carburetor
Vacuum-dependent device to mix fuel with air as it enters the engine to form a combustible mixture. The exact proportions of the mixture will vary with the type of fuel. See also *stoichiometric.*

carburetor icing
Condition when ice is formed on the exterior of a carburetor, caused by high-velocity fuel flow.

carburetor kit
Set of parts and gaskets used to rebuild a specific carburetor.

carburetor restrictor plate
See *restrictor plate.*

carburetor spacer
Block or plate with independent or common runners used to raise the carburetor above the normal opening on a manifold. Typically made from steel, aluminum or plastic composite.

carburetor tag
Tag affixed to a carburetor to identify the model and specifications.

carburetter, carburettor
British spellings of carburetor.

carburize
To treat or combine with carbon.

carburizing flame
Welding flame with excess acetylene.

carcass
Tire casing to which the rubber tread and sidewall are bonded..

Cardan joint
Universal joint with two yokes at right angles to each other and a cruciform-shaped connector between them.

cargo weight rating
Truck's cargo carrying capacity in pounds. The cargo weight rating or CWR is equivalent to the payload minus a 150-pound allowance for each passenger seat, including the driver's seat, in the cab. See also *payload.*

Carrera Panamericana
Legendary Mexican road race, run the full length of Mexico between the Guatemalan and U.S. borders; held five times, from 1950 through 1954. The name has also been used in recent years for a series of much shorter vintage car races on the public highways of northern Baja California.

Carolina stocker
Stock car built for drag racing, but without regard for any recognized rules; same as *southern stocker.*

carrier
Part that holds, positions, moves or transports another object.

carrier bearing
In the differential, bearing that supports the ring gear carrier.

carry the wheels

carrier housing
Housing for the differential assembly.

Carson top
Removable but non-folding padded soft top, usually chopped, used on many customized convertibles and roadsters. The original Carson top was developed by Glen Houser of the Carson Top Shop in Los Angeles and was produced by that firm from 1935 through 1965.

Carryall
Tradename once used by General Motors for a large station wagon built on a truck chassis; predecessor of the Suburban.

carry the wheels
In drag racing, to do a wheel stand.

CART
Championship Auto Racing Teams, 390 Enterprise Court, Bloomfield, Michigan 48013; (313) 334-8500. Sanctioning body responsible for the annual Indycar World Series, which includes all Indycar races except, ironically, the Indy 500 itself, the largest race in the series, which is sanctioned by USAC. CART also sanctions a junior series called Indy Lights.

cartridge rolls
Rolled piece of sandpaper used to deburr or blend sharp edges, such as when porting and polishing cylinder heads.

CAS Registration Number
Chemical Abstracts Service Number used to identify a chemical.

case harden
Heat treatment process that hardens the outer surface of a metal while leaving the core soft and ductile.

cast-iron guide
Valve guide made of cast iron.

cast-iron guide reamer
Left-hand spiral reamer designed for reaming cast-iron valve guides.

castellated nut
Nut machined with vertical notches, resembling the top of a castle wall, to accept safety wire or a cotter pin to lock it securely in place.

caster
On a steered wheel, angle between the spindle axis and the vertical, as viewed from the side. If the spindle axis tilts rearward at the top, the caster is positive.

casting flash
Thin metal extension at the parting edge of a casting when it is removed from a mold. Flash should be removed when the part has cooled.

casting number
Part number cast on a component when it is manufactured.

castor oil
Lubricant made from castor beans.

catalyst
Chemical compound which causes a reaction between other chemicals without itself being affected.

catalytic converter
Emissions-control device in a vehicle exhaust system which uses noble metals such as palladium and platinum to convert unburned hydrocarbons and carbon monoxide to water vapor, carbon dioxide and other less toxic gasses. See photo next page.

catch can, catch tank
Container on a race car's radiator or fuel tank to prevent liquid overflow from spilling on the ground during a hurried pit stop.

cat
Short for *catalytic converter*.

castellated nut

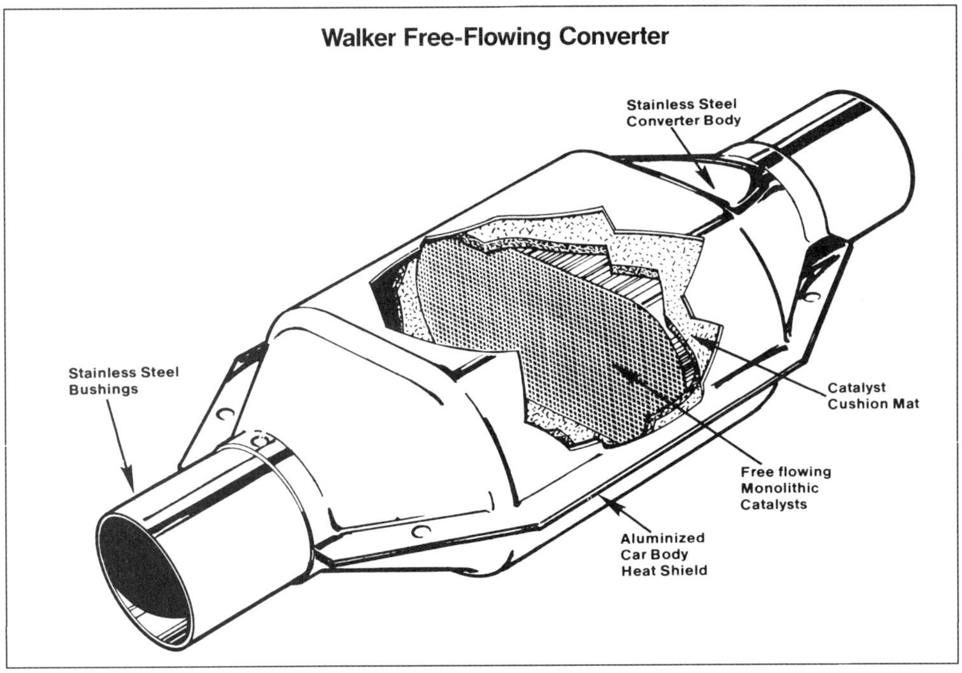

catalytic converter

catch can

cathode
In an electrolytic cell, the negatively charged electrode from which current flows.

caulking compound
Thick viscous compound used as a sealant at joints.

caustic
Salt-based chemical for cleaning engine parts. Can be used for steel, cast iron, stainless steel and magnesium. Will also clean brass and copper, but should not be used for aluminum.

caution flag
Same as *yellow flag*, shown to drivers that a car has either crashed or spun, or that there is an obstruction or safety vehicle on the course, and the drivers are to slow down. Generally, no passing is allowed during a full-course yellow flag.

cavitation
Presence of air in a liquid during pumping, which can affect the flow of the liquid.

CBE
See *cab behind engine.*

CBU
Completely built-up, opposite of *CKD.*

cc
1. Cubic centimeter, an SI measure of volume or, as applied to automobiles, engine displacement.
2. As a verb, to measure the volume of a combustion chamber in cubic centimeters, usually by filling the chamber with liquid and recording the amount as indicated by the *burette*. With this figure and the volume of the cylinder, also in cubic centimeters, the compression ratio can be determined.
3. Close cup, method used to determine the flash point of a flammable liquid.
4. See also *CC grade oil.*

C cam
Pattern used to grind pistons in an oval or cam shape with a 0.009-inch difference between the thrust face and the pinhole side.

CCC
Computer command control.

CCCA
Classic Car Club of America, O'Hare Lake Office Plaza, 2300 East Devon Avenue, Suite 126, Des Plaines, IL 60018; (312) 390-04433. Organization devoted to the preservation of specific luxury cars, American and European, built between 1925 and 1948.

CCEC
Constant current electronic control.

CC grade oil, CD grade oil
API performance specification for diesel motor oil. "C" grade oils for diesel engines hold particulate matter in suspension, whereas "S" grade oils for gasoline engines do not do so.

cc

cc-ing
As a verb, to measure the volume of a combustion chamber in cubic centimeters. See *cc,* def. 2.

CCOT
Cycling clutch orifice tube, air conditioning system.

CCW
Counter-clockwise.

C_d
See *coefficient of drag.*

CD grade oil
See *CC grade oil.*

CDI
Capacitor discharge ignition.

CE
On a truck, horizontal distance from the back of the cab to the end of the frame.

CEC
Combustion emission control.

centering cones
Tapered pieces of metal made to slide on a shaft to align and hold parts with round concentric holes perpendicular to the axis of the shaft.

centering fingers
That part of the boring bar used to center the machine to the center of the cylinder prior to operation.

centerline
1. To bore align, a crucial step when blueprinting an engine.
2. By extension, centerline is sometimes interpreted to mean to blueprint as a whole.
3. Axis of an object, particularly longitudinal.
4. With camshafts, same as *intake centerline*, which pertains to the position at which the cam is installed in the engine relative to the crankshaft.
5. In metalworking patterns and layout, a line indicating the exact center of a given part, from which other details of layout can be determined.

center of gravity
Exact point around which a physical object, such as a car or a part of one, is perfectly balanced in every direction. Abbreviated *cg*.

center of wheelbase
Exact point midway between the front and rear wheels of a vehicle.

center point steering
Steering geometry in which the steering axis passes through the center of the tire contact patch.

center punch
1. For one vehicle to strike another broadside, at a right angle; same as *T-bone*.
2. Tool used to mark the dead center of a given point, generally for drilling. Preceded by a *prick punch*. The center punch has a low angle to keep the drill bit centered. See also *prick punch*.

center-to-center
Distance between the centers of two cylinder bores.

centipoise
Metric unit of dynamic viscosity; one centipoise is defined as the viscosity of water at 20.2 degrees C. Used to indicate the low-temperature operating characteristics of oil, and by the auto paint industry to measure the viscosity of paint. Abbreviated cP.

centistoke
Metric unit of kinetic viscosity; used to indicate the high-temperature operating characteristics of oil. Abbreviated cSt.

centrifugal filter
Rotating oil filter which uses centrifugal force to separate contaminants from oil.

centrifugal supercharger
Mechanically driven forced induction system which uses centrifugal force to increase air pressure.

century mark
100 mph.

ceramic
Material composed of silica and earth elements used as an insulator in spark plugs.

cetane
$C_{16}H_{34}$ or normal hexadecane, hydrocarbon which serves as a primary reference fuel for describing the ignition quality of diesel fuel, in somewhat the same way *octane* serves as a primary reference fuel for describing the ignition quality of gasoline. However, the desired ignition qualities of diesel fuel and gasoline are virtually opposite. A high cetane number indicates a diesel fuel that will ignite quickly from the compression heat. In contrast, a high octane number indicates a gasoline that will *resist* ignition from compression or any other source of heat before the spark plug fires. See also *cetane number*, below.

cetane number
Cetane is assigned an index of 100 while another hydrocarbon, alpha-methylnaphthalene or $C_{11}H_{10}$, is assigned an index of zero. The cetane number of a diesel fuel is simply the percentage of cetane in a mixture with alpha-methylnaphthalene that has the same ignition quality as the fuel being rated. Cetane numbers generally range from 40 to 60.

CFC
See *chlorofluorocarbon.*

CFI
1. Continuous Fuel Injection, a type of fuel injection system that sprays a continuous stream of fuel into the engine.

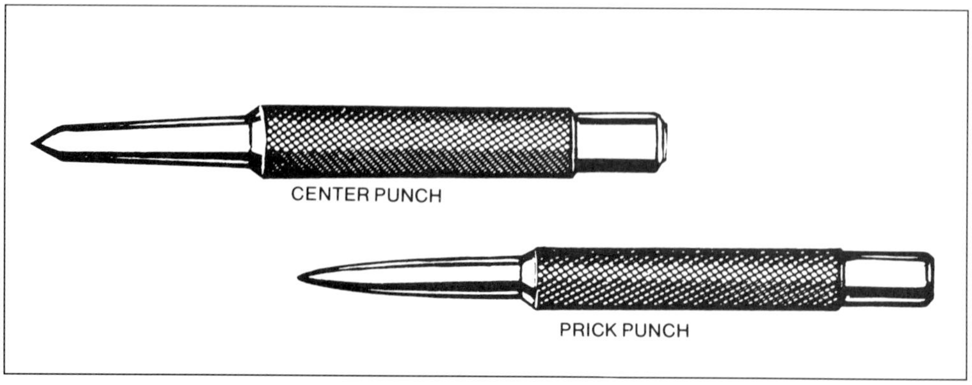

center punch, def. 2, and prick punch

2. Central Fuel Injection, a type of fuel injection system that has two injectors in a throttle body with an electronic control unit.

cfm
Cubic feet per minute, measure of a carburetor's airflow capacity.

CG
See *center of gravity*.

chain drive
Drive system consisting of driving and driven toothed sprockets connected by a roller chain. An example is the timing chain on many engines which enables the crankshaft to drive the camshaft. Chain drives are also common on bicycles and motorcycles.

chain guide
Device used to guide and support a timing chain to reduce *whip*.

chain tensioner
Device or series of devices to keep tension on a chain; may be adjustable guide rails or a hydraulic pressure piston with a rubbing shoe.

chamfer
To remove a hard edge from a part.

chamfering cone
Tapered abrasive sleeve mandrel used to chamfer a cylinder.

champ car
Championship car; older term for *Indycar*.

Championship Trail
Traditional designation of the annual series of races for Indycars, sanctioned in turn by AAA, USAC, and most recently by CART. It is now officially known as the *Indycar World Series*.

channel
On a hot rod based on a pre-1940 car, to lower the body over the chassis, providing a sleeker profile and concealing the frame rails.

Chapman strut
Type of rear suspension with a telescopic strut attached at the top to the chassis and at the bottom to two links which restrict lateral and longitudinal movement. The Chapman strut was developed by Colin Chapman of Lotus from the *MacPherson strut* type of front suspension.

charcoal canister
Pollution control device used to reduce the discharge of harmful gasoline vapors to the atmosphere.

chain drive

charge
1. To fill a battery with electrical energy.
2. To fill an air conditioner with the correct amount of refrigerant for proper operation.
3. Amount of air/fuel mixture to be burned in a cylinder.
4. To drive a racing vehicle aggressively. See *charger*, below.

charger
Top performing driver, one who pushes his car to its maximum.

chase
Process to restore damaged threads.

chasing threads
Manual process using a tap or die to retrace threads on a nut or bolt.

chassis
Lower structure of a vehicle to which the running gear and body are attached. On older cars, the chassis was a separate part of the vehicle with its own frame but, today, it is usually an integral part of the body structure.

chassis dyno
Dynamometer which measures the horsepower and torque actually delivered by the drive wheels, which is usually 15 to 20 percent less than the brake horsepower and brake torque measured at the flywheel on an engine dyno.

chassis punch
Tool used to cut round or square holes in sheet metal.

chassis tuning
Adjusting the running gear (suspension, tires, weight distribution) of a vehicle to different road or track conditions.

cheater slick
Tire made with the same sticky rubber as a drag racing slick, but with a shallow tread cut into the surface to be street legal.

Checker
Checker Motors Corporation of Kalamazoo, Michigan was established in 1923 to manufacture taxicabs. In 1959, the company also began offering its big, roomy sedans to the general public. By the early 1980s, though, there was little need for a car designed primarily as a taxicab. Demand for the Checker diminished and the company went out of business.

check ball, check valve
Device to maintain air or fluid pressure at a predetermined level.

checker, checkered flag
In closed-course competition, a flag waved at a driver to indicate that he has completed a race; the winner of the event is the first driver to be given a checkered flag.

cheek
Plate-like part of a crankshaft that connects the journals together; can act as a counterweight to offset the undesirable twisting effects caused by the power stroke.

chemical fire extinguisher
Type of fire extinguisher that uses dry chemicals to displace oxygen and put out a fire.

chemical gasket
Liquid or putty-like substance used as a substitute for a solid material mechanical seal; usually RTV (room temperature vulcanizing) compounds.

chemiluminescence
Emission of light energy during a chemical reaction other than burning.

chem mill
Chemical milling; same as acid dip.

cherry
In unusually fine shape, as good as or better than new.

Chevrolet
In 1911, William Durant had lost control of *General Motors* and backed Louis Chevrolet, a Swiss-born race driver and engineer, in the development of a new passenger car. It is said that Durant especially liked the sound of Chevrolet's name, as well as his reputation as a driver. In fact, for the first few years, all billboard advertising carried the phonetic spelling of the name until it caught on with the public. Together, Durant and Chevrolet organized the Chevrolet Motor Car Company. Their first car, the only one ever to be designed by Louis Chevrolet, was the 1912 Chevrolet Six Type C Classic. Soon after, trouble developed between the two men. Chevrolet wanted his name associated with quality cars. Durant told Chevrolet that he no longer owned the use of his name and that he, Durant, planned to build a lower-priced Chevrolet to compete with the Ford Model T. In 1914, Louis Chevrolet sold his interest in the company to Durant and left to join his brothers Gaston and Arthur Chevrolet in the formation of the Chevrolet Brothers Manufacturing Company, to produce *Frontenac* race cars and racing equipment. Meanwhile, Durant had built the Chevrolet Motor Car Company into an enormous financial success and was quietly using his profits to buy stock in General Motors. In September of 1916, he was able to walk into a GM board meeting and announce that he once again controlled the corporation. And, of course, he brought his Chevrolet Company into the GM fold.

Chev, Chevy
Chevrolet.

chicane
In road racing, an artificial series of turns marked by pylons or temporary curbs on an otherwise straight, flat course. Generally used to slow down drivers on an exceptionally fast and somewhat dangerous part of a race track.

chilled cast iron
Cast iron hardened by using dry ice to align the molecular structure.

chip
1. Microprocessor, the tiny bit of silicon that controls a computer, as in the black box for a modern ignition or fuel injection system; modified chips to improve OEM performance are expected to be one of the next major advances in aftermarket equipment.
2. Metal removed during a machining process.
3. Nick or ding in paint.

chirp rubber, chirp the tires
To shift quickly enough during hard acceleration that the tires break loose momentarily and leave slight streaks of rubber on the pavement.

chit box
Recreational vehicle, such as a trailer or motor home, so called because of its resemblance to a mobile ticket booth.

chizler
Chrysler product.

chlorofluorocarbon.
Active chemical ingredient used in air conditioners as a refrigerant that, when compressed, removes heat from air. CFC, as it is known for short, is being phased out of use because it is damaging the earth's ozone layer.

choke
See *choke plate*, below.

choke plate
Butterfly valve that closes over the carburetor inlet to restrict air intake and create a richer air/fuel mixture for easier starting and running when the engine is cold.

choke pull-off
Vacuum motor that opens the choke plate under full acceleration.

choke rod
Rod connected to the choke plate.

choke valve
See *choke plate*.

chop
1. In customizing, to lower the *greenhouse* of a car by removing sections of the *A-, B-* and *C-pillars*.
2. In most forms of closed-course racing, to cut in front of another car; same as *close the door* and *shut the gate*—or, for that matter, close the gate and shut the door.

chop, channel, and enamel
Customizer's description of a full restyling treatment of a car, including chopping and channeling to lower it and then painting it a wild color.

chopped flywheel
Lightened flywheel. The surface of the unit is machined to remove excess material and reduce rotating inertia. This particular modification was popular in the early days of hot rodding, when the Ford flathead V-8 was the hottest thing going. However, chopping reduces flywheel strength and durability and, consequently, it fell out of favor when big, powerful V-8s became popular.

chop shop
Facility where stolen vehicles are dismantled and the parts reused or sold illegally.

Christmas tree
Electronic countdown starting system for drag racing. The tree was originally designed with seven vertical lights, five amber, one green and one red, on each side; starting at the top, the ambers come

on at 1/2-second intervals and then the green. If the driver is a "leaver" and starts before the green comes on, he will *red light* and be disqualified. The five-amber setup is still used for amateur classes and for bracket racing, but a single amber light is now the rule in the professional categories.

chrome
See *chromium*.

chrome carnival
Rod and custom show.

chrome-moly steel
Tough steel alloy containing chromium and molybdenum, used for vehicle parts that are subject to high stresses and pressures.

chrome rings
Piston rings plated with hard chrome to increase their durability; must not be used in chrome-plated cylinders.

chrome steel
Any steel alloy containing chromium.

chromies
Chrome-plated wheels.

chromium
Metal used in hard steel alloys, and also to provide a durable and hard surface for engine parts. Found on piston rings, cylinder bores, rod and main journals. Applied with an electrochemical process; not to be confused with the light-duty, cosmetic chrome plating used to decorate automobile parts.

Chrondek
Tradename of a brand of auto race timing equipment.

Chryco
Chrysler Corporation.

Chrysler
Walter P. Chrysler, a Kansas native of German ancestry, worked at General Motors from 1912 to 1919, as works manager and general manager of the Buick Division and as GM vice president in charge of operations. In 1920 and 1921, he was president of Willys-Overland and helped bail that company out of serious financial difficulties. In 1923, he bought the Maxwell Motor Corporation of Detroit and used it as the foundation for his own corporation. Chrysler continued to produce the Maxwell for two more years but, in the meantime, he introduced the first car bearing his own name in 1924. In 1928, he added three more makes to his corporation: *Dodge*, which he bought, and *De Soto* and *Plymouth*, which he originated. For the next 32 years, Chrysler, De Soto, Dodge and Plymouth constituted the Chrysler Corporation line-up. Then, in 1960, the De Soto was dropped. Finally, in 1988, Chrysler acquired *American Motors Corporation* and, with it, *Jeep*. What survived of the AMC passenger car line was renamed *Eagle* but the Jeep, of course, remained the Jeep. Chrysler also owns Italy's *Lamborghini* and has a minority interest in Japan's *Mitsubishi*, which has *badge-engineered* several vehicles for Chrysler over the years.

chuck
Tool used to hold reamers or drill bits.

chuck key
Device to tighten and loosen reamers or drill bits in a chuck.

chute
1. Starting position for a drag race; a car that is properly staged is "in the chute."
2. Fast, straight stretch on an oval track or road course.
3. Parachute, used to slow both drag and lakes cars from high speeds. In drag racing, a chute is required on any car capable of 150 mph or more and, at Bonneville, on any faster than 175 mph.

CI, CID
1. Cubic inches, cubic-inch displacement.
2. CI may also stand for compression ignition, as in a diesel engine.

circle burning
Oval track racing.

circumferential ring expander
Spring-like device used to expand oil control rings against the cylinder wall.

CIS
Continuous injection system; a continuous-flow, mechanically controlled, fuel injection system developed by Bosch.

CIS-E
Continuous injection system-electronic; a continuous-flow, electronically controlled fuel injection system developed by Bosch.

cladding
Layer of one metal or alloy bonded to another, such as a layer of bright metal along a car's rocker panel.

clamp
Tool used to hold parts or assemblies in a desired location.

in the chute

clamping fixture
Special clamp used to hold connecting rods while they are being torqued.

class
Group of race cars with theoretically similar specifications and performance potential. Different systems are used to classify cars for different forms of racing. Some of the standards applied are (a) engine displacement; (b) the ratio between engine displacement and vehicle weight; (c) the ratio between engine horsepower and vehicle weight.

Class F red insulating enamel
Dielectric paint used to aid in the sealing of the interior of an engine and to aid in the quick return of oil to the crankcase. *Glyptal* is a specific brand of such paint.

classic
1. According to the Classic Car Club of America, "a fine distinctive automobile, American or foreign, built between 1925 and 1948." The club maintains a list of the specific makes and models it recognizes as classics.
2. In broader usage, any particularly fine car, regardless of its date of manufacture.
3. A particularly important annual racing event. The Indy 500 is a classic.

clean cut
To shut off a normally aspirated engine at its operating rpm, in order to obtain a reading of the spark plugs at actual operating conditions. A skilled engine builder will be able to determine, among other things, if the fuel mixture is too rich or too lean; if the plugs are too cold or too hot; or if there is too much or too little spark. A clean cut can also be used at the rpm level a misfire or flat spot occurs to help solve the problem. Turbocharged engines cannot be clean cut, due to the high heat generated by the turbo.

clean room
Enclosed area free of dust and dirt, generally with ventilation, where engine components can be assembled with minimal risk of contamination.

clear coat
Transparent coating applied to a painted surface to enhance visual depth.

clearance
Gap between two adjacent parts.

clearance ramp
Area of a mechanical lifter camshaft lobe that makes the transition from the base circle to the flank.

Cleco
A temporary holding device used to fit and refit pieces of metal together before they are permanently welded or riveted. They are installed and removed with Cleco pliers, which fit under the collar and over the plunger of the Cleco to release and secure it.

Clenet
Neoclassic convertible designed by French stylist Alain Clenet and built by his Clenet Coachworks of Goleta, California during the late 1970s and early 1980s.

Cleveland V-8
Ford 351-C (for Cleveland), a 351 CID V-8 built in Cleveland, Ohio. See also *Windsor V-8*.

clip
Major body repair where the front or rear of a vehicle is replaced with the front or rear of another vehicle of the same model.

close-coupled
Vehicle interior with limited rear seating space, as in a *club coupe* or *two-plus-two*.

closed-chamber head
Cylinder head with combustion chambers having large quench areas. On early-model Chevrolet big-block engines, the closed-chamber head has a bathtub-shaped chamber, at an angle on a centerline drawn between the two valves of each cylinder. It was the original combustion chamber design that debuted on the Mark II "mystery" motor in 1963. See also *open-chamber heads*.

closed course
Oval track or road race circuit, as distinguished from a drag strip or lakes course, both of which extend beyond their finish lines into shut-off areas.

closed-end spring
Coil spring with the end loops next to the coils of the spring.

closed-loop fuel system
Computerized system equipped with a sensor which measures the temperature and composition of exhaust gasses. Based on what it reads, the air/fuel ratio can be adjusted for maximum efficiency.

close ratios
Transmission setup with narrow spreads between speeds in individual gears; close ratios are important in drag racing because they allow a minimum drop in engine speed during upshifts. See also *wide ratios*.

close the door, close the gate
In oval track or road racing, to pass an opponent and immediately cut in front of him, blocking his path and preventing him from repassing; or to move over and enter a corner just as the opponent pulls along on the inside of the turn to pass, effectively preventing him from doing so. Same as *chop*, *shut the door* or *shut the gate*.

cloud point
Temperature at which wax begins to separate from oil, causing the oil to look cloudy.

club coupe
Four/five-passenger, two-door body with limited rear seating space; see also *two-plus-two*.

clunker
Poor performing car.

cluster gear
In a manual transmission, a set of three to four gears on a common shaft. See also *countershaft*, def. 2.

clutch
1. Friction device that connects or disconnects the engine and transmission. It allows smooth engagement as the vehicle first gets underway and quick disengagement for shifting gears.
2. The pedal used by a driver to operate the clutch.

clutch cable
Cable which actuates the clutch fork.

clutch can
Same as *bell housing*.

clutch disc
Driven friction plate in a clutch assembly. The disc is forced against the flywheel by the clutch plate.

ClutchFlite
Chrysler TorqueFlite automatic transmission modified for racing with a mechanical clutch in place of its torque converter.

clutch fork
Lever which actuates the clutch release bearing.

clutch-off
To engage the clutch suddenly for a fast start, such as at the start of a drag race.

clutch pack
In an automatic transmission, a group of clutches which apply the power from the torque converter to the different gear sets.

clutch plate
Pressure plate which forces the clutch disc against the flywheel.

CNG
Compressed natural gas, primarily methane, used as a motor fuel.

CO
See *carbon monoxide*.

coach
1. Originally, a large, four-wheeled carriage with an enclosed passenger compartment and a raised, open seat at the front for the driver. From Kóes, a village in Hungary where such carriages originated in the 16th century.
2. In the early years of motoring, an enclosed two-door sedan.
3. Bus.
4. Motorhome.

coachbuilder
Producer of individually designed bodies, or *coachwork*, for luxury cars.

coachwork
Product of a coachbuilder.

coating
1. Paint used to provide color or a weather resistant surface to a vehicle or its parts.
2. Any material applied to a metal surface to increase durability, resist abrasion, reduce friction or act as a heat barrier.

cockpit
Driver's compartment.

COE
Cab-over engine. See *cab over*.

coefficient of drag
Measure of the air resistance of an auto body design; the C_d or C_x, as it's known for short, is affected by the overall body shape and by any air ducts passing through the car for cooling or ventilation, and can be determined accurately only by wind tunnel testing. Overall aerodynamic drag involves not only C_d but frontal area, vehicle speed and air density.

coefficient of friction
Measure of the resistance of one surface moving against another.

cog
Gear, particularly the final drive gear; same as *screw*.

coefficient of water/oil distribution
Ratio of the solubility of a chemical in water to its solubility in oil. Same as *partition coefficient*.

coil
Transformer in the ignition system used to increase low battery voltage to the high spark plug voltage required to ignite the compressed air/fuel mixture. Same as *ignition coil*.

coil bind
In a coil spring, condition where the spring is compressed and the coils touch. Also known as *spring bind*.

coil-over shock
Suspension component consisting of a shock absorber within a coil spring.

coil spring
Spiral-shaped spring. Coil springs are found in many places in motor vehicles but are most familiar for their use in suspension.

coke bottle
Shape of an auto body tucked inward slightly at the middle, somewhat like a Coca Cola bottle.

cold cranking current
Amperage drawn by the starter when an engine is cold.

cold drawn
Process where metal is drawn or rolled into a particular shape or size.

cold manifold
Intake manifold without a pre-heat passage.

cold patch
Process to repair a punctured tire or tube without heat.

cold-start injector
Electronic fuel injector which supplies extra fuel needed to start a cold engine.

cold-start valve
Valve which introduces extra air into the intake manifold during a cold start on a fuel-injected engine.

cold weld
Method of repairing cracks in heads and blocks using tapered plugs to fill the crack. Also called *Irontite* method after the company manufacturing equipment for it.

collector
In an exhaust manifold, a device that collects exhaust gasses from the primary exhaust tubes and funnels them into a single exhaust pipe. See photo next page.

collet
1. Split, coned sleeve to hold small tools or bits in the nose of a lathe.
2. Another name for a *valve keeper*.

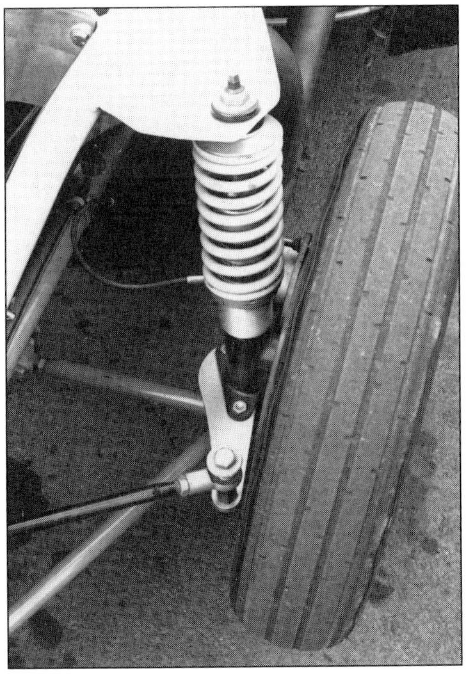

coil-over shock

C

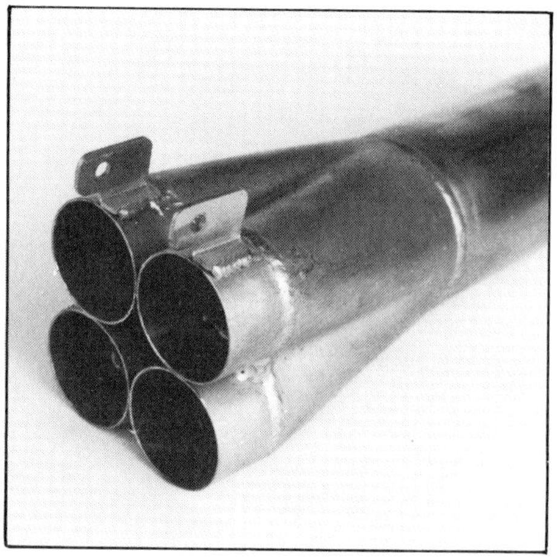

collector

combustion chamber

color-sanding
Light sanding process used to smooth surface imperfections and blend colors after a vehicle has been painted. Generally sandpaper rated 1000-grit or higher is used.

combustion
In an engine, the burning of the air/fuel mixture.

combustion chamber
In an engine, area where combustion takes place, usually a cavity in the cylinder head.

combustion knock
See *knock*.

commutator
Part of the generator or starter used to transfer electrical energy to the armature.

companion cylinders
In an engine, two cylinders that are at TDC (Top Dead Center) at the same time.

comparator
Instrument for comparing a specific measurement, such as length or weight, to a fixed standard.

compensating port
Device to maintain a constant level of fluid in brake lines.

compression
1. The upward stroke of the piston that compresses the air/fuel mixture into the combustion chamber prior to ignition.
2. Short for *compression ratio*.

compression braking
1. On a diesel engine, slowing provided by an engine retarder such as a *Jake Brake*. When a diesel's accelerator is released, the flow of fuel into the engine is reduced but the flow of air continues; thus, no vacuum develops within the cylinders and the engine does not slow down significantly, the way a gasoline engine does. With a retarder, on the other hand, the fuel supply is completely cut off and the exhaust valve timing is altered, so that compression ignition cannot occur despite the build-up of pressure within the cylinders during the compression stroke. That pressure slows the engine and, with it, the vehicle. See also *Jake Brake*.
2. Misnomer for the tendency of a gasoline engine to slow down when the accelerator is released; the flow of both fuel and air into the engine is reduced and, as a result, a vacuum develops in the cylinders that slows down the pistons. It is this vacuum, not compression, that causes the slowing.

compression gauge
Instrument used to measure the pressure created in the cylinder as the piston moves upward on the compression stroke.

compression height
Distance measured from the crown of the piston to the center of the wrist pin.

compression ignition
Operating system in a diesel engine, where air admitted to the cylinder is heated as it is compressed by the upward stroke of the piston; when the piston reaches Top Dead Center, fuel is admitted and immediately ignites from the heat of the compressed air, without an electrical spark.

compression ratio
Relationship between the combined capacities of a cylinder and combustion chamber with the piston at BDC and the capacity of the combustion chamber with the piston at TDC. See illustration next page.

compression ring
Top piston ring used to seal and contain the combustion pressure on top of the piston.

compression seal
Metal seal on a direct fuel injection system to resist compression pressures.

compressor
Machine which generates high air pressure to operate pneumatic tools.

composite materials
Differing materials that are bonded together for added strength, such as fiberglass, carbon fiber, Kevlar and Aramid.

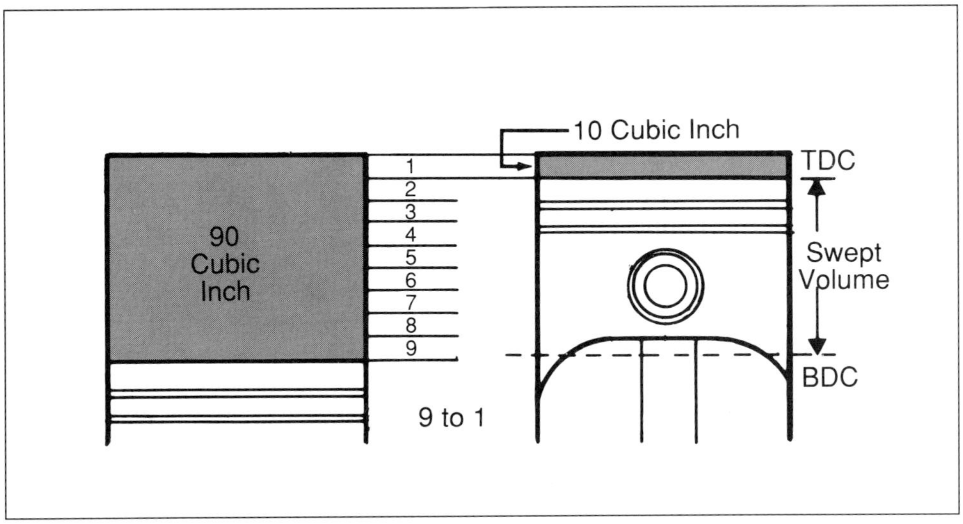

compression ratio

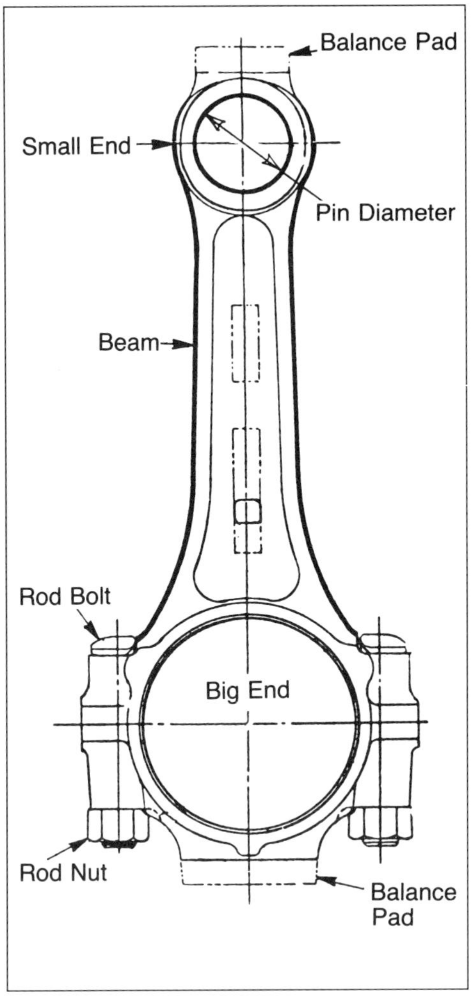

connecting rod

C

composition gasket
Gasket made from a combination of materials, such as steel and press-treated paper or copper and asbestos.

compound low gear
In a four-wheel drive vehicle with a two-speed transfer case, the combination of first gear in the transmission and low range in the transfer case.

compounding
Application of an abrasive paste to smooth out the surface of paint.

computerized air suspension
Type of suspension with rubber bags controlled by an air compressor to maintain a specified ride height determined by road surface conditions.

concentric sleeve
Sleeve on Sunnen honing mandrels to center the mandrel to the drive mount.

concentricity meter
Instrument to check the concentricity of one part in relation to another, such as a valve seat to a valve guide.

concours d'elegance
Literally, French for "contest of elegance." A concours d'elegance is a showing of luxury cars, both classic and modern, in lush surroundings, such as an exclusive country club or the parking area of an expensive restaurant. Awards are given to the vehicles judged best in such features as appearance, luxury, finish and, in the case of classics, authenticity of restoration.

condenser
1. Device which stores an electrical charge, part of a point-type distributor.
2. Radiator-like device used to remove heat in an air conditioning system.

conductance
Ability of a material to transmit an electrical charge.

conductor
Any material that will transmit an electrical charge.

conformability
Degree of ease or difficulty in shaping different metals.

connecting rod
Link between a piston and crankshaft that converts the reciprocal motion of the piston into the rotary motion of the crankshaft.

con rod
Short for *connecting rod.*

contingency money
Payment from accessory and equipment manufacturers to top finishing contestants using their products in a race.

continuity
Ability of an electrical circuit to convey energy from one point to another.

continuous codes
Series of diagnostic computer codes that monitor engine control functions.

continuous flow injection
Non-pulsed fuel injection system that delivers fuel continuously in small increments without pause. Used in throttle body injection systems, but not port injection.

contact patch
Portion of a tire tread in contact with the road surface.

control arm
See *A-arm.*

control cable
Front primary cable used to set a parking brake.

control plunger
In a fuel injection system, a device that is moved by the airflow sensor to regulate fuel delivery to the injectors.

control points
Series of points, holes or flat surfaces used to align body panels during assembly or reconstruction.

control pressure
Amount of fuel pressure needed for a fuel injection system to operate.

conventional cab
Type of truck with the cab behind the engine. Same as *cab-behind engine.*

conventional frame
Chassis frame separate from the body structure.

cook
1. To perform well, as in "he's cookin'."
2. To overheat to the point of irreparable damage.

coolant
Substance used to carry away heat generated by an engine or a machining operation.

coolant fan relay
Electrical device used to energize a coolant fan. The relay uses low-current voltage to energize the high-current fan motor.

coolant reservoir
Tank for storing coolant, connected to the radiator with an overflow hose.

copper-asbestos-copper gasket
Gasket, particularly a head gasket, with a layer of asbestos sandwiched between two layers of copper.

copper gasket
Gasket made from a solid sheet of copper, used in high temperature and high pressure conditions.

copper sulfate
Chemical solution used to detect chrome-plated cylinders and to test crankshafts for *Tuftriding.*

Cord
Front-drive luxury car built by the Auburn Automobile Company of Auburn, Indiana, and named for company owner Erret Lobban Cord. There were two series of Cord cars: the L-29, built from 1929 to 1932, and the 810 and 812, built in 1936 and 1937. However, apart from their front drive, they were totally unalike. In addition to *Auburn* and *Cord,* E. L. Cord's interest included *Duesenberg.*

core
1. Interior of a hollow casting.
2. Used part or assembly, generally stripped of non-essentials, that is to be rebuilt or remanufactured.

core drill
Tool to drill out valve guides before final sizing with a reamer.

core hole
Cavity in a casting caused by the core shifting during manufacture.

core plug
Cavity cast into a part to facilitate the removal of core sand after the casting is complete.

core shift
Condition when one side of a cylinder bore is thicker than the other. Blocks with a lot of core shift should not be bored as much as blocks that have round bores. See also *sonic testing.*

cornering force
Force in *g's* exerted on the tires as a vehicle goes through a turn.

corrected horsepower
Brake output of an engine as observed on a dyno, adjusted for any deviations from the SAE standard ambient temperature of 60 degrees F. (15.6 C.) and barometric pressure of 29.0 inches of mercury (98.2 kilopascals). See also *observed horsepower.*

corrugated metal gasket
Gasket with a single thickness of special hardness tin metal, preformed to concentrate load at points to be sealed. See also *steel shim gasket.*

corsa
Italian for "course," specifically a road racing circuit.

Cosmoline
Tradename for a heavy-grade lubricant used to protect machined surfaces from rust.

Cosworth
British racing engine manufacturer, named for its founders, Mike *Cos*tin and Keith Duck*worth.* Cosworth is best known for its Ford-badged powerplants for Indycar and Formula One racing, though it has also done past development work for Chevrolet, as on the Cosworth Vega.

CO_2
Carbon dioxide.

cough
To damage or destroy an engine.

counterbalance
See *counterweight.*

counterbore
Recess that allows another part to be installed in a block or head into a particular location, such as a valve seat.

countershaft
1. Shaft used to reduce the imbalance inherent in some I-4 and V-6 engines. Usually, two countershafts are used in an I-4, but only one is needed in a V-6.
2. In a manual transmission, the shaft that supports the cluster gear set and rotates opposite the direction of the clutch and driveshaft.

countersink
Taper fluted tool used to chamfer parts.

counterweight
Weight added to a rotating shaft or wheel to offset vibration by balancing the part. Counterweights are used on crankshafts and sometimes on flywheels and driveshafts as well. Also sometimes called *counterbalance.*

coupe
Car with a close-coupled passenger compartment. In the United States, a coupe is generally understood to be a two-door car but, in Europe, the term is sometimes used for close-coupled four-door designs as well.

coupe de ville
Coupe with an open driver's compartment and an enclosed rear passenger compartment. See also *cape top.*

cowl
Part of a vehicle structure between the engine and passenger compartments to which the windshield and dashboard are attached.

C-pillar, C-post
Structural support just behind the rear door or rear quarter window; often the same as the rear quarter panel of the *greenhouse*. See photo p. 18. See also *A-pillar, A-post, B-pillar, B-post.*

cP
See *centipoise*.

CR
See *compression ratio*.

crank
1. Crankshaft.
2. As a verb, to fire up or rev an engine.
3. As a verb, to go fast, as in "he's crankin'."

crankcase
That part of an engine containing and supporting the crankshaft. On most engines, the crankcase consists of the lower part of the cylinder block and the oil pan.

crankcase breather
Tube or outlet that allows crankcase pressure and vapors to escape; in other words, *crankcase ventilation*.

crankcase pressure
Pressure built up in the crankcase by the downward movement of the pistons during the intake and combustion strokes; a form of *back pressure*.

crankcase vapors
See *blowby*.

crankcase ventilation
See *crankcase breather*.

crank kit
Reconditioned crankshaft, furnished with appropriate rod and main bearings.

crankpin
Rod journal of a crankshaft. Also *crank throw* or simply *journal*.

crank rpm
Measurement required for electronic engine control units to determine when ignition should occur.

crankshaft
Shaft with U-shaped cranks that converts the reciprocal motion of the pistons and rods to rotary motion that ultimately turns the wheels and drives the vehicle.

crankshaft counterbalance, crankshaft counterweight
See *counterweight*.

crankshaft arm
Connector, usually unmachined, between the main bearing and the two rod journals on the crankshaft. See also *long arm* and *short arm*.

crankshaft thrust collar
Vertical disc-shaped machined area on the crankshaft against which the flange of the main bearing rides.

crank start
To start an internal combustion engine by hand cranking it to rotate the crankshaft, with the ignition and fuel systems turned on. All ICE vehicles had to be crank started before the electric starter was introduced by Cadillac in 1912, and many cars still had holes in front for hand cranks as late as the 1940s. The principle of the crank start lives on in the kick start for some motorcycles, the prop start for some light aircraft, and the pull cord start for many small-engined devices, from lawn mowers to small outboard boat motors.

crash box
Manual transmission with straight-cut, non-synchromesh gears; with a crash box, a driver has to *double clutch* to avoid crashing or crunching the gears.

cream hardener
Activating ingredient for Bondo.

cream puff
Vehicle in especially fine condition.

creature comforts
Any options and/or amenities that increase vehicle driving pleasure.

critical pressure
Atmospheric pressure at which a gas becomes unstable and possibly volatile.

critical temperature
Temperature at which a flammable gas will ignite.

crocus cloth
Very mild abrasive sandpaper, used to polish parts, such as crank journals.

Crosley
Pioneering effort at an American small car by Powel Crosley, a successful radio manufacturer. The first Crosley had an air-cooled, two-cylinder engine and was built in Richmond, Indiana from 1939 to 1942. The second version of the make had a water-cooled, four-cylinder powerplant and was built in Marion, Indiana from 1945 to 1952.

cross-bolt main cap
Main bearing cap retained with two down-facing bolts and two bolts that intersect at 90 degrees.

cross-drilled crank
Crankshaft with two oil passages approximately 90 degrees apart in the main journals, to provide extra lubrication for the bearings. See photo next page.

crossflow head
Cylinder head with the intake ports on one side and the exhaust ports on the other, so that the gasses flow across the combustion chamber.

cross-hatch
Honing pattern required in the cylinder to maintain the correct amount of oil retention and to facilitate ring rotation in the cylinder. See photo next page.

cross heads
T-shaped part used on diesel engines to open and close two valves at one time.

cross-over pipe
Pipe used to connect both sides of a dual exhaust system to equalize pressure.

cross-over tube
Tube used to transmit liquids or gasses in or around an engine. The *heat-riser* passage in some intake manifolds is an example.

cross-section
Section formed by a plane cutting directly through an object, generally at 90 degrees to the object's centerline.

cross-up
To lose control of a car, allowing it to skid or spin off course.

crow foot
C-shaped, open-end wrench used with an extension to tighten or loosen hard-to-reach fasteners.

crown
Top surface of a piston.

cross-drilled crankshaft

cross-hatch cylinders

crown gear, crown wheel
Ring gear in a differential.

CRS
Cold-rolled steel, carbon steel worked into shape while cold.

CRT
Cathode ray tube, a vacuum tube used in electronic equipment to display information.

crude oil
Petroleum in its natural state as pumped from the ground.

cruise control
Device which will hold a vehicle at a highway speed set by the driver.

cruising
Social outing by generally younger drivers that involves driving a route repeatedly, usually on major city streets, at a slow speed, often for hours at a time. For young men, it is an opportunity to show off their cars and to flirt with young ladies along the way. In the last respect, cruising is a motorized version of the traditional Saturday evening promenade around the town square.

crush
Amount of compression needed to seat a rod or main bearing into its housing bore.

crunch hat
Safety helmet.

crush relief
Area on the edge of the bearing which allows crush to occur.

crush sleeve
Sleeve used to position a pinion gear in the differential that is designed to crush when torqued to a specified pressure.

cryogenic
Extremely low temperature process; used to harden some types of metal parts.

cSt
See *centistoke*.

CTO
Coolant temperature override.

C3I
Computer controlled coil ignition, a system developed by General Motors that uses a computer to monitor, maintain and adjust ignition timing.

cubes
Cubic inch displacement, or CID.

Cunningham
1. American luxury car built by the James Cunningham Company of Rochester, New York from 1907 to 1933. The company survived until 1936 as a coachbuilder, building custom bodies for other makes.
2. American sports car built by the B.S. Cunningham Company of West Palm Beach, Florida from 1951 to 1955. Briggs S. Cunningham's main goal with his Cadillac-, Chrysler- and Meyer-Drake Offenhauser-powered two-seaters was to win the 24 Hours of Le Mans. However,

the best his cars did in that race was third overall in both 1953 and 1954.

cup expander
Small disc used to maintain the seal between the cup and cylinder on a wheel cylinder assembly.

cup seal
Rubber seal inside the wheel cylinder.

cup shim
Spring adjuster with a cup-like shape used to reduce valve spring bounce at high rpm. See also *spring walk*.

curb height
Measurement from the vehicle frame to the road surface, used to detect sagging or broken springs.

curbside
On an RV, the right-hand side of the vehicle, i.e., the side normally next to the curb, as opposed to the *streetside*.

curb weight
What a vehicle weighs ready to drive away, with full loads of water, oil and gasoline, but without passengers or cargo aboard.

curing
1. Drying of paint.
2. Hardening of a catalyzed compound.

custom
Car which has been restyled for a more distinctive appearance. A mild custom may have only a few changes and its identity may be easy to recognize. A wild or rad custom, on the other hand, may completely lose its original identity and become an all-new design.

customize
To restyle a car.

cut
1. Direction and texture of the rows of cutting teeth of a file.
2. To defeat or eliminate a competitor in a drag race.

cut a big one, cut a fat one
To record a particularly quick time or high speed.

cutting brake
Special type of brake master cylinder used on off-road vehicles that has two levers to control how much brake pressure is applied to each rear wheel. One wheel can be braked while the other remains under power, allowing the vehicle to make much sharper turns. Also called *steering brake*.

CV joint
Constant velocity joint, a U-joint which can run at a steady speed without *wowing*.

CVT
Continuously variable transmission.

CVCC
Compound Vortex Combustion Control, tradename of a three-valve, stratified charge combustion chamber design developed by Honda in the early 1970s.

CW
Clockwise.

C_x
See *coefficient of drag*.

cycle
Short for motorcycle.

cycle fenders
Individual fenders for each wheel of a car, similar in shape and style to motorcycle fenders.

Cylgastos gasket
Gasket made with treated asbestos layers bonded on to a perforated tin plate.

cylinder
Hole in an engine block in which the piston moves up and down.

cylinder bore
Diameter of a cylinder.

cylinder deglazing
Process to remove the shiny glazed appearance on the cylinder walls in an engine after extensive use.

cylinder head
That part of an engine which covers the tops of the cylinders and pistons, and usually contains the combustion chambers and valvetrain.

cylinder head gasket
On an engine, gasket used to seal the head to the block against combustion pressures in the cylinders.

cylinder liner, cylinder sleeve
Removable and, therefore, replaceable cylinder wall. See also *dry liner, dry sleeve* and *wet liner, wet sleeve*.

D
Drive, one of the forward gear positions on an automatic transmission. Usually the highest gear available. "D" is sometimes combined with a number, as in "D1" for a lower drive range and "D2" for a higher range.

DA
At a body shop, a dual-action sander.

dago axle
Dropped beam axle for older Fords, designed to "dump" or lower the front end; the term is California slang for San Diego, where this type of axle is supposed to have originated. See also *dropped axle* and *dump*.

Daimler
Gottlieb Daimler and Wilhelm Maybach, both of Bad Cannstatt, Germany, developed a single-cylinder internal combustion engine in 1883 that was the first such powerplant designed to run on gasoline. (Karl Benz's engine, under development at about the same time, ran on naphtha.) Daimler's first application of the engine was in a two-wheeled vehicle, the world's first motorcycle and the only one Daimler ever produced. He also used it in the world's first motorboat. However, it wasn't until 1886, a year after Karl Benz built his first car, that Daimler built an automobile. The Daimler car had one important advantage over the Benz: it had four wheels, not just three. In the late 1890s, Emil Jellinek, an Austro-Hungarian diplomat residing in France, supported the development of a new car by Daimler. The vehicle was actually designed by Maybach and established the layout of a front engine and rear drive that would be the norm in automotive design for much of the century to come. By 1901, Jellinek had acquired distribution rights for the car in several European countries and the United States. To avoid possible legal problems with other automakers who had licenses to use Daimler engines, Jellinek decided against using the Daimler name and, instead, called the car after his daughter Mercedes. In 1902, the Daimler Motor Company adopted the name Mercedes for all of its passenger cars. In 1926, Daimler merged with Benz. The combined companies became Daimler-Benz and their products were renamed Mercedes-Benz. Daimler-Benz is the world's oldest car manufacturer. See also *Benz*, *Mercedes-Benz*.

dampener
Expression sometimes incorrectly substituted for *damper*, below.

damper
1. Friction or hydraulic shock absorber or, with active suspension, an equivalent electronic device.
2. A balancer on the front of the crankshaft to reduce unwanted harmonic vibrations.
3. In a broad sense, any device which reduces or eliminates oscillation or vibration.

Darrin
See *Kaiser-Darrin*.

dash
1. In circle track racing, a short race, usually no more than six laps, for the cars which have the best qualifying times for the main event.
2. See also *dashboard*, below.

dashboard
Full-width interior panel below and behind the windshield, housing the instruments, various accessory controls and the glove compartment; called *dash* for short.

Dash Series
NASCAR race series for four-cylinder, subcompact cars.

Datsun
In Tokyo in 1914, Masujiro Hashimoto built a car of his own design that he called the DAT, a name derived from the initials of three of his supporters—Kenjiro Den, Rokuro Aoyama and Meitaro Takeuchi. In Japanese, "dat" can also mean "hare" which, with its imagery of quickness and agility, was certainly an appropriate name for an automobile. However, the market for private passenger cars in Japan was still limited but there was a growing demand for commercial vehicles. So, during the 1920s, DAT Motor Company focused its efforts on trucks rather than cars. In 1931, Dat introduced a new mini car called the "Datson," meaning "Son of DAT," because it was so much smaller than the

trucks the company had been producing. In 1933, the Datson was renamed slightly. In Japanese, the syllable "son" can mean "damage" or "loss." After a typhoon inundated the DAT factory, "Datson" was changed to "Datsun," in hopes the "sun" would provide protection against such "son" as flooding. Also in 1933, the rights to manufacture the Datsun were acquired by a holding company which, a year later took the name "Nissan." In the early 1980s, the name Datsun was phased out and Nissan became the name of the product as well as of the company. See also *Nissan*.

datum point
In machining, the starting point for measuring an object. Same as *part zero point*.

daylight
In any side-by-side form of racing, to be ahead of a competitor by more than a car length, so that daylight is visible between the two vehicles.

Daytona
Daytona International Speedway, Daytona Beach, Florida; site of several major annual events, including NASCAR's Daytona 500 and Firecracker 400 stock car races and IMSA's 24-Hours of Daytona sports car endurance race.

dB
See *decibel*.

DC
See *direct current*.

D cam
Pattern used to grind pistons in an oval or cam shape with a 0.012-inch difference between the thrust face and the pinhole side.

dead axle
Shaft which connects wheels on either side of a vehicle but which does not transmit power, such as the rear axle on a front-drive car; same as *beam axle* and the opposite of *live axle*.

dead player
In the auto service industry, any vehicle part that is inoperable.

dead spot
Momentary lapse in power as an engine increases rpm. Same as *flat spot*.

deburr
To remove sharp edges from parts.

decarbonize, decarburize
To remove carbon deposits, such as from a combustion chamber. Also *decoke*.

decelerate
To decrease speed.

dechrome
To strip a car of its standard chrome trim, a common custom modification; in bodywork, the removal of all exterior trim to paint the car.

decibel
Measure of the relative loudness of a sound.

deck
1. The flat, mating surfaces of an engine block and head.
2. The trunk on a passenger car; the trunk door is the *deck lid*.
3. As a verb, (a) to machine the deck of an engine block flat, as part of a blueprint procedure, or (b) to dechrome the deck lid.

deck plate
Heavy metal plate bolted to a block deck during cylinder honing to simulate the stresses that pull the cylinder out of round when the head bolts are torqued into place.

decoke
British term for *decarbonize*.

dedicated fixture measuring systems
In bodywork, a fixture used to check the locating or alignment points on a vehicle.

de Dion axle
Final drive system with a differential or transaxle bolted to the frame; exposed, U-jointed half-shafts driving the wheels; and a separate, dead axle, usually a tube, which connects the wheels and holds them upright and also supports the springs. The de Dion axle provides the low unsprung weight of independent suspension with the stability of a solid axle. It is generally identified with rear-wheel drive but has also been used with front-wheel drive, notably on Miller race cars of the 1920s and Cord passenger cars built from 1929 to 1932.

deep dish wheel
Wheel with an extreme positive offset.

deep rolled fillets
Transition radius between a crank journal and the cheeks on the crankshaft.

deep dish wheel

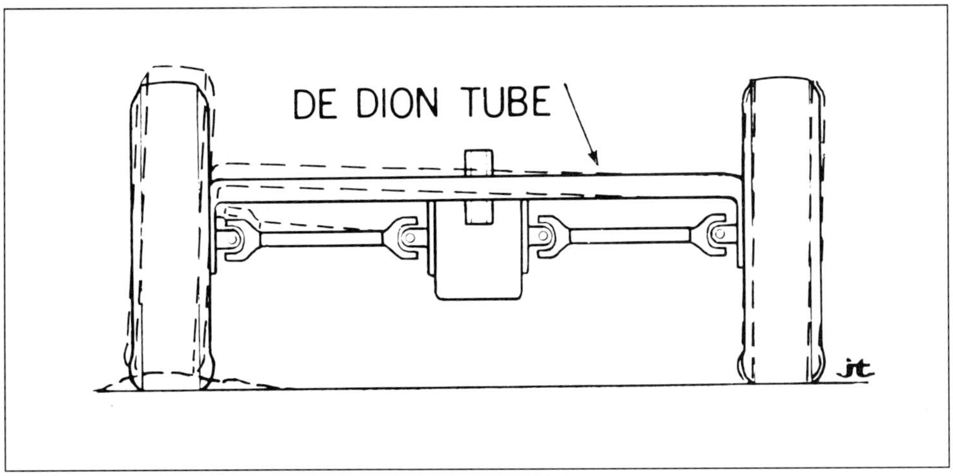

de Dion axle

D

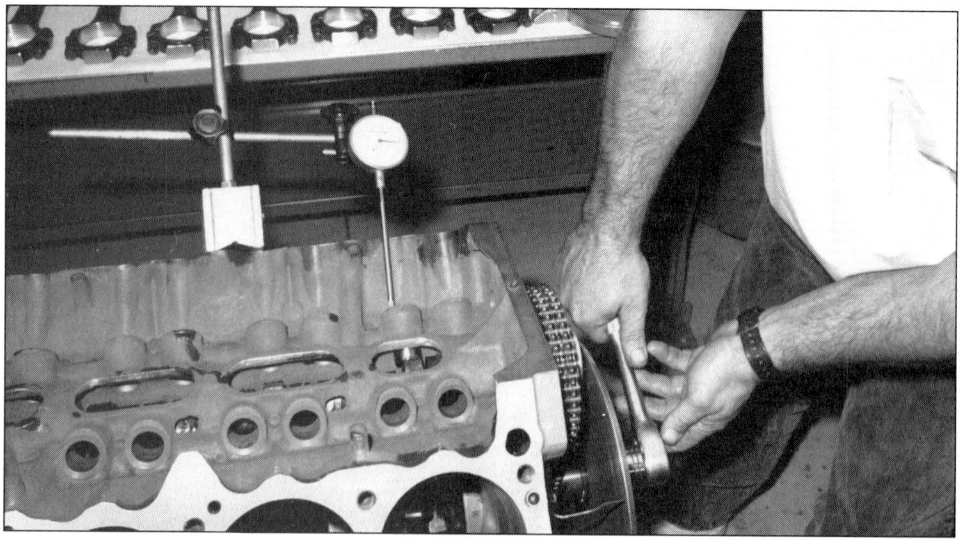
degreeing a cam

deep staging
Drag racing technique, whereby the driver uses minimum *rollout* to avoid *breakout*. See also *rollout*.

deep sump
Oil pan deep enough to keep oil away from the crankshaft at high rpm to reduce *windage*; used on some drag race cars.

deflection
Any axial or radial movement away from the normal or standard axis of a part due to side loading or pressure, such as the loads placed on suspension components during cornering.

degreaser
Chemical which breaks down grease and oil for easier removal.

degreasing
Cleaning parts in a solvent to remove grease and oil contamination.

degreeing a cam
Using a degree wheel and dial indicator to determine the actual timing of valve opening and closing provided by a particular camshaft.

De Lorean
Sports car developed by John Z. De Lorean, a former General Motors executive, and built from 1980 to 1982 by De Lorean Motor Cars Limited in Dunmurry, Northern Ireland. The De Lorean was a rear-engined, two passenger coupe with stainless steel body panels over a fiberglass structure. It also featured gullwing doors. However, the car never caught on with the public, and only an estimated 8000 were ever built. The company filed for bankruptcy and was placed in receivership by the British government in 1982, the forerunner to a decade of legal troubles that would plague De Lorean and his company.

demagnetize
To reduce or remove magnetism from an object.

departure angle
Maximum angle in degrees of a line running rearward and upward from the rear tire contact point to the lowest obstruction under the rear of the vehicle; see also *approach angle*.

depolarize
To remove positive or negative poles from an object.

depressed park
Positioning device on some windshield wipers to move the wiper arms out of sight below the hood level when power is turned off.

depth micrometer
Micrometer designed to measure the depth of holes, slots, recesses, keyways; in thousandths of an inch.

desiccant
Water absorbing material used as a drying agent.

desmodromic valves
Valve system in which positive cam action is used to close the intake and exhaust valves as well as to open them, instead of relying on springs to close them.

Desmond dresser
Tool to resurface large grinding stones.

De Soto
Medium-priced car introduced by Chrysler in 1928 and produced until 1960. The car was named for Hernando De Soto, the 16th century Spaniard who explored much of what is now the southeastern United States and is reputed to be first European to see the Mississippi River.

detergent dispersant
Chemical component in motor oil which loosens dirt and varnish in an engine.

detergent oil
Oil with a detergent additive.

detonation
Irregular combustion of the air/fuel mixture when two flame fronts collide, resulting in a knocking or pinging noise. The second flame front is generally believed to be caused by *auto ignition* of the *end gas*. Detonation is similar to preignition, but there's an important difference: As the term itself suggests, preignition occurs before the spark plug has fired, not after.

Detroit
U.S. auto industry in general, because the *Big Three* (GM, Ford and Chrysler) are all headquartered in the vicinity of this Michigan metropolis. See also *Motown*.

Detroit Locker
Specific brand of locking rear end differential.

deuce
1. 1932 Ford.
2. 1962 through 1967 Chevy II.
3. Two-barrel carburetor.
4. With an initial capital, Deuce was a nickname for the late Henry Ford II.

deuce-and-a-quarter
Buick Electra 225; so called because, when the first Electra 225 was introduced as Buick's top-of-the-line model in 1959, its overall length was 225 inches.

deuce-and-a-half
Truck with a nominal payload of 2-1/2 tons.

DG
Double-groove valve stem; also called *2G*.

diagonal cross-check
Measure of the weight distribution between the right front and left rear wheels, and the left front and right rear wheels; important in setting up a car for oval track racing.

dial
Generally, a measuring instrument with an analog gauge, rather than a digital readout.

dial-bore gauge
Tool to measure inside diameters to 0.0001-inch accuracy, generally used to measure cylinder bores for machining purposes.

dial gauge
See *dial indicator*.

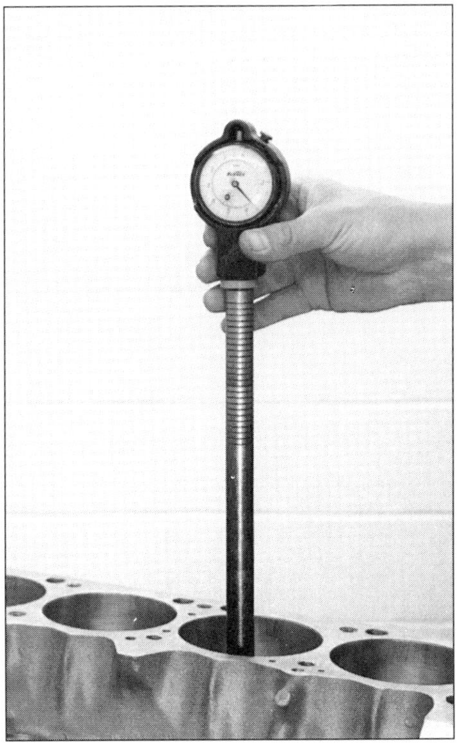

dial-bore gauge

dial-in
1. To set up a car with just the right combination for maximum performance according to current racing conditions.
2. In bracket racing, to set the *Christmas tree* with the interval between starting times for vehicles with different indexes, and to set-up the car to hit the index as close as possible.

dial indicator
Tool to measure straight-line movement, such as valve lift or piston height.

dial under
Under NHRA rules, an option allowed in Stock and Super Stock classes to select a time under, i.e., quicker than, the national index for the class. Dialing under is applied in handicap eliminations where the breakout rule is in effect.

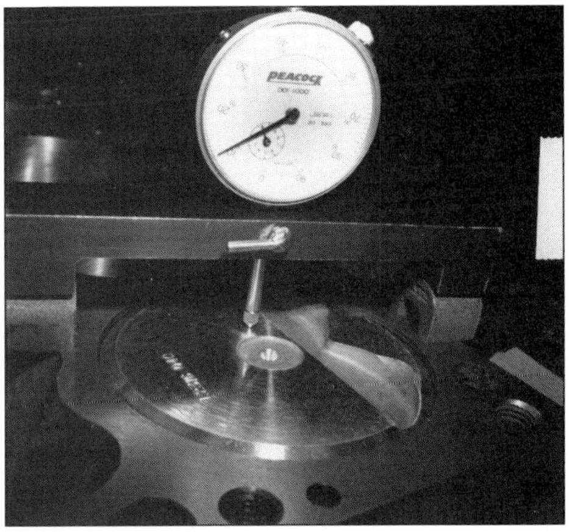

dial indicator

diamond
Collision damage where bodywork has been bent or pushed into the shape of a diamond.

diamond dresser
Tool encasing an industrial grade diamond to reface grinding stones.

diamond lap
Tool to sharpen bits.

diaphragm
Flexible membrane which deflects under hydraulic or pneumatic pressure, causing movement that can pump liquids or air, or perform mechanical work.

diaphragm clutch
Clutch with a shallow, cone-shaped spring disc to provide pressure to the plate.

dice
Tight contest between two cars on an oval track or road course; a dice is often a race within a race, with two competitors battling for a specific position back in the pack.

die
1. Hand tool to cut external threads on a shaft.
2. A tool used to bend or form metal tubing so that the walls do not collapse.

die bar
Bar with a flat hook at one end, used in pairs to pry apart stamping dies and gear-pulley assemblies.

die grinder
High-speed (20,000+ rpm) grinder using rotary files and brushes to grind or clean parts.

diesel engine
Compression ignition engine developed by Rudolf Diesel; even though the word diesel derives from a proper name, it is not usually capitalized. See *compression ignition*.

dieseling
Condition when a spark ignition engine continues to run after the ignition system has ben switched off, usually as the result of hot spots such as carbon deposits in the combustion chambers. Same as *auto ignition* and *running on*.

diff
See *differential*, below.

differential
Gearing device which transmits power from a driveshaft or transaxle to driving axles, and which also allows the wheel on the outside of a turn to rotate faster than the wheel on the inside to prevent tire *scrub*. See photo next page.

differential pressure regulator
See *pressure actuator*.

differential-pressure valve
Device that maintains constant fuel pressure to injectors.

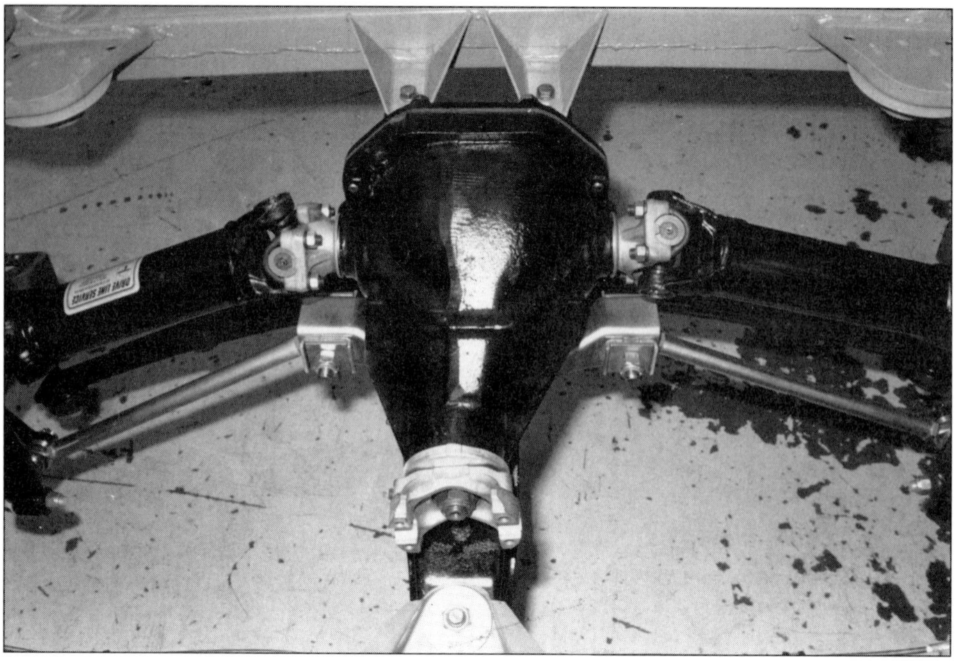

differential

digger
Dragster. The term originated to describe drag cars because they seem to "dig" themselves *out of the hole* as they accelerate from the starting line.

digital instrument
Display which shows some physical quantity, such as mph, rpm, voltage, or fuel supply, with an electronic readout rather than a movable needle; a digital instrument is usually more difficult to read at a glance than an analog instrument. A panel of digital instruments is sometimes referred to as an *Atari dashboard*. See also *analog instrument*. Most Indy cars use digital instruments because many instruments can be displayed on a single panel, without taking up too much space.

dig out
To accelerate suddenly, as at the start of a drag race.

digs
Drag races.

dimmer switch
Hand or foot control for switching back and forth between the high and low headlight beams.

dimple
Process to turn a hole under or down to allow installation of a fastener; to *bell*.

DIN
Deutsches Institut fur Normung or German Institute for Standardization. DIN is the German equivalent of our SAE and sets similar industry standards for measurement.

ding
Small dent or scrape in auto bodywork.

dingle berry hone
Slang for a silicon carbide ball hone or flex hone for cylinder glazing. See *flex hone*.

dipper
Small metal scoop on the bottom of a connecting rod which dips or scoops oil from the pan to lubricate the bearing.

dipper trough
Trough aligned under connecting rods that are fitted with dippers. See *dipper*, above.

dip stick
Metal stick to measure the oil level in an engine or transmission..

direct current
Electrical current which flows in one direction continuously. Abbreviated *DC*. See also *alternating current*.

direct drive
Transmission mode in which the engine crankshaft and the driveshaft rotate at the same speed; a 1-to-1 gear ratio.

direct ignition system
Ignition system that has no distributor; electrical impulses are sent from a modulator directly to the spark plugs.

direct injection
Type of fuel injection that injects fuel directly into the cylinders.

direct layout
Method to scribe lines directly onto metal without using a pattern or template.

directional signals
Flashing lights at either side of both the front and rear of a vehicle used to indicate turning direction. Same as *turn indicator*.

directional tire
Tire with an asymmetrical tread pattern that must be mounted facing forward. When the tires are rotated, a directional tire cannot be taken around and mounted on the other side of the vehicle, because its tread would now be facing backwards. Directional tires can only be switched from front to rear on the same side.

dirt dobber
Circle track race driver who prefers dirt tracks to asphalt.

dirt tracking
Driving on an asphalt track as if it were dirt, throwing the car through corners in exaggerated slides.

DIS
Direct or distributorless ignition system. See *direct ignition system*.

disc brake
Brake system using a caliper and rotor, or disc, to slow or stop a vehicle See photo next page.

dished piston
Piston with a depression in the crown; opposite of *domed piston*.

disc brake

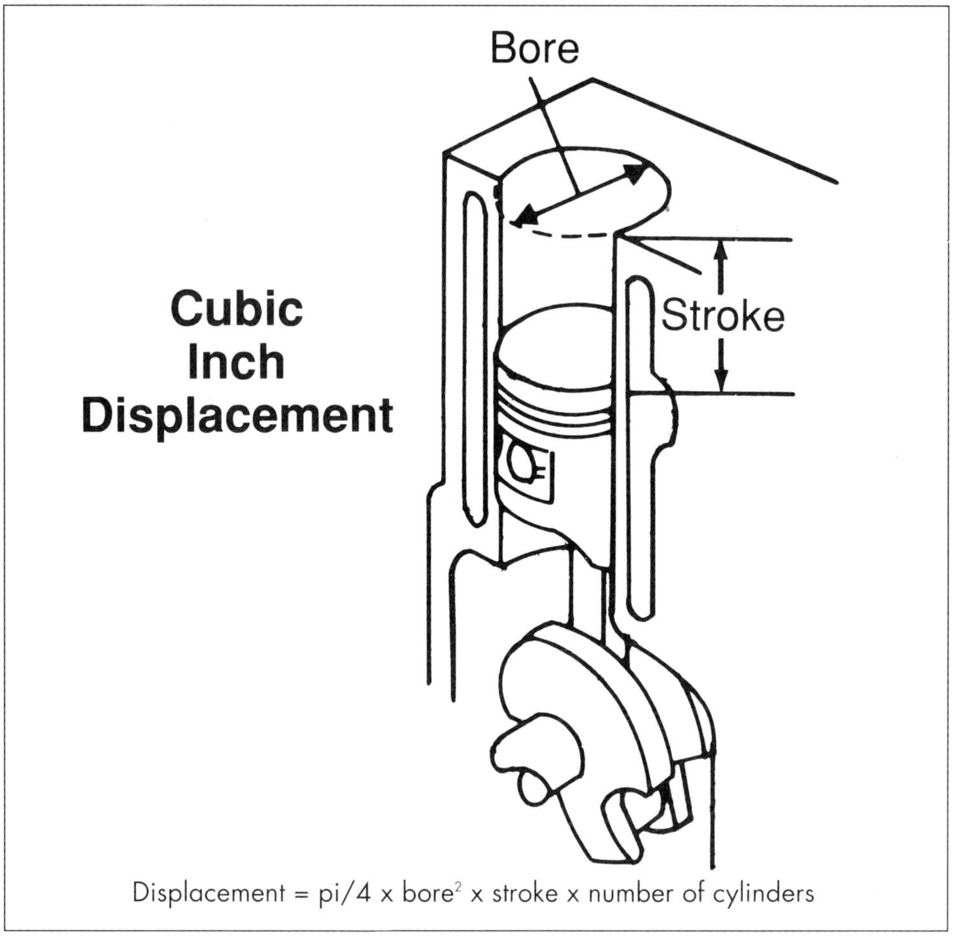

displacement

D

displacement
Volume within an engine's cylinders swept by the pistons as each of them makes one stroke downward, from Top Dead Center (TDC) to Bottom Dead Center (BDC); expressed in cubic inches, cubic centimeters or liters.

distributor
Device used to direct, or distribute, either electrical current to spark plugs or fuel to injectors.

distributor machine
Machine for dynamic testing and calibrating of distributors.

distributor pipe, distributor rail
In a fuel injection system, a pipe to convey fuel from the fuel distributor to an injector.

dive
During hard braking, the tendency of the front part of a vehicle's structure to press down on the front springs as a result of sudden weight transfer to the front. See also *squat.*

divergent nozzle end
Exhaust pipe nozzle end that expands from the pipe inlet to the end.

divergent-convergent nozzle end
Exhaust pipe nozzle that expands and then reduces in size at the end.

DIY
Do it yourself.

dizzy
Slang for *distributor*.

D-Jetronic
Early Bosch fuel injection system.

DNF
In any form of motor racing, did not finish.

Dodge
Horace and John Dodge were early shareholders in the Ford Motor Company and manufactured engines for Ford. In 1914, they formed Dodge Brothers to produce a car of their own design. Dodge cars soon acquired a reputation for ruggedness and were widely used as staff cars and ambulances during World War I. In 1928, Walter P. Chrysler bought out Dodge Brothers and Dodge has been a mainstay of Chrysler Corporation ever since, building not only cars but trucks as well. Chrysler has often emphasized Dodge as the corporation's performance car and that remains true today, with such vehicles as the Daytona, Stealth and Viper all carrying Dodge nameplates rather than Chrysler or Plymouth.

dog
1. In oval track racing, to follow another car extremely close in an effort to spook its driver into making a mistake.
2. Poor performing car.
3. Pin or stub used to mate and drive a gear or assembly.

dog clutch
Simple, splined clutch which cannot be slipped, a common piece of equipment in dirt track cars without transmissions or in the locking hubs of four-wheel-drive vehicles. See also *in-and-out box*.

dog house
1. Housing over an engine or transmission.
2. To a bodyworker, the front fenders, hood, and grille assembly of an automobile.

dog leg
Sharp, angular turn, such as an acute bend on a road racing course.

domed piston

dog tracking
Off-center tracking of the rear wheels in relationship to the front wheels; usually the result of a bent or twisted frame.

DOHC
Dual overhead camshafts, two cams in a single cylinder head; see also *OHC* and *SOHC*.

dolly
1. In sheet metal fabrication or bodywork, a tool used underneath metal being hammered from above to help shape or form it.
2. As a verb, to shape or form metal using a hammer and dolly.

DOM tubing
Drawn over mandrel, a type of seamless tubing that is precise and consistent in both inside and outside diameters; used in race car chassis construction.

domed piston
Piston with a raised crown; opposite of *dished piston*.

donuts
1. Tires, especially big racing slicks.
2. A 360-degree burn-out, commonly performed in high school parking lots and off-road.

dooley
Chevrolet pickup truck with dual rear wheels at each end of the drive axle for added cargo carrying capacity. See also *DRW* and *duallie*.

doorslammer
Full-bodied drag car with functioning doors.

doozie, doozy
See *Duesie*.

DOT
Department of Transportation, the federal agency responsible for establishing and enforcing fuel economy and safety standards for all new cars and light trucks sold in the U.S.

double A-arm, double A-frame
Suspension system using two A-arms or A-frames to connect the chassis to the wheel spindle. The upper arms are usually shorter then the lower units. Also called *double wishbone*. See also *A-arm, A-frame*.

double century, double ton
200 mph.

double clutch
Driving technique to minimize gear clash with a manual transmission that has straight-cut, non-synchromesh gears. The driver depresses the clutch pedal and shifts out of gear. He then releases the clutch and depresses it again before shifting into the next gear.

double hump heads
See *camel hump heads*.

double J rim
Safety bead locks on a wheel rim designed to hold both the outer and inner tire beads securely; the "double J" describes the shape of the locks.

double wishbone
See *double A-arm, double A-frame*.

dowel pin
Round, solid or hollow pin used to align two or more parts.

downdraft carburetor
Carburetor with downward airflow.

downforce
Downward force of air on a speeding vehicle. Properly directed downforce can improve traction and cornering ability.

downshift
To change from a higher gear to a lower one. See also *upshift*.

D-port
Intake or exhaust port shaped like the letter D, usually found with the straight side facing down toward the deck surface. See photo next page.

drafting, NASCAR-style

DQ
In any form of motor racing, disqualified.

draft
To follow another car around an oval track, especially in stock car racing, closely enough to take advantage of the slipstream or partial vacuum created behind it at very high speeds. One vehicle will pull up closely behind another on the straightaway. The front car must penetrate the air while the rear car does not. This causes the rear car to use less horsepower and fuel while traveling at the same speed. The addition of the rear car also extends the envelope of the vacuum, which reduces the amount of drag or air pressure on the front car, and effectively "pushes" the front car along (without physical contact). Therefore, the two cars will both go faster then just one by itself. This principle also extends to more than two cars. That is why you'll often see a train of as many as 10 or more NASCAR stock cars on superspeedways.

draft tube
In an engine, a vent to release crankcase vapors to the atmosphere.

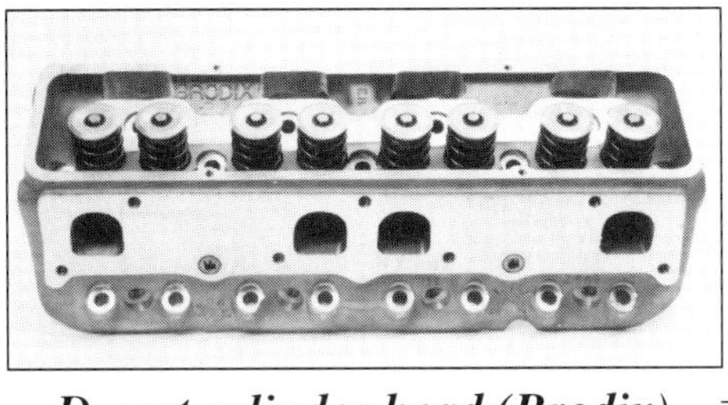

D-port cylinder head (Brodix)

drag
1. Acceleration contest between two vehicles; in *heads-up racing*, the vehicles start together and the first to cross the finish line is the winner. In bracket racing, they're started separately at an interval corresponding to the difference between the indexes for their respective classes.
2. Resistance of air against an object trying to pass through it. See *aerodynamic drag*.

drag coefficient
See *coefficient of drag*.

drag link
Steering component which connects the *Pitman arm* to the *steering arm*.

dragster
Vehicle engineered and constructed strictly for drag racing. In the interest of spectator identification, most other drag cars, even such exotic types as *Altereds* and *Funny Cars*, bear some resemblance to ordinary automobiles. A dragster doesn't; at every level from *Econorail* to *Top Fuel*, it's a pure race car.

drag strip
The standard quarter-mile drag strip uses a paved area 60 feet wide and up to 4000 feet long. A competitor's elapsed time or ET is measured from the Christmas tree to another timing light 1320 feet away; his or her top speed is measured over a 132-foot trap, beginning 66 feet ahead of the 1320-foot mark and finishing 66 feet beyond it. The remainder of the 4000-foot length serves as a shut-off area. The eighth-mile strip is similar in layout but obviously shorter, with the ET being measured over only 660 feet.

draw bar
Bar used to tighten a tool, such as a mill tool, collet or form tool, into its holding fixture on a milling machine.

draw file
Method of drawing a file back and forth at a right angle to the axis of the object being filed; usually leaves a very smooth surface.

drier
1. Small canister located in the air conditioning line used to remove moisture from the refrigerant.
2. Catalyst added to paint to speed the curing time.

drift
1. Controlled slide through a turn with all four wheels broken loose; when done with a Lincoln, it's known as Continental drift.
2. Tool used to separate two Morse Taper joints.

drill geometry
Drill bit angle of 59 degrees, the angle at which experience shows a bit will last the longest and drill the most holes.

D-ring
Control in a drag race car's cockpit to release the chute at the end of a run.

drive axle
Axle or, with independent suspension, axle shafts that transmit power to the drive wheels.

drive by wire
To use an electronic throttle control rather than the traditional mechanical linkage.

drive fit
See *interference fit*.

driveline
See *drivetrain*.

driven plate
Driven friction plate in a clutch assembly. Same as *clutch disc*.

driveshaft
In a front-engined/rear-drive vehicle, the shaft that transmits power from the transmission, through the differential and half-shafts, to the rear wheels.

driver
1. Beyond its obvious definition, driver is used to mean a car for everyday use; same as *beater* or *grocery getter*.
2. Tool used to guide a part into place, such as a valve seat or guide.

drivetrain
The components which deliver power from the engine to the road surface, including the clutch or torque converter, and the transmission, driveshaft and differential or transaxle, and the axle shafts, wheels and tires. The drivetrain does *not* include the engine itself, though the *powertrain* does. The drivetrain is also sometimes called the *driveline*.

driving lamps, driving lights
Auxiliary lights to provide extra illumination for high-speed night driving.

drop
To lower some structural part of a car; see *dago axle*, *dropped axle* and *dump*.

drop-head coupe
British term for two-door convertible; opposite of *fixed head coupe*.

drop forge
To hammer, form or beat hot metal into a specific shape, using a heavy press, weight or hammer.

drop the hammer
To engage the clutch and depress the accelerator suddenly at the start of a drag race, or to suddenly depress the accelerator to the floorboard to increase speed. See *floor it*.

drop-throttle oversteer
See *lift-throttle oversteer*.

dropped axle
Lowered beam axle for older Fords, designed to *dump* the front end; same as *dago axle*.

druid
Deprecating term for a race official or promoter, usually used by disgruntled contestants who have trouble running within the rules.

DRW
Ford pickup with dual rear wheels at each end of the drive axle for added cargo carrying capacity. See also *dooley* and *duallie*.

dry
Process of paint changing from a liquid to a solid state; occurs when the solvents within the paint evaporate.

dry charge battery
Lead-acid battery shipped dry and not filled with electrolyte until put into service.

dry deck
Condition when a piston crown is at the level of the block deck.

dry film lubricant
Graphite- or petroleum-based chemical that bonds to metal and provides a slick, protective coating on parts surfaces at engine start-up, before any oil is circulating. Also called simply *dry lube*.

dry fuel, dry gas
Diesel fuel or gasoline with an additive, usually alcohol, to prevent water from collecting and freezing in the fuel system, and especially in the fuel lines.

dry lakes
See *lakes*.

dry lube
See *dry film lubricant*, above.

dry spray
Condition that occurs when paint is sprayed toward a surface from too great a distance, causing the binders of the paint to solidify before reaching the surface.

dry liner, dry sleeve
Cylinder liner contained by the existing cylinder wall and, therefore, not in contact with the coolant.

dry sump
Crankcase which does not contain the engine's oil supply; for better cooling, the oil is carried in a separate tank outside the engine.

dry weight
Weight of a vehicle without any water or gasoline.

dual bed converter
Catalytic converter that passes exhaust gasses through an upper or front chamber and a lower or back chamber. Usually, one chamber is coated with platinum and palladium and the other with platinum and rhodium, for control of all three major exhaust pollutants, i.e., carbon monoxide, unburned hydrocarbons and oxides of nitrogen. Also called *three-way catalyst*.

dual cowl
Phaeton with separate windshields for the front and rear passenger compartments. See *phaeton*.

dual exhaust
Exhaust system used on high-performance V-type engines, with a separate exhaust pipe and muffler for each cylinder bank.

dual fuel engine
Engine designed to run on two different fuels, either separately as in the case of an engine which can run on either gasoline or propane, or simultaneously, as in the case of an engine which can run on gasoline, alcohol or a combination of the two.

dual-idler gear drive
Timing gear system with two idler gears to enable the crankshaft to drive the camshaft.

dual ignition system
See *twin plug ignition system*.

dual master cylinder
Brake master cylinder with two separate circuits to prevent complete loss of braking. The circuits may be divided between the front and rear brakes, or diagonally, with the left front and right rear as one pair and the right front and left rear as the other.

dual-plane crankshaft
Crankshaft with throws in two planes, at 90 degree angles.

dual-plane manifold
Intake manifold with two air cavities to provide air/fuel mixture to the cylinders. Neither cavity serves cylinders that follow each other in firing order, giving the flow

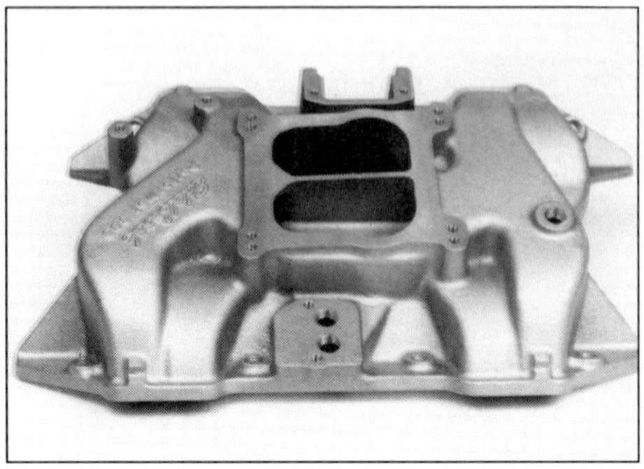

dual-plane manifold

of mixture in each cavity a chance to calm before the next intake pulse.

duallie
Dodge pickup truck with dual rear wheels at each end of the drive axle for added cargo carrying capacity. See also *dooley* and *DRW*.

dual-quads
Two four-barrel carburetors.

duals
Double exhaust system, with two mufflers and two tail pipes.

ducktail
Upswept rear end, usually incorporating a spoiler.

duct
Opening in a vehicle body panel that admits air and directs it to a specific area, such as to the carburetor for the air/fuel mixture, the interior for ventilation, or to the brakes for cooling. See also *scoop*.

ductility
Ability of metal to be formed and shaped without breaking.

duct tape
Heavy-duty, fabric-backed tape originally developed for sealing air conditioning ducts; adheres well with metal, fiberglass, plastic and glass; commonly used for improvised repairs in all forms of racing, from labeling parts to temporarily repairing damaged body parts during the course of a race. Also called *racer's tape*, *silver tape*, *super tape* and *200-mph tape*.

Duesenberg
The Duesenberg brothers, Frederick and August, were already veteran builders of race cars and of marine and aircraft engines when they established the Duesenberg Motor Company of Indianapolis in 1920 to manufacture their first production passenger car. Called the Duesenberg Model A, it had such innovative features as a straight-eight engine with an overhead camshaft and four-wheel hydraulic brakes. The Model A bore a strong resemblance to Duesenberg race cars of the early 1920s and basked in their glory as they won the French Grand Prix in 1921 and the Indy 500 in 1924, 1925 and 1927. E.L. Cord acquired control of the Duesenberg Motor Company in 1926 and commissioned the brothers to develop a new, much larger and more powerful car. The result was the Duesenberg Model J, which debuted in late 1928. It was more than twice as powerful as any other car made in the United States at the time. As if that weren't enough, a supercharged version, the Model SJ, was added to the line. The car went out of production with the collapse of Cord's automotive empire in 1937. Many experts consider the Duesenberg the finest American vehicle of the classic era. In the years after World War II, there were three attempts by members of the Duesenberg family to build an entirely new car, and two efforts to produce a Duesenberg replicar. However, there is not apt to be anything quite like the Model J and SJ ever again.

Duesie
1. *Duesenberg*, one of the greatest cars ever built in the United States. See above.
2. In a broader sense, a Duesie is anything truly fine or outstanding. In this usage, the word is sometimes spelled *doozie* or *doozy*.

dummy
Mannequin used in vehicle crash tests to determine survivability of human passengers.

dummy load
Electrical testing procedure to simulate actual operation of a circuit.

dummy shaft
Shaft that aids in the assembly or disassembly of a parts group. An example is a dummy pinion shaft, which is used to help with the installation of the pinion gear in the differential housing.

dump
1. To defeat a competitor in a drag race.
2. To damage or destroy a component as, for example, "to dump a clutch."
3. To lower the front-end of car.

dumped and tubbed
Vehicle which has been lowered at the front and fitted with oversize wheelwells, or *tubs*, to accommodate big *meats* or tires at the rear.

dump station
Facility where an RV's *black water* and *gray water* can be disposed of.

dump tubes
Straight-through exhaust headers.

dune buggy
See *buggy*.

Durometer
Gauge to test rubber hardness.

Dura Spark ignition
Ignition system designed by Ford.

duration
Amount of time, expressed in crankshaft degrees, that a camshaft lobe holds an intake or exhaust valve open. Also *cam duration*.

dust, dust-off
In motor racing, to defeat or overtake another competitor decisively.

dust shield
Cover or plate to keep dust away from sensitive parts.

Dutched
Bodywork finished with elaborate striping or flame painting of a type popularized in the 1950s by the late Kenneth "Von Dutch" Howard.

dwell
1. In an ignition system, the degrees of distributor rotation during the interval the breaker points are closed. Also called *dwell angle*.
2. Period of time that a honing machine stays at the bottom of a cylinder bore to eliminate taper.

dwell angle
See *dwell*.

dwell meter
Electronic device to measure dwell angle.

dye penetrant testing
Inexpensive, non-destructive method to detect cracks in metal. The process consists of three separate chemicals: a cleaner, a penetrating red dye, and a white developer. After the area to be tested is cleaned, the red dye is sprayed or brushed on and allowed to soak in for a few minutes. Then the developer is sprayed on. Defects show red and smooth areas show white. When the inspection is complete, the area is again cleaned to remove the dye and developer.

Dykem blue
Blue dye used to color metal, primarily so lines and marks can be visibly scribed directly onto the metal surface.

Dykes ring
Compression piston ring, with a cross-section shape like the letter "L," which provides good sealing against cylinders walls at all engine speeds. Named for its inventor, Paul Dykes.

dynamic balance
Process of checking and correcting the balance of a rotating part, such as a crankshaft or wheel, while it is actually in motion. Opposite of *static balance*.

dynamo
DC generator.

dyno, dynamometer
1. Energy-absorbing device for measuring the torque and rpm of an engine, from which horsepower can be calculated. An engine dyno shows output at the flywheel, while a chassis dyno shows it at the drive wheels. See also *brake horsepower, brake torque* and *prony brake*.
2. As a verb, dyno means to test an engine or a vehicle on a dynamometer.

Dzus fastener
Screw-like fastener with a recessed, slot-screw head and a spiral slot in the shank designed to attach to a heavy wire. Developed by William Dzus in the 1930s for aircraft use, the Dzus fastener can be tightened or loosened with only a quarter of a turn and, thus, is ideal for race car body panels that might have to be removed and replaced quickly during a pit stop.

dyno

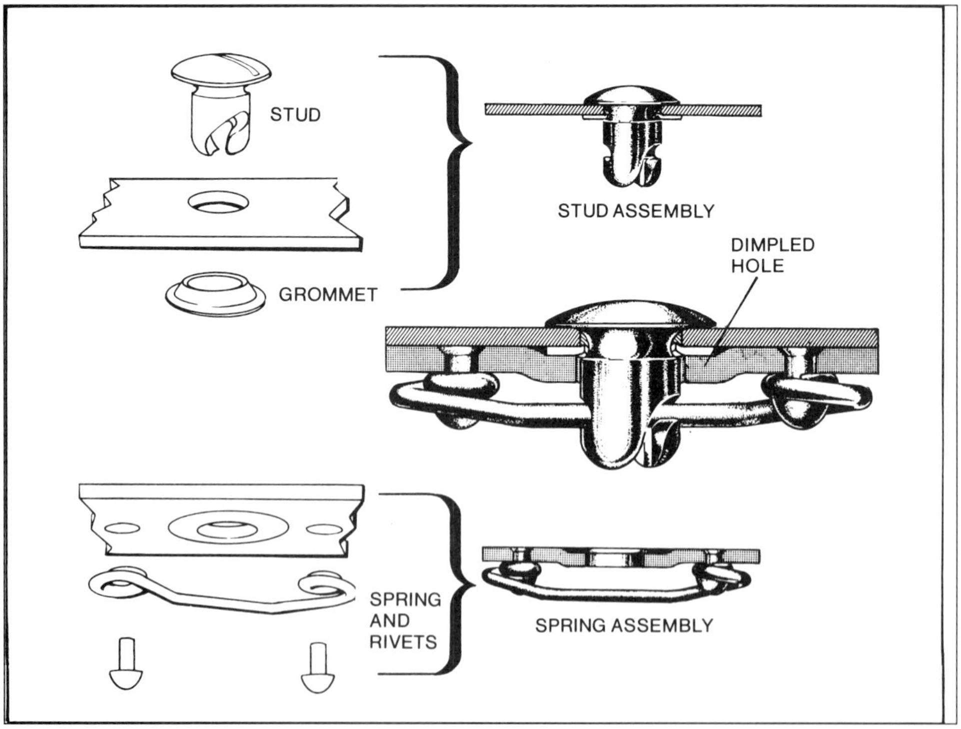

Dzus fastener assembly

E

Eagle
When Chrysler Corporation acquired American Motors Corporation in 1988, it gave the name Eagle to what was left of the AMC passenger car line. Eagle had been used earlier by AMC itself as a model designation for a four-wheel-drive version of its compact sedan and wagon, introduced in 1980.

early apex
Early entry into a corner; i.e., getting to the inside of a turn sooner than usual.

east-west
Transverse or sideways engine placement in a vehicle, as in most small front-drive cars and some mid-engined, rear-drive cars. See also *north-south*.

E cam
Pattern used to grind pistons in an oval or cam shape with a 0.013-inch difference between the thrust face and the pinhole side.

ECC
Electronic climate control, used to regulate the temperature of a vehicle's passenger compartment.

eccentric bearing
Bearing that is thickest at the crown, with the ends a few ten thousandths of an inch thinner.

eccentric sleeve
Sleeve used to offset a mandrel in a Sunnen hone.

eccentricity
Condition when two or more round parts or holes do not share the same central axis.

ECM
Electronic control module, used to control some engine functions.

econobox
Small economy car.

economizer
Device in a carburetor which regulates fuel flow to reduce excessive consumption, particularly under hard throttle.

economy of motion
Minimum effort needed to do a job.

Econorail
Dragster with a single, normally aspirated gasoline engine; category for those who want to race a true dragster but who don't have the budget needed for Top Fuel or Top Alcohol.

ECS
Electronic control system, used to control certain electrical or engine operations.

ECU
Electronic control unit, computer control box for engine management. Same as *ECM*.

ECT
Electronically controlled transmission, linked to a vehicle's electronic control system.

edge loading
Condition when two parts rub together at their edges.

EDM
Electric discharge machine, which uses electrical power to machine parts into specific patterns.

Edsel
Garish-looking, medium-priced car built by Ford Motor Company from 1958 to 1960. It was named after Edsel Ford, the son of the original Henry Ford and the father of Henry II. The car was supposedly the product of intensive market research but bombed with the public and was dropped after less than three model years, at a loss of over $250 million for Ford.

EEC
1. Evaporative emissions control; see *EECS*.
2. Electronic engine control, system which regulates an engine's electrical functions.

EEC-I
1978 Ford electronic engine control system that controlled the ignition advance and retard only.

EEC-II
1979 Ford electronic engine control system that used a crank-mounted ignition sensor and electronic engine control unit.

EEC-III
1980 Ford electronic engine control system that used an oxygen sensor, microprocessor control unit, a series of vacuum switches, and either a variable venturi carburetor or a central fuel injection system.

EEC-IV
Ford electronic engine control system that uses a mass air flow sensor, sequential port fuel injection, electronic fuel injection, speed density sensor, and electronic control unit.

EECS
Evaporative emissions control system, canister filled with activated charcoal to reduce raw fuel emissions.

E85
Fuel blend of 85 percent *ethanol* and 15 percent gasoline; not to be confused with *gasohol,*which is a blend of 85-90 percent gasoline ad 10-15 percent ethanol. See also *M85.*

Edwards
We couldn't leave out a car built by a namesake (but not a relative) of the author's. The Edwards was a sports car built in the early 1950s by industrialist Sterling Edwards of South San Francisco, California. The forerunner of the car was the Edwards Special, a Ford V-8 powered sports racing car built in 1949. The production car was called the Edwards America and appeared in prototype form in 1951 with a Chrysler Hemi engine in a Henry J chassis. Later versions used Oldsmobile, Cadillac or Lincoln engines in a shortened Mercury station wagon chassis. By the time Edwards gave up producing the America in 1955, only half a dozen production cars had been built.

EFI
Electronic fuel injection.

efficiency
Ratio of the actual energy produced by a machine to the potential energy originally supplied to that machine, i.e., output divided by input, expressed as a percentage. In an engine, three important forms of efficiency are *mechanical efficiency*, *thermal efficiency* and *volumetric efficiency*.

egg crate
Cross-hatch grille design, such as traditionally used by Cadillac.

EGR, EGR valve
See *exhaust gas recirculation.*

elapsed time
Abbreviated *ET*, the time in seconds and thousandths of seconds it takes a vehicle to cover a given distance from a standing start; in drag racing, the distance is usually a quarter mile, or sometimes an eighth mile.

elastic limit
Maximum a part will stretch without breaking.

elastomeric seal
Seal made of rubber or similar material.

ELC
Electronic level control, device to regulate the ride height of a vehicle under differing loads.

Eldo
Cadillac Eldorado.

electric vehicle
Vehicle propelled by electric motor(s), using current from rechargeable, on-board storage batteries.

electric welding
See *arc welding.*

electro-hydraulic pressure actuator
Valve providing continuous adjustment of fuel pressure for basic fuel metering on the KE series Bosch fuel injection system.

electrode
1. Either of the terminals in an electrical circuit separated from each other by a gap the current has to cross, such as the center and side electrodes in a spark plug.
2. Rod used in arc welding.

electrolysis
Electrical etching action in metal caused by heat and moving water and leading to structural deterioration.

electrolyte
Solution that conducts electrical current, such as the mixture of sulfuric acid and distilled water in a storage battery.

electromagnet
Device with a coil of wire wrapped around an iron inductor that becomes a magnet when electric current is passed through the coil.

electromagnetic induction
Method of generating voltage by passing a magnet through a coil of wire.

electron
Negatively charged particle of an atom. See also *positron.*

electronic ignition
Ignition system in which transistorized circuits have replaced mechanical breaker points.

elephant foot
Valve adjusting screw with a ball that swivels when it contacts the valve stem.

elephant motor
Chrysler Hemi engine, so called because of its huge displacement and power output, which in stock form is 425 cubic inches, 425 horsepower. See *Hemi.*

eliminations
In drag racing, series of matches between two cars at a time, with the winner of each match advancing to the next round; the winner of the final round is the top eliminator of the series.

Elky
El Camino, a Chevrolet passenger car-based pickup truck. See photo next page.

elliptic spring
See *leaf spring.*

elongation
Stretching of a material.

ELOX
Type of machine that uses an electrical charge to burn away broken bolts or studs in parts.

embedability
Ability of a substance to accept embedding of foreign material.

embossed gasket
Shim-type head gasket with a raised surface.

Elky

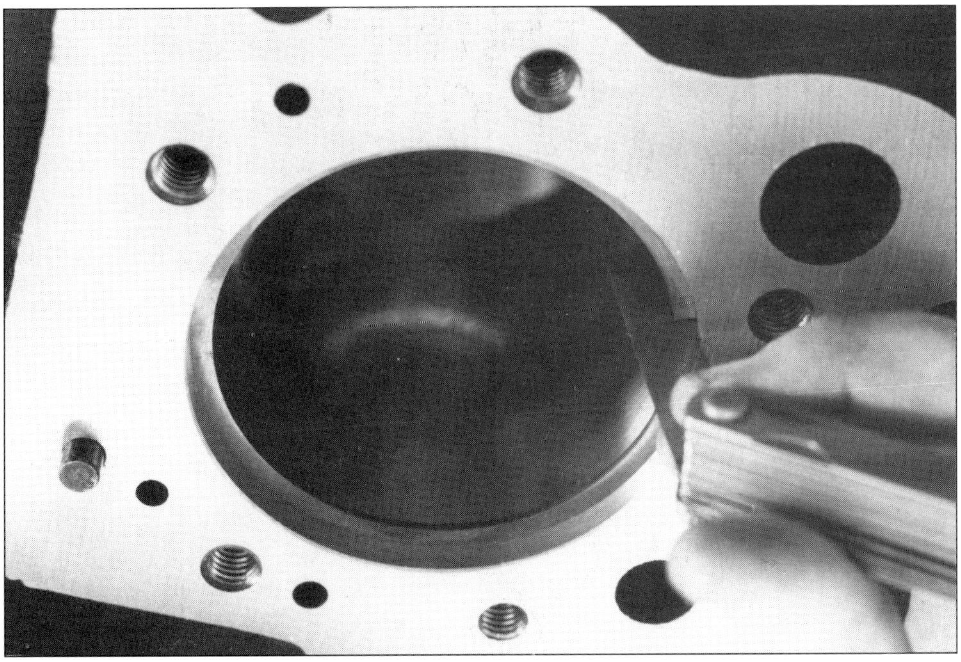

checking end gap

embrittlement
Condition when a part becomes hard and brittle from extended cycling.

emery paper
Corundum-magnesite abrasive coated paper, used as sandpaper.

EMF
Electromotive force, or voltage.

emulsifiable chemicals
Any chemical that will mix with water.

emulsion
Fluid substance consisting of one liquid dispersed and suspended in another, rather than dissolved, such as butter fat in homogenized milk.

emulsion tube
Passageway in a carburetor in which air is mixed with fuel.

emissions control
Any device on a motor vehicle which reduces hazardous exhaust emissions. See *exhaust emissions*.

enamel
Type of paint that dries in two stages, first by evaporation and then by oxidation of the paint film.

end clearance, end play
In an engine, the distance a crankshaft moves longitudinally, i.e., end-to-end, relative to the block. Checking a crankshaft's end play is an important step when blueprinting and assembling an engine.

end gap
Distance between the ends of a piston ring.

end gap file
Tool to file the ends of a piston ring to obtain a specific clearance.

end gas
During combustion, the portion of the air/fuel mixture not yet consumed by the *flame front*; in other words, the last part of the mixture to burn.

endo
To flip a vehicle end-over-end.

end play
See *end clearance, end play*.

English wheel

enduro
Motor race between six and 24 hours long, with an emphasis on endurance and reliability more than sheer speed.

engine bay
Area in a vehicle occupied by an engine.

engine displacement
See *displacement* and *swept volume*.

engine dyno
Dynamometer which measures the output of an engine at the flywheel in brake torque, which can be converted to brake horsepower.

engine management system
Electronic device which monitors, regulates and adjusts the fuel injection and ignition systems to meet varying operating conditions. Same as *ECM* and *ECU*.

engine overhaul
Repair of a powerplant, usually including replacement of such worn parts as the piston rings, main and rod bearings, and gaskets, as well as a valve job. An overhaul is much less extensive than an *engine rebuild* and does not include any replacement or remachining of major parts.

engine paint
Special paint that resists high temperatures and is used on engines. The paint will turn black once the temperature reaches 250 to 260 degrees F.

E-PROM

engine rebuild
Thorough repair and reconditioning of an engine to factory stock specifications, usually including replacement or remachining of all major parts. The block is align-bored and decked, the crankshaft is reground, the camshaft is either reground or replaced, the cylinder head is remachined, and such parts as the pistons, rings, bearings, valves, valve guides, springs and lifters, oil pump, timing chain and gears, and gaskets are all replaced. A rebuild is far more extensive—and expensive—than an *engine overhaul*.

engine stand
Stand which holds an engine and allows it to be turned and rotated for easier access to areas being repaired or modified.

English wheel
Special tool to form sheet metal into body panels. Representing a large "C," it consists of a flat-faced, upper wheel, 6-9 inches in diameter and 3 inches wide; and a lower wheel, the *anvil*, which is smaller in diameter with a curved surface that forms the curve in the panel. Anvils come in varying sizes.

EP
Extreme Pressure, an API-rated lubricant for high loads.

EPA
Environmental Protection Agency, the federal agency responsible for establishing and verifying vehicle exhaust emissions standards; while measuring emissions on new cars, the EPA also measures fuel consumption for CAFE requirements established by the DOT. Still another EPA responsibility is regulating the handling and disposal of toxic wastes.

EP, EP lube
See *extreme pressure lubricant*.

E-PROM
Eraseable programmable read only memory, a computer chip whose bits can be erased and reprogrammed, used in engine management systems.

equalizer
1. Device in the brake system which balances the side-to-side tension of the cable used to engage the emergency brakes, so that, in an emergency situation, one side doesn't lock before the other.
2. Tube which balances pressure between dual exhaust pipes.

equal length headers
Exhaust system with tubes of equal length from each cylinder to the collector. See *exhaust headers*.

Equa-Lok
Ford limited-slip differential.

ergonomics
Science of adapting a workplace to the worker, so that the work will be lighter and easier. In a motor vehicle, ergonomics is applied to making the layout of the driver's compartment comfortable and efficient.

esses
Series of S-shaped bends back and forth on a road-race course.

EST
Electronic spark timing

ESV
Experimental safety vehicle, i.e., one-off prototype to test specific safety features.

ET
See *elapsed time*.

ethane
C_2H_6, a minor component of natural gas, used as a fuel and a refrigerant.

ethanol, ethyl alcohol
C_2H_5OH, a form of alcohol sometimes blended with gasoline to produce gasohol; ethanol is also the form of alcohol found in alcoholic beverages.

Ethyl
Tradename for tetraethyl lead, a fuel additive which improved octane rating. Ethyl was also used incorrectly as a generic

name for so-called high-test or premium gasoline containing tetraethyl lead. The use of lead in gasoline is now severely restricted and will eventually be prohibited, effectively outlawing Ethyl. See also *tetraethyl lead.*

ethylene glycol
$HOCH_2CH_2OH$, colorless liquid used as an antifreeze, a solvent, and in some resins. Sometimes referred to simply as *glycol.*

ETI
Equipment and Tools Institute, 1545 Waukegan Road, Glenview, IL 60025; (312) 729-8550.

E-Town
Englishtown, New Jersey; site of the annual NHRA Summernationals.

Eurostyle
Custom styling treatment which usually involves lowering a car; fitting it with a front air dam, side skirts and rear spoiler; and finishing the exterior, including parts normally chromed or painted flat black, in a single color. When a Eurostyle package is offered either by an OEM or aftermarket supplier, it's also likely to include a high-performance engine and heavy-duty suspension.

even-fire
In a V-6 engine with either a 60- or 90-degree block, a conventional crankshaft with two connecting rods attached to each of the three crank throws will not allow smooth, even firing. An even-fire crankshaft has the individual journals on each throw staggered in relation to each other to provide even firing, and thus reduce engine vibration.

Excalibur
Brooks Stevens was the stylist of such vehicles as the Jeep Wagoneer and Studebaker Hawk GT. He first applied the name Excalibur, after King Arthur's sword, to a Henry J-based sports car he designed and built in the early 1950s. That plan was abandoned in 1955 when Kaiser went out of the passenger car business and the Henry J chassis was no longer available. Stevens revived the Excalibur name for an entirely different car, basically a replica of the Mercedes-Benz SSK roadster of the late 1920s. Called the Excalibur SS, this car was introduced in 1963 by the Excalibur Automobile Corporation of Milwaukee, Wisconsin. It was originally built on a Studebaker chassis, but Stevens switched to a Chevrolet Corvette chassis when Studebaker suspended production in 1966. By 1970, the Excalibur continued to use a Chevrolet engine but now had its own chassis. Over the years, the Excalibur has duplicated the evolution of Mercedes-Benz styling from the late 1920s into the 1930s. The most recent Excalibur resembles the Mercedes of the late 1930s and has been available as a sedan and even a stretch-out limousine, as well as the traditional roadster.

excessive crush
Condition when a pair of bearing shells are installed into a smaller than specified housing bore, causing the shells to deform and leading to premature bearing failure.

exhaust back pressure
Resistance to free flow of gasses in the exhaust system. A slight back pressure, 7.0 or 8.0 pounds per square inch, is desirable for a smooth flow of exhaust gasses and to prevent evacuating the combustion chamber so quickly that cold air could flow back up the pipes and damage the extremely hot exhaust valves.

exhaust emissions
Noxious products of combustion in an engine, particularly unburned hydrocarbons, carbon monoxide and oxides of nitrogen.

exhaust gas analyzer
Instrument to measure the various types and quantities of gasses in engine exhaust.

exhaust gas recirculation
Recycling of some exhaust gasses back through the intake manifold to lower combustion temperature, and thus reduce the emission of oxides of nitrogen. The process is called *EGR* for short, and the control for it the *EGR valve.*

exhaust gas speed
Exhaust gasses travel through the header pipes at approximately 200 to 300 feet per second; in other words, it takes only 0.010 of a second for the gasses to travel 3.0 feet.

exhaust headers
Special type of exhaust manifold, usually with steel tubes of equal length that have a scavenging effect, to duct exhaust gasses from the exhaust ports to the pipes in the exhaust system. See also *exhaust manifold.*

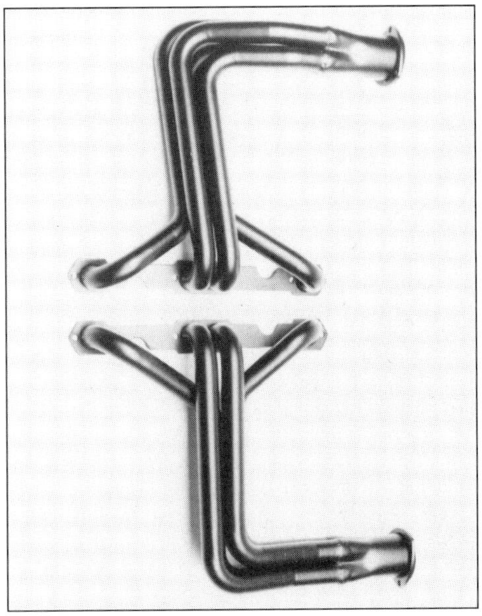

exhaust headers

exhaust manifold
Component, generally cast iron, with passages of varying lengths, to duct exhaust gasses from the exhaust ports to the pipes in the exhaust system.

exhaust ports
Passages in the cylinder head (or, in an F-head or L-head engine, in the block) which duct burned gasses from the combustion chambers to the headers or exhaust manifold.

exhaust stroke
Upward stroke of the piston forcing burned gasses out the open exhaust valve(s).

exhaust system
Tubing, muffler(s) and catalytic converter that direct exhaust gasses from the engine to discharge them at the rear of the vehicle into the air.

exhaust valves
Valves which open to release burned gasses from combustion chambers and into the exhaust system.

exothermic
Chemical reaction, such as combustion, that gives off heat.

expansion plug
See *freeze plug.*

expandable pilot
Device used for grinding valves that positions the grinding wheel so that it is concentric with the valve. An expandable pilot can be adjusted to fit various valve guide sizes.

expansion valve
Valve to relieve high pressure within a system, such as the valve between the expansion tank and radiator in a vehicle's cooling system.

expansion tank
See *surge tank*.

external combustion engine
Powerplant which burns fuel externally, rather than within the cylinders, such as a steam engine.

Extrude Hone
Tradename for a process that removes material by pushing an abrasive putty under high pressure through a passage, such as an intake runner, in order to enlarge the passage and smooth the surface. Not a replacement for a conventional porting technique, when extensive reworking is required.

eyeball
To estimate visually, rather than actually measure with a tape or ruler.

eyes
Light beams that operate an electronic race timing system.

F

F.
Fahrenheit, the traditional measure of temperature in the United States.

fab shop
Shop dedicated to making, or fabricating, parts.

face
Flat seal area on the head of a valve; in other words, the *valve face*.

face angle
Factory specified angle of the valve face.

factor
Mathematical evaluation used by the NHRA to assign production cars to specific stock classes, using estimates of true horsepower and curb weight, rather than factory claims.

Factory Experimental, FX
Type of drag racing car developed in the 1960s by Dodge and Plymouth, and Ford and Mercury, using their biggest and most powerful engines in relatively light vehicles. The FX was a forerunner of the *Pro Stock*.

factory recall
See *recall*.

factory spec
Factory specification, i.e., a manufacturer's recommended dimension, clearance or tolerance. See also *blueprint*.

factory team
Racing team openly supported by a vehicle manufacturer.

factory tool
Tool designed by a vehicle manufacturer for a specific function on a specific make and model.

fad car, fad T
T-bucket with a bobbed pickup bed patterned after the street rod built by Norm Grabowski and featured on the 1960s TV series "77 Sunset Strip." Despite the ephemeral implications of the word "fad," the fad car is an enduring style that has inspired several repro rods.

fadeaway fenders
On some cars of the 1940s, front fender design which flowed back and blended into the front door panel. Fadeaway fenders appeared on the 1941 through 1947 Packard Clipper, and the 1946 through 1948 Chrysler, DeSoto, and Dodge, and later became a popular customizing technique.

false air
Excess air in a fuel injection system, more than is needed for combustion.

false guide
Valve guide insert that is not an original part of the cylinder head, used to replace worn integral valve guides.

fan
1. Rotating device with blades designed to push or pull air, such as the fan at the front of an engine that moves cooling air through the radiator.
2. The incorrect technique used to apply paint by waving a spray gun back and forth with the wrist.
3. The spray pattern of a paint spray gun.

fan belt
Endless belt which transmits power from a pulley driven by the crankshaft to a pulley driving the fan and other engine accessories.

fan blade
See *fan*.

fan clutch
Thermostatically controlled device that engages or disengages a radiator cooling fan according to need. When a vehicle is in slow traffic on a hot day, the fan clutch engages to keep air flowing through the radiator and prevent overheating. On the other hand, when the vehicle is at highway speed on a cool day, the fan clutch disengages because the combination of vehicle movement and moderate temperature enables the radiator to provide adequate cooling without the fan. The fan clutch may have either a viscous or electro-mechanical coupling.

fan hub
Mounting surface for the fan.

fanning
The use of pressurized air through a spray gun to speed up the drying time of a finish, which is not recommended.

fan shroud
Rubber or metal duct used to direct air from the fan to the radiator.

fastback
Autobody style with a roofline that extends in a single, simple curve from the windshield to the rear bumper.

fat fendered

fast idle
Engine idling speed in the 1300 to 1800 rpm range.

fast idle cam
Cam-shaped lever in the carburetor to raise the idle speed of an engine when it is cold.

fast idle screw
Screw in the carburetor for adjustment of the fast idle speed.

fast idle solenoid
Electro-mechanical device in the carburetor for adjustment of the idle speed.

fat fendered
Cars with separate, bulbous fenders, especially those built from 1936 through 1948.

fatigue
Tendency of metal or other material to break and fail under repeated or extended stress.

fatigue strength
Measurement of a material's resistance to fatigue, depending on pressure, temperature, lubrication and other variables.

featheredge
In bodyworking, the technique of blending the edges of an undamaged area of a body panel into the area of the same panel that has been repaired and repainted. See photo next page.

feathering
To modulate the throttle lightly and smoothly for precise, controlled changes in engine speed. Generally used by a race driver during the entry, apex and exit of a turn. A driver who uses this technique is known as a *featherfoot*, the opposite of a *leadfoot*.

feature car
Vehicle displayed at a custom car show for appearance money, and not in contention for any of the show's major trophies.

Federal version
Vehicle that meets U.S. Federal exhaust emissions standards, but not the stricter California State standards. Also called a *49-state car*.

feed holes
Holes to supply oil or coolant in an engine.

feeler gauge
Strip of metal machined to a specific thickness, used to measure the distance between or within parts, such as spark plug gap.

felt dust seal
Engine seal made of felt, normally used on the front crankshaft pulley, to keep dust and dirt out of an engine.

fender cover
Cover draped over a vehicle fender to protect the fender's finish while a mechanic is reaching over it to work on the vehicle.

Fenderside
GMC narrow-bed pickup truck. See also *Stepside*.

Ferrari
Enzo Ferrari, a former race driver, directed the Alfa Romeo factory racing team from 1930 to 1937. He built his own first cars, two roadsters which he called the Auto Avio Tipo 815, in 1940. The Tipo 815 had a Fiat chassis with a small, straight-eight engine of original design. In 1946, Ferrari established Auto Construzione Ferrari in Modena, Italy, and began building the legendary sports and racing cars bearing his name. In recent years, the company has become part of the Fiat complex and Enzo Ferrari has died, but the firm continues to produce some of the world's most splendid automobiles.

ferrous metal
Metal, such as steel, consisting of or containing iron.

ferrous wheels
Vehicle wheels made of iron or steel alloy.

FF
1. Ferguson Formula, four-wheel-drive system developed in the 1960s by Harry Ferguson, Ltd., which featured a variable torque split between the front and rear wheels, depending on road conditions; if the rear wheels began to slip, the front ones received more power, and vice versa. FF was used on several Formula One and Indycars in the late 1960s and was the forerunner of the AWD and 4WD systems in high-performance cars today.
2. Formula Ford, an entry level, highly competitive class of racing car, open wheeled, and containing a stock 1600cc Ford engine. Many of the top racing drivers in the world got their start in FF racing. Because the engines are restricted to stock with no modifications, driver skill, rather than equipment, is a more important factor.

F-head
Engine design with intake valves in the cylinder head and exhaust valves in the block; also called *IOE* for intake over

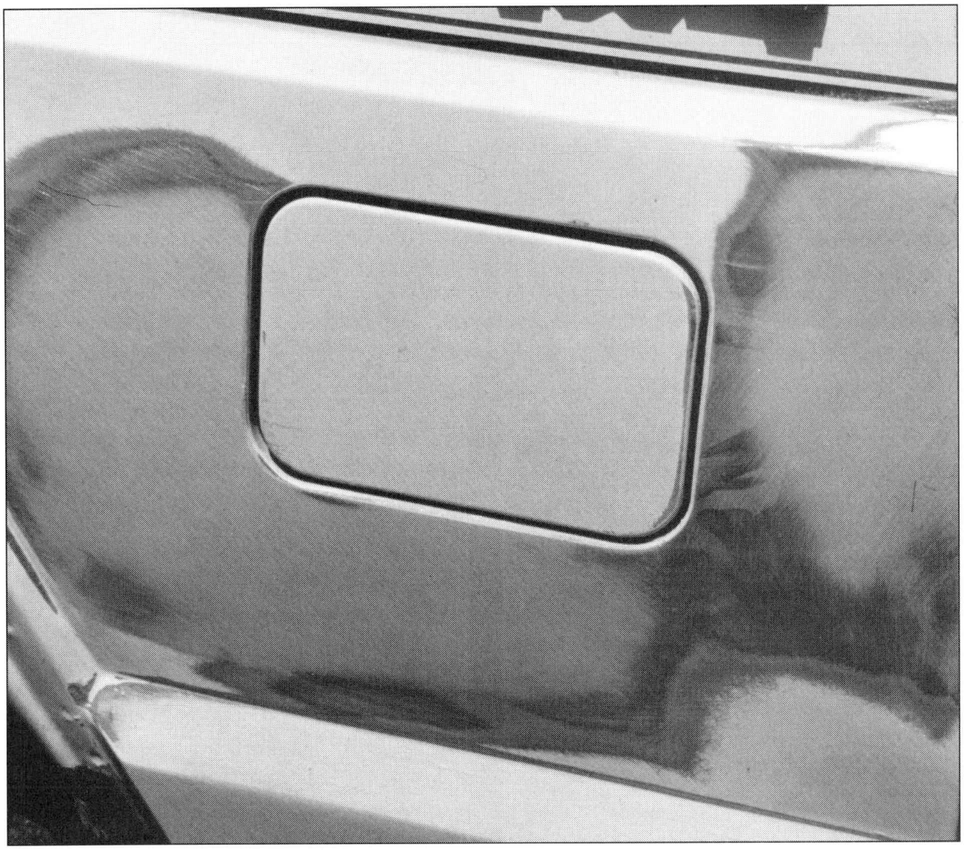

featheredge

exhaust. The idea is—or was—that the exhaust valves, which are subject to greater heat than the intakes, can be cooled better in the block than in the head. The last F-heads from major automakers were offered by Rolls-Royce and Willys in the 1950s.

FI
See *fuel injection*.

FIA
Federation Internationale de l'Automobile, 8, Place la Concorde, 75008 Paris, France; 011-33-1-42-65-99-51. An international association of national automobile clubs and the parent organization of FISA, which sanctions and regulates major international auto racing series, notably Formula One. The U.S. affiliate of FISA is ACCUS.

Fiat
Fiat was formed in Turin, Italy in 1899 as Fabbrica Italiana Automobili Torino. Over the years, it has evolved into a huge complex, producing not only automobiles but commercial vehicles, ships, airplanes and railway rolling stock. It also dominates the Italian automobile industry, and includes *Alfa Romeo, Ferrari* and *Lancia* among its subsidiaries. An estimated 90 percent of the motor vehicles produced in Italy come from Fiat or one of the companies it owns.

Fiberglas
Tradename for Owens Corning fiberglass reinforced plastic, or *FRP*; fiberglass, with a lower case "f" and a second "s," is the generic term for the product.

fiber optics
Method of transmitting light through a transparent fiber filament.

fiber timing gears
Camshaft timing gears made of a composite fiber material which reduces gear noise.

field
Electrical force in the space around electrically charged particles. Imaginary lines of force start at protons, or positively-charged particles, and end at electrons, or negatively charged particles.

field coil
Electromagnet in a DC generator that produces electrical current.

field terminal
Electrical terminal connecting the field coil to the voltage regulator.

15-Year Rule
NHRA regulation banning stock cars more than 15 years old from competing at the association's major drag meets.

fifth wheel
1. Bicycle-like wheel towed behind a test vehicle, driving highly sensitive instruments separate from those built into the vehicle, especially a speedometer and odometer which record precise acceleration, speed and distance figures.
2. See also *fifth-wheel hitch*, below.

fifth-wheel hitch
Hitch with a slotted, wheel-shaped platform on a tow vehicle into which a kingpin on a *fifth-wheel trailer* locks to connect the trailer to the vehicle. A fifth-wheel hitch for a recreational trailer is usually designed to fit into a pickup bed, directly above the truck's rear axle, so that the entire hitch weight is applied to the axle. A *semi tractor* is a heavy-duty, commercial application of the same principle.

fifth-wheel trailer
Trailer with an extended top front section, under which is the built-in kingpin that attaches to a *fifth-wheel hitch*.

filled
On a custom car, seams in welded body panels concealed with smooth lead, putty, or plastic.

filled axle
On a hot rod, an I-beam axle with concave portions reinforced with added metal.

filler
In bodyworking, material used to fill dents and smooth damaged body surfaces. Filler is often referred to incorrectly as "bondo." However, Bondo, with a capital B, is a tradename for a brand of plastic body filler, and it should not be used to describe all body fillers.

fillet
On a crankshaft, the radius connecting a journal to the crank cheek.

fillet weld
Weld deposit of filler metal, approximately triangular in shape. Usually made when welding a T-joint or 90-degree intersection.

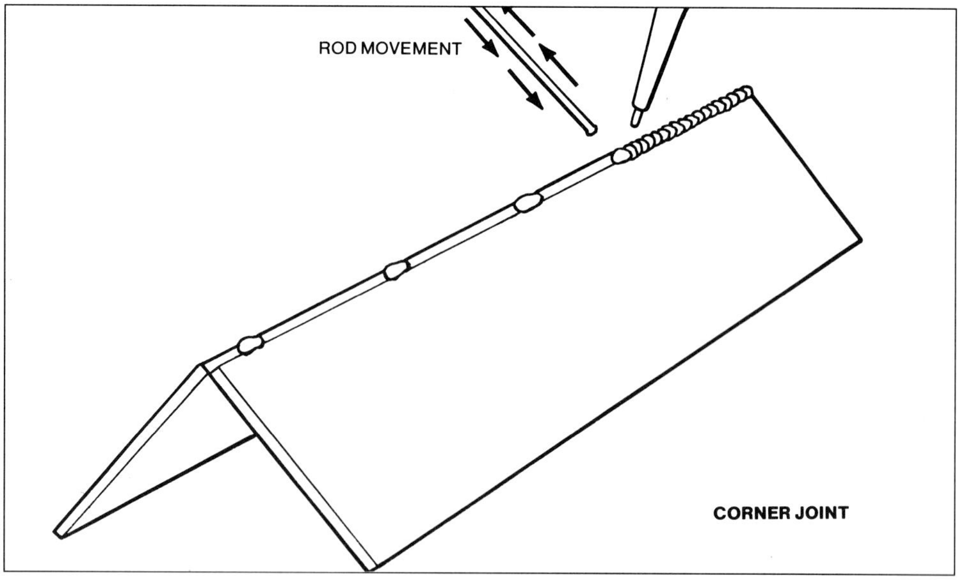

fillet weld

filter
Device containing porous material which removes suspended particles of dirt or contaminants from either gasses, including air, or liquids, including gasoline and oil.

final drive
Pinion, ring and differential gears which transmit power to the drive wheels.

final drive ratio
Ratio between the ring and pinion gears in the final drive.

fire bottle
See *fire extinguisher*, below.

fire extinguisher
Device to put out fires. There are three different types: Class A, for ordinary combustibles such as paper, cloth, wood and upholstery; Class B, for flammable liquids such as gasoline, grease and oil; and Class C, for any fire involving live electricity.

fire point
Lowest temperature at which a flammable liquid produces sufficient vapor to flash near its surface and continues to burn. Usually 10 to 30 degrees C. higher then the *flash point*.

fire suit, flame suit
Aluminized, fire-resistant driving suit.

firewall
Partition between the engine and passenger compartments. On a front-engined vehicle, the firewall is part of the cowl, ahead of the passenger compartment. On a mid- or rear-engined vehicle, it is behind the passenger compartment.

FISA
Federation Internationale du Sport Automobile, a division of the FIA which sanctions and regulates major international auto racing series. See *FIA*.

fish eye
Crater-like openings on a newly painted surface, caused by the presence of water, oil or a silicone-based material.

fish-eye mirror
Wide-angle mirror, providing a broader view than a standard mirror. Fish-eye mirrors are often used on motor vehicles, especially on RVs, as rearview mirrors, or as parts of them, to give the driver a broader picture of what's behind the vehicle. While fish-eye mirrors broaden the view, they also reduce the scale, so many of them are marked with such warnings as "Objects in mirror are closer than they appear."

fishtail
To lose traction at the rear wheels, allowing them to slither from side to side, out of control.

five-point seat belt
Safety belt system with a single buckle and a two-part lap belt (two points), two shoulder belts (two points) and a crotch belt (one point) to restrain the driver in a crash. See also *four-point seat belt*.

5-6-7
1955, '56 and '57 Chevrolets.

five-window coupe
Coupe body with rear quarter windows; the five windows are the two in the doors, the two in the rear quarters, and the one at the rear. See also *three-window coupe*.

fixed caliper disc brake
Brake system with the caliper attached to a mounting bracket and pads that adjust themselves to rotor position and thickness. See also *floating caliper disc brake*.

fixed head coupe
British term for two-door hardtop; opposite of *drop head coupe*.

fixed tappet
Solid valve lifter or cam follower.

flame cutting
Using a welding torch, fitted with a special cutting head, to cut metal.

flame-front
Leading edge of the burning air/fuel mixture during combustion.

flame-harden
To heat-treat metal with a flame of specific temperature in order to increase the metal's surface hardness and wear resistance.

flame kernel
Initial shape of a freshly ignited charge of air/fuel mixture which, during the first few milliseconds of combustion, resembles a kernel of corn.

flame-out
Ignition failure while a vehicle is in motion.

flame propagation, flame travel
Expansion of the burning air/fuel mixture, from the *flame kernel* at the spark plug throughout the combustion chamber.

flame suit
See *fire suit*.

flame travel
See *flame propagation*, above.

flange
Flat plate which joins a pipe or other part to a flat base surface for ease of removal, replacement and sealing.

flanged bearing
1. Bearing which has a step on its outside diameter, allowing it to maintain a specific position or distance.
2. Main bearing which has a flange to control the *end play* of the crankshaft.

flanged sleeve
Cylinder sleeve which has a step or ledge at the top to allow the sleeve to be set at a specified depth in the block.

flange gasket
Gasket which seals the surfaces of a flanged part and a base surface, such as a gasket for the exhaust manifold flange.

flange nut
Fastener which incorporates a flange or washer thrust surface.

flank
The flat part of a camshaft lobe.

flapper valve
Usually referring to any ball valve operated with a vacuum or pressure diaphragm motor, because the diaphragm flaps back and forth during use.

flared
Wheelwells emphasized with raised edges.

flash
1. Excess material found around the parting edge of a cast or forged part.
2. Process that occurs when paint is drying and the first coat appears dull prior to final drying, when the surface shows a high gloss.

flash chrome
Chrome-plating 0.001 to 0.004 inch thick, which offers good wear resistance for certain engine parts.

flash point
Lowest temperature at which a flammable liquid produces sufficient vapor to flash near its surface, but without continuing to burn. Usually 10 to 30 degrees C. lower than the *fire point*.

flat-out

flash time
In auto painting, the paint manufacturer's recommended interval for a coat of paint to dry before applying another coat, to avoid runs, drips or sags.

flat four, flat six
Opposed four- or six-cylinder engine, such as those of the VW Beetle and Porsche 911, respectively.

flathead
Engine with intake and exhaust valves in the block, rather than in the head; the head itself is a simple, flat slab. Also called *L-head*, because the piston and valves are side by side and require an L-shaped combustion chamber. Without question, the most famous flathead of all time was the Ford V-8 built from 1932 through 1948.

flat motor, flatty
Ford flathead V-8.

flat-out
At full throttle, using every bit of a vehicle's power.

flat spot
Momentary lapse in power as an engine increases speed.

flat tow
To tow one vehicle on all four wheels behind another vehicle.

flat tappet
Mechanical valve lifter; also the contact surface.

flat track
Dirt oval without banked turns.

flex-hone
Cylinder deglazing hone that uses a silicon carbide ball attached to spring-like wires that flex; informally called *dingle berry hone*.

flexible flyer
Dragster chassis with a light, flexible structure to allow maximum weight transfer. The forward engine mounts, for example, are not bolted to the frame; they merely rest on top of small brackets, allowing the engine block to lift up and back slightly as the car comes out of the chute and shifting an added bit of weight to the rear wheels for better traction.

flex joint
Flexible connection, such as between the steering column and steering gear.

flint paper
Sandpaper with a flint-base abrasive.

flip
To overturn a vehicle

fliptop
Convertible with a retractable hardtop that literally flips back into the rear deck. The only significant production example of such a car ever produced by a major U.S. automaker was the Ford Skyliner, built from 1957 through 1959.

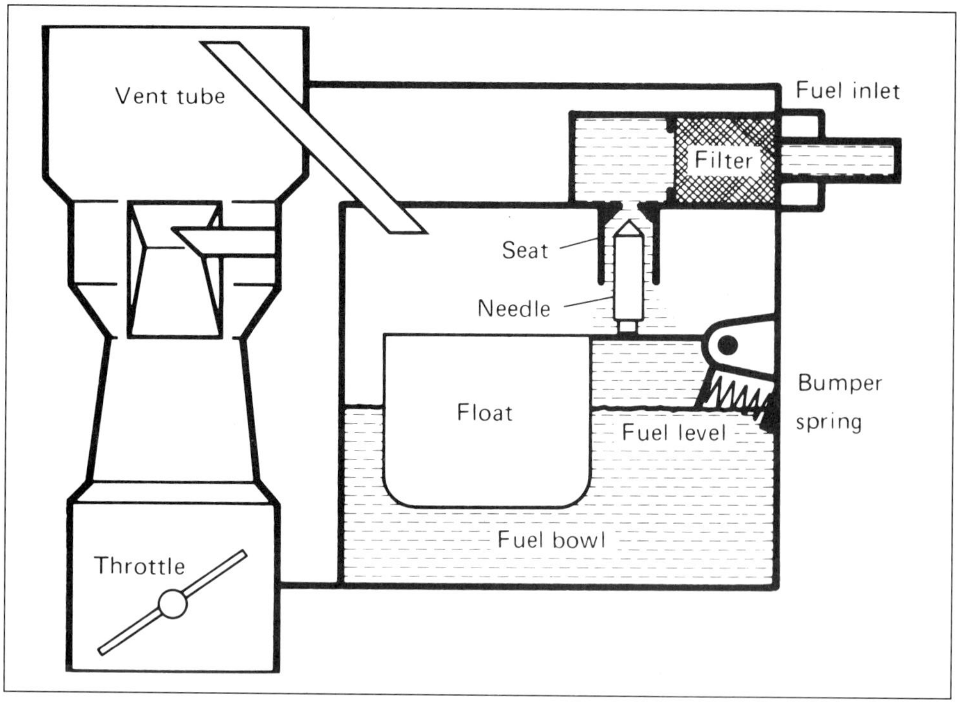

float, float bowl (Holley)

flopper

float
In a carburetor, a buoyant device, usually a small metal tube, which floats on top of the fuel in the float bowl or chamber and, as it rises or drops, closes or opens a valve that regulates the amount of fuel entering the bowl.

float bowl, float chamber
Fuel reservoir at the bottom of a carburetor. Also called a fuel bowl.

floater
See *full floating axle.*

floating caliper disc brake
Brake system in which only one of the two pads is energized and moves the caliper so that it is caught between both pads. See also *fixed caliper disc brake.*

floating piston
Piston with a *floating piston pin*; see below.

floating piston pin
Piston pin that rotates freely within the pin bore on the connecting rod.

floating axle
See *full-floating axle* and *semi-floating axle.*

flog
To push a vehicle hard, to the point of abusing it.

flood
During a cold start, to pump more fuel into the combustion chambers than can be ignited.

floored, floor it, floorboard it
To run at full throttle, with the accelerator pushed to the floor.

floorboard
Sloped portion of the *floorpan* immediately behind the *firewall.*

floorpan
Body panel, or combination of panels, forming the floor of a vehicle's interior compartment, including not only the passenger area but, in a van or wagon, the interior storage area as well.

flopper
Funny Car, so called because of the way the entire fiberglass body shell flops up at the front for access to the engine, chassis and driver's compartment.

flow bench
Machine which measures the airflow through intake or exhaust ports of cylinder heads. Measurements are made in cubic feet per minute (cfm), in increments of .050-inch of valve lift.

flush bucket
Racing slang for an oversize carburetor that feeds in more air/fuel mixture than the engine can handle.

flux
Chemical powder or paste that cleans the base metal and protects it from atmospheric contamination during soldering or brazing. Flux consists of chemicals and minerals that properly clean and protect different types of metals. Each type of metal joining requires a specific formulation of flux. Flux is not used in *fusion welding*, except as a coating over *arc welding* rod or in *submerged arc welding*.

flyboy
Drag competitor who races only as a hobby, as opposed to one who is a full-time professional; same as *weekend warrior*.

fly cutter
Variable-size, single-bit cutting tool used on a milling machine.

flying kilometer, flying mile
International standards for maximum speed records; a vehicle making a record attempt is allowed a running start so that it enters the measured kilometer or mile at the highest possible speed. See also *standing kilometer, standing mile*.

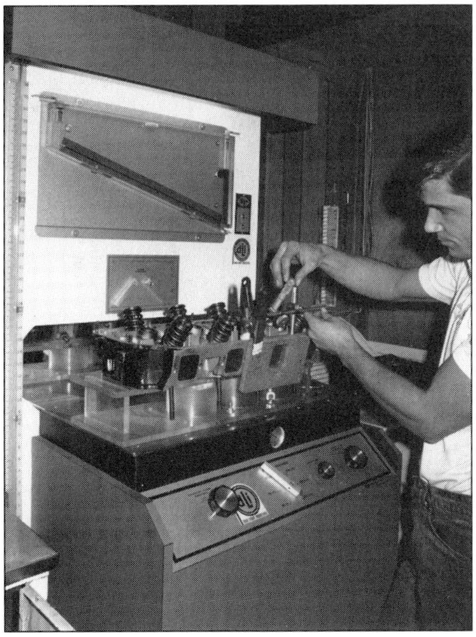

flow bench

flywheel
Heavy, round metal plate mounted on the end of the crankshaft that serves as a vibration damper and balance member, smooths out the individual power pulses as the cylinders fire and, in a vehicle with a manual transmission, acts as part of the clutch to transmit power to the gearbox. The rim of the flywheel is toothed to mesh with the starter motor gear.

fold
Process used to bend a piece of material, usually doubled back to form a 180-degree bend.

follower
See *lifter*.

FoMoCo
Ford Motor Company or any Ford product; derives from the tradename used by Ford's parts division.

foot in the carburetor, foot in it
Accelerator pushed to the floor; a driver who is accelerating rapidly, or refuses to lift off the throttle and yield during an attempted pass, is said to have his "foot in it." See also *floor it*.

footprint
Portion of a tire tread in contact with the ground.

foot-pounds
Measure of torque. One foot-pound is the force required to lift one pound one foot. Ten foot-pounds is the force required to lift one pound ten feet or ten pounds one foot—or, for that matter, two pounds five feet or five pounds two feet, or any other combination with a product of ten. Some engineers prefer to limit use of the term "foot-pounds" to the torque needed to tighten a bolt or nut properly, and to use "pounds-feet" to describe the torque produced by an engine. See also *pounds-feet* and *torque*.

footwell
In a passenger vehicle, area for a passenger's feet.

forced induction
Intake system that allows air or air/fuel mixture to flow into an engine at greater than atmospheric pressure. A *supercharger* is the most obvious example of forced induction, but a *ram-tuned* intake manifold could also be considered a form of it.

force-fit
Same as *press fit*.

Ford
Henry Ford built his first experimental car in 1896. In the early 1900s, he helped organize the Detroit Automobile Company, which was known briefly as the Henry Ford Company before he left it and it became the Cadillac Automobile Company. In 1903, he organized the Ford Motor Company in the Detroit suburb of Dearborn. In 1908, he introduced the Model T, a car inexpensive enough that Ford Motor Company's own workers could afford to buy it. In the early 1920s, Ford expanded to the other end of the market. Henry M. Leland, who had replaced Ford at the company that became Cadillac, left Cadillac in 1917 to form the Lincoln Motor Company to produce a precision-built luxury car. The first Lincoln appeared in 1920. The car was a fine one but, within a couple of years, Leland had financial problems and Ford bought him out and absorbed Lincoln. In 1928, the now-dated Model T was replaced by the Model A. Another major breakthrough came in 1932 when Ford introduced its low-priced V-8. It wouldn't be until 1955 that Ford's principal competitor, Chevrolet, would offer a V-8. In 1939, Ford began to fill the marketing gap between the Ford and Lincoln by introducing the medium-priced Mercury. In 1958, an attempt to expand in the medium-priced field with the Edsel proved one of the most disastrous mistakes in Ford's history. Today, Ford has two principal passenger car divisions, Ford and Lincoln-Mercury. It builds cars under the Ford name in Australia, Argentina, Brazil, Canada, Mexico, Germany and the United Kingdom. Ford's British properties also include A.C., Aston Martin and Jaguar. Finally, Ford has a minority interest in Japan's Mazda Motor Company.

forked eight, forked six
V-8 or V-6 engine.

F

four-barrel carburetor (Holley)

Fordor
One-time Ford designation for a four-door sedan. See also *Tudor.*

forge
To form a metal object into a desired shape with blows from a hammer, press or other machine. Pistons, connecting rods and crankshafts are examples of engine parts that are often made by forging.

forging flash
Remnant of metal on a forged part, usually squeezed out of a mold used to shape the part while it is being forged.

forming charge
Initial charge applied to a new battery.

formula car
In international racing, a single-seat, open-wheeled race car built to a particular set of specifications or formula. There are several different formulas, but by far the most prestigious is *Formula One*, see below.

formula libre
Literally, free formula, a type of road racing open to any and all comers, without any limits on engine size, bodywork, or other design features; the European equivalent of *run what ya brung.*

Formula One
FISA category of single-seat, open-wheeled cars for international Grand Prix racing. The annual Formula One World Championship series includes races on six continents to determine both driver's and constructor's championships.

49-state car
See *Federal version.*

forward rake
Attitude of a car with the front lower than the rear; a customizing technique and also sometimes used on race cars to create extra downforce at high speed. A Funny Car is a good example.

fossil fuels
Solid, liquid or gaseous fuel formed underground by chemical and physical changes in plant and, to a lesser degree, animal matter, under extremely high temperature and pressure conditions for extended geological time periods. Coal, petroleum and natural gas are all fossil fuels.

foul
In drag racing, to leave before the green light flashes, causing a red light and immediate disqualification.

four-banger
Four-cylinder engine or a vehicle equipped with one.

four-barrel carburetor
A carburetor with four *venturis.*

four-bolt mains
In an engine, a main bearing cap held in place with four bolts. Generally found in high performance or heavy-duty (truck) engine blocks. See *Main Cap.*

four-by
4x4, see below.

4x4, 4x2
A 4x4 is a four-wheeled vehicle with four-wheel-drive, while a 4x2 is a four-wheeled vehicle with two-wheel-drive. The latter should never be referred to as a 2x4; that's a piece of lumber.

four cammer
V-type engine with dual overhead camshafts on each cylinder bank, such as the Cosworth and Ilmor racing powerplants.

four-gas analyzer
Device used to measure the amounts of carbon monoxide, carbon dioxide, oxides of nitrogen and oxygen in exhaust gasses.

four on the floor
Four-speed manual transmission with a floor-mounted shift lever.

four-point seat belt
Safety belt system with a single buckle and a two-part lap belt (two points) and two shoulder belts (two points) to restrain the driver in a crash. See also *five-point seat belt.*

four-stroke cycle
Cycle of engine operation in which combustion occurs in each cylinder on every other revolution of the crankshaft. The four strokes are (1) intake or induction; (2) compression; (3) combustion, power or expansion; and (4) exhaust.

four-valve head
Head design, usually with hemispherical combustion chambers, with four valves per cylinder; the most common form of multi-valve head.

four-wheel drift
Controlled four-wheel slide on a paved surface. A four-wheel drift is similar to a power slide on dirt in that the driver uses the throttle rather than the steering to control the car, but the drift on pavement occurs at higher speed and involves less skidding sideways than the slide on dirt. The harder bite on pavement makes the drift a more difficult, more precise maneuver. See also *drift*, *power slide*.

4WD
Four-wheel drive; same as *4x4* but not necessarily the same as *FWD*.

four wheeling
Off-highway travel in a four-wheel-drive vehicle; same as *jeeping*.

4WS
Four-wheel steering.

fractionating tower
In oil refining, a distilling device which separates, or fractionates, various compounds in crude oil by their different boiling points.

fraction drill
Drill bit that is measured in fractions of an inch.

frame
Substructure of a vehicle that supports the bodywork and powertrain and is supported, in turn, by the suspension and wheels.

frame alignment
Measurement of a vehicle's frame to determine whether or not it is aligned according to factory specifications.

frame rack, frame machine
Device to straighten or align vehicle frames that have been twisted. Also called a *jig*.

Frantz Oil Filter
Tradename of an oil filter that uses a roll of toilet paper as its filtration medium; it filters approximately 10 percent of the oil supply at a time.

Frazer
Sedan built by Kaiser-Frazer Corporation from 1946 to 1951, named for company co-founder Joseph W. Frazer.

free-flow exhaust
Exhaust system with reduced back pressure.

free standing deck
Type of engine block construction in which the cylinders are cast into place without being tied by the deck to the outer walls. This allows coolant to circulate around the very top of the cylinders, usually blocked off by the deck, and eliminates out-of-round stresses on the cylinders when the head bolts are tightened.

freeze crack
Crack in an engine caused by the expansion of coolant as it freezes and turns to ice.

freeze plugs
Disc- or cup-like metal plugs in a cylinder head or block, inserted into holes left in the casting through which the core was removed. The plugs open into cooling passages and will pop loose as safety valves if the coolant freezes and expands, thus preventing freeze cracks.

Frenched
Body part which is normally separate, but which has been molded into another, larger portion of the body. Headlight rims are a common example; on production cars, they're usually detachable but, when they're Frenched, they become molded, integral parts of the front fenders.

French seam
Fabric seam in which the edge of the material is tucked under and sewn on the inner side; commonly used on a *landau top*.

frequency valve
Valve used to regulate or stabilize the air/fuel mixture on a fuel injected engine; a part of the Lambda system.

friction ball joint
Non-load carrying ball joint in a suspension system.

frontal area
Area in square feet of a vehicle's cross section, as seen from the front; frontal area is one of four major factors contributing to aerodynamic drag, the others being Cd, vehicle speed and air density.

front chute
See *front straight*.

front clip
In bodywork, replacing the damaged front part of a vehicle, extending back as far as the cowl or A-pillar, with another, undamaged front part from a similar model.

front drive
Drive system which transmits power through the front wheels; same as *front-wheel drive*. See also *FWD*.

Frontenac
1. In 1914, when Louis Chevrolet had a falling out with William C. Durant and left the Chevrolet Motor Car Company, he joined his brothers Gaston and Arthur in forming the Chevrolet Brothers Manufacturing Company to produce both passenger cars and race cars, as well as racing equipment for other makes, using the name Frontenac after a 17th century French explorer of Canada. The passenger car never got beyond the prototype stage, but the brothers did build some successful race cars. In fact, Gaston Chevrolet drove a Frontenac to victory in the 1920 Indianapolis 500. The racing equipment was also successful, particularly the "Fronty Ford" line for the Model T. See also *Chevrolet*.
2. Louis Chevrolet's old adversary, William C. Durant, had the gall to use the Frontenac name on a car he marketed in Canada from 1931 to 1933. It turned out that Louis Chevrolet had not protected the Frontenac name in Canada, so there was nothing he could do to stop Durant from using it there.
3. Ford also used the Frontenac name in Canada, on a version of the compact Falcon sold in 1959 and 1960 by Canadian Lincoln-Mercury dealers.

front-end rack
Machine to check and adjust front-end alignment on a vehicle.

front engined
Vehicle with the engine at the front, ahead of the passenger compartment. A front-engined car may have *front drive*, *rear drive* or *all-wheel drive*.

front roll center
Center determined by front suspension geometry around which the forward part of a vehicle tends to roll. See also *rear roll center* and *roll center*.

F

front steer
Steering gear positioned ahead of the front wheel centerline.

front straight
Front straightaway on a circle track race course, such as the straight at the Indianapolis Speedway between turns four and one. The start-finish line is usually midway down the front straight. Also called *front chute*.

front-to-rear brake bias
Difference or balance of brake pressures between the front and rear brake cylinders or calipers, to control overall vehicle braking. Specifically, greater brake pressure is usually needed at the front because of the forward weight bias in most front-engined cars, especially those with front drive, and because of weight transfer toward the front during hard braking.

front-wheel-drive
Drive system which transmits power through the front wheels; same as *front drive*. See also *FWD*.

Fronty
See *Frontenac*.

FRP
Fiberglass reinforced plastic; see *Fiberglas*.

fruit cupper
Amateur driver, especially in sports car racing; the term derives from the small cups often awarded as trophies in such competition.

fry
Overheat.

fudge factor
Allowance for extra time or material when working on a vehicle.

fuel
1. Generally, any combustible liquid or gas that can be used as an energy source for an engine.
2. As slang in most forms of racing, any combustible liquid other than gasoline; methanol and nitromethane are two of the most widely used fuels.

fuel block, fuel log
Manifold that distributes fuel to two or more carburetors.

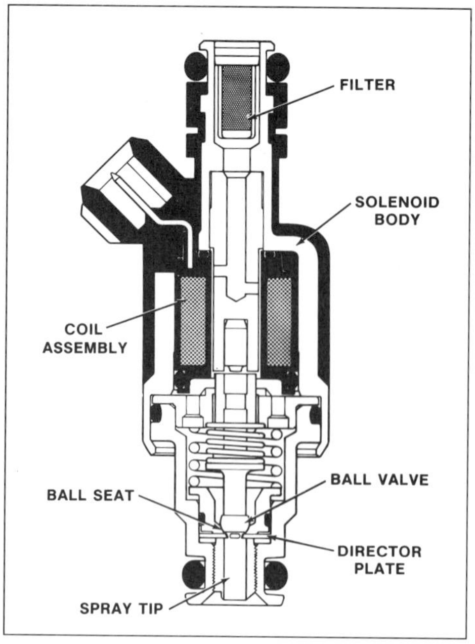

fuel injector

fuel cell
Special fuel tank for a race car, containing a bladder and baffling, designed to minimize fuel spillage if the vehicle crashes.

fuel distributor
Mechanical or electro-mechanical device to route fuel to injectors.

fueler
Race car, especially a Top Fuel dragster, running on a fuel other than gasoline, such as methanol, nitromethane or a combination of the two.

fuelie
1. As applied to production cars, a fuelie was one with fuel injection rather than carburetion, such as a 1957 Corvette fuelie. The term is seldom heard today, now that virtually all production cars have fuel injection.
2. In drag racing, fuelie is sometimes used as a general term for the fuel categories, specifically Top Fuel and Funny Car.

fuel injector
Device, mechanical or electromechanical, which meters fuel in an engine.

fuel line/hose
Rubber or metal tube to carry fuel from the tank to the carburetor or injection system.

fuel log
See *fuel block, fuel log*.

fuel map
Topographic-like chart showing interrelationships of rpm, fuel flow and ignition on a particular engine.

fuel rail
In an FI system, a conduit to deliver fuel from a fuel distributor to an injector.

fuel pump
Mechanical or electrical device to deliver fuel from the tank to the carburetor or fuel injectors.

fuel lines, send and return
1. Send lines supply fuel to the carburetor or fuel injectors.
2. Return lines return fuel that is not used by the carburetor or injectors to the fuel tank, and are also used to cool the carburetor and injectors.

fuel separator
Device which separates fuel and water so that only fuel is allowed to go into the engine.

fuel wash
Condition that sometimes occurs when a new or rebuilt engine is flooded during the initial start-up, causing raw fuel to wash away the assembly oils and allow metal-to-metal contact.

full bore, full chat
Full throttle.

full floater
See *full-floating axle*, below.

full-floating
Any part that rotates or moves within another part, such as a floating piston pin or, below, a *full-floating axle*.

full-floating axle
Drive axle in which the axle shafts do not support the vehicle weight; their sole function is to transmit power to the drive wheels. Each axle shaft rides in two roller bearings within the axle housing and the housing, in turn, supports the wheels as well as the vehicle weight. Full-floating axles are frequently used on race cars because, if an axle shaft breaks, the wheel is still supported by the axle housing and will not fall off.

Funny Car

full-flow
Type of oil filter through which all the oil from the oil pump flows, with no bypass.

full house
Engine that has had every normal hot rodding modification. A full house engine isn't necessarily full race. Even though it's been thoroughly reworked, a full house engine may be set up for street use rather than racing.

full-load
Engine delivering its maximum output.

full-load enrichment
Injection of extra fuel into an engine at full-load conditions.

full-metallic brake linings
See *sintered brake linings*.

full race
Engine built for maximum racing performance. A full race engine is usually but not necessarily *full house*. Even though it's built for racing, it may have some parts that haven't been modified.

full race cam
Camshaft ground for maximum performance.

fume
Airborne dispersion of minute solid particles arising from the heating of a solid material, which may produce an oxide of the solid.

Funny Car
1. In drag racing, a vehicle with what's essentially a dragster chassis covered with a lightweight, plastic replica of a passenger car body. Also called a *flopper*.
2. Before the term identified a specific drag category, funny car in all lower case letters was a generic term for any unusual or unorthodox racing vehicle; the mid-engined Lotus Ford was considered a funny car, for example, when it first appeared at Indy in the early 1960s.

furnace brazing
Welding process to repair complex cast iron castings. It involves heating the casting to 1300 degrees and gas welding the part with a special cast-iron welding rod.

fuse
1. As a noun, a safety device to limit the amount of current in an electrical circuit. The fuse usually consists of a wire or strip of an easily melted metal, set in a plug and placed in a circuit. If the current becomes too strong, the fuse melts and breaks the circuit.
2. As a verb, to join two pieces of metal by melting them together.

fusion welding
Type of welding in which the metal pieces to be joined are heated to a liquid state along the welding seam. Usually, filler metal of the same or similar kind is added to the molten puddle and allowed to cool, forming one continuous piece of metal.

FWD
1. Generally understood to mean *front-wheel drive*, as on most contemporary small cars, not *four-wheel drive*, *4WD* or *4x4*.
2. Despite that general understanding, FWD has been the tradename for a line of heavy trucks produced since 1912 in Clintonville, Wisconsin, by a firm called the Four Wheel Drive Auto Company from 1912 to 1960, and the FWD Corporation since 1960. FWD is well known for its 4WD or 4x4 trucks, but has also produced vehicles in such multi-drive axle configurations as 6x4, 6x6, 8x6, 8x8, 10x8 and 12x10.

FX
See *Factory Experimental*.

F

G

g
Gravity, the rate at which physical objects are attracted toward the center of the earth; 1.0 *g* equals an acceleration rate of 32.174 feet per second per second. Unlike most single letter abbreviations, this one is usually written in lower case rather than as a capital, and is always italicized.

gage
Alternative spelling of *gauge*, see separate entry.

galling
1. Generally, surface wear caused by rubbing.
2. Specifically, in an engine, the welding-up and tearing apart of metals due to over exposure to extremely high temperatures, such as can occur in an inadequately lubricated valvetrain. See also *scoring*.

galloping hinge
Connecting rod.

galvanic reaction
Electrical reaction caused by heat and water passing at high flow rates through metal pipes and/or parts.

galvanize
Electrochemical zinc coating process used on ferrous metals to retard or prevent rust formation.

gap
Space between two adjacent parts or surfaces.

gas
In most forms of racing, gasoline as distinguished from *fuel*.

gas class
Any drag racing category limited to vehicles that run on gasoline rather than *fuel*, such as Gas Coupe/Sedan or Gas Dragster.

gas guzzler
Vehicle with excessive fuel consumption; new cars classed as gas guzzlers under DOT rules are subject to a special tax based on how far off they are from CAFE requirements.

gas hog
Same as *gas guzzler*, above.

gasohol
Mixture of gasoline and 10 to 15 percent alcohol, usually ethanol.

Gasoline Alley
Infield garage area at Indy.

gas ports
Series of holes drilled from the crown of a piston to the top ring groove to allow combustion pressure to blow the ring against the cylinder wall for a more effective seal.

gas shock
Tubular shock absorber with two separate compartments, one containing regular shock absorber fluid and the other a gas, usually nitrogen. The gas keeps the fluid under pressure, which helps prevent the gas from aerating or foaming.

gasket
Piece of thin, compressible material, such as cork, rubber or soft metal, placed between two surfaces in order to seal them, retaining pressure and preventing leakage, such as the head gasket between an engine's cylinder head and block.

gasket cement
Liquid, gel or paste material used to bond gaskets to their mating surfaces.

gasket shellac
Liquid form of *gasket cement*, see above.

gate
1. The cash collected for paid admissions to a racing event; the size of the gate often determines the amount available for prize money.
2. Starting position for a drag race.
3. As a verb, to take the lead in a drag race right at the start, at the gate; similar to *hole shot*.

gauge
1. Instrument which shows some physical quantity, such as mph, rpm, voltage or fuel supply, either with a movable needle on a dial (*analog instrument*) or with an electronic numerical readout (*digital instrument*).
2. Measure of the thickness of sheet metal or the diameter of wire. Different materials are measured with different gauges. American or Brown and Sharp Gauges are used for aluminum or brass sheet, U.S. Standard Gauge for steel sheet or iron plate, and American Wire Gauge for wire.

gauging point
Starting point for measuring a part.

GAWR
Gross axle weight rating, the maximum allowable weight, fully loaded, on a given axle, front or rear.

GCWR
Gross combination weight rating, the maximum allowable weight, fully loaded, of a given combination of tow vehicle and trailer.

gear
1. One cogged device that meshes with and drives another. Both gears may be circular as with a *ring and pinion*, or one may be straight and the other circular as with a *rack and pinion*.
2. Personal belongings or equipment.

gear backlash
Measurable gap or slack between gears.

gear carton
Transmission housing.

gear drive
System of two or more gears, such as a gear drive that transmits rotary motion from the crankshaft to the camshaft.

gear-rotor pump
Type of pump that uses Sun gears to transfer liquid. The gear-rotor pump passes the liquid between the gears, rather than around their circumference, and limits the amount of air that can be introduced to the liquid. Also called *gerotor*.

gear shift
Control, usually a lever on either the floor or the steering column to change gears in the transmission.

gel coat
First layer applied in a female mold for fiberglass, before the mat or cloth layers; the gel coat can be color impregnated.

General Motors
What would become the world's largest automaker had its beginnings in 1904, when William Durant, a successful carriage manufacturer of Flint, Michigan, joined the board of directors of the Buick Motor Car Company. During the next four years, Durant gained control of the company and built it into one of the four leading American automakers, the others being Maxwell-Briscoe, REO and Ford. As early as 1907, Durant and Benjamin Briscoe of Maxwell-Briscoe proposed a merger of those four makes. However, Henry Ford and R.E. Olds both wanted $3 million in cash for their respective companies, an amount Durant and Briscoe did not have. When the deal fell through, Briscoe went his own way but Durant persisted in his ambition to build his own automotive conglomerate. In 1908, he founded the General Motors Company, merged Buick into it and, during 1908 and 1909, he acquired Oldsmobile, Cadillac and Oakland (which later became Pontiac). Meanwhile, Durant had also bought out a number of smaller, less desirable companies, stretching GM's resources to the limit—and sometimes beyond. Durant had a flamboyance that did not set well with bankers and, in order to raise needed capital, he had to relinquish control of the company. But he was not through yet. For the story of how he later regained control of GM, see *Chevrolet*. In recent years, GM has again stretched its resources and, at this writing, is reorganizing and downsizing. However, it is still the largest automaker in the world. The corporation has six automotive divisions in the United States, Buick, Cadillac, Chevrolet, Oldsmobile, Pontiac and Saturn, plus GMC trucks. The Chevrolet Division also markets the Geo line of cars, built in joint ventures with three Japanese firms, Isuzu, Suzuki and Toyota. In fact, GM is part owner of Isuzu. Pontiac also markets a car under its own name that is produced by Daewoo in Korea. The corporation also produces the Vauxhall and Lotus in England, Opel in Germany, SAAB in Sweden, and Holden in Australia.

GEN-III system
Fuel and ignition engine management system developed by General Motors in 1988.

generator
Electrical generating device which converts mechanical energy from a drive belt into electrical energy in the form of direct current. Since 1970, the DC generator has been replaced by the AC *alternator*, which is a more efficient device for producing electrical energy.

gerotor
See *gear-rotor pump*.

get off it, get out of it
To release the accelerator and slow down.

get with the program
Organize to do a job properly, whether it is tuning an engine or driving a race car.

g force
Measurement of the force exerted on a vehicle during acceleration, deceleration or cornering, expressed in units of gravity or *g*'s. See *g*.

gilhooley
In dirt track racing, a *spin out*.

Gilmer belt drive
Accessory drive system using a cogged belt for positive engagement with both drive and driven gears. A Gilmer belt is often used to drive a *GMC supercharger* on a drag race car.

girdle
Heavy-duty main bearing support for a racing engine; in addition to holding the bearings, the girdle also stiffens the lower end of the block.

G.I. spacer
Device to correct worn out piston ring grooves by enlarging them. A special ring spacer is installed with the piston ring once the ring groove has been machined oversize.

glass
Fiberglass reinforced plastic, or *FRP*.

glass bead cleaning
Process using abrasive glass bead particles propelled by compressed air to clean parts. The unit is called a *glass beader*.

glass-wrapped
Vehicle with a fiberglass body.

glaze
Smooth, glossy surface.

glaze breaker
Tool to remove the slick surfaces sometimes found on parts that have been rubbed together.

glove box, glove compartment
Small, enclosed storage area in the front passenger compartment of a vehicle. The glove compartment is usually either in the dash on the passenger's side or in a central console between separate front seats.

goat

glow plug
In a diesel engine, an electrical plug which pre-heats the combustion chamber to aid in cold starting.

glycol
See *ethylene glycol.*

Glyptal
Specific brand of dielectric paint. See *Class F red insulating enamel.*

GM
General Motors Corporation. See *General Motors.*

GMC
Truck building division of *GM.*

GMC supercharger
Roots-type blower originally developed by GMC for use on two-stroke diesel truck engines and later adapted for gasoline racing engines, particularly for drag racing. Different size GMC superchargers were designated by the number of cylinders—3, 4, 6 or 8—in the engine for which the specific unit was intended, and the cylinder capacity of that engine in cubic inches, which was 71 across the board. Thus, the two most popular units, the 4-71 and 6-71, were designed for 4- and 6-cylinder engines, respectively, both with cylinder capacities of 71 cubic inches. The first successful application of a GMC 6-71 blower in a dragster is generally attributed to Ernie Hashim in the mid-1950s.

GN
See *Grand National.*

goat
Pontiac GTO.

gobble
To run extremely fast.

go button
Accelerator.

gofer
Errand boy—or should we say errand person?—on a racing team or at a repair shop. The term evolved from the words "go for." See also *parts chaser.*

Go Kart
Originally, a specific brand of racing kart, but often used as a generic term. See *kart.*

gold
Trophy.

goodies
1. High-performance equipment on an engine.
2. Prizes, especially merchandise, for race winners or car show participants.

goosed moose
Car with a severe *forward rake.*

gourd guard
Helmet.

gow job, gow wagon
What a *hot rod* was called in the 1940s before it was called a hot rod. The latter term eventually prevailed, probably because it was catchier, but consider that the fortunes of Petersen Publishing Company might have been founded on a magazine called not *Hot Rod* but *Gow Job*! Then there would've been *Popular Gow Jobbing*, *Street Jobber*, and, of course, the *NGJA.*

gow out
To dig out of the hole (accelerate quickly) in a gow job.

GP
1. General Purpose; GP was a military designation for the World War II Willys 4x4 which evolved into the name Jeep.
2. See *Grand Prix.*

GPH
Gallons per hour.

GPM
Gallons per minute

governor
Device that limits maximum engine rpm and, with it, maximum vehicle speed.

Grand National
Premier series of NASCAR stock car races; abbreviated *GN.*

Grand Prix
Literally, French for "grand prize." In its strictest racing usage, the term refers to an international series of Formula One events which determine the annual world driving championship. In a broader sense, it is often used by race organizers and promoters to describe any particularly important event. The 24-hour race at LeMans, for example, is known as the Grand Prix d'Endurance, or "Grand Prize for Endurance." And an annual USAC midget race that used to be held every Thanksgiving in southern California was

gourd guard

called the Turkey Night Grand Prix. The spelling Gran Prix, without the "d," is incorrect.

grand touring
See *GT*.

granny gear
In a 4x4, the combination of low gear in the transmission and low range in the transfer case. See also *compound low*.

gravity casting
Process that uses gravity to pull material to the bottom of a mold during casting.

gray market
Individual importation of a foreign-made car into the United States and private modification of it to meet U.S. safety and emissions laws, without dealing with the authorized U.S. distributor for the particular marque.

gray market parts
Parts that are not covered by the manufacturer's warranty because they were not sold through an authorized dealer.

gray water
In an RV, used wash water from the kitchen and bathroom.

grease
1. Semi-solid petroleum product used as a lubricant.
2. As a verb, to lubricate a vehicle.

grease cap
On a wheel, cover to keep lubricant in the spindle hub.

green, green flag
Flag used to signal the start of a race. The green is common to most forms of motorsport except international Formula One Grand Prix races, where the national flag of the host country is used instead.

green goo
See *green Loctite*, below.

greenhouse
Upper portion of a passenger car body; the structure above the beltline, including the windows, pillars and roof.

green Loctite
Anaerobic compound used to secure parts together in the absence of air; used in high temperature, such as for valve guides, cylinder sleeves and seats. Informally referred to as *green goo*.

grenade motor
Engine that is expected to provide very high horsepower for a very short time before it blows up.

grenaded motor
Engine that has blown up.

grid
1. In road racing, arrangement of the race cars in qualifying order on the front straight prior to the start.
2. Wire mesh, such as is sometimes used in a *grille*, see below.

grille
Ornamental opening at the front of a vehicle through which air is ducted to the radiator.

grind
1. The specific contour of a camshaft's lobes, such as a *quarter-race* grind.
2. Any long race where the emphasis is on endurance more than performance.
3. As a verb, to use an abrasive wheel to remove material from a metal object.

grinding sleeve
Abrasive sleeve with a rubber mandrel mounted in a drill motor to remove burrs from metal parts.

grip
Traction.

grit
Fine dust or dirt.

grocery getter
Car for everyday transportation; same as *beater* and *driver*.

grommet
1. Reinforced eyelet through which a fastener is attached.
2. Rubber sleeve-like part through which wires are passed through to prevent chafing.

groove
1. Specific path through a turn in either oval track or road racing. Also called the *racing line*.
2. Recess in a part to hold a ring or snap ring.

gross horsepower, gross torque
Maximum engine output as measured on a dyno, using modified intake and exhaust systems and with most engine accessories removed. See also *net horsepower, net torque*, as well as *corrected horsepower, corrected torque* and *observed horsepower, observed torque*.

gross valve lift
Valve lift including the running valve clearance.

ground
In a single-wire system, any metal part of a vehicle's structure that is directly or indirectly attached to the battery negative post; used to conduct current from a load back to the battery

ground effect
Reduced air pressure under a vehicle, provided by such devices as an air dam and side skirts; the weaker pressure below allows the normal pressure above the vehicle to push it downward slightly for a better grip on the road.

ground-end spring
Spring that has ground or flattened ends to fit the spring perches or retainers.

growler
Electrical device used to test generator armatures for shorts and defects.

GT
Gran turismo, Italian for "grand touring." Technically, the term has come to mean a sports car with enclosed coupe rather than open roadster bodywork.

GTO
Gran turismo omologato, Italian term for GT cars that have been *homologated*, i.e., enough have been built to qualify them for racing as regular production vehicles rather than as prototype or experimental units. Ferrari was the first manufacturer to call a specific model a GTO, then Pontiac borrowed the term for its pioneering muscle car. Ironically, the Ferrari GTO was never homologated but the Pontiac was!
2. In IMSA racing, a category for non-turbocharged sports cars.

guide
1. Generally, a part to align or direct another part along a predetermined path.
2. Specifically, the support for the valve stem in the head.

guide liner

guide block
Metal or hard rubber block used to maintain timing chain tension.

guide driver
Tool used to install valve guides at their proper location and height.

guide hone
Tool to grind the inside diameter of a valve guide.

guide insert
See *false guide*.

guide knurler
Tool to recondition a valve guide by reducing its inside diameter.

guide liner
Thin bronze metal sleeve used to repair worn-out valve guides.

guide-mounted seal
Seal that mounts directly on to the valve guide; used to wipe oil from the stem as it reciprocates down and up.

guide plate
Metal plate on the cylinder head to keep the pushrod aligned with the rocker arm.

guide rail
Device to keep the timing chain aligned in the correct position on an engine.

guide reamer
Special piloted reamer to cut a valve guide to a particular size.

guide shoe
Hard rubber or plastic part used to maintain tension on the timing chain of an overhead cam engine.

guide seal
Seal to prevent oil from being drawn into the valve guide.

gullwing
Coupe body type with the doors hinged at the top so that they open upward rather than forward; cars that have had gullwing designs include the Mercedes-Benz 300SL coupe of the 1950s, as well as the Bricklin of the 1970s and DeLorean of the 1980s.

gulp valve
Valve to pass crankcase vapor to the intake manifold; an early form of *positive crankcase ventilation*, used particularly on some British cars.

gum
Residue left when gasoline is allowed to set for a long time.

gumballs
1. Rotating red lights in a hemispherical housing on top of a police car or other emergency vehicle.
2. Drag racing tires made of a particularly soft, sticky compound.

gun drilled oil holes
Holes drilled to allow oil to be fed to the piston pin.

gun it
To rev an engine suddenly.

gusset

gusset
Triangular piece of metal to add extra strength at corners, such as on frame members or roll cages.

gut
To remove non-functional parts of a car, especially interior fittings and upholstery, to reduce weight. See also *bare out*.

guts
1. Internal structure of an auto body.
2. In general, the essential working parts of a device; see also *innards*.

gymkhana
Maneuverability contest for sports cars; competitors are clocked individually over an extremely tight course. See also *autocross* and *slalom*.

GVWR
Gross vehicle weight rating, the maximum a vehicle should weigh fully loaded, with all passengers and cargo aboard.

H

hack
1. Originally a term for taxicab, derived from the British "hackney," meaning a coach for hire. Hack now means any passenger car for everyday driving; in other words, a *beater* or *grocery getter*.
2. As a verb, in customizing, to cut out sections of bodywork, as when the vehicle is channeled, chopped or sectioned.

hack saw
Saw to cut metal.

hairpin
1. On the road or on a race course, a turn of more than 90 degrees.
2. Crankshaft.

half-moon key
See *Woodruff key*.

half shaft
In the final drive assembly, the individual axle shafts on either side of the differential that transmit power to the drive wheels.

halogens
Group of elements that includes astatine, bromine, chlorine, fluorine and iodine. The halogens are nonmetallic and electronegative.

halogen lamp, halogen light
High-output lamp used as a headlight, driving light or fog light which has one or more gaseous halogens, such as iodine, inside the bulb. In a halogen atmosphere, a tungsten filament can carry higher current for a given filament size, and thus produce a more brilliant white light. See also *quartz halogen, quartz iodine*.

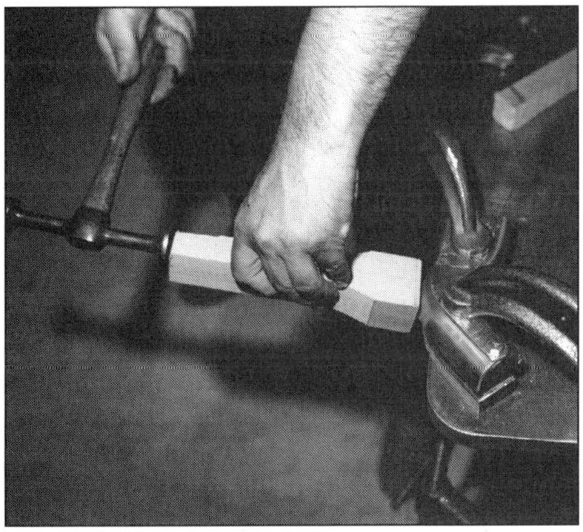

hammerforming

hammerforming
To form or shape metal by hitting it with hammers, mallets or corking tools over, onto or into a base form, which is known as the hammerform.

handicap
In drag racing, a system that allows two cars from different classes to race each other. See *bracket racing*.

handler
1. Driver who knows how to get the most out of his car.
2. Car that the most can be gotten out of.

hang a left, hang a right
To turn left or right.

hang it out
To throw the rear end of a car into a deliberate slide around a turn.

hard chrome
Heavy chrome plating applied to a metal surface to make it more durable and resistant to wear, as opposed to the lighter chrome plating applied for cosmetic bright work.

hard edge
Sharp corner where two surfaces meet.

hardener
Chemical component of epoxy used to start the catalytic reaction and harden the mixture.

hard face
Application of hard material to a surface to improve its durability and wear resistance. An example is the application of stellite to valve seats.

hardness test
Technique for determining the hardness of a metal. See *Brinell test* and *Rockwell test*.

hard parts
Internal parts used to rebuild an engine.

hard pedal
Condition in an overloaded vehicle when the brake pedal is depressed but the vehicle

does not stop because the inertia of the load is greater than the braking power. The load literally overrides the brakes.

hard solder
Solder that requires a temperature of more then 1000 degrees F. to melt.

hardtop
Short for hardtop convertible, an oxymoronic term for a body type with a fixed roof styled to look like a convertible with the top up. The distinguishing feature of the hardtop was its lack of a B-pillar; when the windows were lowered, there was a clear, open sweep from the A-pillar at the windshield to the C-pillar at the rear quarter. The hardtop in both two- and four-door form was popular from the 1950s until the 1970s. It was discontinued because federal vehicle rollover requirements made a B-pillar necessary.

hard throttle
Accelerator pressed to the floor.

harmonic
Rhythmic vibration of a moving part or assembly.

harmonic balancer, harmonic damper
Balance wheel or shaft that reduces or eliminates unwanted harmonics. See also *balance shaft* and *damper*.

hatchback
Passenger car body on which the rear decklid has been replaced with a full-height, opening hatch that includes the rear window, allowing larger items of cargo to be loaded and unloaded more easily. The hatchback usually also has a folding rear seat to increase cargo capacity.

hat
On a constant-flow fuel injection system, pipe-like housing for the injector.

hat trick
Three successive victories in the same annual event.

hauler
Top performer, referring to either a car or its driver.

hauling the mail
Performing at peak efficiency. One only wishes that the United States Postal Service could *haul the mail*.

hazardous waste
Any substance that is poisonous or contains carcinogens. The EPA lists all materials that are considered toxic.

H-beam rod
Connecting rod that has an H-beam shaped cross-section.

HC
See *hydrocarbon*.

HD
Heavy duty.

HDRA
High Desert Racing Association, 12997 Las Vegas Boulevard South, Las Vegas, Nevada 89124; (702) 361-5404; Professional off-road racing organization founded by the late Walt Lott and staging desert races in Nevada and adjacent states.

harmonic balancer

head
See *cylinder head.*

headache rack
Rack at the rear of a truck cab interior to prevent a load from crashing through the rear window and possibly injuring the occupants.

head bolts
Bolts which fasten the cylinder head to the block.

header
1. Free-flowing exhaust manifolding used on high-performance cars. See *exhaust manifold.*
2. In auto racing, a vehicle crash.

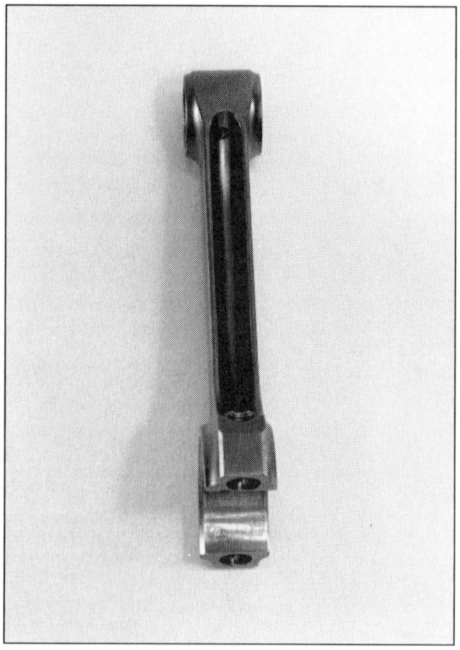

H-beam rod

header tank
In a cooling system, the reservoir at the top of the radiator.

head gasket
Gasket to seal an engine's cylinder head to the block. See also *gasket.*

head gasket notch
On a diesel engine, series of one to four notches to measure the thickness of a head gasket in order to control piston-to-head clearance.

head saver shims
Shims to compensate for cylinder head material removed during resurfacing; especially important on overhead cam heads in order to maintain correct cam drive chain tension.

headlamp, headlight
Lights on the front of a vehicle to illuminate the road at night.

headlight delay
System to turn off the headlights automatically after the driver has left the vehicle with the light switch still on.

head stock
Part of a machine, such as a lathe or crankshaft and camshaft grinder, containing the drive motor and gearing.

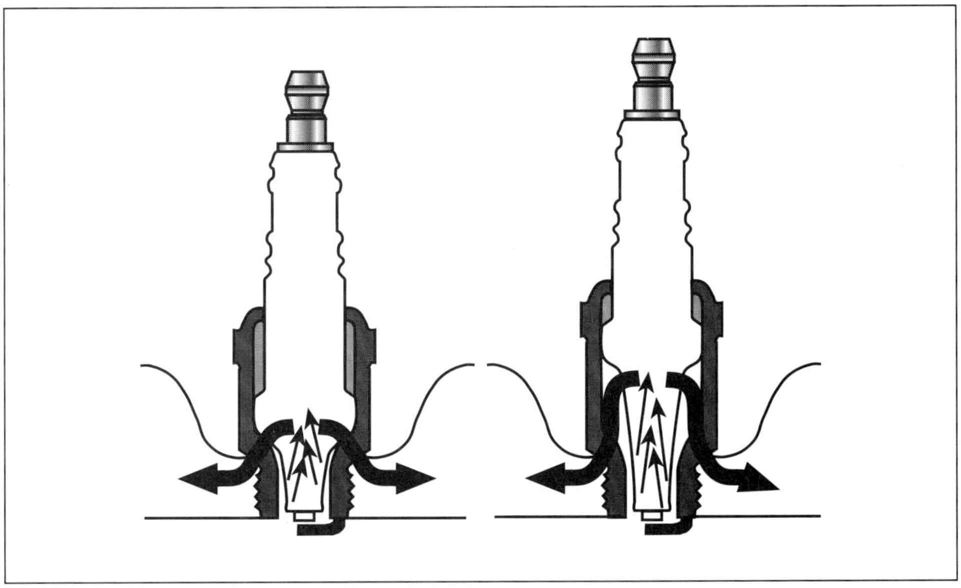

heat range

heads-up display
Images of a vehicle's instruments projected on the inside of the windshield, where they are in the driver's direct line of view and can be read without the driver's eyes being diverted from the road. Abbreviated *HUD*.

heads-up racer
Race driver who is very good at what he does.

heads-up racing
Direct, wheel-to-wheel competition, with no handicap.

heater
Device to warm a vehicle interior to make passengers more comfortable on cold days.

heat exchanger
Device that transfers heat from a warmer medium to a cooler one, the way a radiator transfers heat from its coolant into the atmosphere.

heating value
Measure of the heat released when a fuel is burned. In laboratory testing, the heating value of a fuel includes the latent heat of the water produced during combustion as it condenses and becomes liquid; this is the higher heating value or *HHV*. In an automobile engine, the heating value does not include the latent heat of the water, because the water is exhausted as steam and not condensed; this is the lower heating value or *LHV*.

heat range
Measure of a spark plug's ability to transfer heat from the tip of the insulator into the cylinder head. A plug that is too "hot" may cause pre-ignition, while a plug that is too "cold" may foul or misfire, and reduce horsepower. The range is determined by the distance heat must travel from the tip to the shell—the longer the distance, the hotter the plug.

heat riser
Valve between the exhaust manifold and head pipe, to divert exhaust heat to the crossover port to warm the intake manifold.

heat tab
Small aluminum disc, with a lead center designed to melt at 260 degrees, which can be attached to a cylinder head or block to indicate if the engine has been overheated.

heat treatable
Metal alloys that can be hardened by heating after they have been shaped; such alloys are marked with the letters "H" or "T."

heat treatment
Process that adds strength and brittleness to metal. Most, though not all, metals have a critical temperature at which their grain structure changes. This involves controlled heating and cooling of the metal to achieve the desired change in crystalline structure.

heavy-duty shock absorbers
Shocks with stiffer damping for either (a) supporting heavier loads or (b) increasing high-speed stability.

heavy-duty vehicle
According to Title 40 of the Code of Federal Regulations, "Any motor vehicle rated at more than 8500 pounds GVWR or that has a vehicle curb weight of more than 6000 pounds or that has a basic vehicle frontal area in excess of 45 square feet."

heel
1. On a camshaft, bottom-most portion of a cam lobe. See also *base circle*, *lobe*.

2. On a ring-and-pinion gearset, innermost part of a gear tooth.

H

heel-and-toe
Applying the toe of one's right foot to the brake pedal while applying the heel to the accelerator; the object is slow the vehicle as it enters a turn, while keeping engine revs up by *blipping* the throttle when downshifting.

heel-to-toe clearance
Space between the brake drum and the heel and toe of the brake shoe.

HEI
High Energy Ignition, a General Motors high voltage ignition system.

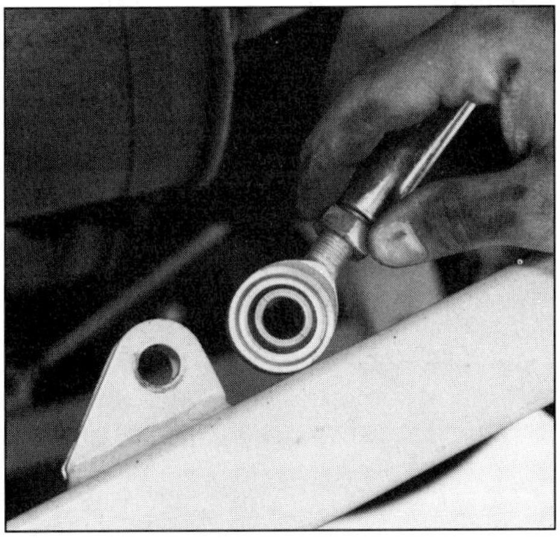

Heim joint

Heim joint
Spherical rod-end joint often used in race car suspension because it allows extremely precise adjustment of wheel position.

426 Hemi

Heliarc welding
Tradename of a tungsten inert-gas form of welding developed by Linde Welding and Cutting Systems. See *TIG welding*.

helical
Shaped like a helix or spiral. A coil spring is an example and, in fact, is sometimes called a *helical spring*.

helical gear
Gear cut with the teeth at a slanted angle to the gear's shaft or circumference. In a helical gearset, the loads are smooth and constant and, as a result, the gears are relatively quiet in operation.

Heli-Coil
Screw thread inserts, consisting of coil springs made of wire with a diamond-shaped cross-section, matching standard thread sizes. Heli-Coil inserts are best known for their aftermarket use to repair damaged screw threads, but are also used by some automakers as original equipment screw threads.

helper springs
Auxiliary suspension to increase a vehicle's carrying capacity, especially on the rear wheels. Generally, helper springs are progressive, i.e., they don't come into play until the main springs are heavily deflected.

Hemi, hemi head
Cylinder head with hemispherical combustion chambers. The hemi chamber is literally half of a sphere, allowing room for extra large valves, or even a multi-valve arrangement, and providing an ideal shape for smooth, even combustion. Chrysler popularized the concept in American production cars with its "Firepower" Hemi, offered as a regular production option from 1951 through 1958, and 426 Hemi, offered as a high-performance option from 1964 until 1971. In 1992, Chrysler resumed limited production of the 426 hemi block as a Mopar aftermarket product for those rebuilding or restoring Chrysler products originally equipped with that engine.

hemi cammer
Engine with both hemispherical combustion chambers and overhead camshafts.

hemispherical combustion chamber
See *Hemi, hemi head*, above.

Henry
Ford product.

Henry J
Small two-door sedan built by Kaiser-Frazer from 1950 through 1954, named for Henry J. Kaiser. A badge-engineered version of the Henry J was marketed by Sears as the *Allstate*. In addition, during the early 1950s, the Henry J chassis served as the basis for at least three attempts at producing an American sports car: Stirling Edwards' *Edwards* America, Brooks Stevens' original *Excalibur*, and Howard "Dutch" Darrin's *Kaiser-Darrin*.

HEPA
High-efficiency particulate air filter, which prevents solid particles of material from entering an engine's intake system. HEPA filters are 99.97 percent efficient in trapping particulates.

heptane, n-heptane
C_7H_{16} or normal heptane, hydrocarbon which serves as a primary reference fuel with an index of zero, combined with octane with an index of 100, for describing the anti-knock quality of a gasoline blend, i.e., the ability of the blend to resist premature ignition from compression or any other source of heat before the spark plug fires. See also *octane* and *octane number*.

herringbone gear
Gear with teeth cut in the V-shaped pattern of the small bony extensions on a herring's spine.

hertz
Unit of frequency of any regularly repeated event, the number of times that event occurs with a given period of time, such as a vibration, or the reversal of direction in a flow of alternating current. One hertz is the same as one cycle per second. The term was named for Heinrich R. Hertz, a 19th century German physicist.

Hg
Chemical symbol for mercury.

HHV
Higher heating value; see *heating value*.

highboy
Hot rod, usually a roadster based on an early model car, such as a *deuce*, which has been left at its stock height; that is, it hasn't been *channeled* or *sectioned*.

high gear
The highest speed in a transmission, such as fourth gear in a four-speed; high gear is usually either a direct drive or overdrive.

The Corvette pulls a hole shot; the Mustang is holed.

high gearing
Drive ratio which applies maximum engine output at a relatively high road speed. High gearing is important in lakes competition or any other form of racing where the emphasis is on sheer speed rather than acceleration. The term can be confusing because a high gear has a numerically low ratio. For example, 2.5-to-1 would be a high gear but is obviously a lower ratio than, say, 4.5-to-1. Thus, the term "high gear ratio" should be avoided because it's impossible to tell which is supposed to be high, the gear or the ratio. See also *low gearing*.

high-lift cam
Camshaft which provides increased valve lift, compared with the standard camshaft for the particular engine.

high-lift rocker arms
Rocker arms which provide increased valve lift, compared with the standard rocker arms for the particular engine.

high pedal
1. Position of the brake pedal when it is adjusted near the top of its upward travel.
2. On a Ford Model T, the position of the clutch pedal when engaging high gear in the transmission.

High Risers
1. Raised cylinder heads offered for the Ford 427 cubic-inch V-8 during the 1960s. The taller heads had room for intake ports 2.34 inches high, 0.79 inch higher than standard 427 heads. The higher ports were straighter for more direct flow of air/fuel mixture toward the combustion chambers. The heads provided substantial gains in horsepower between 5000 and 7000 rpm, which made them excellent for racing but unsuitable for street use. High Riser heads required a special High Riser intake manifold that would not fit other versions of the 427. See also *Low Risers* and *Medium Risers*.
2. A name assigned to any manifold that places the carburetor(s) above the original design location. The manifold lengthens the port runners to increase low-speed engine response and power.

high spot
Outward curvature on a normally flat surface.

high swirl port technology
Cylinder head design with high-speed airflow to pack more air/fuel mixture into the combustion chamber. A familiar engine using such technology is the four-cylinder Pontiac *Iron Duke*.

high tension wire
Wire that transmits high voltage from the coil to the distributor.

hi-po
High performance.

hi-rev kit
Set of auxiliary springs to keep roller lifters in contact with camshaft lobes.

history
Something destroyed or damaged beyond repair, as in "this engine's history."

hitch
Device attached to the rear of a vehicle, enabling it to pull a trailer. Hitches are rated according to the gross weight of the trailers they can pull: Class I, up to 2,000 pounds; Class II, up to up to 3500 pounds; Class III, up to 5,000 pounds; and Class IV, from 5,000 to 15,000 pounds.

hitch ball
Steel sphere, from 1-7/8 to 2-5/16 inches in diameter, on top of the end of a hitch on a tow vehicle. The tongue at the front of the trailer has a cup-like end that fits over the hitch ball and secures to it.

hitch pin
See *hitch receiver*, below.

hitch receiver
Underneath the rear of a tow vehicle, a heavy, square steel tube into which a removable shank supporting the hitch ball is inserted. The shank has a hole in it that aligns with holes on either side of the receiver. A pin, called the *hitch pin*, is then inserted through the holes to hold the shank in the receiver.

hitch weight
The load applied to a tow vehicle hitch by the trailer tongue. For stable towing, the hitch weight should be from 10 to 15 percent of the trailer's gross weight.

HO
High output.

hog
1. Any large vehicle, such as an older, oversize Cadillac or Lincoln.
2. Among motorcyclists, specifically, a Harley-Davidson.

hog out
To enlarge openings or passages in an engine, as when it's bored or ported.

hold the road
To steer and handle well at high speeds.

hole
1. Cylinder.
2. Starting position for a drag race.

hole shot
Beating a drag competitor right at the start of a race; that is, when coming out of the *hole*, usually with a faster reaction time. The winner pulled a *hole shot* and the loser was *holed*.

hollow
Concave area in a body panel.

hollow domed piston
Piston with a compression dome that is of equal thickness across the top.

hollow flank
Concave or indented flank on a camshaft lobe.

hollow pushrod
Tubular pushrod, hollow inside.

homologated
See GTO.

honcho
Someone in charge; from a Japanese military term, "hancho," meaning "squad leader."

Honda
Honda Motor Company was established by Soichiro Honda in 1947 and began producing motorcycles the following year. By 1960, it had become the largest and most successful motorcycle manufacturer in the world. In 1962, Honda produced its first small car, a two-seat convertible with a 360-cc, 4-cylinder engine, and featuring dual overhead cams and hemispherical combustion chambers. The company's motorcycle engineering experience showed in the little car's final drive, with a separate chain to each rear wheel. Honda's first major breakthrough as an automaker came with the 1972 Civic, a state-of-the-art small car with Honda's exclusive *CVCC* engine, which it met U.S. emissions standards with. Four years later, production of the Civic passed one million units and it was joined in the Honda lineup by another, slightly larger car, the Accord. Honda was the first Japanese motor company to establish a *transplant* in the United States. It began building motorcycles at a plant near Marysville, Ohio, in 1979. Automobile production began at a separate, larger facility adjacent to the motorcycle plant in 1982. Today, the Marysville auto factory produces both the Accord and the Civic. In 1990, the Honda Accord became the best-selling car in the U.S.

hone
1. Generally, a fine-textured grinding stone for sharpening an edge, as on a razor, or polishing a surface.
2. In auto mechanics, specifically, a rotating tool with three legs, each holding a fine-textured grinding stone, used to enlarge and smooth the inner surface of a hole. Hones are used to finish the inner surfaces of such items as engine cylinders, valve guides and brake cylinders.

hone mandrel
Part of the hone holding the grinding stones.

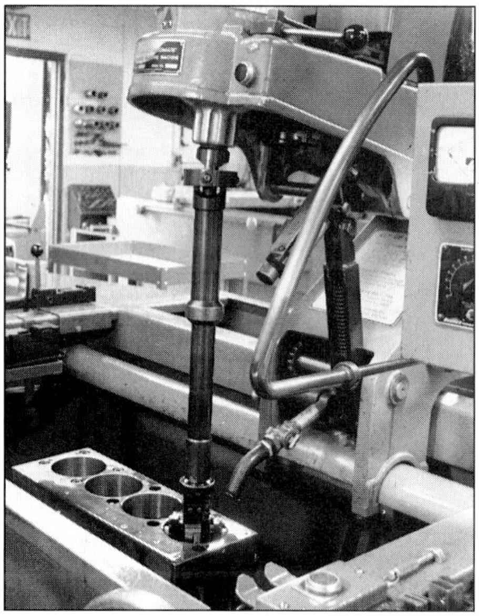

honing machine

honing machine
Stationary machine, such as the Sunnen CK-10, which drives an individual cylinder hone.

honk
To beat another car, especially in a drag race.

honker
Top performing car.

honk on
To perform well.

hood
Opening body panel ahead of the cowl, covering the engine compartment on a front-engined vehicle, and what may be the luggage compartment on a mid- or rear-engined one.

hood scoop

hood scoop
Air duct in the hood to allow air to flow directly to the engine. See *ram air.*

hook up
1. In drag racing, to set the car up for the best possible traction off the starting line. A driver who *launches* well, with a lot of *bite,* is said to be "hooked up."
2. In oval track racing, to enter a *draft.*

hooligan
In dirt track racing, a consolation event; cars which failed to make the show for the main event run together in the hooligan, which is usually held just before the main.

hop up
To modify an engine for increased performance.

horse car
Ford Mustang.

horsepower
Measure of the work an engine can perform. Horsepower can be described as the ability to move a given weight a given distance—i.e., to apply leverage—in a given period of time. One horsepower is equal to 33,000 pounds-feet of torque per minute or 550 pounds-feet per second. There are several ways of expressing horsepower. See also *brake horsepower, corrected horsepower, gross horsepower, indicated horsepower, net horsepower* and *observed horsepower*, as well as *torque.*

Hotchkiss drive
A live axle rear suspension system for rear-wheel-drive vehicles in which a live axle is located with longitudinal leaf springs. The springs also support the rear of the vehicle, so it is a very simple system. In fact, the basic design is a carryover from horse carriages. In 1970, Chevrolet found that placing one of the shocks ahead of the axle and placing one behind it would eliminate torque-induced wheel-hop under hard acceleration and braking, keeping the Hotchkiss drive suspension current. It is still used today.

hot dog
Another term for a top performer in almost all forms of racing; see also *weenie*.

hot drawn
Process to induce strength and improve grain structure in metal as it is heated and pulled through dies or rollers.

hot iron
Early term for *hot rod*, see below.

hot rod
Passenger car, usually American made, which has been rebuilt or modified for higher performance and a distinctive, functional appearance. An important characteristic of the hot rod is that it's built primarily for straightaway speed or acceleration, such as lakes or drag competition, rather than for *road racing—street racing* maybe, but road racing rarely.

hot setup
Particular combination of components and modifications that results in maximum performance.

hot shoe
Top race driver, one who consistently gets maximum performance out of his vehicle.

hot spot
1. In a combustion chamber, a localized area where excessive heat can build up such as around the spark plug or exhaust valve, and possibly cause *preignition*.
2. Among bodyworkers, an area on an auto body where corrosion is likely to occur.

hot tank
Vat containing a mixture of hot water and a caustic chemical to strip oil, paint and rust from engine parts. Use extreme caution when working around a hot tank.

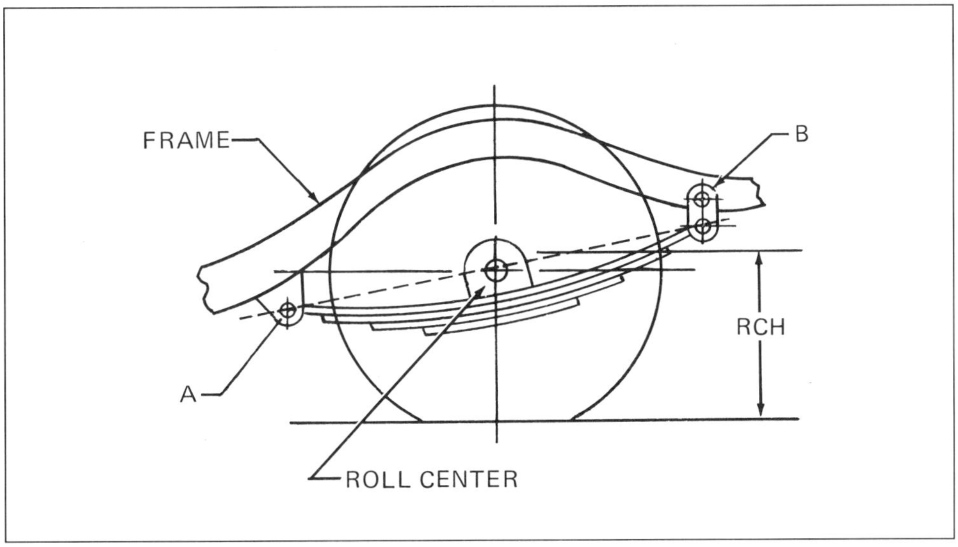

Hotchkiss drive

hot tank gloves
Long-sleeved rubber gloves that help protect the user of a hot tank.

hot weld
Technique for joining pieces of cast-iron together that involves preheating them to 1300 degrees F. and then oxyacetylene welding them.

hot-wire sensor
Device inside the mass airflow meter that uses heat from electrical current passing through the wire to measure airflow and density.

housing bore
Inside diameter of a bearing housing.

HPV
Human-powered vehicle, such as a bicycle.

HRS
Hot-rolled steel, formed while hot.

H shift pattern
H-shaped arrangement of gear shift positions for a manual transmission.

HSS
High-speed steel, an extremely hard alloy used to make cutting bits and blades.

hub
Center of a wheel.

hub cap
Wheel covering.

HUD
See *heads-up display*.

Hudson
The Hudson Motor Car Company of Detroit was founded in 1909 by Roy D. Chapin, with financial backing from J.L. Hudson of the famous Detroit department store of that name. Hudson merged with *Nash* in 1954 to form the *American Motors Corporation*. In 1957, both the Hudson and Nash nameplates were dropped in favor of *Rambler*. Roy D. Chapin, Jr., son of Hudson's founder, later became president of AMC. The corporation was absorbed by Chrysler in 1988.

huffer
Supercharger.

Hummer
See *Humvee*, below.

hummingbird suspension
Lightweight independent front suspension once used on some dragsters; it featured extremely high frequency springs which oscillated very rapidly, reminding some of a hummingbird's wings.

Humvee
HMMWV or High Mobility Multipurpose Wheeled Vehicle, a GM diesel-powered, four-wheel-drive vehicle developed by AM General and built in a variety of configurations for both military and civilian use. The Humvee—or *Hummer*, as it's also known—was particularly conspicuous during the Persian Gulf War in early 1991.

hybrid
1. Vehicle with two separate propulsion systems, such as one with both an internal combustion engine and an electric motor or motors. The two may be interrelated, as when the internal combustion engine is used to charge the batteries supplying the electric propulsion system, or they may be independent, as when the internal combustion engine is used for long-distance cruising and the electric system for city driving.
2. Vehicle with major components from more than one source, such as the Shelby Cobra of the 1960s, which combined a high-performance Ford V-8 engine with a light-weight British A.C. chassis.

hydraulic valve lifter
Lifter which uses oil pressure to adjust its length and maintain zero valve clearance. The hydraulic lifter compensates for wear, eliminates the need for periodic valve adjustments and operates more quietly than a mechanical lifter.

hydraulics
On a low rider, hydraulic ram units installed at each suspension point to raise or lower the ride height. Sometimes referred to as "hydros."

hydrazine
H_2NNH_2, a highly explosive jet fuel sometimes used as an additive in fuel for drag racing.

Hydro, hydro
1. With a capital "H," Hydra-matic, a brand of automatic transmissions built by General Motors.
2. Hydraulic valve lifter.
3. See *hydraulics*, above.

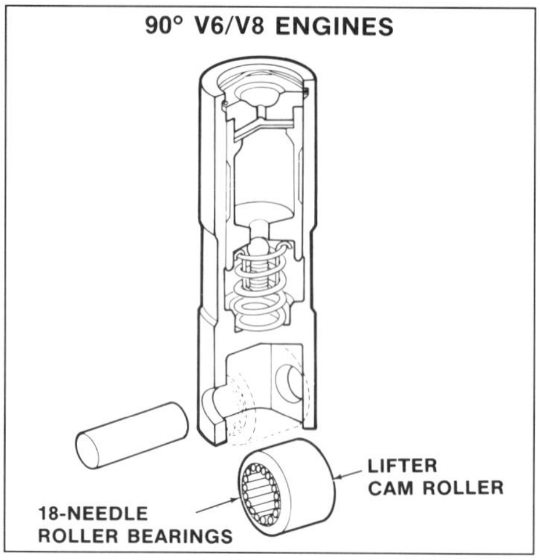

hydraulic valve lifter

hydro cam
Camshaft especially designed for use with hydraulic valve lifters.

hydrocarbon
HC, any of a large number of organic compounds consisting of hydrogen and carbon, obtained mainly from petroleum and coal tar. Gasoline is a mixture of hydrocarbons. Two important subcategories of hydrocarbon fuels are paraffins—including methane, ethane, propane and butane—and aromatics, including benzene, toluene and xylene.

hydrocarbon emissions
See *exhaust emissions* and *unburned hydrocarbons.*

hydrometer
Device to measure the specific gravity of a liquid. Hydrometers are used, for example, to find the electrolytic quality of battery fluid and the amount of glycol in radiator coolant.

hydroplaning
See *aquaplaning.*

hydrostatic gauge
Instrument for measuring liquid volume, such as a fuel gauge.

hydrostatic lock
Condition in an engine block when leakage allows liquid to fill a cylinder and block movement of the piston.

hydrostatic testing
Testing the structural integrity of tanks or other containers with water under high pressure.

hygrometer
Instrument to measure the relative humidity in the atmosphere.

Hypalon wire
Special dielectric wire covering used for high tension spark plug wires.

hypoid gears
In a final drive assembly, spiral bevel gears that allow the pinion to be placed below the center of the ring gear. This, in turn, allows the driveshaft and, with it, the floor of the vehicle to be lower.

I

I-beam axle
Beam axle with an I-shaped cross-section.

I-beam rod
Connecting rod with an I-shaped cross-section.

ICE
Internal combustion engine.

i.d.
Inside diameter of a tube or pipe, i.e. the diameter of the inner walls.

ideal air/fuel ratio
See *Stoichiometric air/fuel ratio.*

IDI
Indirect injection; system in which fuel is injected into a prechamber and ignited before entering the main combustion chamber.

idiot box
Automatic transmission.

idiot light
Red warning light used on the dash panel in place of some specific instrument, to indicate that a malfunction has occurred. See also *warning light.*

idiot proof
Product designed to be as simple as possible to operate.

idle circuit
System within a carburetor which meters fuel when the engine is running at low rpm. As the engine gets underway and gains speed, the idle circuit phases out of operation and the main fuel metering system takes over.

idle mixture screw
On a carburetor, the screw used to adjust engine idle speed.

idle speed
Engine speed at minimum throttle and load, with the transmission in neutral.

idler arm
Lever which balances the pitman arm in a vehicle's steering geometry. The pitman arm converts the rotary motion of the steering gearbox to lateral motion of the centerlink. The centerlink, in turn, connects the pitman arm to the idler arm on the opposite side of the system and causes the idler to duplicate the movement of the pitman. See also *pitman arm.*

idler gear
Gear connecting two other gears so both of the latter will rotate in the same direction.

I-4
Inline four-cylinder engine. See *inline.*

If you can't find 'em, grind 'em!
Admonition to a driver who misses a shift.

IFS
Independent front suspension. See *independent suspension.*

ignition
The firing of a spark plug to ignite compressed air/fuel mixture in a combustion chamber.

ignition coil
See *coil.*

ignition distributor
See *distributor.*

ignition map
Topographic-like chart showing the precise advance and retard of the ignition on an engine with electronic controls.

ignition points
See *points.*

ignition switch
Switch which turns on a vehicle's ignition system. It is usually operated by a key which can also be turned to activate the starter motor and start the engine.

ignition system
Electrical circuitry that provides the spark at the right moment to ignite the mixture in the combustion chamber. Its major components are the battery, ignition switch, coil, distributor, high-tension wiring and spark plugs.

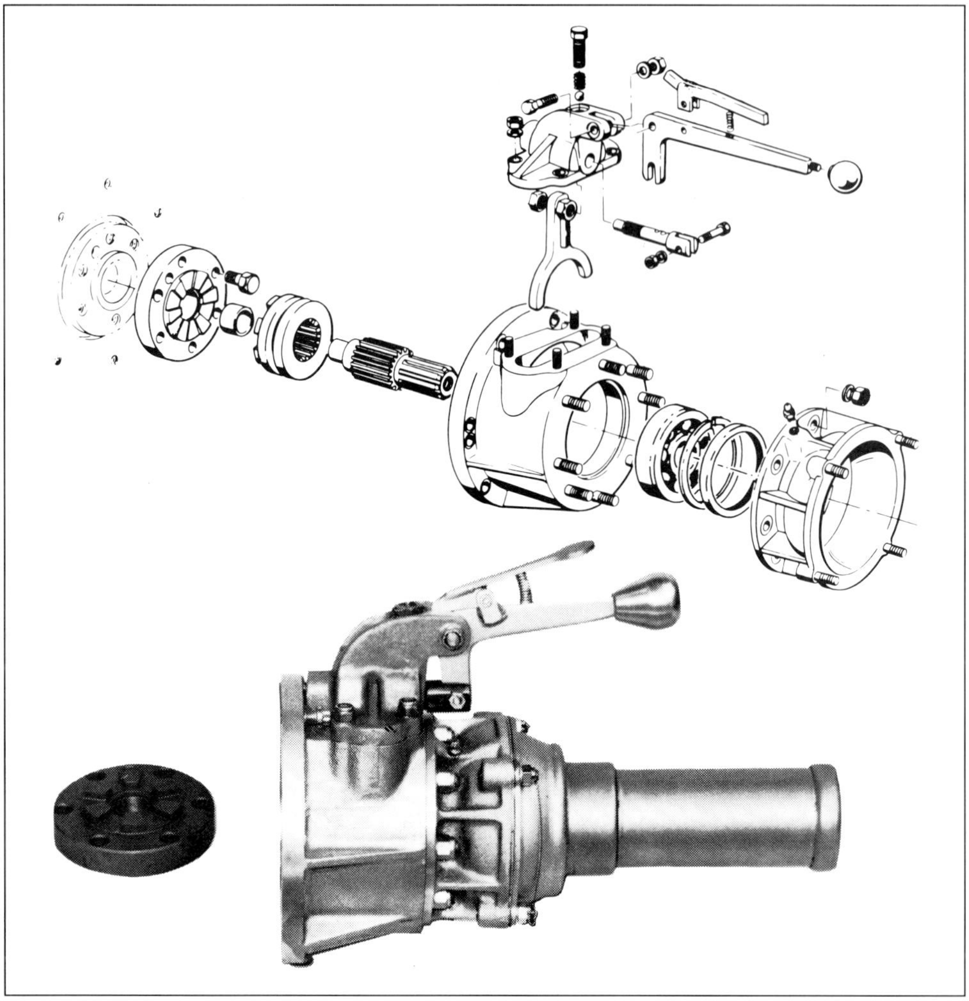

in-and-out box

ignition temperature
Lowest temperature at which a combustible material will ignite in air and continue to burn independently of the heat source.

ignition timing
Timing of the spark relative to piston top dead center, expressed in crankshaft degrees.

I head
Overhead valve engine with both the intake and exhaust valves directly over the piston. The valves are actuated through pushrods and rocker arms by a camshaft located in the block.

IHRA
International Hot Rod Association, P.O. Box 3029, Highway 11E, Bristol, Tennessee 37624; (615) 764-1164. Drag racing sanctioning body.

IHP
See *indicated horsepower*.

IKF
International Karting Federation, 4650 Arrow Highway, Suite 4B, Montclair, CA 91763; (714) 625-5497. Major kart race sanctioning body.

Ilmor
Chevrolet racing engine developed by Mario *Il*lien and Paul *Mor*gan.

IMCA
International Motor Contest Association.

IMEP
See *indicated mean effective pressure*.

impact failure
Failure of a part or parts caused by repeated impact or off-square seating.

impact hardness
Hardening of a part or parts caused by repeated impact.

impact particle cleaning
Method of cleaning parts by air-spraying them with small, abrasive glass beads. Same as glass bead cleaning.

impact tools
Pneumatic tools, i.e., those powered by compressed air, such as an impact wrench.

impeller
Rotor which transmits motion, as in a centrifugal pump, supercharger, turbine or fluid coupling.

Imperial
Traditionally, Chrysler's biggest, most luxurious and most expensive car line. The first Chrysler Imperial was built in 1926. From 1954 to 1975, the Imperial was marketed as a separate make in its own right. It was dropped in 1975 and then revived briefly in 1981 and 1982. It was revived again in 1990, this time simply as a stretched-out version of Chrysler's front-drive *K car*.

IMS
Indianapolis Motor Speedway, which is in Speedway, Indiana, not Indianapolis. See also *Indy*.

IMSA
International Motor Sports Association, P.O. Box 10709, Tampa, Florida 33679; (813) 877-4672. Road racing sanctioning body.

inadequate crush
Lack of proper crush in a pair of bearing shells, allowing too much clearance between the bearings and the shaft; if not corrected, inadequate crush will lead to premature bearing failure.

in-and-out box
Racing transmission with neutral and a single, direct-drive forward gear, using a dog clutch and splined shaft with a fork for shifting in or out of gear.

inboard brakes
Brakes mounted at the inboard end of an axle half shaft, near the chassis centerline, instead of outboard at the wheel. Inboard brakes are part of the vehicle's *sprung weight*, while outboard brakes are part of the *unsprung weight*.

inch-pound
Unit of torque. One inch-pound is the force needed to lift one pound one inch. Twelve inch-pounds equal one foot-pound.

independent suspension
Type of suspension, front or rear, in which the wheel on one side of the vehicle reacts separately from the corresponding wheel on the other side. Compared with a *beam axle*, independent suspension reduces *unsprung weight,* takes up less space, and can be engineered to provide both a smoother ride and more stable handling.

index
1. In drag racing, elapsed times assigned to various classes to calculate starting time differences for handicap or bracket racing.
2. To examine and adjust rod journal spacing and alignment.
3. Installing the camshaft relative to crankshaft position so that the valves open and close at precisely the right moment. See *degreeing a cam.*

indicated horsepower, indicated torque
Indicated horsepower and torque are calculated from IMEP or *indicated mean effective pressure*. The indicated figures represent the actual output developed within the cylinders, before the losses due to friction that occur by the time the output reaches the flywheel, where the brake horsepower is measured. See also *brake horsepower, brake torque*.

indicated mean effective pressure
Average of the pressures developed within a cylinder during a full four-stroke cycle of intake, compression, combustion and exhaust. The IMEP can be measured with a device called an *indicator* and is the basis for calculating the indicated engine output. See also *indicated horsepower, indicated torque*.

indicated speed
Speed as shown by the speedometer.

indicated torque
See *indicated horsepower, indicated torque*.

indicator
Instrument for measuring *indicated mean effective pressure*.

indirect measurement
Use of such tools as a telescoping gauge to measure areas of parts, such as an inner diameter of a cylinder, that are not accessible for direct measurement. The distance between the ends of the gauge is then measured with a micrometer.

induction
1. Process in which a magnet or electrically charged object transmits magnetism or electrical current in a nearby object without any physical contact between the two objects.
2. Synonym for "intake," as in induction manifold or induction port, particularly in British usage. See *intake manifold* and *intake port*.

Indy
1. Indianapolis Motor Speedway, site of the world's most famous 500-mile race, held every Memorial Day weekend. The track is 2.5 miles long, with two long straightaways on the sides and short "chutes" on each end connected by four corners struck on a radius of 840 feet. Indycars today lap this circuit with *average* speeds in excess of 220 mph. It was originally paved with bricks, hence the nickname "Brickyard." See *Indy 500*.
2. Indianapolis Raceway Park, site of the NHRA U.S. Nationals on Labor Day weekend.

Indycar
Open-wheeled racing vehicle built expressly for Indy and CART racing.

Indycar

induction coil
In an ignition system, a primary coil which receives low-voltage direct current from a power source, such as a battery, when the ignition points are closed. When the points are opened, the current is interrupted, transmitting high-voltage direct current by induction to a secondary coil.

induction hardening
Process using electric coils placed next to a part to harden the surface of that part.

Indy 500
Race held every Memorial Day weekend at Indianapolis Motor Speedway by USAC for Indycars. The first race was held in 1911, and won by Ray Harroun in the "Marmon Wasp." Since that time, the Indy 500 has become an American classic, and is the single largest spectator-attended sporting event in the world. Although officials won't release figures, it is estimated that over 500,000 people attend the event each year.

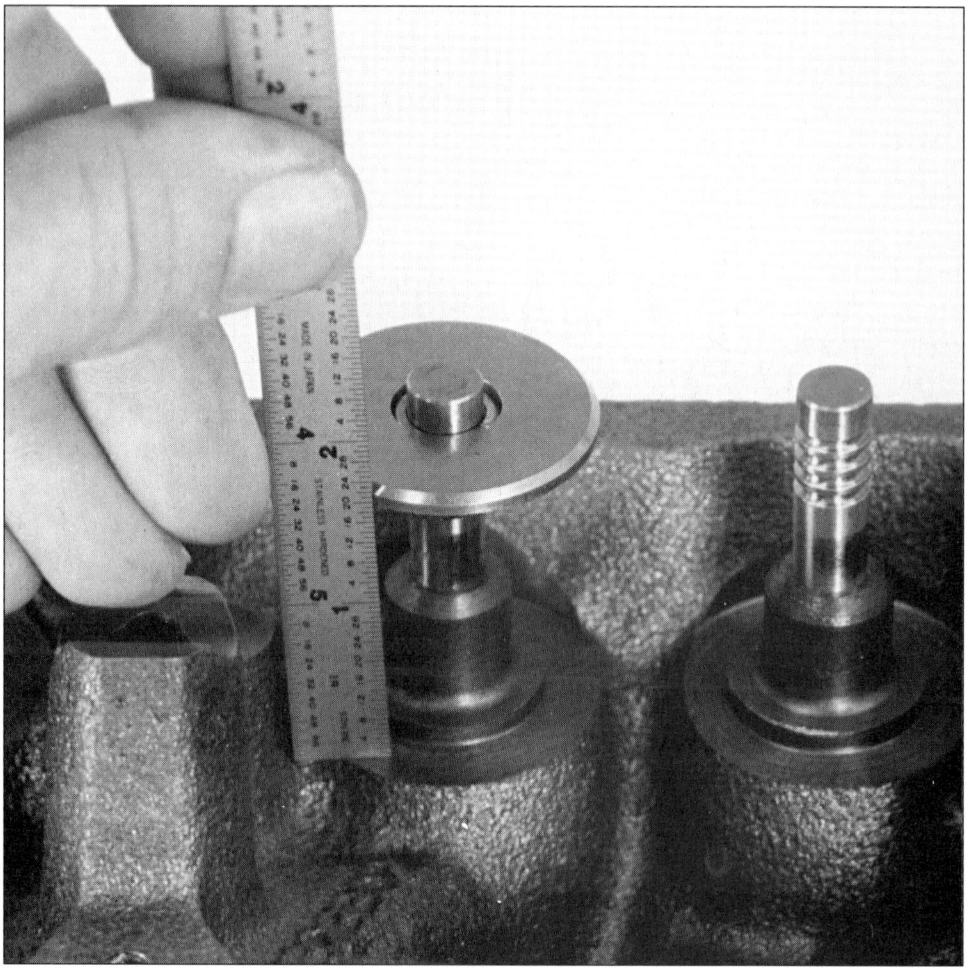

installed height

inertial scavenging
Exhaust system which uses the momentum of flowing gasses to pull even more gasses through.

infield
Area enclosed by an oval track or road course.

information center
Electronic display in the cockpit of some luxury cars which shows such data as the date, time, inside and outside temperatures, trip distance traveled, trip average speed and fuel consumption, amount of fuel left, maximum distance before refueling and much else.

information sheet
Form used to record information about a vehicle during measurement or assembly.

in Hg
Inches of mercury, unit of pressure.

inhibitor
See *rust inhibitor*.

in H_2O
Inches of water, unit of pressure.

injected
Engine equipped with fuel injection rather than carburetion.

injection valve, injector
See *fuel injector*.

injector body
Housing for a fuel injection system.

injector fuel
Fuel stored within the injector body prior to use.

injector tube
Copper or brass tube used in diesel cylinder heads to cool fuel injectors and seal combustion pressures.

inlet
Like *induction*, a synonym for *intake*.

inline
Engine with its cylinders in a single line; most inlines are four- or six-cylinder, though there are a few threes and fives as well and, prior to 1950, there were a number of inline eights. See also *straight*.

innards
Internal parts, of an engine or transmission.

input shaft
In a vehicle's transmission, the shaft that receives power from the engine, via the clutch or torque converter, and delivers it to the transmission gears.

insert valve guide
Replaceable valve guide, as opposed to an *integral valve guide*.

insert valve seat
Replaceable valve seat, as opposed to an *integral valve seat*.

installed height
Distance from the valve stem end to the valve spring seat.

instant center
The imaginary center point around which a given wheel appears to pivot when a vehicle's structure rolls from side to side. See illustration next page.

intake manifold
Component, generally cast iron or aluminum, with passages of varying length, to duct incoming air/fuel mixture from the carburetor, or air alone in an injected engine, to the intake ports.

intake ports
Passages in the cylinder head (or in a L-head engine, in the block) which duct incoming air/fuel mixture, or air alone in an injected engine, from the intake manifold to the intake valves. See photo next page.

intake stroke
Downward stroke of the piston, creating a vacuum that draws air/fuel mixture through the intake valves into the cylinder.

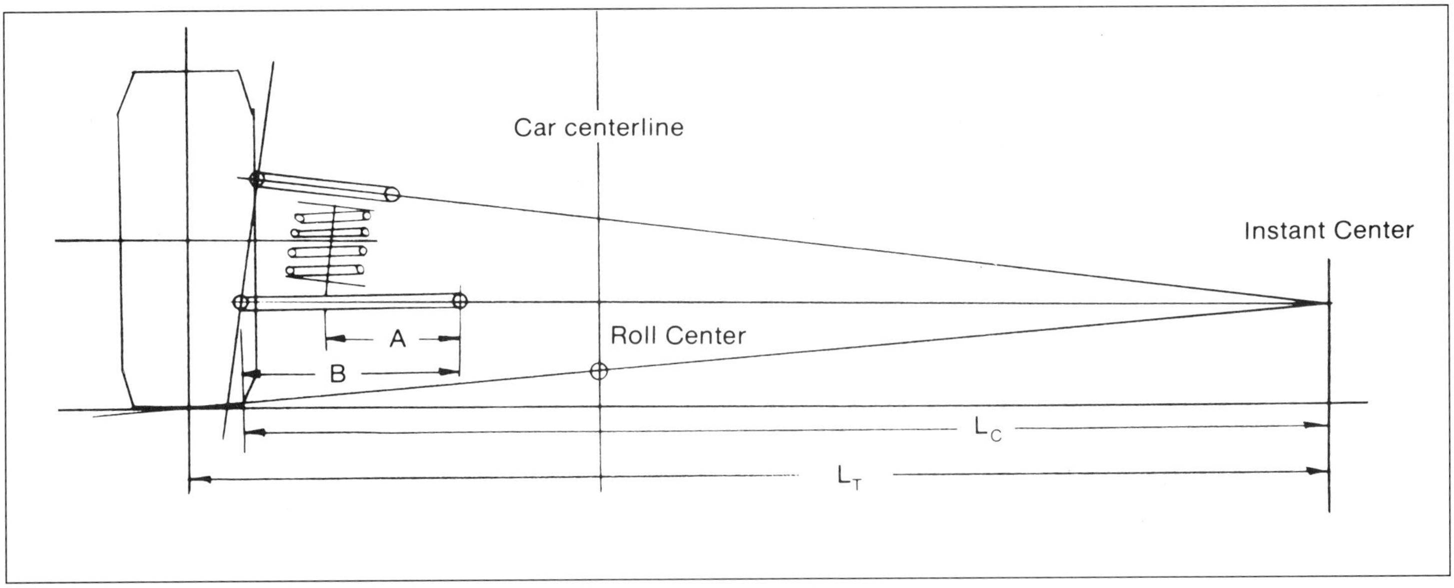

instant center

intake ports

intake valves
Valves which open to admit air/fuel mixture from the intake ports into the cylinders.

integral valve guide
Valve guide machined into the cylinder head, as opposed to a removable or *insert valve guide*.

integral valve seat
Valve seat machined into the cylinder head, as opposed to a removable or *insert valve seat*.

integral power steering
Steering system with a built-in power assist.

interaxle differential
In *all-wheel drive* or full-time *four-wheel drive*, a third differential between the front and rear differentials, usually at the *transfer case*, to prevent bind or wrap-up between the front and rear axles, especially going around corners.

intercooler
On an engine with supercharging, including turbocharging, a radiator-like heat exchanger between the supercharger and the engine which cools the air, or air/fuel mixture, that has been heated by compression in the supercharger. The object is to increase the density of the air or mixture. See photo next page.

interference angle
See *interference valve angle*, below.

interference fit
Condition when two parts of different dimensions must be pressed together; usually a 0.0005- to 0.007-inch difference.

interference valve angle
Difference between the valve seat angle and the valve face angle, usually only one or two degrees.

intermediate gear
Any transmission gear between low and high. In a three-speed, second is the only intermediate gear. In a five-speed, on the other hand, second, third and fourth are all intermediate gears.

International
International Harvester Company of Chicago was established in 1907 and, for its first four years, it built both cars and trucks. In 1911, however, it dropped its car line to devote its efforts entirely to commercial vehicles. Today, it is best remembered for its Scout line of sport utility vehicles, introduced in 1961. Twenty years later, the company discontinued the Scout and, since 1981, it has built only medium- and heavy-duty trucks. These still carry the International nameplate, though the company is now called Navistar.

in the chute
Staged for a drag race.

inverted start
Oval track race where the cars are started in opposite order of their qualifying times, i.e., the slowest cars up front and the fastest ones at the rear. The object is to provide exciting action by forcing the faster cars to work their way up through the pack.

IOE
Intake over exhaust, same as *F-head*.

IROC
International Race of Champions, 45 Park Road, Tinton Falls, New Jersey 07724; (908) 542-4762. Annual series for top drivers from various forms of oval track and road racing who are invited to compete in identical spec cars. Originally, the cars

intercooler (Buick V6)

were Porsche 911s and, later, Chevrolet Camaros. At this writing, the IROC series uses specially built Dodge Daytonas, with NASCAR stock car-type tube frames and front-mounted V-8 engines with rear drive.

Iron Duke
151-cubic-inch, four-cylinder, cast-iron engine introduced by Pontiac in 1978 and since used in numerous smaller General Motors cars and trucks. The Iron Duke is sometimes confused with a similar 153-cubic-inch four used in the Chevy II in the 1960s, but the two units have no significant parts in common.

Irontite
Tradename for a process to repair cracks in cast-iron cylinder heads and blocks, using tapered plugs to fill the crack.

IRP
Indianapolis Raceway Park; see *Indy*.

IRS
Independent rear suspension. See *independent suspension*.

I-6
Inline six-cylinder engine. See *inline*.

ISCA
International Show Car Association, 3225 Mally Drive, Madison Heights, MI 48071; (313) 588-5568. Promoter of International Championship Custom Car Shows.

Isky
Brand of camshafts and valvetrain components produced by pioneer hot rodder Ed Iskenderian.

isoblock
Rubber insulator block used for motor mounts.

isolator
Rubber or synthetic device used to separate two or more parts and to reduce vibration.

isomers
Chemical compounds with the same molecular weight and atomic composition but with differing molecular structures. As an example, the hydrocarbons *isooctane*, see below, and *octane* are isomers. A molecule of either has eight carbon atoms and eighteen hydrogen atoms, but they are arranged differently. In octane, they are in a straight carbon chain while, in isooctane, they are branched.

isooctane
$(CH_3)_2CHCH_2C(CH_3)_3$, a hydrocarbon with an octane number of 100, used in combination with n-heptane, which has an octane number of zero, to define octane numbers of less than 100. See also *octane* and *octane number*.

Isuzu
Japanese automaker, Isuzu Motors Limited. Isuzu means "fifty bells" and is the name of a river which flows through an area in Ise province which contains one of the most ancient and revered Shinto shrines in Japan. Isuzu is a successor to the Tokyo Ishikawajima Shipbuilding and Engineering Company, which was founded in 1916 and, according to Isuzu, was Japan's first manufacturer of automobiles. Isuzu was adopted as a vehicle name in 1934 and became the company name in 1949. Since 1971, General Motors has owned about one-third of Isuzu.

J

jack
Mechanical or hydraulic device to lift one corner or one end of a vehicle to change a wheel and tire. A simple jack should not be used to support a vehicle for prolonged work on the undercarriage. For that, the vehicle should be supported securely on *jack stands* or *ramps*.

jacking
1. In oval track racing, modifying the suspension to raise or lower one corner of the chassis, in order to alter the car's weight distribution for better handling.
2. On a vehicle with a high roll center because of swing axles, such as at the rear of the early Volkswagen Beetle and Chevrolet Corvair, the tendency of the body to roll in tight, fast corners, allowing the outboard wheel to tuck under at a severe negative camber and jack up that side of the car.

jack rabbit start
Sudden acceleration from a standing start.

jacketed gasket
Gasket with metal grommets around water and bolt holes to increase strength.

jackshaft
Auxiliary shaft used on most overhead camshaft engines to drive the fuel pump, oil pump and distributor. The jackshaft is located in the block and is driven by the timing belt or chain.

jack stands
Portable stands, adjustable for height, which support a raised vehicle at axles or frame members so that a mechanic can work underneath safely and with adequate clearance. The vehicle is lifted with a *jack* and then lowered on to the jack stands' appropriate support points.

Jack the Bear
Top performing driver.

Jacobs Brake
See *Jake Brake*.

Jacob's ladder
On some rear-wheel-drive race cars, a triangular control linkage to center the rear axle assembly.

Jaguar
British car manufacturer currently owned by Ford Motor Co. In 1922, William Lyons, a motorcycle enthusiast and salesman, joined forces with William Walmsley, who built aluminum sidecars, to form the Swallow Sidecar Company. They built their first car in 1927, a Morris-based Cowley Swallow. The company continued to build cars, coming out with a SS100 Jaguar model in 1935. After World War II, the company was reorganized as Jaguar Cars Ltd., and began developing premier sports and racing cars. In 1966, Jaguar merged with the British Motor Corporation, which later became the British Leyland Motor Corporation. During the 1970s and much of the 1980s, Jaguar's sales slipped and its reputation suffered from poor quality control standards. In 1990, Jaguar was purchased by Ford Motor Co., and has since undergone significant changes, which have resulted in positive improvements, both on and off the racing track.

Jake Brake
Engine retarder produced by the Jacobs Vehicle Equipment Company for heavy-duty truck diesels. When a diesel engine's accelerator is released, the flow of fuel into the engine is reduced but the flow of air continues; thus, no vacuum develops within the cylinders and the engine does not slow down significantly the way a gasoline engine does. With a Jake Brake, on the other hand, when the accelerator is released, the fuel supply is cut off and the timing of the exhaust valves is altered. During the intake stroke, air is admitted to the cylinders as usual, and during the compression stroke, that air is compressed. The exhaust valves are opened early, before Top Dead Center, relieving the pressure, but not before there has been enough build-up of pressure to slow the engine. With the fuel cut off and the exhaust valves opening early, compression ignition cannot occur, so there is no combustion or power stroke to counteract the slowing effect of the pressure build-up during the compression stroke. The net effect is that the engine slows down and, with it, so does the vehicle. See also *compression braking*.

jalopy
1. Old, dilapidated automobile.
2. In dirt track racing, a type of low-budget race car rebuilt from an older vehicle.

jam nut
Thin nut tightened against a standard size nut to lock it into place.

J cam
Pattern used to grind pistons in an oval or cam shape with a 0.017 inch difference between the thrust face and the pinhole side.

Jeep
Name applied to Willys MB and Ford GPW 1/4-ton military four-wheel-drive vehicles during World War II and apparently derived from the initials *GP* for "general purpose." Since 1945, Jeep has been a registered trademark of, successively, Willys Motors, Kaiser Jeep, American Motors, and currently, Chrysler Corporation. It is *not* a generic term for four-wheel-drive vehicles.

jet cleaner

jeeping, jeep trail

jeeping
Operating a four-wheel-drive vehicle, especially off the road. The term dates from the late 1940s or early 1950s when the Jeep was the only readily available, short-wheelbase four-wheel drive vehicle.

jeep trail
Back country road or trail considered suitable only for short-wheelbase four-wheel-drive vehicles like the original Jeep.

jet
Orifice through which a liquid or gas can be transmitted at a controlled rate, such as in a carburetor or fuel injection system.

jet car
Race car powered with a jet aircraft engine, generally for open course competition, such as at dry lakes or drag strips. Jet cars are often used as crowd-pleasing exhibitions at major car shows and drag races.

jet cleaner
Self-contained parts cleaning machine that sprays a caustic liquid through high pressure nozzles on parts as they rotate on a platform inside; similar in operation to a dishwasher.

jet valve
In a stratified charge engine, a small intake valve located in a pre-combustion chamber that admits a highly concentrated air/fuel mixture. That mixture, in turn, helps ignite a much leaner mixture in the main combustion chamber. Perhaps the best known example of this technology was in the CVCC engine developed for the Honda Civic in the early 1970s.

jig
1. In bodywork, large device for straightening the frame of a damaged vehicle.
2. A fixture or framework for holding work and for guiding a machine tool to the work; used for such tasks as locating and spacing drilled holes and for *jig welding*, below. See photo next page.

jig welding
Welding of components which are held together temporarily in a *jig*. In this term, "jig" is a word in its own right and need not be capitalized, unlike the abbreviated qualifiers in *MIG welding* and *TIG welding*.

Jimmy
Although recently used by the GMC truck division of General Motors as a designation for specific, short-wheelbase sport-

jig, jig welding

utility vehicles, Jimmy is a traditional popular term for all GMC products. Jimmy superchargers, Roots-type blowers originally designed for GMC diesel truck engines, are widely used in drag racing.

JIS
Japanese Industrial Standard, Japan's equivalent of the SAE in the United States or DIN in Germany.

Johnson rod
Mythical automotive component blamed for any problem or malfunction that can't be tracked down and corrected.

jounce
In a vehicle suspension system, the retraction inward of the springs and shock absorbers when a wheel hits an obstruction; jounce is followed by *rebound.*

journal
Areas of a rotating part, such as a crankshaft, crank throw, camshaft or axle, supported by bearings. The bearing surfaces are mated to insert bearings that support and position the part. During an engine overhaul, measurement of the crank, crank throw and cam bearings and their conformity to original factory specs is used to determine if the bearings should be reused, reconditioned or replaced.

J rim
On a vehicle wheel, a groove around the outer edge to provide a lock for the tire bead. The result is better tire-to-wheel retention under heavy side loadings around corners.

judder
Low frequency vibrations in the clutch or brakes, with the frequency increasing with rotational speed; usually a sign of imbalance caused by excessive wear.

jug
Carburetor.

juice
1. Current in a vehicle's electrical system.
2. Special racing fuel, particularly nitromethane.
3. Hydraulic fluid, such as brake fluid.

jump
1. In drag racing, to start from the line suddenly and unexpectedly, before a competitor is ready to go. A driver who tries to jump against a *Christmas tree* runs the risk of a *red light.*
2. In forms of racing with a *rolling start*, to begin accelerating rapidly through the field before the green flag is waved, generally coming off the last turn. If the jump is blatant and potentially dangerous, the starter most likely will refuse to wave the green, and force the field to take another pace lap.
3. In off-road use, an obstacle that causes a fast-moving vehicle to become airborne.
4. As a verb, to *jump start*, see below.

jump start
To start a vehicle with a discharged battery by connecting that battery with *jumper cables* to draw electrical current from a good battery.

jumper cable
Pair of cables to connect two batteries for a *jump start.*

jumper wire
Wire used to bypass electrical circuits for testing purposes.

Junior Fueler, Junior Stocker
Older drag racing terms for lower class fuel dragster and stocker, respectively; no longer in official use.

junk
Anything, from a small part to a complete vehicle, that is too badly worn or damaged for further use.

junk box
1. Well-worn or damaged vehicle ready to be scrapped, also called a *junker.*
2. Vehicle rebuilt from well-worn parts.

junker
Same as *junk box*, def. 1., above.

junky
Person or company in the vehicle salvage business.

junk yard
Facility selling used parts for vehicles; same as *bone yard.*

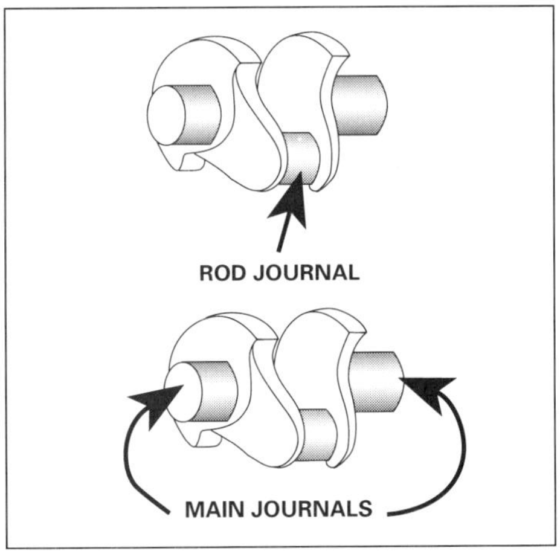

crankshaft journals

K

k

1. In SI decimal or base 10 units, the letter "k" stands for "kilo," derived from a Greek word for 1,000, and indicates 10^3 or 1,000 of a unit. Familiar examples are: the *kilogram* (kg), a unit of weight equal to 1,000 grams; the *kilohertz* (kHz), a unit of frequency equal to 1,000 hertz; the *kilometer* (km), a unit of length equal to 1,000 meters; the *kilopascal* (kPa), a unit of pressure equal to 1,000 pascals; and the *kilowatt* (kw), a unit of power equal to 1,000 watts.
2. In computer science, "k" stands for "kilobyte," which is somewhat more than 1,000 bytes. A computer operates not on a decimal or base 10 system, but on a binary or base 2 system and a kilobyte is 2^{10} or 1024 bytes.

Kaiser

Passenger car built from 1946 to 1955 by Kaiser-Frazer Corporation of Willow Run, Michigan. The company derived its name from its two principals, Henry J. Kaiser, a successful ship builder during World War II, and Joseph W. Frazer, a former president of Graham-Paige Motors Corporation. Cars were produced with both men's names, though the Frazer was phased out in 1951. Kaiser-Frazer bought Willys and, with it, Jeep in 1953. By the mid 1950s, production was suspended of both Kaiser and Willys passenger cars. Kaiser-Frazer sold its Willow Run plant to General Motors, moved its headquarters to the Willys facilities in Toledo, Ohio, and changed its name to Kaiser-Willys Sales Corporation. In 1963, it changed its name again to Kaiser Jeep Corporation. Finally, in 1970, the company was bought out by American Motors Corporation, which changed it to simply Jeep Corporation. See also *American Motors Corporation*, *Frazer*, *Henry J*, *Jeep* and *Willys*.

Kaiser-Darrin

American sports car designed by Howard "Dutch" Darrin and originally manufactured by Kaiser-Frazer, beginning in 1953 and 1954. The car had a fiberglass body on a Henry J chassis and a Willys 6-cylinder, F-head engine. After Kaiser-Frazer got out of the passenger car business, Darrin discovered nearly 100 of the cars were in storage. He bought them, equipped many of them with Cadillac V-8 engines and continued to market them until the supply ran out in 1958.

Kamm

Wunibald Kamm, German automotive engineer who demonstrated in the early 1930s that a chopped off or ducktail rear body shape could be just as effective aerodynamically as a long, tapered tail. His type of design is often referred to as a *Kamm back* or *Kamm tail*.

kandy apple

Rich red finish, similar in color to a candied apple, popular on kustom kars.

kart

Miniscule race car, with small tires at the four corners of its simple tube frame and a small-displacement, single-cylinder engine, usually mounted at the driver's right. Generally, the kart has no bodywork and the driver rides in a simple bucket seat out in the breeze. During the early days of karting in the late 1950s, one of the most popular makes was the *Go Kart* and that name is still used, albeit incorrectly, as a generic term for such vehicles. See also *IKF*.

K car

Compact front-drive car introduced by Chrysler Corporation in 1981 as the Dodge Aries and Plymouth Reliant. During the 1980s, the K car became a mainstay for Chrysler and, by the early 1990s, it served as the basic platform for virtually all Chrysler, Dodge and Plymouth passenger vehicles, including mini-vans, built in North America.

KD set

Knocked down package of automobile components, manufactured at a main factory but designed for final assembly at a remote plant. Automakers often use KD sets for vehicle assembly in foreign countries.

Keenserts

Thread repair system that uses special inserts to replace stripped or damaged threads.

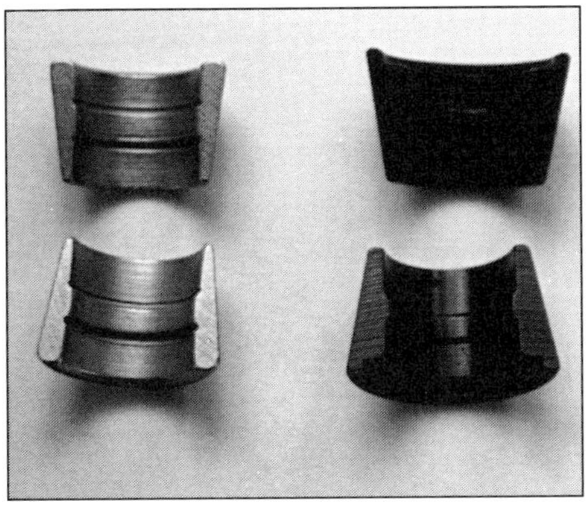

keepers

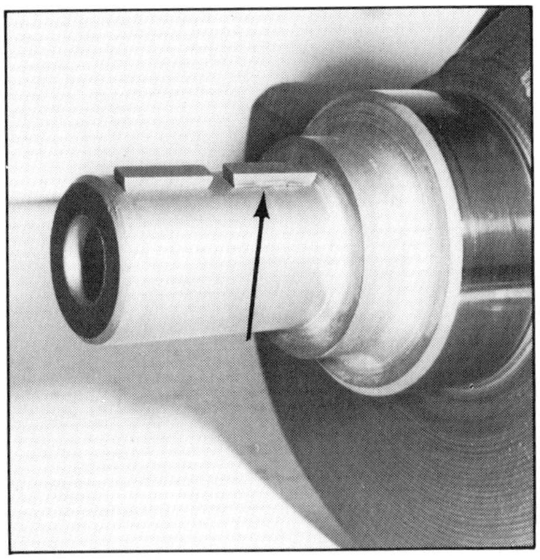

keyway, with keys

kemp

keepers
Tapered metal, key-like locking devices, generally used in pairs, to hold valve retainers in place on the valve stem.

keeper grooves
Grooved areas on the valve stem for the *keepers*, see above; the grooves may be square or round, and single or multiple.

KE-Jetronic
Modified continuous electronic fuel injection system produced by Bosch Corp. The system uses a Lambda sensor to monitor oxygen content within the exhaust gas stream to correct for over lean or rich conditions.

kemp
Kustom car or *lead sled*.

keystone ring
Double-tapered compression piston ring, shaped like a keystone.

keyway
Groove milled into a shaft or part to accept a square, round or half-moon piece of metal.

kg
Kilogram, see *k*.

kHz
Kilohertz, see *k*.

kickdown
In an automatic transmission, a downshift to the next lower gear which occurs when the driver applies full throttle, as when passing another vehicle on the highway or starting up a steep hill.

kick out of gear
To shift into neutral.

kickpad
Area along the bottom inside of a car door which is often kicked accidentally by passengers getting out of the vehicle and, thus, gets scuffed.

kickup
Section of a chassis frame raised to clear suspension parts or axles.

kill switch
On a race car, a switch to disconnect the electrical system in an emergency.

kingpin
On a front beam axle or on some early independent front suspension systems, a nearly vertical shaft around which a steered wheel pivots. On modern independent front suspension systems, kingpins have been replaced by *ball joints*.

King Kong
Hemi-engined Dodge or Plymouth, particularly in stock car racing during the 1960s and 1970s.

kit car
Knocked down vehicle designed for assembly by the private hobbyist. The kit includes body and some chassis parts but is usually meant to be used with salvaged powertrain and suspension components. See also *KD*.

K-Jetronic
Continuous mechanical fuel injection system produced by Bosch.

km
Kilometer, see *k*.

knock
Noise within an engine caused by abnormal, out-of-sequence combustion such as

knock-off hub
(Courtesy Corvette Fever)

detonation or *preignition*. A specific fuel's resistance to knock is indicated by its *octane number*.

knock-off
Counterfeit, such as a cheap auto part illegally packaged as a popular brand.

knock-off hub
Single, large wing nut used to attach an automobile wheel to a splined stub axle. The knock-off hub was once popular on sports and racing cars because the wing nut could be knocked loose by striking one of its ears with a hammer, allowing a much faster wheel change than with a normal four- or five-bolt hub. However, it was outlawed for passenger car use because it was alleged to be a danger to pedestrians.

knock sensor
Electrical device that detects *knock* in an engine and adjusts ignition timing to eliminate it.

knuckle
See *steering knuckle*.

KOEO
Key on, engine off: testing procedure in which the ignition key is turned on but the engine is not running.

KOER
Key on, engine running: testing procedure in which the engine is running.

kPa
Kilopascal, see *k*.

kustom
Spelling of "custom" koined by George Barris, a noted Kalifornia kustomizer, and later borrowed by many of his kontemporaries and kolleagues.

kw
Kilowatt, see *k*.

L

L
Low, one of the forward gear positions on an automatic transmission. Usually the lowest gear available.

lacing
Method of mending cracks in cylinder heads or blocks, using threaded repair plugs. Adjacent plugs are installed with their threads overlapping to lock in place and seal the crack.

lacquer
Type of paint which dries by solvent evaporation only; must be rubbed out to produce the desired gloss. Increasing environmental legislation has severely restricted, and in some instances, prohibited the use of lacquer paints for automotive refinishing.

ladder bars
Chassis device on a drag car designed to minimize rear *axle windup,* attaching to the frame at one point and to the axle at two points. See also *Jacob's ladder.*

ladder frame
Chassis frame with parallel side members and perpendicular cross members, giving it the appearance of a ladder.

lady foot
Tapered pry bar with one end that resembles a small foot.

Lagonda
British luxury and sports car. Wilbur Gunn, an American engineer, emigrated to England in the late 1890s and built the first Lagonda car there in 1900. The name is actually a French spelling of a Native American Indian word for "Buck Creek," a stream near Gunn's hometown of Springfield, Ohio. In 1947, Lagonda became affiliated with Aston Martin which, in turn, was acquired during the 1980s by Ford Motor Company.

lakes
Dry lakes, such as those in the Mojave Desert in California or at Bonneville in Utah; because of their long, flat surfaces, the lakes are ideal for high-speed trials.

lakes pipes
Straight exhaust pipes, without mufflers, running along the lower edges of a hot rod's body; such pipes were developed to reduce exhaust back pressure during high-speed runs at the dry lakes, but non-functioning lakes pipes are now sometimes used for styling effect on street machines.

lakester
Hot rod with a narrow, streamlined body but fully exposed wheels, designed for lakes competition; the lakester is designed for minimum frontal area. See also *belly tank.*

LA Kit
A reconditioned crankshaft supplied with the appropriate size bearings and an installation kit. The name is derived from "lay the crank."

lambda
1. Greek equivalent of the letter "L" which, in automotive use, refers to a sensing device used in exhaust systems to measure the proportion of oxygen in the exhaust gasses and, from that proportion, to determine the air/fuel ratio of the incoming mixture. If the air/fuel ratio deviates from the ideal or *stoichiometric ratio,* a microprocessor attached to the lambda sensor will make appropriate corrections in the fuel delivery system.
2. By extension, lambda is sometimes used to mean the ideal air/fuel ratio itself. See *stoichiometric ratio.*

lambda control, lambda sensor
See *lambda,* above.

Lamborghini
Exotic Italian sports car, introduced in 1963 by Ferruccio Lamborghini, who, up to that time, had been a successful tractor manufacturer. During the 1980s, Nuova Automobili Ferruccio Lamborghini SpA was acquired by Chrysler Corporation.

laminar airflow
1. Generally, the smooth, continuous movement of one layer over another of a gas or liquid.
2. In an engine, specifically, the movement of the main body of air or air/fuel mixture through the intake manifold and ports as it flows over the *boundary layer.* Because of

surface friction along the wall, the boundary layer moves more slowly than the main body of air or mixture.

laminate
1. As a noun, a structure consisting of two or more layers of material. A common example is safety glass, such as that used for automobile windshields, which consists of a layer of tough but transparent plastic between two layers of glass.
2. As a verb, to fabricate such a structure.

laminated case
Container with walls made of two or more layers of material. A safety fuel cell is an example.

laminated core
Center of an electromagnetic device, such as an ignition coil, made of several metal plates.

Lancia
Italian car, originally developed by Vincenzo Lancia in 1906 and still in existence today as a part of Fiat.

land
Part of the exterior wall of a piston, between the ring grooves, separating and supporting the rings.

landau
In the classic era, a semi-convertible body with a folding top over the rear passenger compartment; the opposite of a *brougham* or *town car*. The most famous landau appeared in the film "Sunset Boulevard," starring Gloria Swanson and William Holden.

landau bar, landau iron
Ogee- or S-shaped trim sometimes applied to C-pillars or *sail panels*. On classic convertibles and landaus, the bar was a functioning part of the convertible top mechanism; in modern applications, the device is non-functioning and is used as an ornament on vehicles with fixed roofs rather than on convertibles.

landau top
In modern usage, passenger car roof wholly or partially covered with vinyl to give it a convertible-like appearance.

lap
1. One complete trip around an oval track or road course.
2. As a verb, to gain a lead of a full lap over another car in a race, in other words, to "lap him."

lap weld
Type of welding seam where one layer of metal is overlapped on another layer by approximately half an inch and then the two are welded together.

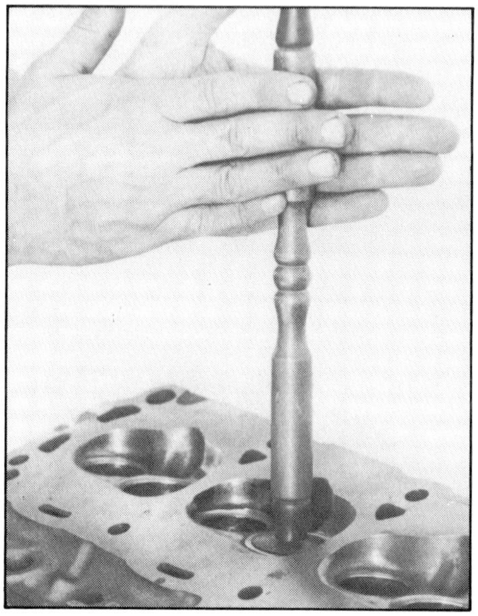

lapping, with lapping stick

lapping
Valve grinding process using a paste-like grit on the face of the valve. The valve is then rotated back and forth, grinding the seat and face area to provide a perfect seal.

lapping compound
Paste-like grit used for *lapping*, above.

lapping stick
Wooden stick with a rubber suction cup on one end which attaches to a valve head to rotate it back and forth when *lapping*, above. The stick is rubbed rapidly between the palms of the hands.

La Salle
Medium-priced car built by the Cadillac Division of General Motors from 1927 to 1940. The La Salle was meant as a less expensive alternative to the Cadillac and, as such, competed with other medium-priced GM makes, particularly Buick and Oldsmobile. The car was named after Robert Cavelier La Salle, a 17th century French explorer of the Mississippi Valley.

lash
Clearance between two parts, such as between a valve and a rocker or lifter.

lash pad adjusters
Small, round pieces of metal of varying thickness, used for accurate adjustment of valve clearance. See *valve adjusting shims*.

late apex
Late entry into a corner, i.e., getting to the inside of a turn later than usual. The car will usually be moving toward the outside of the track or roadway as it comes out of the corner.

lateral acceleration
As a car goes around a corner, the lateral acceleration is the centrifugal force, expressed in *g*'s, tending to push the vehicle sideways toward the outside of the turn.

lateral link
Suspension component positioned to resist side-to-side movement of the wheel.

lateral runout
Side-to-side movement of a wheel as it rotates.

lateral weight transfer
Momentary shift of a vehicle's center of gravity from the inside tires to the outside tires as the result of cornering forces. Equalizing the lateral weight transfer is a key element in chassis tuning.

launch
In drag racing, a good start off the starting line.

lay a patch, lay a scratch
Same as *lay rubber*.

lay on it
To go fast. See also *lean on it*.

lay on the iron
In track racing, to cut inside another car on a turn, crowding it away from the apron or apex and out of its groove. See also *lean on it*. See photo next page.

layout
Lines scribed on a piece of metal or other material to simplify the bending or machining of the material. See photo next page.

lay on the iron

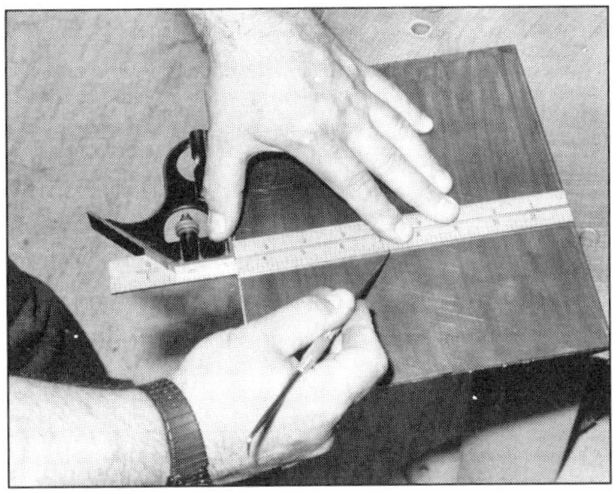

layout

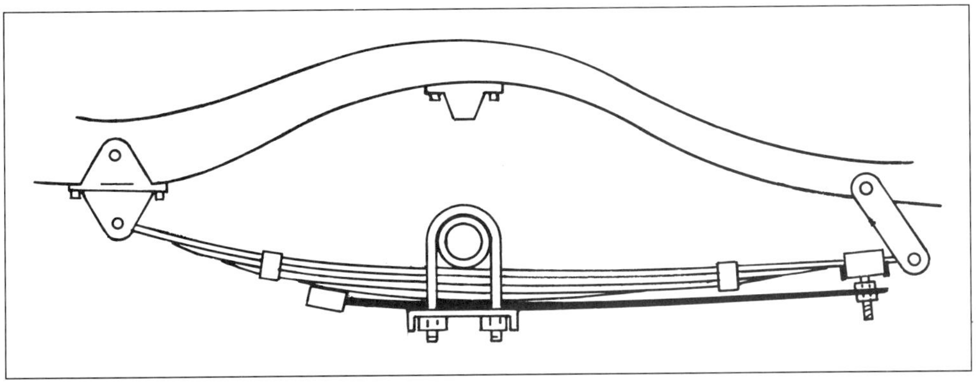

leaf spring

lay rubber
To leave streaks of rubber on the pavement during hard acceleration.

LCD
1. Liquid crystal display, a type of readout on some digital instruments, using liquid crystal film sealed between glass plates that becomes opaque when an electrical current is applied to it. See also *LED*.
2. In mathematics, lowest common denominator.

lead
1. Soft, heavy, malleable metallic element used as a solder and as a filler to cover seams or holes in bodywork.
2. As a verb, to apply such filler.
3. Short for *tetraethyl lead*, a compound formerly used to improve gasoline octane numbers, as well as to provide upper cylinder lubrication but which, for general automotive use, has been virtually legislated out of existence because of its toxicity.

leadfoot
Driver who goes faster than is really necessary, whether on the race course or the street, in such a manner as to cause harm to the equipment or other competitors.

leading link
Suspension component attached to the chassis behind the wheel and positioned to resist fore-and-aft movement of the wheel.

lead sled
Same as *kustom* or *kemp,* though lead sled is sometimes used deprecatingly to describe a car with an excessive amount of lead or Bondo covering mediocre sheet metal work.

leaf spring
Type of vehicle suspension consisting of one or more long, narrow strips of metal, usually steel, or plastic, such as fiberglass, mounted between the frame and axle. Leaf springs may be either longitudinally or laterally positioned relative to the frame. Generally, they are *semi-elliptic* in form, though there have been historic examples of longitudinal leaf springs that were *quarter-elliptic* or even fully elliptic in form. Both longitudinal and lateral leaf-spring assemblies have usually had multiple steel leaves and have been used with solid axles. An important exception is the late-model Chevrolet Corvette which, since the mid 1980s, has had transverse-mounted, single-leaf springs made of fiberglass, used with fully independent suspension front and rear.

leakdown test
Test using air injected at a pressure of 100 pounds per square inch into the spark plug hole or injector port of a cylinder to determine the amount of leakage past the rings, valves or gaskets.

leaker
Engine or car not well prepared; it may literally leak coolant or lubricant.

lean mixture
Air/fuel mixture with a higher than normal proportion of air.

lean on it
Same as either *lay on it* or *lay on the iron* which, however, are not the same as each other.

lean out
1. To increase the proportion of air in the air/fuel mixture.
2. To decrease the percentage of nitro in a fuel mixture.

leaver
Drag race driver who starts too soon and red lights, thereby forfeiting the race.

LED
Light emitting diode, a type of readout on some digital instruments, using a semiconductor diode that emits light when an electrical current is applied to it. See also *LCD,* def. 1.

left-hand thread
Thread pattern on a bolt or screw that requires that it be tightened by being twisted counterclockwise, or to the left at the top.

leg it
To go fast.

leg out of bed
On a damaged engine, a rod that has broken through the cylinder block wall.

Le Mans
Road racing circuit in France, scene of the Grand Prix d'Endurance, an annual 24-hour race that is one of the world's most famous sports car events.

Le Mans start
Method of starting a road race with the drivers standing across the track from their cars. When the starting flag is dropped, the drivers run to their vehicles, jump in, start their engines and take off. The system originated at Le Mans, hence the name, but is no longer used there for safety reasons.

lemon
Vehicle, especially a relatively new one, with an inordinate number of defects.

Lemon Laws
Federal and state laws to assure that the buyer of a defective vehicle will receive proper repairs by the dealer or replacement by the manufacturer.

length-to-diameter ratio
On a coil spring, the ratio of the wire diameter to the overall spring length, a measure of the spring's overall effectiveness.

letter drill bits
Series of drill bits that are cataloged alphabetically, "A" being the smallest with a diameter of 0.234 inch and "Z" the largest with a diameter of 0.413 inch.

letter stamps
Individual metal stamps used to imprint letters of the alphabet onto metal parts.

level
1. Tool used to level or adjust parts to a horizontal plane.
2. Amount of a liquid in a system, such as ATF, coolant, fuel or oil.

lever
Arm used to transmit force and motion.

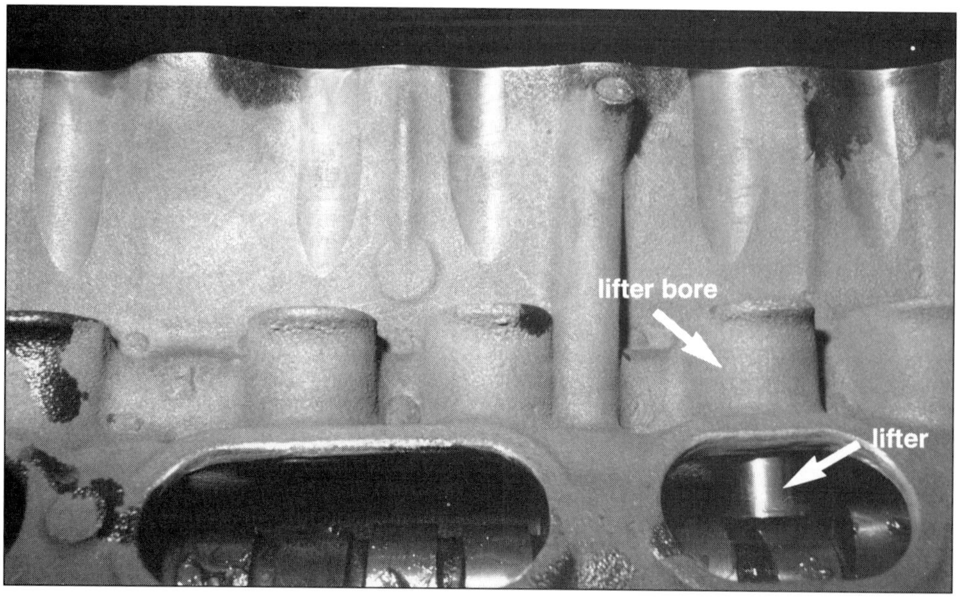

lifter bore (Chrysler)

Lexan
Plastic material that is transparent yet heat resistant and shatterproof; tradename owned by General Electric. Lexan is commonly used as the material on race car rear windshields.

L-head
Engine with intake and exhaust valves in the block, parallel to the cylinders and pistons, rather than above them in the head. In cross-section, the cylinder and combustion chamber look like an inverted letter "L," hence L-head. See also *flathead.*

LH-Jetronic
Bosch pulsed electronic fuel injection system that uses a mass airflow sensor with a digital control unit.

LHV
Lower heating value. See *heating value.*

lid
Cylinder head on a flathead or L-head engine.

lift
1. Amount of the opening of a valve (valve lift) or the amount of rise generated by the lobe of the camshaft (cam lift). See *lobe.*
2. Aerodynamically, an upward force caused by airflow around a moving vehicle that tends to lift the vehicle slightly. Spoilers are designed to counter such lift and push the vehicle toward the ground. See *spoiler.*

liftback
Vehicle body with a one-piece, rear *liftgate,* hinged at the top and incorporating the rear window. Basically the same as a *hatchback.*

lifter
Part between the camshaft and pushrod on an *OHV* engine, or between the camshaft and valve stem on an *OHC* engine.

lifter bore
In the cylinder head or block of an engine, the hole in which a valve lifter is located.

liftgate
Rear opening on a hatchback or liftback. See *liftback,* above.

lift it
To get off the throttle.

lift kit
Suspension package consisting of new springs, longer multiple shocks and lift blocks, along with various other steering and chassis components to raise the vehicle body above the frame or tires. If the vehicle has a separate frame and body, the kit is called a *body lift kit*; with unibody vehicles, it is called a *suspension lift kit*.

lift-throttle oversteer
In a rear-wheel drive vehicle, a loss of grip at the drive wheels when the throttle is lifted during fast cornering, causing the rear of the vehicle to swing toward the outside of the turn, or *oversteer*. A technique, when applied correctly, that can adjust for *understeer*. Same as *drop-throttle oversteer*. See also *oversteer* and *understeer*.

light it off
To start an engine.

light-duty vehicle
According to Title 40 of the Code of Federal Regulations, "Any motor vehicle rated at 8500 pounds GVWR or less which has a vehicle curb weight of 6000 pounds or less and which has a basic vehicle frontal area of 45 square feet or less."

light the rugs, light the weenies
To smoke the drive tires at the start of a drag race.

light up
To perform a burn-out.

lights
Timing lights at the end of the drag strip.

lime deposits
Condition in a vehicle's cooling system when the lime present in water-based coolants comes out of solution and coats the engine's water passages. Lime deposits can be removed from cast-iron parts with phosphoric acids or by baking the part at approximately 700 degrees F.

limited slip differential
Final drive system in which the difference in rotating speeds between the two axle shafts, and with them, the two drive wheels, is mechanically limited to prevent wheelspin on slippery surfaces. The limited-slip differential is sometimes referred to as a posi or Posi-Traction. Strictly speaking, though, Posi-Traction is a Chevrolet

lift kit

light up

tradename and not a generic term. See also *Posi-Traction*.

limo, limousine
1. Formal sedan, generally chauffeur-driven, with a transverse glass partition separating the chauffeur from the passengers. The limo is frequently though not necessarily a *stretchout*.
2. Bus or van used to carry passengers to and from airports or railroad stations.

Lincoln
The Lincoln Motor Company was established in 1920 by Henry Martyn Leland, who had been in charge of Cadillac for 14 years, both before and after it became part of General Motors. Leland named his new car after the 16th president of the U.S., Abraham Lincoln. Unfortunately, Leland soon ran into financial difficulties and, in 1922, Henry Ford bought the company and Leland resigned a few months later. Today, the Lincoln is produced by the Lincoln-Mercury Division of Ford Motor Company and is Ford's premium luxury vehicle line.

line
1. In drag racing, the starting line or staging position.
2. In oval track or road racing, a specific path through a turn; in other words, a *groove*.

line job
Beating a drag competitor right at the start of a race; same as *hole shot*.

line mechanic
Mechanic who works on the repair line at a dealership. The line mechanic is usually a specialist in a particular automotive system, such as the engine, transmission or brakes.

liner
1. Sleeve, usually made of steel, used to repair a worn cylinder.
2. Bronze insert used to repair a worn valve guide.
3. Short for *streamliner*, as at Bonneville.

line ream
In engine work, to ream bearings or bushings to proper size after they have been installed.

line setting card, line setting tag
Card or tag provided by a car or truck manufacturer that lists a particular vehicle's specifications and equipment.

linkage
Series of levers and rods to transmit movement from one part to another.

linkage power steering
Steering system with a power assist attached directly to the steering rods.

liquid-filled gauge
Instrument filled with clear liquid to dampen vibrations that could affect the instrument's reading.

liquified petroleum gas
See *LPG*.

liter
SI unit of capacity, corresponding to 1,000 cubic centimeters or milliliters, 61.023744 cubic inches, or 0.2641721 gallons.

litmus
Purple coloring matter obtained from various lichens which turns blue in alkaline solutions and red in acid solutions. In practical use, absorbent paper impregnated with litmus is dipped in the solutions to determine their alkalinity or acidity.

little end
Smaller end of a connecting rod, i.e., the piston pin.

live axle
Axle through which power is applied via a differential and halfshafts, as opposed to a non-powered *dead axle*.

L-Jetronic
Bosch pulsed electronic fuel injection system with a vane-type airflow sensor and analog control unit.

LNG
Liquified natural gas, primarily *methane*, CH_4, which has been converted to a liquid by chilling it to 260 degrees below zero F. LNG is proposed as a substitute for gasoline because it is cleaner burning and its octane number, 130, is the highest of any readily available fuel. However, LNG mileage is less than 50 percent that of gasoline and it has to be stored under pressure in a special tank. See also *CNG* for *compressed natural gas*.

load
1. In any car or truck, the demand for power placed on an engine. At low speeds on a level roadway, the load is relatively light. At high speeds or over hilly terrain, the load is much greater.
2. In a commercial vehicle, the cargo.
3. As a slang term, particularly in drag racing, load can mean fuel, especially nitro.
4. In chassis tuning, load is the amount of weight placed on a tire. See *vertical load*.

load range
The weight a tire will support at a specific inflation pressure.

load meter
Instrument on a honing machine to show the amount of material that can be removed from the part being honed, and also show any taper at the top and bottom of the part.

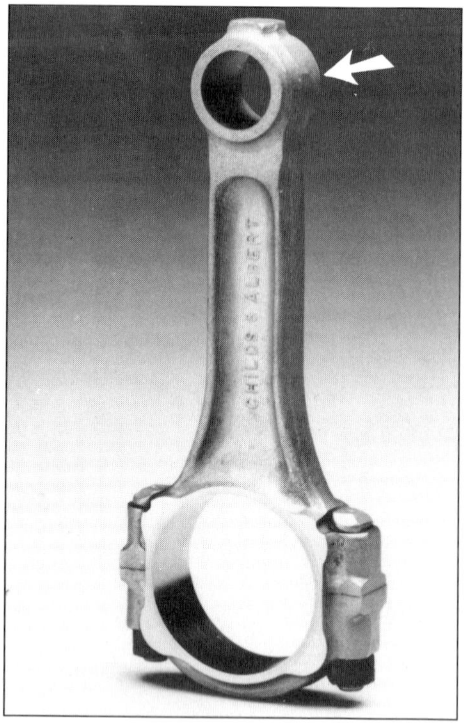

little end

lobe
Part of a camshaft that actuates a valve lifter. The lobe is egg-shaped, and the various areas are labeled the *flank*, *ramps*, *nose* and the *base circle* or *heel*. See illustration next page.

lobe centers
On a camshaft, the number of degrees between the centers of the intake and exhaust lobes.

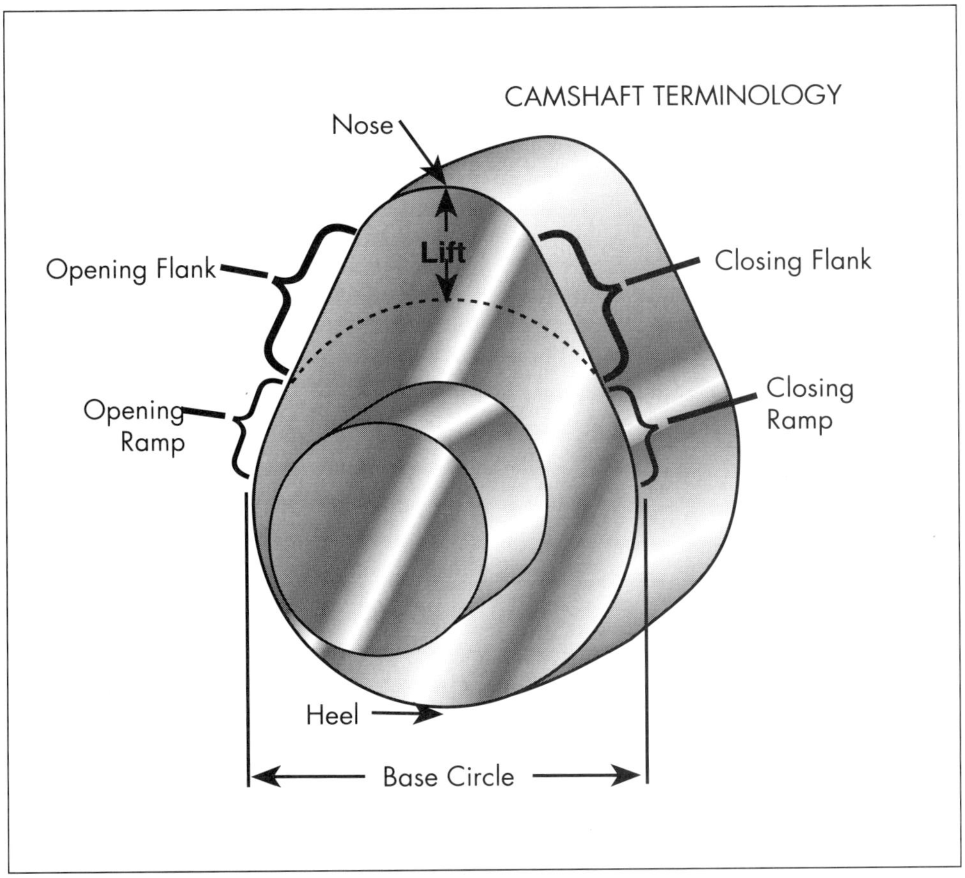

camshaft lobe

locked rear end
Rear driving axle without any differential action; the wheels on either side rotate at the same speed around turns as well as on the straightaway. Not the same as a *locker* or *locking rear end*, which locks on the straightaway but which allows one wheel to rotate freely around turns.

locker
See *locking rear end.*

locking hubs
On a four-wheel-drive vehicle, *dog clutches* in the front hubs that allow the front wheels to be disengaged from the front axle shafts when the forward part of the four-wheel-drive system is not in use. Occasionally, locking hubs are also installed at the rear, to allow the rear wheels to be disengaged from the rear axle shafts when the four-by-four is *flat towed* behind another vehicle. In either case, the purpose is to prevent the wheels from turning the final drive gears and causing unnecessary wear.

locking rear end
Final drive with a differential which, on the straightaway, acts as a locked rear end but, around turns, applies power through one wheel only and allows the other to rotate freely. Also referred to as a *locker.*

locking torque converter
In an automatic transmission, a hydraulic torque converter with a mechanical clutch that locks at cruising speeds, providing a positive connection that eliminates converter slippage to improve efficiency and fuel economy.

lock nut
1. Nut designed to lock into place when it is screwed down tightly.
2. One nut screwed down tightly on another to lock the latter into place.

lock-to-lock
Number of turns of the steering wheel from its full left to full right positions, or vice versa.

Loctite
Tradename for an extensive line of adhesives and sealants used in vehicle and engine assembly. Loctite *Threadlocker* compounds are basically *anaerobic* liquids that fill spaces between mated metal parts, such as threads on nuts and bolts; in the absence of oxygen, the compounds harden from liquid to solid, locking the parts into place. *Threadlocker* compounds are color-coded blue for medium-strength, green for medium- to high-strength, and red for high-strength. The higher the strength, the more difficult the eventual disassembly of the parts will be.

long arm
Throw on a crankshaft which has been *stroked.*

longbed
Cargo box on a long-wheelbase pickup truck; a longbed is usually seven or eight feet in length, compared with only six feet for a *shortbed.*

long block
Engine assembly consisting of the block, crankshaft, camshaft, bearings, pistons, rings, connecting rods, oil pump, oil pan, timing covers, seals, cylinder heads and intake manifolding, all installed. See also *short block.*

long gear
Final drive with high gearing, i.e., a numerically low gear ratio; same as *tall gear* and opposite of *short gear.*

loop
In track racing, a spin. A loop is usually caused by a deliberate maneuver to avoid a collision with another car, rather than an unintended loss of control.

loose
1. Tendency of a vehicle to oversteer excessively. See photo next page.
2. Slippery track or road surface.

loper
Big, high performance engine that idles roughly and noisily, due to an aggressive camshaft profile. Same as *rumper.*

loose

louvers

lo po
Low performance; opposite of *hi po*.

lose fire
To stall an engine.

lost foam casting
Casting method using a model part made from styrofoam. The foam part is pressed into a sand mold. Molten aluminum or iron is then poured into the mold. The hot metal evaporates the foam part and takes the shape left by it in the sand.

Lotus
British racing and sports car manufacturer, founded in 1952 by Colin Chapman. The company began with a two-passenger kit car and eventually produced a broad spectrum of high-performance vehicles, from two- and four-passenger sports coupes to single-seat racing vehicles that won the Formula One World Championship and the Indy 500. During the 1950s, Chapman introduced his *Chapman strut* rear suspension on the Lotus Elite coupe. Lotus has also done development work for other manufacturers, such as on the chassis and suspension for *DeLorean*. In the 1980s, Lotus Cars Ltd. was acquired by General Motors.

loud pedal
Accelerator.

louvers
1. Slotted openings in auto body panels to admit or emit air for cooling or ventilation.
2. Series of movable, flat metal plates used to reduce or block airflow through a radiator.

lover cover
Scattershield between the driver's legs on a front-engined, single-seat drag car.

love taps
In circle track racing, a facetious reference to the bumping and shoving that often occurs among cars running in a closely packed group or *train*.

low end
Low engine speed.

low-end power
Horsepower at low engine speed, usually the output during first 25-to-30 percent of the rpm range.

lower
To reduce the ride height of a car by modifying the suspension, such as by cutting a coils from the coil springs.

lower A-arm, lower control arm
Lower member of a double-A-arm suspension assembly.

lower end
Crankshaft, main bearing and connecting rod bearing assembly in an engine; same as *bottom end.*

lower entry
Bottom of a wet cylinder sleeve in an engine block.

lower entry sleeve
Cylinder sleeve to repair a worn *lower entry*, see above.

lowering blocks
On a vehicle with a solid axle above semi-elliptic leaf springs, lowering blocks may be placed between the axle and springs to drop the ride height of the chassis and, with it, the body, relative to the axle.

lower mount
In a vehicle, a support for the engine or transmission that is below the crankshaft centerline.

low gear
First gear, the lowest speed in a transmission.

low gearing
Drive ratio which applies maximum output at a relatively low road speed. Low gearing is important in drag racing or any other form of competition where the emphasis is on acceleration rather than sheer speed. The term can be confusing because a low gear has a numerically high ratio. For example, 4.5-to-1 would be a low gear and 2.5-to-1 a high gear, even though 4.5-to-1 is obviously a higher ratio than 2.5-to-1. Thus, the term "low gear ratio" should be avoided because it's impossible to tell which is supposed to be low, the gear or the ratio. See also *high gearing*.

low pedal
1. Position of the brake pedal when it is adjusted near the bottom of its downward travel, near the floor when it is fully depressed.
2. On a Ford Model T, the position of the clutch pedal when engaging low gear in the transmission.

low rider
Vehicle which has been lowered not only with suspension modifications but with wheels much smaller than standard. The theme is carried through to the interior, where even the steering wheel is smaller than usual. Another common feature of the low rider is a hydraulic jacking system on the front suspension which allows the front end to be raised and lowered rapidly.

Low Risers
Standard height cylinder heads originally developed in the early 1960s for the Ford 406-cubic-inch V-8 and later used on both the 427- and 428-cubic-inch engines as well. Low Risers had intake ports 1.93 inches high and differed from standard 427 heads mainly in having slightly larger valves, though not as large as those in *High Risers* and *Medium Risers.*

LPG
Liquified petroleum gas, predominantly *propane*, C_3H_8, but also usually containing some *butane*, C_4H_{10}, both of which are gaseous in a natural state but become liquified when compressed. LPG is used for gas appliances in RVs. It is also proposed as a substitute for gasoline because it is cleaner burning and its octane numbers, 125 for propane and 91 for butane, are relatively high. However, LPG mileage is only about 75 percent that of gasoline, it costs more and it has to be stored under pressure in a special tank.

LPO
Limited production option, item of new car equipment available only on a restricted basis. A high-performance package for police use is an example of an LPO.

LSR
Land speed record, the maximum velocity attainable by a land-based vehicle. There are two basic types of LSR cars, those that are wheel-driven by internal combustion engines and those that are thrust-driven by jet or rocket engines.

lubricant
Substance, usually petroleum based, used to coat moving parts to reduce friction between them.

lubrication system
Oil pump, tubing, filters and oil passages in an engine that circulate lubricant to moving parts.

lug bolts, lug nuts
Fasteners used to hold the wheels on a vehicle.

lugging
Running an engine at lower than normal rpm, causing it to *balk.*

lug wrench
Wrench designed for removing or replacing lug bolts or lug nuts on vehicle wheels. The lug wrench that comes as standard equipment on a production car or truck usually also serves as a pry bar for removing the hub cap, as well as a handle for pumping the jack up or down.

L

LU-Jetronic
Bosch pulsed electronic fuel injection system similar to the L-Jetronic unit but has a lambda sensor. The "U" designates this unit as a U.S.-only version.

lumbar support
Support in a seat for the lumbar region of the occupant's body, i.e., the area between the lowest ribs and the pelvis.

luminosity probe
Tune-up instrument which displays rpm and degrees of ignition timing on either gasoline or diesel engines.

lump
Engine, especially a big heavy one.

lunch
To severely damage or destroy; for example, a race driver who pushes his engine too hard may *lunch* it.

M

machine
General term for any car, though among hot rodders, it usually means a later model. See also *street machine.*

machinist dye
Dye used to coat metal so that it can be marked with a scribe for *layout. Dykem Blue* is an example of a machinist dye.

MacPherson strut
Type of front suspension with a coil spring mounted directly above a shock absorber, developed in the 1950s by Earle S. MacPherson for Ford of England. The MacPherson unit is attached to the vehicle structure at the top of the coil spring. The wheel hub is attached at the bottom of the strut and is located by a *lateral link* and *anti-roll bar* or by a lower *A-arm.* The virtues of the MacPherson strut are that it is simple, space-saving, and inexpensive. A similar type of rear suspension for rear-wheel-drive cars was later developed by Colin Chapman of *Lotus* and is known as the *Chapman strut.*

mag
1. Magneto, an electrical device which combines the functions of a generator and distributor, and provides greater ignition efficiency at higher engine speeds. See also *magneto.*
2. Light alloy wheel. True mag wheels are made of magnesium but, because that material is costly and difficult to maintain, it's rarely used for street wheels. The so-called mag wheels on most cars are actually made of aluminum.

Magnaflux
Dry, magnetic, non-destructive test, or *NDT,* to check for cracks in iron or steel parts. The part is subjected to a strong magnetic field while magnetic particles are sprinkled on the surface. Any crack acts as a new magnetic pole and causes the particles to collect at that point.

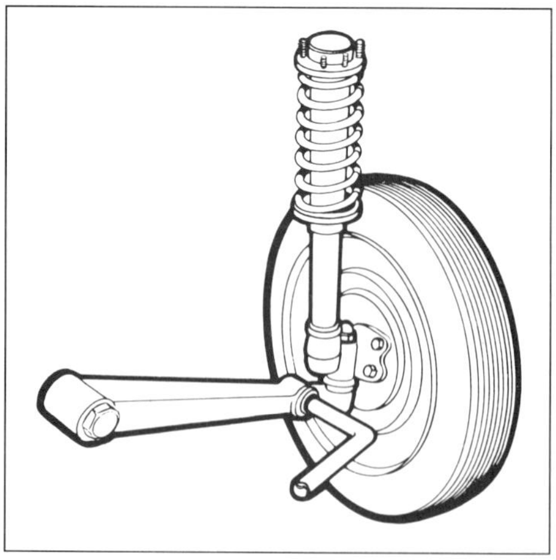

MacPherson strut

Magnaglow
Wet, magnetic and ultraviolet light, non-destructive test, or *NDT,* to check for cracks in iron or steel parts. The part is coated with a liquid containing magnetic particles and then subjected to a strong magnetic field that causes the particles to gather along any cracks. The ultraviolet light is then used to locate the particles.

magnesium
Silver-white metallic element that is highly ductile and malleable, and is the lightest in weight of all structural metals. Should not be confused with *manganese.*

magnetic particle test
Non-destructive test using a magnet and magnetic particles to check an iron or steel part for cracks. See *Magnaflux* and *Magnaglow.*

magnetic pick-up
Part of an electronic ignition system that uses a magnetic field to trigger an amplifier that generates voltage to fire the spark plugs.

magneto
In an ignition system, an electrical device which both generates and distributes current to fire the spark plugs. A magneto does not need an external source of current, such as a battery, and the intensity of its voltage increases with engine speed, whereas the intensity of a battery ignition's voltage decreases. Thus the magneto is the better for racing engines. For road vehicles, though, a battery is needed for the lights and other electrical accessories, so a battery ignition is preferable. See photo next page.

magnetos

main bearings

M

main
1. Main bearing, see below.
2. Feature event, especially at an oval track race.

main bearings
Bearings which support and locate the crankshaft in the engine block.

main cap
In an engine block, structural device which holds the main bearings and crankshaft in place.

main hoop
In a race car, a *rollbar* placed immediately behind the driver's seat.

main journals
In an engine, the journals that fit into the block to support the crankshaft.

mains
See *main bearings* and *main cap.*

major diameter
On a bolt, largest in diameter of the threads.

major overhaul
Engine repair procedure that includes replacement of the pistons, rings, rod and main bearings, timing chain and gears, and gaskets, plus a valve job. Not to be confused with a *rebuild.* See also *minor overhaul.*

major tune-up
Engine maintenance procedure that includes the replacement or adjustment of the plugs, points, condenser, cap and rotor, plus adjustment of the valves and overhaul of the carburetor. Obviously, these procedures only apply to engines with point-type distributors and carburetors. The use of electronic ignitions, hydraulic camshafts and fuel injection has virtually eliminated the need for a major tune-up. See also *minor tune-up.*

make the show
To qualify for a race.

malleability
Ability of a metal to be formed through hammering, bending or similar metal-fabricating processes.

mallet
Hammer with a rubber or rawhide head.

mandrel
Tool used to position parts for machining, such as to align valve grinding wheels to valve seats on cylinder heads.

mandrel tube bender
Hydraulic or mechanical machine with dies and mandrels to bend tubing so that the walls do not collapse. Not to be confused with a *crush bender.*

manganese
Grayish white or grayish red metallic element, hard and brittle, rusts like iron but is not magnetic. Manganese is used in alloys of iron, steel, aluminum and copper and should not be confused with *magnesium.*

manganese bronze
Alloy of copper and zinc containing up to 3.0 percent manganese, used for toothed wheels and gears.

manganese steel
Hard, malleable, ductile steel alloy containing 12 to 14 percent manganese, used for drill bits.

manifold
Conduit-like device used to duct gasses into or out of an engine. See *exhaust manifold* and *intake manifold.*

manifold gauge set
Set of instruments to measure vacuum or pressure in an engine's intake or exhaust system.

manifold heat control
Flapper valve in the exhaust manifold which diverts heat to the intake manifold.

manifold pressure
Positive pressure in the intake manifold measured in pounds per square inch or bars.

manifold vacuum
Negative pressure in the intake manifold measured in inches of mercury.

manometer
U-shaped tube used to measure the pressure of a gas or liquid, acting on a column of water or mercury. The gas or liquid is fed into one arm of the U. If its pressure is greater than the pressure of the atmosphere, it will raise the column of water or mercury in the other arm of the U.

MAP
Manifold absolute pressure, the pressure in an intake manifold relative to the atmospheric pressure of 14.7 pounds per square inch (psi).

MAP sensor
Manifold absolute pressure sensor, instrument to measure the *MAP*, above.

marbles
Bits of dirt or rubber debris on the outer edge of a race track, outside the racing *line*. A car forced "onto the marbles" will generally lose traction and become unstable.

Marcel
Spring assembly in the clutch drive plate, which absorbs the high input of energy when the clutch cover is released against the flywheel.

margin
On an exhaust or intake valve, the material between the face and head of the valve. The minimum thickness should be no less than 2/3 of the thickness when the valve was new, or approximately 1/16 inch.

Mark
One of a series of cars, usually identified by a Roman numeral, such as the Lincoln Continental Mark VII or Mark VIII. Not the same as *marque.*

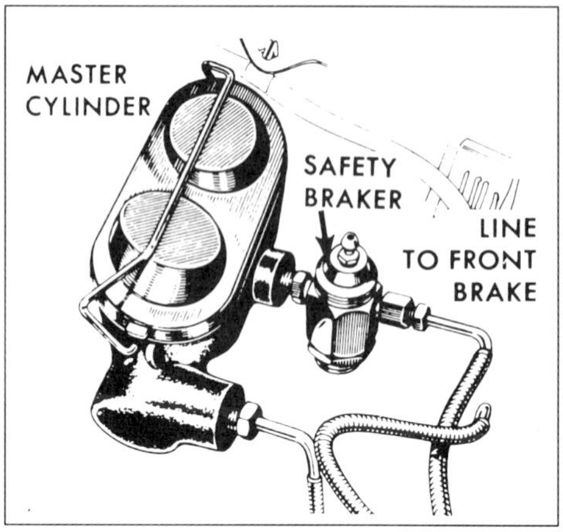

master cylinder

marque
French for "make," as in make of car. Not the same as *Mark.*

marriage
On an automaker's assembly line, the installation of the powertrain in a vehicle's chassis.

Maserati
Italian racing and sports cars, built by Officine Alfieri Maserati SpA, which was founded by Alfieri Maserati and three of his brothers in 1926. Generally, the Maseratis built race cars, including one that Wilbur Shaw drove to victories in the Indy 500 in 1939 and 1940. The few road cars they did build were meant for drivers of professional skill, not for lay people. By 1947, the brothers had sold their interest in the company and left to form OSCA, for Officina Specializzata Costruzione Automobili, where they built small sports cars until 1967. Meanwhile, the original Maserati company began turning its attention to sports and touring cars, a focus it retains to this day. Since 1975, Maserati has been owned by Alejandro de Tomaso, who has also produced cars under his own name, including the famous De Tomaso Pantera.

masking
1. Prior to painting a vehicle, covering its trim and windows with paper and tape.
2. Modifying intake ports with air dams to direct airflow in a desired direction.

mass
Measure of the amount of matter contained in a given quantity of a gas, liquid or solid.

mass airflow sensor (MAS)
In an engine, a device that measures airflow into the intake manifold. This information is fed into the engine's computer, which uses this data, along with other information supplied by various sensors, to calibrate the optimum air/fuel ratio to suit the current driving conditions.

master cylinder
Hydraulic reservoir for the brake system which, when the brake pedal is pressed, supplies hydraulic pressure to send fluid to the wheel cylinders which, in turn, force the brake linings or pads against the drums or discs to slow or stop the vehicle.

master kit
Engine parts kit that contains a crankshaft, bearings, camshaft, bearings, lifters, oil pump, timing chain, pistons, rings, gasket sets and core plugs. Abbreviated *MK.* See photo next page.

match bash, match race
Two-out-of-three, or three-out-of-five series of races between two drag competitors.

mat fabric
Fiberglass with an irregular strand structure.

Material Safety Data Sheets
See *MSDS.*

Mayflower
Plymouth, so called after the small replica of the Mayflower sailing vessel sometimes used as a Plymouth trademark.

Mazda
Japanese automaker. The Mazda name was first used on a three-wheeled motorcycle in 1931 by Toyo Kogyo Kaisha, or Orient Industry Company. "It was named Mazda," a company publication explains, "after Ahura Mazda, the wise lord, supreme deity and creator of the world;

master kit

The god of light in Zoroastrianism." The company did not get into serious production of passenger cars until 1960. Since then, it has become renowned as the only automaker in the world to make on ongoing success of the *Wankel rotary engine*. In 1984, Toyo Kogyo Kaisha became Mazda Jidosha Kaisha, or Mazda Motor Company. Mazda has close ties with Ford Motor Company in this country, and the two market *badge-engineered* versions of some of each others products.

MCU
Microprocessor control unit, the *black box* which operates a vehicle's various electrical systems. Also called ECM or electronic control module.

mean
Top performer; driver or car tough to beat in a race, as in "he is a mean driver."

mean motor scooter
Top performing car, especially in drag racing.

meat
Structural metal, especially in an engine block.

meats
Big tires, such as drag racing slicks.

mechanical efficiency
In the mechanical transfer of horsepower and torque, the percentage of the input contained in the output. In an engine, for example, the mechanical efficiency is the percentage of the *indicated* horsepower and torque, the amount produced in the combustion chambers, contained in the *brake* horsepower and torque, the amount delivered at the flywheel. The latter is always less than the former because of losses in friction and heat, and in the power needed to operate the valve gear, the oil pump and other engine accessories. In the drivetrain, the mechanical efficiency is the percentage of the horsepower and torque at the flywheel contained in the horsepower and torque delivered at the drive wheels. Again, the latter is always less, this time because of losses in friction and heat in the transmission and final drive.

mechanical valve lifter
Valve lifter that provides direct cam-to-pushrod contact or, on *OHC* engines, direct cam-to-valve contact. The mechanical lifter provides more positive operation than its hydraulic counterpart but requires periodic adjustment, which the hydraulic lifter does not.

mechanical seal
Seal formed by direct metal-to-metal contact.

Medium Risers
Standard height cylinder heads offered for the Ford 427-cubic-inch V-8 during the 1960s, with the same larger, light-weight valves as High Risers but with intake ports 2.34 inches high, 0.38 inch less than High Risers and 0.41 inch more than Low Risers. Medium Risers could be used with any standard 427 intake manifold and did not need the special manifold used with High Risers. See also *High Risers* and *Low Risers*.

M85
Fuel blend of 85 percent *methanol* and 15 percent gasoline. See also *E85*.

MEK
Methyl ethyl ketone, $CH_3COCH_2CH_3$, highly flammable liquid used as a cleaning solvent.

melt
To damage or destroy by overheating.

melt down
Among racers, a description of what happens to pistons that have seized in an engine because of such problems as too lean a mixture or preignition.

melting point
Temperature at which a solid substance becomes a liquid as it is heated. The melting point is the same as the *freezing point*, i.e., temperature at which a liquid substance becomes a solid as it is chilled.

MEMA
Motor and Equipment Manufacturers Association, P.O. Box 13966, Research Triangle Park, NC 27709-3966; (919) 549-4800.

meniscus
Top of a column of liquid in a tube, such as water or mercury in a manometer. The meniscus is concave when the walls of the tube are moistened and convex when the walls are dry. Either way, the height of the meniscus is measured at the center of the column.

M

MEP
Mean effective pressure; in an engine, the average pressure developed within a cylinder during a full four-stroke cycle. See *brake mean effective pressure* and *indicated mean effective pressure*.

Merc
1. With a hard "c," Mercury.
2. With a soft "c," Mercedes-Benz.

Mercedes, Mercedes-Benz
In 1901, Emil Jellinek, who was an Austro-Hungarian diplomat residing in France, acquired distribution rights to a new car developed by the Daimler Motor Company of Bad Cannstatt, Germany. To avoid possible legal problems with other automakers who had licenses to use Daimler engines, Jellinek decided against using the Daimler name and, instead, called the car after his daughter Mercedes. In 1902, Daimler adopted the name for all of its passenger cars. In 1926, the Daimler Motor Company merged with Benz and Company of Mannheim, Germany to form the Daimler-Benz Company, whose products were renamed Mercedes-Benz. See also *Benz* and *Daimler*.

Mercer
American sports car, produced in Mercer County, New Jersey from 1910 to 1925. The *Mercer Raceabout*, a roadster introduced in 1911, was a rival of the *Stutz Bearcat*.

mercury
1. Heavy, silver-white metallic element which has a melting point of approximately 38 degrees below zero F. and, as a result, is a liquid at normal temperatures. Mercury is used in such measuring instruments as barometers, manometers and thermometers. It also combines with most other metals to form alloys called amalgams.
2. With a capital "M," a medium-priced car introduced by Ford Motor Company in 1939 to compete with such makes as GM's Buick and Oldsmobile. The Mercury was named not for the mineral but for the Roman messenger of the gods, whose name implied swiftness. Today, the Mercury is a product of the Lincoln-Mercury Division of Ford. See also *Merkur*.

mercury column
Manometer containing mercury. See *manometer*.

Merkur
German for *Mercury*, used as a product name for some of the higher performance cars produced by Ford of Germany.

metal conditioner
Chemical compound used to remove light surface rust from metal prior to bodywork and painting.

metal pickling
Condition when metal is exposed to acids or to electroplating, causing the metal to become hard and brittle.

metallic brake linings
Brake linings made of metal particles that have been fused or *sintered* together into solid material. Metallic linings can withstand higher temperatures than *organic brake linings*.

metallic paint
Paint containing very fine glittering metallic particles, making the paint sparkle and look somewhat grainy. Metallics were introduced in the sixties and are very popular today. Metallics are a little more difficult for an inexperienced painter to apply properly because the particles can lay down at different angles and thereby reflect light differently. Also, if the paint is applied too thick and too wet, the metallic particles can settle out or fall, causing non-uniform patterns, often described as a *blotchy* appearance.

meter
1. SI unit of linear measure, equal to 3.28084 US feet or 39.37008 US inches.
2. Short for *dynamometer*.
3. As a verb, to regulate or measure the flow of a gas or liquid.

metering rods
Tapered rods that control fuel flow in a carburetor.

metering slit
Small, narrow opening used to meter fuel output in a fuel injector.

metering valve
1. In a carburetor, a valve used to deliver a specified amount of air or fuel.
2. In a vehicle brake system with discs at the front and drums at the rear, a valve in the brake system used to delay pressure to the front brakes to keep them from locking.

methane
CH_4, colorless, odorless, flammable gas and the simplest of the hydrocarbons; the primary component of *natural gas*, formed naturally by the decomposition of vegetable or other organic matter. See also *CNG* and *LNG*.

methanol, methyl alcohol
MH_3OH, a form of alcohol used as a racing fuel in Indycars and in some drag racing classes. Methanol is poisonous and burns without a visible flame. For use as a road fuel, it is mixed in a blend of 85 percent methanol and 15 percent gasoline, called *M85*, with the gasoline providing a visible flame as well as easier cold starting.

metric system
See *SI*.

Mexineering
Improvised back-country repairs, using only tools and parts right at hand. The term originated among travellers in the rugged back country of the Baja California peninsula as a tribute to the ability of rural Mexican drivers to keep their vehicles running under even the most adverse circumstances.

MG
British sports car, built from 1924 to 1980. The initials stood for Morris Garages, the dealer for Morris automobiles in Oxford, and the first MGs were simply Morrises that the Oxford facility modified for higher performance and fitted with sportier bodywork. MG was absorbed by Morris which, in turn, merged with Austin in 1952 to form the British Motor Corporation. In 1970, BMC became part of British Leyland, which phased the MG out of production 10 years later. Currently, the rights to the MG name and design are controlled by Rover, which has announced plans to produce a new MG line by the mid 1990s.

microfinish
Machine process used to smooth the surface of a part in order to reduce friction against that surface.

micrometer
1. A tool used to measure parts to within 0.0001 (one ten-thousandth) of an inch or, with a metric micrometer, 0.002 (two thousandths) of a millimeter. For maximum precision, the *mike*, as it is called for short, has a range of only 1.0 inch or, with a

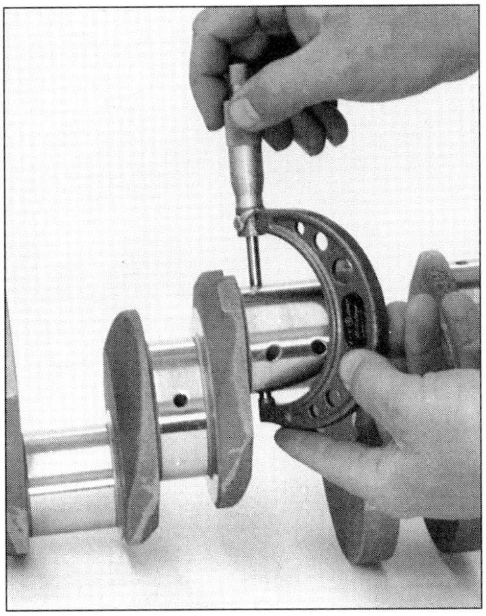

micrometer

metric unit, 25 millimeters. To measure an object of slightly more than 5.0 inches, it would be necessary to use a mike specifically designed for objects between 5.0 and 6.0 inches.
2. SI unit of linear measure, 0.000001 (one millionth) of a meter, same as a *micron*.

microinch
US unit of linear measure, 0.000001 (one millionth) of an inch.

micron
SI unit of linear measure, 0.000001 (one millionth) of a meter, same as *micrometer*, def. 2.

mid-engined
Chassis layout with the engine behind the driving compartment but ahead of a rear final drive assembly. Not the same as *rear-engined*.

midget
Small oval-track racing car, essentially a scaled down sprint car.

midnight auto parts, midnight auto supply
Stolen parts.

MIG welding
Metal inert gas welding. The metal is a spool of wire fed through a sheet of inert gas, usually 25 percent helium and 75 percent argon. The wire becomes the electrode and melts. Therefore, it must be continuously fed to the weld puddle. Stainless steel, steel, aluminum and other metals that can be fusion welded can also be MIG welded. See also *TIG welding*.

mike
1. Shortened name for a *micrometer*.
2. As a verb, to use a micrometer.

mil
U.S. unit of linear measure, 0.001 (one thousandth) of an inch.

mild steel
Steel alloy with a low carbon content, usually between 0.08 and 0.35 percent. While not as strong as higher-carbon steels, mild steel costs less and is easier to machine, shape and weld.

mill
1. Engine.
2. As a verb, to use a *milling machine* to remove metal from an object.

mill file
Fine-toothed hand file.

milling machine
Machine used for removing metal from an object by planing or boring.

milliampere
SI unit of electrical measure, 0.001 (one thousandth) of an ampere.

millimeter
SI unit of linear measure, 0.001 (one thousandth) of a meter.

Mini
British small car, introduced in 1960 as the Morris Mini Minor and Austin Seven, the latter name recalling the classic Austin Seven of the 1920s and 1930s. Designed by Alec Issigonis, the Mini was the first modern car to combine a transverse front engine with front-wheel drive, along with wheels pushed out toward the four corners of the boxy body. The idea of a transverse engine with front drive was not new; it was first tried in 1904 by an American designer, J. Walter Christie. But Issigonis was the first to demonstrate that it was a key to the most efficient use of space in a small car, and the Mini's layout has since become the norm for small car design throughout the world. In 1970, the Morris Mini Minor became known simply as the Mini and no longer carried Morris or Austin nameplates.

minimum thickness
On a disc brake rotor, the minimum thickness needed to dissipate heat and prevent the rotor from warping.

mini stock
In oval track racing, category for four-cylinder, subcompact sedans.

milling cylinder head on milling machine

minor diameter
On a bolt, smallest in diameter of the threads.

minor overhaul
Engine repair procedure that includes replacement of the piston rings, rod bearings, head and manifold gaskets, plus a valve job. Not to be confused with a *rebuild*. See also *major overhaul*.

minor tune-up
Engine maintenance procedure that includes the replacement or adjustment of the plugs, points and condenser, plus adjustment of the ignition timing. Necessary only with engines equipped with point-type distributors. See also *major tune-up*.

Mitsubishi
Japanese automaker. The name means "three diamonds," which is the corporate emblem. Mitsubishi is not Japan's largest automaker but it is part of one of that country's largest conglomerates, employing some 10 percent of the Japanese work force and turning out 12 percent of the gross national product. Mitsubishi built its first automobiles in 1917 but produced only about 20 before deciding to concentrate on commercial vehicles. It did not begin modern production of passenger cars on a serious scale until 1960. Mitsubishi has close ties with Chrysler Corporation, which offers several models that are badge-engineered versions of Mitsubishi products.

MK
Master kit, an engine parts kit that contains a crankshaft, bearings, camshaft, bearings, lifters, oil pump, timing chain, pistons, rings, gasket set and core plugs. Sometimes referred to redundantly as "MK kit," which would mean "master kit kit."

MKT
Engine parts kit that contains all the items in an *MK*, plus timing gears.

MMC
Metal matrix composite, a mixture of ceramic and metal which is light in weight and resistant to high temperatures.

model year
Vehicle's year of manufacture as designated by the automaker. The model year does not coincide with the equivalent calendar year and, in fact, usually precedes it by several months and sometimes by as much as a year. For example, a car designated as a 1993 model may actually be introduced as early as January 1992.

modesty panel, modesty skirt
Metal or fiberglass panel below the bumpers which conceals chassis components. An air dam serves as a modesty panel, though its main purpose is aerodynamic rather then aesthetic.

modified
Term used rather broadly in several forms of racing to describe a car which retains a semblance of a passenger car body but is otherwise reworked, or modified, for higher performance.

modulator
1. In electronics, a device which varies the amplitude, frequency or phase of electromagnetic waves.
2. In an automatic transmission, device which regulates hydraulic line pressure to meet differing load conditions. At full throttle or under a heavy load, the modulator increases pressure to give the clutches a firmer grip. At light throttle or under a light load, the modulator decreases pressure for smoother shifts.

modular wheel
Vehicle wheel made with separate inner, outer and central hub sections, bolted or riveted together.

module
Semi-conductor control for an electronic ignition system; the proverbial *black box*.

modulus of elasticity
Point at which a material, such as a piece of sheet steel, has been bent too far to snap back to its original shape.

molded
Adjoining body panels which have been reworked, usually with either Bondo or lead, into a smooth, unbroken surface.

molded hose
Section of hose, such as radiator hose, formed with permanent bends to fit into a specific space in the engine compartment.

moly
Short for *molybdenum*, see below.

molybdenum
Hard, heavy, silver-white metallic element, used in some steel alloys to harden and strengthen them.

molybdenum disulfide
MoS_2, compound of molybdenum and sulfur, a black powdery solid sometimes added to oil or grease to improve their lubricity.

moly lube
Lubricant made with molybdenum disulfide, used during engine building, especially on a camshaft, to provide lubrication during the initial startup of the newly assembled engine.

moly ring
Piston ring with a fused molybdenum coating that improves sealing between the ring and cylinder wall.

camshaft with moly lube

moment of inertia
In physics, the tendency of a body to resist angular or rotational acceleration. In automotive terms, the tendency of a vehicle to resist cornering. If the vehicle's main masses—the engine, transmission, final drive, and passenger or cargo loads—are widely dispersed over the vehicle's length, as they are, say, in a *stretch limo*, the moment of inertia will be high and the vehicle will not want to go around corners very fast. If, on the other hand, the main masses are concentrated, as they are in a *mid-engined* sports car or GT, the moment of inertia will be low and the car will be capable of cornering much faster. That is one of the reasons why, when rules permit it, modern race cars are usually mid-engined.

MON
Motor octane number. See *octane number*.

Monel
Alloy, primarily of nickel and copper, tough and strongly resistant to corrosion and high temperatures; used in high stress areas of engines, such as exhaust valves. Monel (with one L) was named for A. Monell (with two Ls), an American manufacturer of the early 20th century who developed the material.

money grabber
In stock car racing, a driver who enters and starts a race but quits after a minimum number of laps, collecting appearance money without competing seriously.

money pit
Vehicle that is expensive to restore and maintain.

monitor
Electronic sensor which measures a variable characteristic either constantly or on demand, compares the measured value against a pre-established limit, and signals corrective action if the value is inconsistent with the limit. The *lambda sensor*, which measures the proportion of oxygen in exhaust gasses in order to determine the stoichiometric accuracy of the incoming air/fuel mixture, is an example of such a monitor.

monkey motion
Imprecise or excessive movement in a mechanical device, such as in an improperly adjusted carburetor linkage or stick shift mechanism.

monobloc
Engine block with the cylinders and crankcase in one casting.

monocoque
Unitized autobody frame structure with stressed sheet metal panels. A monocoque tub is often used for open-wheeled race cars, because of its strength and rigidity.

monster truck
Truck, usually a pickup, with huge oversize wheels and tires, and special heavy-duty powertrain components to drive them. The tires are big enough that the monster truck can be driven up and over standard size passenger cars, crushing them. Bob Chandler pioneered the concept with his "Big Foot" in the early 1980s.

Moon discs
Simple, smooth hub caps which cover wheels completely. Because they're better aerodynamically than exposed wheels, or most other hub caps for that matter, Moon discs are popular for lakes cars. They were developed by the late Dean Moon, a pioneering hot rodder.

Mopar
Chrysler product. Mopar, which stands for "Motor Parts," originated as the trademark of Chrysler's parts division. However, the term is widely used by enthusiasts to describe any Chrysler high performance car, particularly their *muscle cars*.

Moon disc

Morgan
British sports car. Morgan Motor Company Limited was founded in 1910 by H.F.S. Morgan to build three-wheeled cars. They featured a single, chain-driven drive wheel at the rear and two wheels at the front featuring independent suspension with sliding pillars and coil springs. Morgan introduced its first four-wheeled car, the 4/4, in 1936, with the same front suspension. The three-wheeled design was dropped in 1952, but the four-wheeled Morgan has continued to this day with only minor cosmetic changes. After being in production for more than half a century, it has become its own *replicar*.

Morris
British passenger car. W.R. Morris, later Lord Nuffield, began manufacturing automobiles in 1913. During the 1920s, his company took over development and production of the Morris-based *MG* sports car. Morris also acquired two other automakers, Wolseley in 1927 and Riley in 1938. Morris, MG, Wolseley and Riley merged with Austin in 1952 to form the British Motor Corporation and all five makes became badge-engineered versions of each other. In 1970, they were absorbed into British Leyland and, one by one, were phased out of production.

M

motor
1. Technically, a motor is a device which converts electrical energy to mechanical energy, while an engine is a device which burns a combustible fuel to develop heat energy which, in turn, is converted to mechanical energy. Out in the real world, though, nobody pays much attention to that distinction any more and motor has become a widely used synonym for engine. 2. As a verb, to travel by car. When said with emphasis, motor can mean to travel very fast as in "he's motoring!"

motorhome
Self-contained *RV*, or recreational vehicle, built on a bus or truck chassis, with both a driving compartment and complete living facilities. Not to be confused with *mobile home*.

motor mounts
Supports for the engine and transmission on a vehicle's frame, made of hard rubber to absorb vibration, and partly encased in

muffler

steel. In a conventional front-engine, rear-drive car or truck, there are at least three mounts, one on each side of the engine and one under the rear of the transmission.

motor mouth
Overly talkative person, same as *ratchet jaw*.

motor oil
Liquid lubricant formulated expressly for use in engines.

MoTown
Detroit, center of the U.S. auto industry. The term is contracted from "Motor Town" and became famous as the name of a Detroit-based record company.

Motronic
Bosch electronic fuel injection and ignition management system. The device monitors the engine's fuel requirement, plus temperature, altitude and rpm, then conveys its readings to a microprocessor which, in turn, adjusts fuel flow and ignition for efficient operation.

mountain motor
Big block V-8, generally either a Chevrolet or Ford, enlarged to at least 500 cubic inches and often to between 600 and 800 cubic inches.

mouse milk
Additive for oil or fuel.

mouse motor
Chevrolet small-block V-8; so called because, when it was introduced in 1955, it was relatively small for its displacement. See also *rat motor*. Legend has it that the terms evolved in response to the nickname bestowed upon Chrysler's famed Hemi engine, the *Elephant*.

MS
Military Standard, a system of grading the quality of fasteners and other items of hardware, particularly for aircraft use. MS was developed by the military services but has also been adopted by the civil aircraft industry and is the formal designation of what is called "aircraft quality." Sometimes referred to redundantly as "MS Standard" which would mean "Military Standard Standard."

MSDS
Material Safety Data Sheet. A sheet containing specific information about hazardous materials. Required by *OSHA* to be displayed at any workplace where such materials are used.

M/T
Trademark used by the late Mickey Thompson for aftermarket equipment he manufactured and distributed.

MTBE
Methyl tertiary butyl ether, $CH_3OC_4H_9$, oxygenated compound used to raise the octane number of gasoline.

MTEG
Mickey Thompson Entertainment Group, P.O. Box 25168, Anaheim, California 92825; (714) 938-4100. Organization founded by the late Mickey Thompson to promote stadium races for off-road vehicles.

mud boggin'
See *boggin'*.

mud flap
Flap hanging down behind a tire, particularly on a large truck or semi-trailer, to deflect mud, gravel or spray kicked up by the tire, and prevent any such debris from striking vehicles following behind.

mud plug
On a dirt track race car, a cap installed in the center of a wheel to keep out mud.

muffler
Silencing element in a vehicle exhaust system.

muffler bearing
Non-existent part used to make fun of (or in the case of shady mechanics, to rip off) someone with little or no mechanical knowledge.

muffler clamp, muffler hanger
Bracket that holds the muffler in place.

mule
Race car used primarily for practice or testing. In off-road racing, the equivalent of a mule is a *prerunner*.

multi-fuel vehicle
Vehicle with an engine modified to run on more than one fuel, such as gasoline and LPG or gasoline and methanol.

multiple disc clutch
Clutch with two or more driven plates separated by floater plates. Multiple disc clutches allow smaller diameter flywheel and clutch assemblies, which allows the engine and transmission to be mounted lower in the chassis, thereby also lowering the center of gravity.

multi-point injection
Electronic fuel injection system in which the fuel is injected into each separate port rather than into a single point in the intake system.

multi-viscosity oil
Motor oil formulated to have a low viscosity for easier flow in cold weather and a high viscosity for better protection in hot weather.

multi-valve head
Cylinder head design with more than one intake and/or one exhaust valve per cylinder; multi-valve heads have been built with anywhere from three to six valves per cylinder, but the most common type is the four-valve head. Like many good ideas, this one has been around awhile; the first four-valve head was used on a Peugeot race car built in 1911.

Muncie
Gearbox, particularly a four-speed manual, produced at a General Motors transmission plant in Muncie, Indiana.

Muroc
Muroc dry lake, one of the early Mojave Desert sites used for Southern California Timing Association speed trials. "Muroc" is a reverse spelling of "Corum," the name of the family which owned the land. In 1939, the dry lake was incorporated into what became Edwards Air Force Base and its name was changed from Muroc to Rogers dry lake. Today, it is the unpaved strip used for space shuttle landings at Edwards.

muscle car
High-performance vehicle with a big-block engine in a lightweight, mid-size chassis and two-door body, usually with heavy-duty suspension. The Pontiac GTO, introduced in 1964, was considered the first muscle car. By the late sixties, all of the domestic manufacturers offered at least one muscle car, resulting in a horsepower race and fierce competition both on and off the race track. The idea died out in the early 1970s, partly because of high insurance rates and partly because of government demands for reduced exhaust emissions and improved fuel economy. However, the muscle cars built from 1964 through 1973 remain popular with collectors, enthusiasts and hot rodders.

mushroom lifter
Valve lifter with a foot larger in diameter than the body. Mushroom lifters provide more surface area for the cam lobe to act upon and, thus, allow more aggressive cam profiles.

MVMA
Motor Vehicle Manufacturers Association, 7430 2nd Avenue, Suite 300, Detroit, Michigan 48202; (313) 872-4311. Trade association of the major U.S. auto and truck makers.

muscle car

mushroom lifter

N

N
Neutral position on an automatic transmission shift quadrant. See *neutral*.

NACA duct
Bottle-shaped, low-drag air intake design developed by the National Advisory Committee for Aeronautics or NACA, the predecessor of the National Aeronautics and Space Administration or NASA; sometimes incorrectly referred to as *NASA duct*.

nail it
To apply full throttle.

NASA duct
Incorrect reference to *NACA duct*, see above.

NASCAR
National Association for Stock Car Auto Racing, P.O. Box 2875, Daytona Beach, Florida 32115; (904) 253-0611. The major sanctioning body for stock car racing.

nasty car
NASCAR stocker.

Nash
In 1917, Charles W. Nash, a former president of General Motors, bought the Thomas B. Jeffrey Company of Kenosha, Wisconsin. Jeffrey had been in business since 1902, building Rambler and Jeffrey cars, as well as the Jeffrey Quad four-wheel-drive truck which saw widespread military use during World War I. With the Nash takeover, the firm became the Nash Motor Company and the vehicles became Nash cars and trucks. In 1950, for a new compact car, Nash revived the Rambler name Jeffrey had once used. Nash merged with Hudson in 1954 to form the American Motors Corporation. In 1957, both the Nash and Hudson nameplates were dropped in favor of Rambler. The corporation was absorbed by Chrysler in 1988. See also *AMC* and *Rambler*.

natural gas
Mixture of flammable hydrocarbons, occurring naturally in the earth and consisting mainly of methane with smaller amounts of ethane, butane and propane. See *methane*.

needle bearing

NDRA
Nostalgia Drag Racing Association, P.O. Box 9438, Anaheim, CA 92802; (714) 539-6372. Organization staging drag races for older cars, including muscle cars, built before 1984.

NDT
Non-destructive test, method of testing parts for cracks without causing damage.

necking
Narrowing of the stem and radius area of an exhaust valve caused by acids and other corrosives created as combustion by-products.

nearside
Side of a vehicle near the curb. Same as *curbside*, and the opposite of *offside* or *streetside*.

needle-and-seat
Assembly which regulates fuel flow into the carburetor float bowl. When the fuel level in the bowl drops, the needle moves off the seat, allowing more fuel to enter the bowl. When the fuel level rises in the bowl, the needle moves back on to the seat and shuts off the fuel flow.

needle bearing
Small roller bearing in which the rollers are small-diameter, needle-like units.

negative pole, negative post
Negative terminal on a battery, usually the smaller of the two terminals, and may also be color-coded green or black in contrast to the positive terminal color-coded red.

negative camber
Inward tilt at the top of the wheels on a vehicle, as viewed from the front or rear, measured in degrees. See also *positive camber* and *camber*.

negative offset
Wheel rim placed inward from the center of the mounting flange. See *wheel offset*.

neoclassic
Modern car designed to resemble the classics of the late 1920s and early 1930s. The *Excalibur* is a good example.

neoprene
Type of synthetic rubber resistant to oil, heat, light and oxidation, which makes it an excellent material for sealing.

nerf
In oval track racing, to bump or shove another car.

nerf bars
Small tubular bumpers at the front and rear of an oval track race car. Nerf bars have also sometimes been used on hot rods for styling effect in place of conventional bumpers, and on off-road vehicles for a variety of purposes.

net horsepower, net torque
Maximum engine output as measured on a dyno, using standard intake and exhaust systems and with all engine accessories in place. Net figures are often up to 30 percent less than *gross horsepower, gross torque*.

net valve lift
Valve lift minus the running valve clearance.

neutral
With either an automatic or manual transmission, shift lever position which disengages all transmission gears and, thus, disconnects the engine from the drive wheels.

Neway cutter
Fixed angle valve seat cutting tool, using a series of carbide blades to machine the valve seat surfaces at clean, well-defined angles.

NG
No good, such as junk parts. NFG is a more common acronym, however the definition is not suitable for publication.

n-heptane
C_7H_{16}, normal heptane, a hydrocarbon with an octane number of zero, used in combination with *isooctane*, which has a number of 100, to define octane number of differing blends of gasoline. See *octane number*.

NHRA
National Hot Rod Association, P.O. Box 5555, Glendora, California 91740; (818) 914-4761. Major drag race sanctioning body.

NHTSA
National Highway and Traffic Safety Administration, the agency within the Department of Transportation responsible for establishing and enforcing automotive safety regulations.

nib
Diamond-tipped tool used to resurface grinding wheels.

nibbler
Tool used to cut sheet metal with small cuts or "nibbles."

nib cutter

nib cutter
Auto painting tool used to trim down high points, sags, runs or particles stuck on freshly applied paint.

nickel
Hard, silver-white metallic element that is malleable, ductile and magnetic, and used in alloys. It is also resistant to oxidation and, for that reason, is used in electroplating.

Nikasil
Tradename of a coating applied to the interior walls of cylinder sleeves to reduce friction and improve sealing at high temperatures.

Nissan
Japan's second largest automaker and the world's fourth largest. In 1933, a holding company called Nihon Sangyo, or Japan Industries, purchased the rights to manufacture a new small car, the Datsun, developed by the DAT Motor Company. A year later, the holding company adopted its Tokyo stock market abbreviation, "Ni" from "Nihon" and "San" from "Sangyo," or "Nissan," as its corporate name. In 1934, it became the first Japanese automaker to produce more than 1,000 cars, when the Datsun exceeded that figure. None of Nissan's domestic competitors had ever before built more than a few hundred cars in their entire histories. The first car to be called a Nissan rather than a Datsun was the Nissan 70 sedan, introduced in 1937 and built with outdated tooling purchased from an American automaker, Graham-Paige. Generally, in the years that followed, the company's smaller, less expensive products were called Datsuns, while its larger, more expensive ones were named Nissans. By 1980, Nissan management had decided that policy confused the company's image internationally, so the Datsun name was phased out and all of the company's cars and trucks became Nissans. That lasted until 1990, when the company introduced a new, larger, more expensive car that it felt should be distinguished from smaller, less expensive Nissans, so it was called the *Infiniti*. That is a made-up name that has no meaning at all and has left the company's image once again confused. See also *Datsun*.

N

nitride
1. Compound containing nitrogen, which is electronegative, with another element or a metal, which is electropositive.
2. As a verb, to place steel in a heated nitrate solution, which transforms the surface of the steel into a nitride and makes it stronger and harder.

nitro
See *nitromethane*.

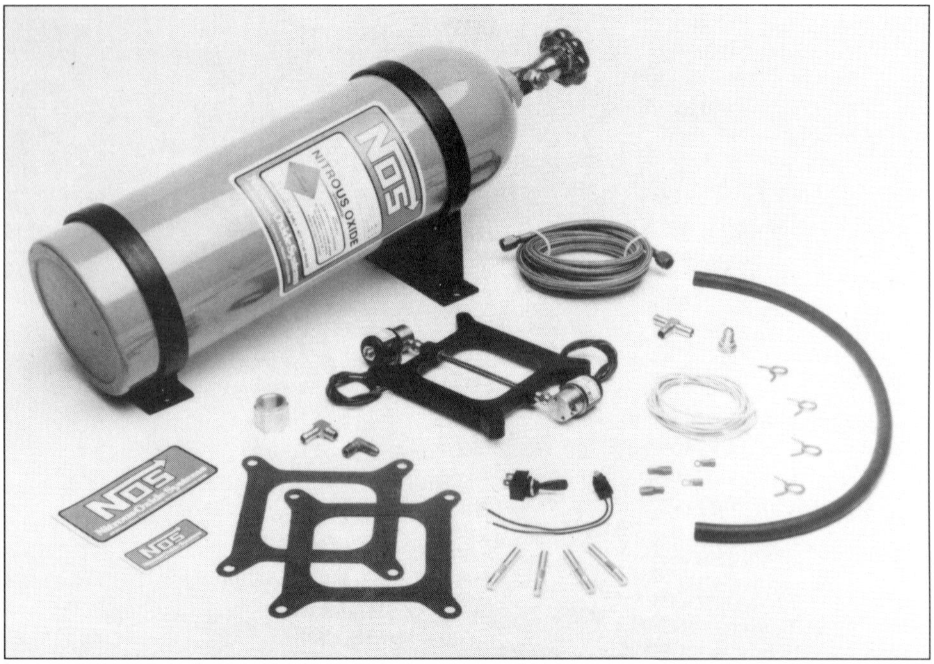

nitrous oxide

nitromethane, nitro
CH_3NO_2, a highly combustible liquid that serves as the main ingredient in drag racing fuels.

nitrous oxide
N_2O or laughing gas, a non-flammable, non-explosive gas which acts as an oxidizing agent with gasoline or methanol to increase the rate and efficiency of combustion, thereby increasing horsepower; often referred to simply as nitrous. Nitrous oxide systems are popular with hot rodders because they deliver relatively large, albeit temporary, horsepower gains without any internal engine modifications. Not to be confused with *NOx*.

NO
Normally open, said of an electrical circuit that is usually on.

nodular cast iron
Cast iron treated while molten with an alloy that causes the formation of nodular or spheroidal graphite, i.e., graphite in small, round lumps. Sometimes referred to as ductile iron or spheroidal graphite iron; used to make such parts as cylinder blocks and heads.

Nomex
Tradename for a fire-resistant fabric used for race drivers' apparel.

normalize
In metalworking, to raise the temperature of low- or medium-carbon steel 50 to 100 degrees F. above its critical temperature range and then allow it to cool slowly in still air. This will refine the grain structure and stress-relieve the metal.

normally aspirated
Engine which relies on vacuum in the intake manifold and cylinders to draw in air or air/fuel mixture; in other words, an engine without the forced induction of *supercharging* or *turbocharging*.

north-south
Longitudinal or lengthways placement of an engine in a vehicle, as in most front-engine, rear-drive cars. See also *east-west*.

NOS
1. New old stock; original, unused parts for older cars.
2. Nitrous Oxide Systems, a manufacturer of N_2O injection equipment.

nose
1. Front end of a vehicle.
2. Uppermost part of a camshaft lobe, which generates the most lift. See *lobe*.

nose over
In racing slang, an engine or other system that is starting to self-destruct.

nose plug
Threaded, tapered plug used to repair cracks around the injector hole on a diesel engine cylinder head.

notchback
Sedan or coupe body on which the *rear deck* forms a separate bulge from the *greenhouse*, as opposed to a *fastback* on which the greenhouse flows smoothly into the rear deck.

NOx
Oxides of nitrogen, a product of high-temperature combustion and an exhaust pollutant; not to be confused with *nitrous oxide*.

NPN
Silicon transistor with three terminals, two negative and one positive.

NSRA
National Street Rod Association, P.O. Box 9438, Anaheim, CA 92802; (714) 539-6372

NTP
Normal temperature and pressure. Same as *STP*, def., 2.

NTPA
National Tractor Pullers Association, 6969 Worthington-Galena Road, Suite J, Worthington, OH 43085; (614) 436-1761.

number stamps
Individual metal stamps used to imprint numbers onto metal parts.

nut runner
Air-powered wrench.

Nylatron
Hard, nylon-based plastic material used to make engine and suspension parts.

O

Oakland
1. The Oakland Motor Car Company was formed in August of 1907 in Pontiac, Michigan, by Edward M. Murphy. Shortly thereafter, Murphy died, and his company was acquired by General Motors. Oakland operated as a separate division, creating a popular model in 1926 called the Pontiac Six. The Pontiac Six soon outsold all other Oakland models combined, and in 1932, the name Oakland was phased out, and the Pontiac Motor Co. was formed. See also *Pontiac*.
2. Northern California city which is the site of the Oakland Roadster Show, one of the nation's most famous displays of hot rods and customs, held annually since 1950.

OAH, OAL, OAW
Overall height, length and width, respectively.

OBD
See *onboard diagnostics*.

observed horsepower
Brake output of an engine as observed on a dyno, before being adjusted for any deviations from the SAE standard ambient temperature of 60 degrees F. (15.6 C.) and barometric pressure of 29.0 inches of mercury (98.2 kilopascals). See also *corrected horsepower*.

octane
1. C_8H_{18}, an isomer of *isooctane*, $(CH_3)_2CHCH_2C(CH_3)_3$.
2. Shortened form of isooctane, which serves as a primary reference fuel for describing the anti-knock quality of a gasoline blend, i.e., the ability of the blend to resist premature ignition from compression or any other source of heat before the spark plug fires. See also *octane number*, below, and *cetane*.

octane number
Isooctane is assigned an index of 100 while another hydrocarbon, normal heptane or n-heptane, is assigned an index of zero. The octane number of a gasoline blend is simply the percentage of isooctane in a mixture with n-heptane that has the same anti-knock quality as the fuel being rated. An octane number of 85, for example, would mean that the blend had the same anti-knock quality as a mixture of 85 percent isooctane and 15 percent n-heptane. There are actually two different methods for finding octane numbers. The research octane number or *RON* is determined under mild operating conditions at an engine speed of 600 rpm, while the motor octane number or *MON* is determined under harsher conditions at 900 rpm. The *anti-knock index*, which is the octane number shown on pumps at gasoline stations, is simply an average of the MON and RON. See also *heptane*, *isooctane*, and *octane*.

octane booster
Additive for gasoline used to increase the octane number.

o.d.
Outside diameter of a pipe or tube.

odd-fire
In a V-6 engine with either a 60- or 90-degree block, a conventional crankshaft with two connecting rods attached to each of the three crank throws will not allow smooth, even firing. The result is an odd-fire engine. However, the problem can be corrected with a crankshaft that has the individual journals on each throw staggered in relation to each other to provide even firing and, thus, reduce engine vibration. See also *even-fire*.

odometer
Instrument which shows the distance a vehicle has gone. All cars and trucks have an odometer which cannot be reset—at least not legally—and shows the accumulated mileage since the vehicle came off the assembly line. In addition, many cars and trucks have a separate trip odometer which can be reset to keep track of the distance of a specific trip.

OEM
Original equipment manufacturer.

off-highway, off-pavement
See *off-road*.

office
Driver's compartment.

off-road
Term which really means *off-highway* or *off-pavement*, because most so-called off-road activity actually takes place on some form of road or *jeep trail*, however primitive it may be.

offset
1. Condition when two parts are not directly in line with one another.
2. See *wheel offset*.

offset rods
Rods on which the beam section is not directly centered over the bearing housing.

offside
Side of a vehicle away from the curb. Same as *streetside* and the opposite of *curbside* or *nearside*.

off-the-line
To *launch* from the starting line in a drag race.

Offy
1. Offenhauser racing engine built by Meyer-Drake, the classic American racing engine. Originally designed by Harry Miller in the 1920s, the engine was later produced by Fred Offenhauser. Offenhauser, in turn, sold the manufacturing rights to Lou Meyer and Dale Drake so that he could devote his time to the hot rod equipment business. But his name stuck on the racing engine.
2. Any item of equipment produced by Fred Offenhauser or Offenhauser Equipment Company, such as an Offy manifold or Offy valve covers.

ogee
S-shaped curve, as in a *landau bar*.

OHC
Overhead camshaft, a camshaft mounted in the cylinder head rather than in the block. See also *DOHC* and *SOHC*.

ohm
SI unit of electrical resistance. When one volt produces a current of one ampere, there is a resistance of one ohm. Named for Georg S. Ohm, a 19th century German physicist.

Ohm's law
In a *DC* circuit, the current in amperes is directly proportional to the electromotive force in volts and inversely proportional to the resistance in ohms. In an *AC* circuit, resistance is replaced by impedance, also in ohms.

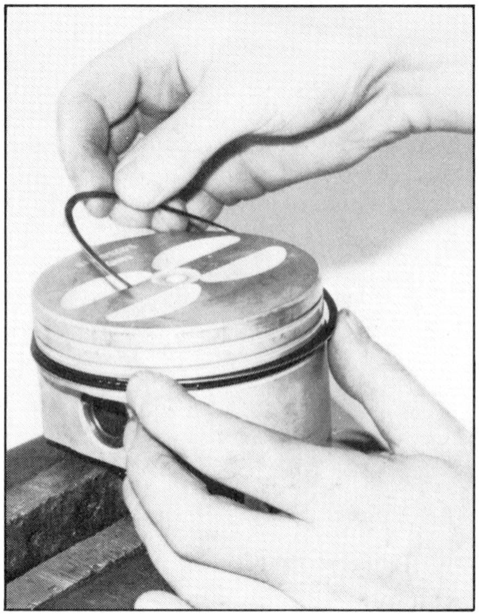

oil control ring

ohmmeter
Instrument to measure electrical resistance in ohms.

OHV
1. Overhead valve, setup with the valves in the cylinder head but driven via pushrods by a camshaft in the block.
2. Off-highway vehicle, i.e., one intended for *off-road* use

oil-air separator
Device to prevent aeration of oil.

oil bath filter
Engine air filter that forces incoming air through a bath of oil that traps dirt and dust before the air goes on through the intake system and into the engine.

oil burner
1. Diesel.
2. Older car or truck with excessive oil consumption, a condition often evident from a smoking exhaust pipe.

oil canning
Sheet metal popping from convex to concave, or vice versa, the way the bottom of an old-fashioned oil can used to pop as its contents were drained.

oil control ring
Bottom piston ring which scrapes oil from the cylinder wall.

oil-cooled piston
Piston cooled by a jet of oil sprayed under the piston dome; used in some diesels and endurance-racing engines.

oil cooler
Device to cool engine oil or automatic transmission fluid. On some race cars, oil coolers are also used to cool manual gearbox and final drive lubricants.

oil dipper
In early, low-powered engines, a small scoop located on the bottom of the connecting rod that dips into a trough of oil to lubricate the rod bearing and crankshaft journal.

oil filter (System One)

oil filter
Device to clean suspended particulates, such as combustion by-products, from engine oil.

oil-fouled plug
Spark plug with its electrode tip coated with oil, preventing an effective spark for combustion.

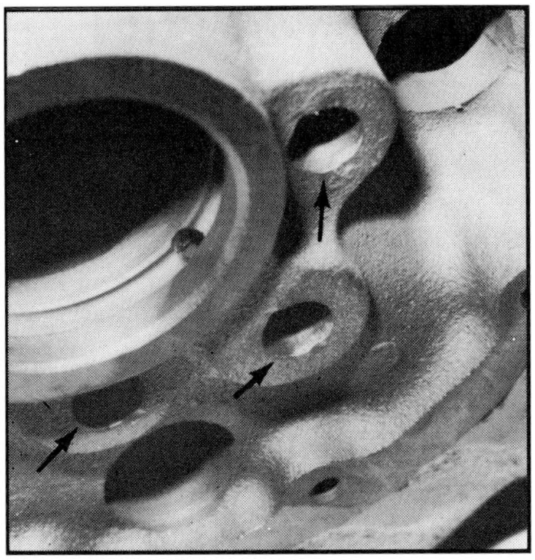

oil galleries

oil gallery
Passages within the engine block and cylinder head through which oil is transmitted.

oil pan
Part of the engine that contains the oil supply, usually at the bottom of the block. Same as *crankcase, oil sump* or *sump*.

oil pressure
Pressure applied by the *oil pump* to force oil to flow throughout the engine.

oil pump
Pump which applies pressure to force oil to flow throughout the engine.

oil ring
See *oil scraper ring*, below.

oil ring expander, oil ring separator
Thin metal strip used to keep constant pressure on the oil ring rails against the cylinder wall.

oil ring rails
Two thin metal rings used to scrape oil from the cylinder walls.

oil scraper ring
Second ring on the piston, used to scrape off and drop into the pan any oil left on the cylinder wall by the *oil control ring*.

oil slinger
Metal disc installed between the crankshaft timing gear and the engine pulley to force oil centrifugally away from the timing cover seal.

oil sump
See *oil pan*.

Oldsmobile
America's oldest automaker. Ransom Eli Olds established the Olds Motor Works in 1896. Five years later, he introduced his most famous car, the Oldsmobile Curved Dash Runabout. It became the world's first mass-produced automobile, rising from 425 units in 1901 to 6500 by 1905. Olds himself left the company in 1904 to establish another firm, REO, using his initials for its name. General Motors took over Olds in 1909. The Oldsmobile Division has become known as an engineering leader among GM makes, introducing such innovations as the Hydra-Matic automatic transmission in 1940; the short-stroke, high-compression, OHV V-8 engine in 1949; the full-size, front-drive Toronado in 1966; and the DOHC, multi-valve Dual Quad four-cylinder engine in 1989. Other GM makes have later adopted some of these items, but Olds was usually the first to have them.

omnibus
Short for the French *voiture omnibus*, or "carriage for all," and the origin of our word *bus*.

on a pass
Making a good, fast run, especially in drag racing.

onboard diagnostics
Computer system permanently installed on a vehicle to analyze problems affecting engine performance, such as malfunctions in the fuel or electrical systems. See photo next page.

onboard fire extinguishing system
Fire extinguishing system permanently installed on a vehicle. The unit is placed in the driver's compartment with two or more nozzles generally located inside the driver's compartment, near the engine and fuel tank. The system emits a dry chemical when activated by a driver or safety crew in the event of a fire. Nearly all race sanctioning bodies require some type of onboard fire extinguishing system.

one-off
Individual, purpose-built vehicle with no immediate plan for mass production.

one-piece oil ring
Oil ring designed with the oil rails and the expander or separator combined in a single part.

one-way clutch
On some twisting tools, a friction or ratchet clutch that allows motion in one direction only.

on the bubble
In a vulnerable position, generally referring to the last available spot on a starting grid

oil pump (Chevy)

onboard diagnostics (Indycar)

prior to the end of qualifying, when the possibility of getting bumped from the field still exists. See *bubble, bump spot* and *bump*.

on the cam
Operating an engine in its most responsive rpm range.

on the grid, on the line
In starting position for a race.

on the piano
Misplaced; a part or tool which can't be found when it's needed is "on the piano."

on the wood
Accelerator all the way to the floor.

oodle
To run an engine at idling speed.

Opel
Adam Opel was well established in Ruesselsheim, Germany as a manufacturer of bicycles and sewing machines when, in 1898, the company entered the auto industry. It began by buying the rights to a car called the Lutzmann and producing it as the Opel-Lutzmann. The company was family-owned until the late 1920s, when it became a joint-stock company. By 1929, the majority of the shares were acquired by General Motors and Opel became GM's German subsidiary. Opel is best known in this country for small cars sold here by Buick dealers in the late 1950s and again in the 1970s.

open chamber head
Cylinder head with combustion chambers having no *quench areas*. See also *closed chamber heads*.

open course
Auto race course which extends beyond the finish line into a shut-off area, such as a drag strip or a dry lake like Bonneville.

open end spring
Coil spring with the end loops apart from the coils of the spring, as opposed to a *closed end spring*, which has end loops pressed against the adjacent coils.

open structural member
Flat body panel with open access from the rear.

open the tap
Increase speed.

opposite lock
In dirt track racing, especially, turning the steering wheel opposite the direction the vehicle is traveling in an effort to control or correct oversteer.

opposed engine
Engine with two cylinder banks 180 degrees apart, such as the flat four in the Volkswagen Beetle, the flat six in the Porsche 911, or flat 12 in the Ferrari Testarossa. Also sometimes referred to as a *pancake engine*.

organic brake linings
Brake linings made of organic materials, i.e., carbon-based compounds, combined with asbestos, or magnesium silicate, which is non-organic; in recent years, though, glass and synthetic fibers have been replacing asbestos. Organic linings wear well at lower operating temperatures. They are also quiet in operation and low in cost and, as a result, they have been traditionally favored in production passenger cars. See also *metallic brake linings*.

O-ring
Round rubber or plastic ring used as a seal, such as at the ends of hydraulic cylinders.

ORV
Off-road vehicle, one ruggedly built and with high ground clearance for use over unpaved terrain.

OS
See *oversize*.

oscilloscope
Electronic instrument which displays the oscillations of varying voltage or current on the screen of a cathode ray tube. An appropriate *'scope*, as it is called for short, can be useful in diagnosing engine electrical performance.

OSHA
Occupational Safety and Health Administration, federal agency concerned with regulating safety and health hazards in work places.

ottoscope
Medical examination device with a light and magnifying lens originally developed for ear, nose and throat specialists, "borrowed" by auto technicians to inspect spark plugs and other small parts.

Otto cycle engine
Four-stroke cycle engine, invented in Germany in 1876 by Nikolaus August Otto. The four strokes are (1) intake or induction; (2) compression; (3) combustion, power or expansion; and (4) exhaust. Combustion occurs in each cylinder on every other revolution of the crankshaft.

O_2 sensor
See *oxygen sensor.*

outboard brakes
Brake assembly at the outer or wheel end of an axle half-shaft, as opposed to inboard brakes mounted at the inboard end of the half-shaft, near the centerline of the car. See also *inboard brakes.*

outer race
In a roller bearing, the race nearest the outside of the hub.

outgas
To release gas embedded in a solid, such as a plastic or composite material, as a result of heat generated during machining or curing. For example, when Plexiglass is machine cut, the operation may produce enough heat to release formaldehyde from the plastic.

out-of-round
Condition of a circular part when its diameter varies; in other words, it is not perfectly circular.

out-of-square
Condition of a square or rectangular part when its vertical sides are not at right angles to its horizontal sides.

out of the box
Absolutely stock, without any modifications.

out of the chute, out of the gate, out of the hole
In a drag race, coming off the starting line.

out to lunch
Worthless. A car which always finishes near the bottom of its class is "out to lunch."

oval
Circular or oval-shaped race track.

oval port
Intake or exhaust port that is oval in shape. Generally used in low-to-medium performance cylinder heads; not for high performance use. Best exemplified by big-block Chevy 241 and 820 castings, both medium-performance cast-iron heads with oval-shaped intake ports. The high performance versions of these heads use square or rectangular intake ports. See *D-Port.*

over, overbore
To enlarge the cylinders of an engine beyond their stock diameters, generally in increments of thousandths-of-an-inch. .030-inch and .060-inch are the most common amounts. See also *bore* and *bored-and-stroked.*

overcenter pre-load
In the steering gear, adjustment of the sector shaft's resistance to turning.

overdrive
Transmission ratio of less than 1-to-1, such as 0.85-to-1, to reduce engine rpm at highway cruising speed for smoother, quieter operation and better fuel economy.

overhaul
See *major overhaul* and *minor overhaul.*

overlap
1. Point in valve timing when the intake valve starts to open before the exhaust valve is fully closed; momentarily, both are open at the same time.
2. In bodyworking, new paint sprayed onto old.

overlay cam
Camshaft with hard face material welded to the flank and nose areas, increasing lift and decreasing wear.

overpull
To pull a body panel slightly beyond where it is supposed to be so that, when pulling pressure is released, the panel will spring back to the correct position.

oval port (intake, big-block Chevy)

overrev
To run an engine at excessive speed, usually beyond its *red line*, or rpm limit.

oversize
Part such as a bearing, piston or valve stem that is larger in diameter than its original specification. Abbreviated *OS.*

oversquare
Cylinder with the bore greater than the stroke.

overspray
Overlap of dry paint particles from a spray gun on areas that were not meant to be painted.

overstaging
Placing a vehicle at the start of a drag race ahead of the usual staging position; the same as *deep staging* and the opposite of *backstaging.*

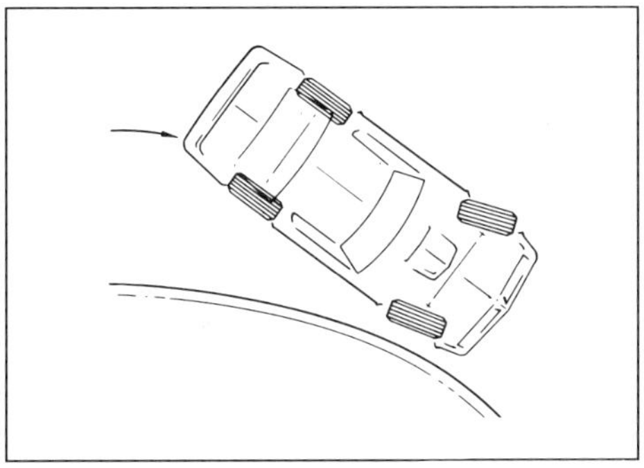

oversteer

O

oversteer
Condition in cornering where the slip angles of the rear tires are greater than the slip angles of the front tires; the rear end of the vehicle tends to break loose and slide outward. The opposite of *understeer.*

overstroke
Condition when a hone is driven through a cylinder and the ends, top and bottom, extend past the cylinder length.

oxidation
Combination of a substance with oxygen, forming an oxide. A common example occurs when iron absorbs oxygen from water to form ferric oxide, a fancy term for plain old rust.

oxide
Compound formed when a substance combines with oxygen. See *oxidation*, above.

oxides of nitrogen
NOx, an oxide formed by the combination of nitrogen and oxygen during high-temperature combustion of air/fuel mixture; an exhaust pollutant. See also *NOx*.

oxidize
1. To form an oxide.
2. In welding, the effect of applying excess oxygen, causing metal to vaporize. See *oxidizing flame*.

oxidizer, oxidizing agent
1. Substance that causes oxidation.
2. In automotive use, an additive which increases the oxygen content of air/fuel mixture to improve combustion efficiency. An example is *nitrous oxide*.

oxidizing flame
In gas welding, a flame with excess oxygen that may cause metal to *oxidize*, def. 2.

oxygenater
Same as *oxidizer, oxidizing agent*.

oxygen cutting
Process of cutting metal by the chemical reaction of oxygen and the metal at high temperatures.

oxygen sensor
Sensing device used in exhaust systems to measure the proportion of oxygen in the exhaust gasses and, from that proportion, to determine the air/fuel ratio of the incoming mixture. If the air/fuel ratio deviates from the ideal or *stoichiometric ratio*, a microprocessor attached to the oxygen sensor will make appropriate corrections in the fuel delivery system. See also *lambda*.

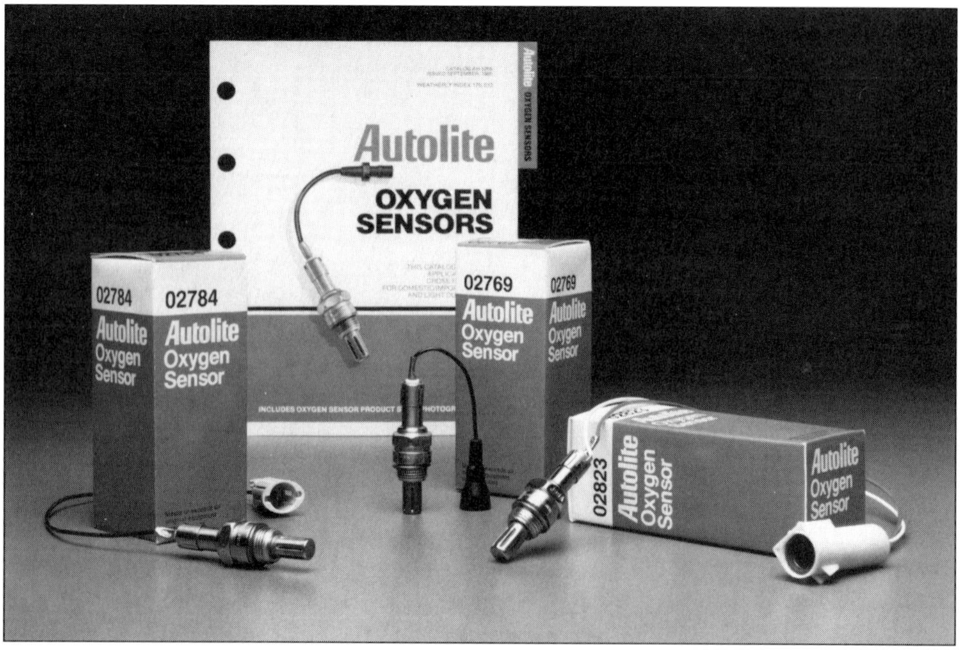

oxygen sensors

P

P
Park position on an automatic transmission shift quadrant, which locks the transmission and prevents the vehicle from being moved.

pace car
Passenger car, usually a convertible, used in closed-course racing to lead the field up to speed for a *rolling start.* When a yellow caution flag or light is displayed, the pace car goes back out in front of the race cars to hold them down in speed until the hazard that prompted the yellow is cleared.

pace lap
In closed-course racing, the last lap just before the start, as the pace car leads the field up to speed. See photo next page.

pacer
1. In oval track racing, a driver who runs at steady, consistent speeds.
2. With a capital "P," the name for a controversially styled passenger car produced by American Motors Corporation from 1974 to 1980.

package
Special combination of optional equipment and accessories offered for a new car. The package usually sells for less than the total for the individual items if they were all ordered separately.

Packard
American classic luxury car, built from 1899 to 1958, named for brothers J.W. and W.D. Packard who founded the company. Throughout much of its history, the Packard was strictly a luxury car but, in the mid 1930s, the firm also started building lower-priced models. Packard did not fare well in the years after World War II and, in 1954, merged with the Studebaker. The very last Packards, built in 1957 and 1958, were simply *badge-engineered* Studebakers.

pad
See *brake pad.*

paddock area
In closed-course racing, the designated areas behind or near the pit area where race cars, transporters, and at some courses, garages, are located. The paddock area is where the cars are tuned and prepared for qualifying and racing. In drag racing, which does not have a separate pit lane on the track, the area where race cars and transporters are kept is referred to as the *pits.*

pal nut
Thin, pressed-steel nut used to lock a regular nut into place. See also *lock nut*, def. 2.

pan
See *oil pan.*

pancake engine
Opposed engine, such as a *flat four* or *flat six.* The Porsche 911 series uses a pancake six-cylinder engine.

P&G check
Measuring engine specs, especially displacement, using instruments made by P&G Manufacturing, which do not require disassembly of the engine. The P&G check provides a quick, easy way to determine the legality of a race car competing in a class with a displacement limit.

panel beater
Body and fender worker. The term originated in England, circa 1900, when automotive body parts were made by hammering or "beating" them out of flat sheet metal by hand. Panel beating was recognized as a highly skilled and respected trade, adopting the European craftsmen system of skilled masters training apprentices over a period of years. Today, the term is used somewhat more generically to describe the typical body shop worker.

panel nut
Thin nut used to hold fittings or other parts to a firewall or bulkhead.

panel truck
Enclosed light truck or van without side windows aft of the front doors or B-pillars.

Panhard rod
On a *beam axle* or *de Dion axle* rear suspension, a transverse rod that attaches to the vehicle's frame at one end and to the axle at the other end, providing lateral location of the axle and preventing the chassis and body from moving side to side relative to the axle. The idea appears to

pace car leading the field on a parade lap prior to the pace lap

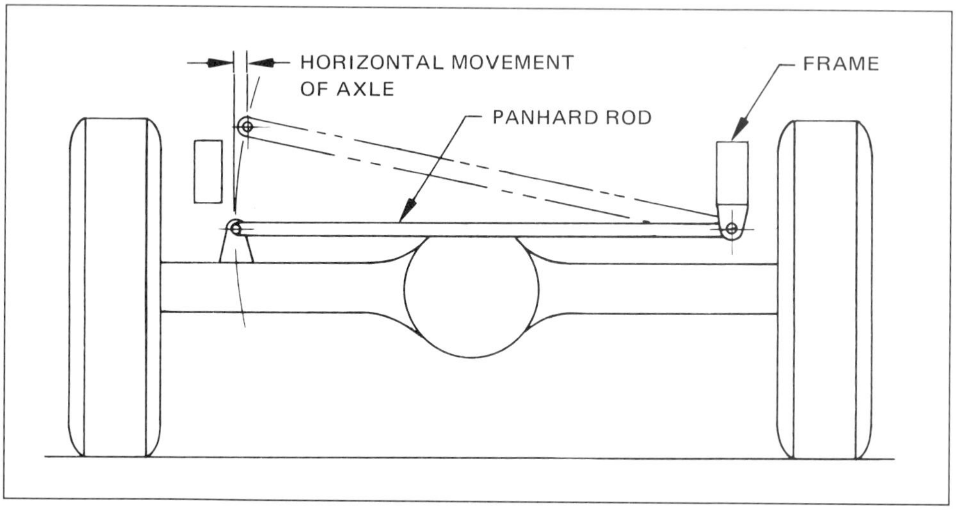

Panhard rod

have been first used on an early model of the Panhard, a French car built from 1889 to 1967.

pan rails
Sides on an oil pan which bolt to the block.

parade lap
In closed-course racing, a lap or laps before the start of an event, as the pace car leads the field of race cars around the track at a moderate speed, prior to the *pace lap.* The purpose of a parade lap is two-fold: it allows the drivers to warm-up tires and engines prior to the start of the race while giving the fans a good look at the cars at slower speeds. It also helps to build anticipation.

parasitic drag
Interference with the aerodynamic efficiency of an auto body caused by small obstructions, such as windshield wipers, door handles and outside mirrors.

parallel circuit
Electric circuit in which two or more electric devices are individually connected to the same circuit and ground. The positive poles of the devices are all connected to one conductor and the negative poles to another conductor. Because each device is individually connected, the failure of one device does not interfere with the operation of any other device. See also *series circuit.*

parallel linkage
Steering linkage with equal-length tie rods.

parent metal
Original metal on a body panel to which another piece of metal has been added.

parking brake
Mechanical braking system with cables that can be actuated to lock the front or rear wheels when a vehicle is parked.

particulates
Solid matter, mainly soot from burned carbon, in a vehicle's exhaust.

partition coefficient
See *coefficient of water/oil solubility.*

parting edge
Excess material found around the edge of a part that has been cast in a two-piece mold. Same as *flash.*

part out
To sell an engine or a complete vehicle piece by piece, instead of as a single assembly.

parts changer
Mechanic who keeps replacing parts randomly until a particular malfunction is corrected, instead of diagnosing the problem beforehand to determine what specific parts are needed.

parts chaser
Vehicle—or person—used by an auto repair shop or a racing team for errands, including buying parts.

parts washer
Machine used to clean parts.

pass
A run down a drag strip.

PAW
Plasma-arc welding. See *plasma.*

pawl
Ratchet tooth that can lock a device. For example, the Park position on an automatic transmission uses a pawl to lock the transmission.

payload
Maximum allowable weight of cargo a vehicle can carry. The payload is calculated by subtracting the curb weight of the vehicle and a 150-pound allowance for

each passenger from the gross vehicle weight rating or *GVWR*.

PC seals
Perfect Circle valve stem seals that have Teflon inserts to wipe the stems clean.

PCV
See *positive crankcase ventilation*.

PDI
Pre-delivery inspection. The process of checking and adjusting a new car prior to customer delivery.

peak
Maximum. Peak horsepower, for example, is the highest output an engine can deliver.

peaked
Body panel with raised beading worked into it for styling effect.

peak out
To reach the engine speed at which maximum horsepower is developed.

pearlescent paint
Color paint with fine mica particles blended into the pigment, giving a similar, but less dramatic effect than a *tri-coat*. Although the effect of the pearlescent color is not as pronounced as a tri-coat, it isn't as expensive or as hard to repair. The first three mica-based pearlescent colors were introduced on the 1982 Corvette and have grown tremendously in popularity. See also *tri-coats*.

pedal-to-the-metal
Accelerator pressed to the floor.

peel, peel rubber
Same as *lay rubber*.

peen
1. Ball-shaped end of a hammerhead, used to shape metal by pounding it.
2. As a verb, to use a peen.

peg
Highest possible reading on a speedometer or odometer; often, there's an actual peg on the dial which prevents the needle from going any farther.

PEL
Permissible exposure limit, the maximum length of time a person should be exposed to any hazard or hazardous material, as established by OSHA; expressed as a time-weighted average limit or ceiling exposure limit.

pen
To draw or design.

PERA
Production Engine Remanufacturers Association, 512 East Wilson Avenue, Glendale, CA 91206; (818) 240-8666. Formerly the Production Engine Rebuilders Association (1969-1973) and the Western Engine Rebuilders Association (1946-1969).

percent
The ratio of nitromethane in a fuel mixture; for example, *running on 80 percent*, means using 80 percent nitromethane and 20 percent methanol.

perimeter frame
Passenger car chassis frame with beams surrounding the floor of the passenger compartment.

Permatex
Brand of engine and transmission sealants.

petcock
Small valve or faucet for draining liquids, such as the one on the bottom of a vehicle's radiator, or at the end of a *burette*.

Peugeot
French auto maker, established by the Peugeot brothers in 1889, as a subdivision of their business, Les Fils des Peugeot Freres. It is the world's second oldest car manufacturer (after Daimler-Benz). One of Peugeot's most remarkable early achievements was a racing engine developed in 1911 that had such prophetic features as dual overhead camshafts, pent roof combustion chambers with centrally located spark plugs, and four valves per cylinder. It became the most imitated racing engine in history and strongly influenced such designers as Ettore Bugatti, the Duesenberg brothers and Harry Miller. The company has never been able to establish a lasting presence in the United States, and officially withdrew from the U.S. market in 1991. However, it remains a solid fixture in the European market.

phaeton
Two- or four-door, four/five-passenger open body, usually without roll-up windows; a popular body type in the 1920s and 1930s. See also *tub*.

pH level
Measure of the acidity or alkalinity of a solution, using a scale of pH0 to pH14, with pH0 being the most acid, pH7 being neutral, and pH14 being the most alkaline.

phosphor bronze
Alloy of copper, lead, tin and less than 1.0 percent phosphorus. It is hard, tough, low in friction and resistant to wear, and is used for such parts as wrist pins, piston pins, as well as for bushings in rocker arms, water pumps and steering knuckles.

phosphoric acid
H_3PO_4, a colorless and odorless acid used to remove rust from steel and cast iron.

pickle fork
Tool used to separate suspension components, such as ball joints, for repair or replacement.

pickup
1. Type of truck with an open cargo bed behind an enclosed cab.
2. Vehicle acceleration.

pickup coil
Engine speed sensor in an electronic ignition system.

pickup tube
Tube used to transmit fuel or oil from a storage tank. See photo next page.

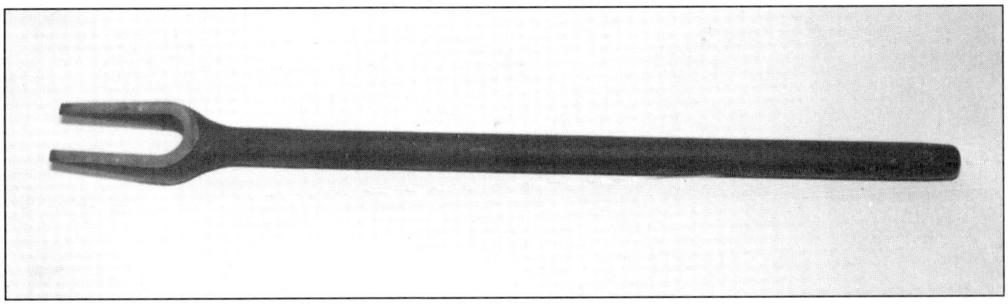

pickle fork

P

oil pump pickup tube

Pierce-Arrow
American classic luxury car, built from 1901 to 1938. The company was founded by George N. Pierce in Buffalo, New York. Its early products were known variously as the Pierce, the Arrow and the Great Arrow, until the firm finally settled on Pierce-Arrow in 1909. In styling, the Pierce-Arrow had headlights fared into the front fenders as early as the 1920s, a feature that did not appear on most other cars until several years later. Pierce-Arrow did not survive the depression years and went out of business in 1938.

pig
1. Unattractive or ill-performing vehicle.
2. Bar of cast metal.

Pikes Peak
Mountain in central Colorado, 14,110 feet high. Pikes Peak is one of the highest points in the United States that can be reached by automobile and is the setting for an annual auto racing hill climb held on or about the Fourth of July. The mountain was named after Zebulon Pike, an American explorer who led an early expedition to the peak. However, it is spelled Pikes, not Pike's.

pilot
1. Driver.
2. Device to support and guide the valve wheel carrier while grinding a valve seat.

pilot bearing
Bearing at the output end of an engine's crankshaft which supports the transmission's input shaft.

pilot hole
Small hole drilled into a part to serve as a guide for a larger size drill bit through the same location.

pilot model
First vehicle of a new design to be built on the assembly line before full-scale production begins. The pilot model serves to test the assembly procedures developed for the new design and is usually put together more slowly and deliberately than the later production models.

pilot shaft
Shaft used to align parts during assembly.

pin
Threaded tapered metal part used to repair cracks in castings, such as an engine block or cylinder head. See *pinning*, below.

PIN
Product identification number, a four-digit code used to identify hazardous material during transport.

ping
Mild *knock*. See also *detonation* and *preignition.*

pink slip
Vehicle ownership certificate. To "go for the pinks" or "race for the pinks" is to run for actual ownership of the competitor's car, generally during a street drag race.

pinning
Using a series of tapered threaded pins to repair a crack in a casting. The pins are screwed into predrilled holes so that they overlap each other from one end of the crack to the other.

pinch bar
Pry bar used to position or move equipment.

pinion
Small gear, such as the pinion at the end of the steering shaft in a *rack-and-pinion* steering system, or the pinion at the end of the driveshaft in a *ring-and-pinion* final drive assembly. A pinion may also be a small ring gear, such as the planet gears in a *planetary gearset.*

pinion bearing
Bearing, usually a double roller type, used to support the pinion gear in the differential housing.

pinion seal
Oil seal for the pinion gear in a ring and pinion.

pintle
Valve-like part of a fuel injector that controls the fuel spray pattern.

pintle hook
Vertical pin that can be installed at the rear of a vehicle to which a tow bar can be attached.

pipes
Dual exhaust system.

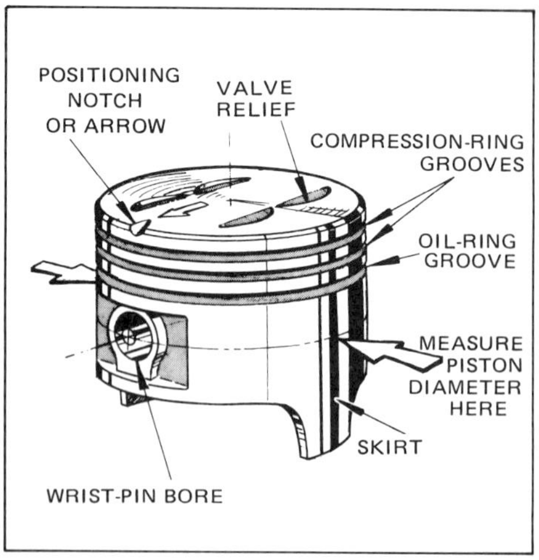

piston

piston
In an engine, a reciprocating, tubular-shaped component that moves up and down within a cylinder. The piston is forced down on the combustion or power stroke, pushing on the connecting rod which, in turn, revolves the crankshaft, converting reciprocating motion to rotary motion.

piston crown
The top of the piston, also used as a reference point to measure compression height. Some piston crowns have recesses (referred to as "dished" pistons) or domes to decrease or increase compression, respectively.

piston oiler
Device that injects oil from underneath into the piston to help carry away heat from the inside of the *piston crown*.

piston pin
Small, tubular-shaped shaft that connects the piston to the connecting rod. Piston pins are either *press-fit* or held in place with internal snap rings. Also called *wrist pins*.

piston rings
Rings that fit into grooves in the outer walls of pistons, just below the crown, to seal combustion pressures and to scrape oil from the cylinder walls.

piston ring expander
Tool used to expand piston rings in order to get them around the piston during installation.

piston ring land
See *ring land*.

piston skirt
Lower end of a piston, generally the part below the hole for the *piston pin*.

piston skirt expander
Device inserted behind the piston skirt to force the skirt out toward the cylinder wall and reduce excessive piston-to-wall clearance.

piston speed
Velocity of a piston in feet per minute as it reciprocates up and down in the cylinder. The term should really be qualified as "average" or "mean" piston speed, because it is not steady. The piston accelerates, decelerates, reverses direction, then accelerates, decelerates, and reverses direction again. However, it is possible to calculate the average or mean speed at any given rpm.

piston-to-valve clearance
Distance between the intake and exhaust valves on the one hand and the piston on the other hand, when the valves are at or near the overlap period and the piston is at or near top dead center.

pit crew performing pit stop in pits

pit crew
Personnel responsible for servicing a race car during pit stops on the track side of the pit wall, or the *hot pits*, as well as those supporting the team effort on the infield side of the wall, or the *cold pits*. There is usually a limit on the number of crew members who can be on the track side of the wall during a pit stop. The crew members on the infield side of the wall include those responsible for timing and communications.

pitch
Rotating motion of a vehicle's sprung mass about its lateral axis—or y axis—compressing the springs at one end of the vehicle and extending those at the other end.

pitman arm
Steering lever which converts the rotary motion of the steering gear to the linear motion of the centerlink.

pits
Trackside service facilities for vehicles competing in a race. In oval track or road racing, the pits are usually along the main straightaway where vehicles can stop for refueling and repairs during a long-distance event. They are divided into the *hot pits*, on the track side of the pit wall, where the pit crews service the cars during a race, and the *cold pits*, on the infield side of the wall, where the crews' equipment and supplies are kept. In drag racing, the pits are usually off to one side in the parking area, away from the strip. The *pits* should not be confused with the *paddock area*.

pit stop
Visit to the pits by a race car during an event to refuel, change tires, perform minor repairs, or sometimes simply for consultation. If the stop is for any reason other than quitting the race, the pit crew tries to get the car ready to go back out on the track as quickly as possible. Races are sometimes won by fractions of seconds and the time spent in the pits may be the difference between winning and finishing back in the pack.

pit wall
See *pits*, above.

pizza cutters

pizza cutters
In drag racing, extremely narrow front wheels used to reduce *rolling resistance.*

plain vanilla
Ordinary, without frills, such as a low-priced economy car.

planetary gearset
Circular gearset with three distinct elements: (a) a central or sun gear, (b) three or four planet gears which rotate around the sun gear, and (c) an internally toothed ring gear which rotates around the planet gears. The gearset's ratios can be varied by stopping any one element and allowing the other two elements to rotate. By combining two or more planetary gearsets, additional ratios can be obtained. Planetary gearsets are generally used in overdrives and in automatic transmissions.

planet carrier
Cradle that holds the planet gears in a *planetary gearset.*

planing
See *aquaplaning.*

plant it
To apply full throttle, same as *punch it, punch out.*

plasma
In welding, an inert gas, such as argon or nitrogen, heated to as high as 50,000 degrees F. (27,760 C.), which ionizes the gas so that it becomes electrically conductive. Plasma-generated electric arcs are used for both metal cutting and welding.

plastic deformation
Point at which any flexible material, such as a piece of sheet metal, has been bent far enough that it will not spring back to its original shape.

plastic filler
Two-part, putty-like material used to fill dents and to smooth imperfections in body panels. *Bondo* is a brand of plastic filler.

Plastigauge
Brand of plastic gauge, a plastic, string-like material used to measure bearing clearance. A piece of plastic gauge is placed between a crankshaft journal and its matching bearing. The specified torque is then applied to the bolts holding the bottom cap on the connecting rod, squeezing the plastic gauge. The bolts are removed, and the flattened plastic gauge is then taken out and measured to determine the bearing clearance.

platform
Basic understructure of a car or truck, including all *running gear.* One of the most versatile platforms in recent automotive history was Chrysler's K car, introduced in 1980 and used in the years since for everything from Dodge and Plymouth subcompacts to Chrysler mid-size luxury cars, as well as for the Dodge Daytona sports coupe and the Chrysler, Dodge and Plymouth minivans.

Plexiglas
Brand of transparent, lightweight plastic sometimes used for windows on enclosed race cars in place of glass.

plenums

plenum
Cavity containing a gas, such as air or air/fuel mixture, under higher than atmospheric pressure. A typical example is the plenum in the intake manifold just beneath the carburetor.

plow
See *understeer.*

plug
1. Spark plug.
2. Threaded tapered metal part used to repair cracks in castings, such as an engine block or cylinder head. See also *pin* and *pinning.*

plug weld
Circular weld made through a hole in one piece of tubing, connecting with another piece slipped inside.

plunger
Part of a hydraulic valve lifter that moves up and down depending on oil pressure.

plies
Layers of cord, fiberglass or steel in a tire carcass.

Plymouth
Low-priced car introduced by Chrysler in 1928 to compete with Chevrolet and Ford. The car's name came from Plymouth Rock in Massachusetts, where the pilgrims landed from the Mayflower in 1620. In fact, a stylized representation of the Mayflower

pony car

has traditionally served as the Plymouth's emblem. The car is produced and marketed by the Chrysler-Plymouth Division of Chrysler Corporation.

ply rating
Index of a tire's strength. Originally, the ply rating was simply the number of plies in the carcass. With modern, improved ply materials, though, it is possible to achieve the equivalent of an x-ply rating with fewer than x plies. In other words, the ply rating is now often greater than the number of plies.

PN
Part number, alphanumeric designation of a part or tool in a catalog.

pneumatic tools
Tools powered by air pressure; also called *impact tools.*

points
See *breaker points.*

polar moment of inertia
See *moment of inertia.*

pole
In oval track or road racing, the starting position on the inside of the front row. Theoretically, the car on the pole is ahead at the start of the race because it has no other cars to pass before reaching the first turn. The pole is usually awarded to the fastest qualifier, except in the case of an inverted start, when it goes to the slowest qualifier.

police options
High-performance equipment for a new car ordinarily available only to law enforcement authorities, and not to the general public.

polished
Intake and exhaust passages which have been refinished with the smoothest possible surfaces, eliminating rough spots sometimes left by factory casting techniques.

polymerization
Chemical reaction in which many small molecules combine to form larger, more complex molecules, with a higher molecular weight and different chemical properties.

poly lock
Type of rocker arm lock nut that has a set screw to add extra force so that the assembly will not vibrate or rotate loose.

Poncho
Pontiac, see below.

ponies
Horsepower, as in "there's a lot of ponies under the hood."

Pontiac
What is now the Pontiac Division of General Motors originated as the Oakland Motor Car Company of Pontiac, Michigan in 1907. Oakland was acquired by General Motors two years later and, as the Oakland Division of GM, it offered the first Pontiac in 1926. The new make soon outshone the old one and, by 1932, the Oakland name was phased out. The Pontiac was named for its city of origin which, in turn, was named for an 18th century chief of the Ottawa Indians.

pony car
Compact two-door, four-passenger, sports-styled coupe or convertible following a long hood, short deck body style; specifically, the Ford Mustang, Chevrolet Camaro, and Pontiac Firebird, and, during the late 1960s and early 1970s, the American Motors Javelin, Plymouth Barracuda and Dodge Challenger. The word "pony" refers to the trim-size and agile handling of such cars, and is also an oblique tribute to the Mustang as the pioneer of the concept.

Pooch
Porsche.

pop
Special racing fuel, particularly one with nitromethane.

pop-off valve
Spring-loaded relief valve that literally pops off its seat under excessive pressure. Its purpose is to limit or prevent the build-up of too much pressure or boost, such as in a turbocharger.

poppet valve
Valve consisting of a disc at the end of a vertical shaft, used for both intake and exhaust in a four-stroke cycle engine.

pop rivet
Fastener used to hold flat pieces of metal together. A rivet consists of a small shaft of metal, with a head at one end that is larger in diameter than the shaft. The shaft is pushed into a hole through the pieces of metal as far as the head will let it go. Pressure is then applied to the opposite end of the shaft, causing it to burst or pop into a second head, thus sealing the device in place and securing the pieces of metal to each other. Usually, rivets will be placed in a row, near the edges of the metal.

pop the clutch
To engage the clutch suddenly, as in a fast start or rapid shift.

porcelain
Hard, white, non-porous translucent ceramic material used in spark plugs to

P

insulate the center electrode from the spark plug shell.

porcupine head
Cylinder head on the Chevrolet big-block or *rat motor*. When the valve covers are removed, the valve stems appear to stick out at odd angles, like the needles on a porcupine.

Porsche
German sports car. The Porsche company was actually founded by Dr. Ferdinand Porsche in Gmund, Austria in 1948, but moved to Stuttgart, Germany two years later. Dr. Porsche had designed the Volkswagen in the 1930s for Adolf Hitler and the first sports cars to bear his name were VW-based. These evolved in the Type 356, the car that made Porsche's name internationally. Today, the company builds a broad line of generally expensive sports cars. It also does consulting work for other manufacturers.

port
See *exhaust port* and *intake port*.

portable boring bar
Tool for boring engine cylinders that can be used without the engine being removed from the vehicle.

portable crank grinder
Tool that can resurface rod journals without removing the crankshaft from the engine.

port bowl
Area of the port next to the valve head.

porting
To enlarge intake and exhaust passages for better engine breathing. An engine which is ported is usually *polished* and *relieved* at the same time.

port injection
Fuel injection system that injects directly into the individual intake ports.

port runner
Partition in the intake manifold that directs air or air/fuel mixture to the individual cylinders.

Pos-A-Traction
Brand of tires, tubes and wheels, *not* a limited-slip differential. For that, see *Posi-Traction*.

posi
Term for limited-slip differential derived from Posi-Traction, a Chevrolet tradename, but often used generically. See *limited slip* and *Posi-Traction*.

porting

positive camber
Outward tilt at the top of the wheels on a vehicle, as viewed from the front or rear, measured in degrees. See also *camber* and *negative camber*.

positive crankcase ventilation
Engine emissions control system that prevents crankcase vapors from passing into the atmosphere by ducting them into the intake system to be burned with the air/fuel mixture.

positive displacement pump
Engine-driven air or liquid pump which displaces substantially the same amount of air or liquid per revolution, regardless of engine speed. A Roots-type supercharger is an example of a positive displacement air pump.

positive offset
Wheel rim placed outward from the center of the mounting flange. See *wheel offset*.

positive pole, positive post
Positive terminal on a battery, usually the larger of the two terminals, and may also be color-coded red in contrast to the negative terminal, color-coded green or black.

Positive Traction
Buick limited-slip differential.

positive wiping seal
Valve stem seal that maintains positive contact with the valve stem to wipe off excess oil.

Posi-Traction
Chevrolet limited-slip differential. See also *Anti-Spin* (Oldsmobile), *Equa-Lok* (Ford), *Positive Traction* (Buick), *Safe-T-Trak* (Pontiac), *Sure-Grip* (Chrysler), *Trac-Lok* (Jeep), *Traction-Lok* (Ford) and *Twin-Grip* (AMC).

post
Battery terminal.

post-start
Time from cold-start to warm-up of an engine.

pot
1. Carburetor.
2. Short for *potentiometer*, see below.

potentiometer
1. Electrical instrument for measuring an unknown voltage or potential difference relative to a known voltage. *(Cont.)*

power slide

2. Three-terminal *variable resistor* with an adjustable center connection; used to adjust volume in radio receivers.

pounds-feet
Measure of torque. One pound-foot is the force required to lift one pound one foot. Ten pounds-feet is the force required to lift one pound ten feet or ten pounds one foot—or, for that matter, two pounds five feet or five pounds two feet, or any other combination with a product of ten. Some engineers prefer to limit the use of the term "pounds-feet" (lbs-ft.) to the torque produced by an engine, and to use "foot-pounds" (ft-lbs.) to describe the torque needed to tighten a bolt or nut properly. See also *foot-pounds* and *torque*.

poured bearings
Bearing formed by pouring molten *babbit* into bearing journal housings, allowing the material to cool, and then align-boring it to a specified size.

pour on the coal
To accelerate rapidly.

pour point
Lowest temperature at which an oil, whether a fuel or a lubricant, will flow freely.

powder puff race
In auto racing, an event strictly for women drivers.

power brakes
Brakes with a hydraulic or vacuum assist that reduces the effort required of the driver to slow or stop the vehicle.

power break
In starting a drag race in a car with an automatic transmission, holding down the brake pedal firmly while revving the engine, then simultaneously releasing the brake and flooring the accelerator to get the quickest possible break from the starting line.

power hop
See *axle tramp*.

power oversteer
Loss of traction at the rear wheels as the throttle is applied while cornering; the rear of the car will swing toward the outside of the turn.

power shift
Same as a *bang shift* or *speed shift*.

power slide
Controlled four-wheel skid used in dirt track racing to maintain speed through a turn. In a power slide, the driver controls the vehicle with the throttle rather than the steering; applying power will force the car to the outside of the turn, while easing off will allow the car to drift to the inside. See also *drift*.

power steering
Steering system with a hydraulic assist that reduces the effort required of the driver to steer the vehicle.

power stroker hone
A honing machine used to recondition connecting rods that utilizes a power driven cradle to stroke the rod back and forth during the machining process.

power take off
On some four-wheel-drive transfer cases, an output shaft for driving external accessories, such as a winch.

power-to-weight ratio
Relationship of horsepower to vehicle weight; a 100-horsepower car which weighs 2000 pounds has 0.05 horsepower per pound. Do not confuse with *weight-to-power ratio*.

powertrain
Combination of the engine, transmission and final drive. Not the same as *drivetrain*.

power valve
Carburetor valve which opens during acceleration to increase the fuel flow.

ppm
Parts per million, the number of parts of a particular substance in a total of one million parts, used as the measure of exhaust pollutants. For example, the amount of unburned hydrocarbons in exhaust can be expressed as the number of parts of hydrocarbons in a total of one million parts of exhaust.

prang
Collision of vehicles.

precombustion chamber
Small, supplementary combustion chamber in which air/fuel mixture is ignited. The precombustion chamber is usually identified with diesel engines, where such a chamber contains an air intake valve, a fuel injector and a glow plug. However, they have also been used in some gasoline engines, such as the Honda CVCC.

preheater
In a diesel, a glow plug used to heat the precombustion chamber before the engine is started.

preheating
In welding, heating the weld area of metal beforehand to avoid thermal shock and stress during the welding itself.

preignition
Premature combustion of air/fuel mixture *before* the spark plug fires, resulting in a knocking or pinging noise. Preignition can have a variety of causes, from hot carbon deposits in the combustion chamber to *auto ignition* of the mixture. It is similar to *detonation*, but there's an important difference between the two: Detonation occurs *after* the spark plug has fired, not before.

preload
1. In chassis tuning, to transfer weight from one side of the car to another to compensate or adjust for the calculated lateral weight transfer during cornering.
2. Pressure applied to a part during assembly or installation.

prerun
1. To test a rebuilt engine before installing it in the vehicle.
2. To reconnoiter an off-road race route. See *prerunner*.

prerunner
In off-road racing, a vehicle built for reconnoitering the route of an upcoming event. In some cases, the prerunner vehicle doubles as a chase truck, carrying replacement parts, fuel and other supplies in case the racing vehicle breaks down.

prelube
To apply lubricant to the parts of a rebuilt engine before firing it up.

press-fit
To fit one part into another by pressing them together, generally with a hydraulic press. For example, some types of wrist pins are press-fit to attach the connecting rod to the piston.

pressure-balanced ring
On a piston, a compression ring that has a ceramic coating for better sealing against the cylinder wall.

pressure bleeder
Tool to remove or bleed air from a vehicle's brake system.

pressure drop
Loss in fuel pressure at the output end of an overly long fuel line.

pressure relief groove
On a piston, a small groove cut into the ring land between the grooves for the compression and scraper rings to equalize combustion pressure between those two rings.

pressure test
Procedure for testing an engine block and heads for external leaks. Water passages are blocked off and air is forced into the engine under pressure, usually at about 60 PSI. Soapy water is then sprayed on the engine and bubbles will form wherever there are leaks.

pressurized carburetor
On a turbocharged engine, a carburetor which mixes fuel with air under pressure from the turbo.

prick punch
Small, hand-held tool used to make a small mark, to act as a guide for a *center punch*. The prick punch has a finer point and higher angle than the center punch, and its mark makes it easier to locate the center punch. See also *center punch*.

primary brake shoe
On a drum brake, the front or leading shoe.

primary circuit
1. Electrical circuit of the primary windings in an ignition coil.
2. Main fuel passage in a carburetor, feeding the main jet.

primary damage
In bodyworking, the damage sustained during initial impact in a collision.

primer
First coat of paint applied to vehicle bodywork, usually providing a dull, flat finish. The primer is often the most important coat of paint. In addition to protecting the body from rust, it also seals off old paint and provides adhesion for the top coats.

primer-sealer
An undercoat of paint which provides adhesion for the topcoat, and which seals old painted surfaces or new primer coats that have been sanded.

primer-surfacer
High-solids primer which fills small imperfections in bodywork, and which usually must be sanded.

prindle
Standardized shift pattern for automatic transmissions, i.e., *PRNDL*.

production
Standard factory version; same as *stock*.

progressive-rate springs
Vehicle suspension springs which stiffen under load. The *spring rate*, in pounds per inch or newtons per millimeter, increases as the springs deflect under added weight.

Prometheus
Acronym, somewhat tortured, for Program for European Traffic with Highest Efficiency and Unprecedented Safety, a joint research and development effort established in 1986 by major European automakers to study how telecommunications technology can improve the safety and efficiency of European roads. Prometheus was a personality in Greek mythology who stole fire from the gods of Olympus and gave it to man. No, we don't get the connection, either.

prony brake
On an older *dynamometer*, a friction device to measure engine output. The prony brake consisted of a hinged collar, or brake, clamped around a drum splined to the end of the engine's driveshaft. Attached to the collar was an arm which, at its other end, bore down on a scale. As the drum was rotated by the engine, it tended to take the collar with it. But the rotation of the collar was prevented by the arm, and the force necessary to stop the motion of the arm was shown on the scale. That force in pounds was multiplied by the length of the arm in feet, providing a torque figure in *pounds-feet*. The use of the prony brake is the source of the terms *brake horsepower* and *brake torque*.

propane
C_3H_8, gaseous fuel that becomes liquid when compressed. Propane is similar to butane, but has the advantage of a freezing point of 44 degrees below zero F., whereas butane freezes at 31 degrees above zero F.,

making it unsuitable for use in winter weather. Both propane and butane are forms of *LPG*, or *liquified petroleum gas*.

proportioning valve
In a vehicle brake system, a hydraulic valve which varies the braking force at the front or rear wheels, depending on pedal pressure, vehicle load and front-to-rear weight transfer, in order to provide efficient braking without wheel lock-up.

Pro Stock
Drag racing category for compact passenger cars with big block V-8s, displacing a maximum of 500 cubic inches. Pro Stock rules allow a drag racer to assemble a latter-day equivalent of a muscle car or Super Stock which, of course, are no longer available as production models. Under NHRA rules, a Pro Stock may use a big V-8 and rear drive in a late-model chassis and body designed for front drive; thus the category influenced the development of the *silhouette car*.

Pro Street
Compact passenger car with a heavily modified big-block V-8 and rear drive built for street use. The Pro Street is obviously patterned after the Pro Stock drag car but, because it doesn't necessarily conform with racing rules, it's sometimes even wilder. The Pro Street may have a blower, for example, an item not allowed in Pro Stock. Many Pro Street cars also have a narrowed rear axle with oversized rear tires. During the 1980s, the Pro Street became a pre-eminent form of hot rod.

Pro Stock

Pro Street

protest
To accuse a competitor in a race of a rules violation; usually, the protest is filed by the racer who finished immediately behind the one being challenged.

prototype, proto
1. An individually built test version of a new car design.
2. In sports car racing, an individually built vehicle running in a category where entries do not have to be *homologated*.

PSI
Pounds per square inch, US unit of pressure or stress.

psych
To intimidate a competitor, particularly at the start of a drag race, in hopes of provoking him into a driving mistake that will cost him the match. In road or oval track racing, the technique is to constantly put pressure on the driver in front by "filling his mirrors" and feigning a pass, in hopes of forcing him into a mistake.

PTO
See *power take-off*.

puck
1. Slang for *brake pad*.
2. Valve adjusting shim.

puffer
Supercharger.

pull
Condition when the brakes are applied and the vehicle veers to one side or the other without being steered in that direction.

puller
Tool designed to remove a specific part from a vehicle by pulling it off or out, such as a *brake puller* or *gear puller*.

pulley
Belt-driven, wheel-shaped device used to drive engine accessories.

pulsed air injection, pulsed air system
Device in an exhaust emissions system which injects pulses of fresh air into the exhaust to aid in the burning of the exhaust gasses.

pulse period, pulse time
See *pulse width.*

pulse ring
Ring found on a crankshaft that triggers a sensor used with the onboard computer to control ignition timing.

pulse width
Time in milliseconds that a fuel injector is open and delivering fuel.

pump gas
Standard gasoline, without any special additives for higher performance; any motor fuel dispensed at gas stations and available to the general public. Some classes of racing particularly amateur ones, specify pump gas only.

pump screen
Filter to remove particles of debris from oil pump gears.

pump-up
Condition when a hydraulic valve lifter has developed more pressure than needed to keep the lifter in contact with the cam, preventing the valve from seating properly.

punch
Fuel, same as *pop.*

punch it, punch off
To apply full throttle; same as *plant it.*

pure stock
Vehicle which conforms to all original factory specifications.

purge
To eliminate unwanted air or liquid from a system.

pur sang
French for "pure blood" or "thoroughbred," sometimes used to describe a particularly fine car, especially such French classics as the Bugatti or Hispano-Suiza.

push
See *understeer.*

push bar
Bar on the front of a *push car* to prevent damage to either vehicle when push-starting a race car.

push car
Vehicle, usually a truck rather than a car, used to push-start a race car which doesn't have a self-contained starting system.

pusher
Rear-engined vehicle, particularly a motorhome.

pushrod
On an engine with overhead valves, but not overhead camshafts, the pushrod is a tubular device which transmits motion from the camshaft to the rocker arm, and, via the rocker arm, opens and closes the valve.

pushrod tube
Passage from the engine block to the cylinder head which houses a pushrod.

push start
To start one vehicle by pushing it with another. The pushed vehicle should have its ignition turned on and the transmission in gear but with the clutch pedal depressed. As the two vehicles get up to speed, the one doing the pushing should drop back, and the driver of the pushed vehicle should pop the clutch, engaging the transmission and, hopefully, starting the engine.

pussycat
Smooth, quiet-running vehicle.

put it to the wood
Yet another term for applying full throttle.

put on the trailer
To defeat a racing competitor decisively and, in effect, force him to load his race car on the trailer and take it home.

putter
Custom car that is not built for high performance and is treated very gently, merely for "putting around."

putty
Another name for *body filler.*

pyrolysis
Decomposition of a compound by exposure to high heat.

pyrolytic oven
Oven which uses pyrolysis, with temperatures from 650 to 710 degrees F., to remove grease, oil and rust from the surfaces of engine parts.

pyrophoric
Having the quality of igniting spontaneously when exposed to air.

pyrometer
Instrument to measure extremely high temperatures, beyond the range of a conventional thermometer. A tire pyrometer, for example, is used to measure racing tire temperatures, which generally range from 200 to 250 degrees F.

Q

Q-jet
Rochester Quadrajet four-barrel carburetor introduced by GM's Rochester Products Division (RPD) in 1965. The Q-Jet has small primary bores with triple venturis for precise fuel control at idle and partial throttle, and large secondary bores with increased air capacity for heavy throttle demands.

quad
1. Four-barrel carburetor.
2. Four-wheel-drive vehicle; the 1940 Willys design that evolved into the Jeep was originally called the Quad.
3. Headlight arrangement with four separate lenses, two on either side of the front end.

Quad 4
High performance four-cylinder engine developed by GM's Lansing Automotive Division in the 1980s that features 2 camshafts (DOHC) and 4 valves per cylinder. The H.O. version produced 180 bhp and 160 lb-ft. torque. Quad 4 engines were used by Pontiac, Buick, Oldsmobile and Chevrolet.

quadrant
1. One quarter of a circle; an arc of 90 degrees.
2. Device which shows the position of the gear lever for an automatic transmission. See also *PRNDL.*

Quadra-Trac
Full-time, four-wheel-drive system offered by Jeep on its larger vehicles. Quadra-Trac features an inter-axle differential with limited slip.

quad ring
Rubber or plastic sealing ring with square sides.

quad valve head
Cylinder head with four valves, two intake and two exhaust, per cylinder.

qualify
To earn a starting position for a race, usually by demonstrating a vehicle's performance in an individually timed run or series of runs.

quarter-elliptic spring
One-half of a semi-elliptic spring, cantilevered so that one end is attached to the chassis frame and the other to the axle.

quarter-mile
Standard distance for a drag strip, though there are also eighth-mile and even occasional half-mile strips. The time it takes a vehicle to travel a quarter-mile from a standing start is a universally recognized measure of performance.

quarter panel
Body shop term for a front or rear corner of a vehicle body.

quarter-race cam
Camshaft reground for slightly better than stock performance; not to be confused with a *quarter-speed cam.*

quarter-speed cam
Camshaft that operates at one-fourth crankshaft speed. A conventional half-speed cam rotates once every time the crank turns twice; a quarter-speed cam rotates once while the crank turns four times.

quartz halogen, quartz iodine
Type of high-output lamp used as a headlight, driving light or fog light which has a quartz bulb containing one or more gaseous halogens, such as iodine. In a halogen atmosphere, a tungsten filament can carry a higher current for a given filament size, and thus produce a more brilliant white light. However, the filament also operates at higher temperatures than in a conventional lamp, requiring a bulb of quartz rather than glass. See also *halogens* and *halogen lamp, halogen light.*

Quattro
Full-time, four-wheel-drive system offered by Audi, primarily for improved traction in adverse highway conditions, such as rain or snow, and not for off-road travel.

quench
To harden a metal or alloy, such as steel, by heating it and then cooling it suddenly by plunging it into water or oil.

quench area

Shallow, flat surface within a combustion chamber that is very close to the top of the piston at top dead center. The limited clearance between the quench area and the piston can be used to squeeze air/fuel mixture toward the center of the combustion chamber. In addition, the flat surfaces of the quench area and piston provide conductive cooling that reduces the temperature of the end gasses during combustion and that, in turn, suppresses detonation. Unfortunately, an extensive quench area reduces a combustion chamber's breathing ability, while the tendency to cool the end gasses results in higher levels of unburned hydrocarbons, one of the most significant exhaust emissions. A combustion chamber with little or no quench area will have better breathing and, consequently, will develop higher horsepower, and will also produce fewer unburned hydrocarbons. However, the combustion chamber capacity will be larger and, to achieve a high compression ratio, domed pistons will be needed. A cylinder head with an extensive quench area is a *closed-chamber head*, while one with little or no quench area is an *open-chamber head*. The Chevrolet big-block is one engine that has been available with either type of head but, because of its emissions problem, the closed-chamber version was phased out during the early 1970s. Quench area is also sometimes referred to as *squish area*.

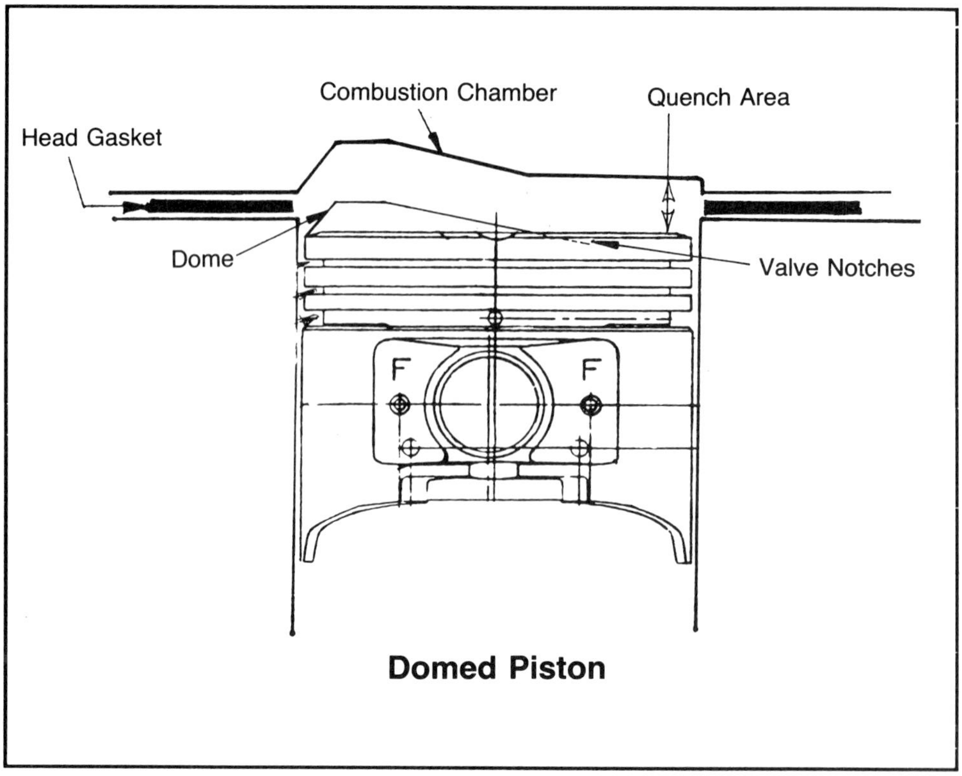

quench area

quick change

On some race cars, a special rear axle center section with gears that can be removed and replaced in just a few minutes, allowing rapid switches in final drive ratio to meet varying track or strip conditions.

quill

Round part of a drill press that can be moved up and down and supports the drill chuck.

Q ship

An innocent-looking vehicle with outstanding performance. The term derives from a type of vessel used by the British Navy during World War II; the Q ship looked like an ordinary freighter but was equipped with concealed heavy armament. See also *sleeper*.

R

race

race
Groove, edge or track in or on which a rolling or sliding part moves. For example, the balls in a ball bearing move in a *race*.

racer
Competition driver. The term is also sometimes applied to a racing vehicle.

racer's tape
See *duct tape*.

rack-and-pinion
Steering assembly with a gear, or pinion, at the end of the steering shaft, engaging a horizontal toothed bar, or rack, which has tie rods at either end attached to the steering arms.

racy bopper
Auto racing groupie.

rad
Radical, a term sometimes used to describe a highly modified engine or vehicle.

radial-ply
Tire design with carcass plies at 90-degree angles to the centerline of the tread, as well as separate belts or plies directly under the tread. See also *bias-ply* and *bias-belted ply*.

radial runout
Condition of a wheel-and-tire assembly when it is out of round; in other words, the radius from the hub to the tread varies.

radiator
Heat exchanger which uses circulating water, or a mixture of water and an additive such as *ethylene glycol*, to discharge an engine's combustion heat into the atmosphere.

radius arms, radius rods
Longitudinal suspension arms used to position a *beam axle*. The rods are usually attached to the chassis frame behind a front axle but ahead of a rear axle. See also *torque arms* and *trailing arms*.

radiused
1. A procedure used to reduce the radius diameter where the valve stem meets the valve head.
2. A type of valve seat that is ground with a radial valve seat grinder to enhance airflow around the valve.
3. Wheelwells that have been cut to a perfectly circular shape, emphasizing and outlining the wheels and tires.

ragged edge
Absolute limit of a car's potential. A racing vehicle that's running on the ragged edge doesn't have any further margin in performance or handling.

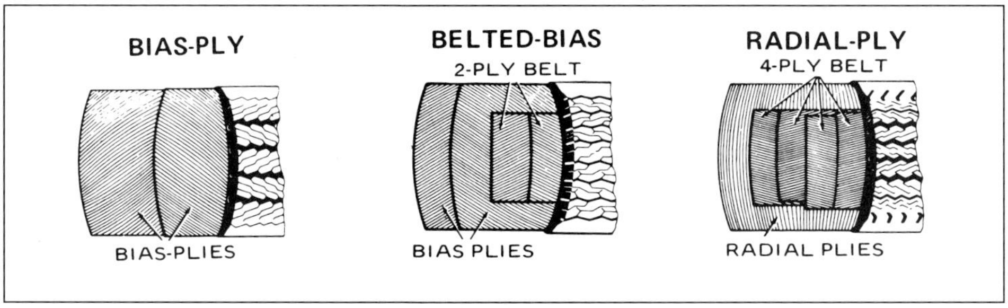

radial-ply

ragtop
Convertible with a fabric top.

rail, rail job
Early dragster without full bodywork, and exposed, bare frame rails. The idea of the rail was to reduce weight to an absolute minimum, even at the loss of aerodynamic efficiency. At the speeds dragsters now reach, though, aerodynamic efficiency has become more important than minimum weight and the frame rails are usually covered with smooth body panels.

rake
Suspension and/or structural design or modifications to lower one end of a car relative to the other end, in the name of aerodynamic efficiency. Generally, the front end and the windshield are raked.

rally
Driving contest, generally for sports cars, in which specified average speeds must be maintained over particular distances. The rally is a test of driving precision rather than vehicle performance.

ram air
1. Intake scoop or duct designed to direct as much air as possible into the carburetor or fuel injection system without supercharging. Unlike *ram induction* and *ram tubes*, ram air doesn't rely primarily on resonance to increase the volume of airflow.
2. With capital letters, the name given to a high performance Pontiac muscle car engine, which was first offered on the 1965 Pontiac GTO. Displacing 389 cubic inches, it produced 360 bhp and 424 lbs-ft. of torque. In 1969, another version was offered, called the Ram Air IV, with a displacement of 400 cubic inches, a peak horsepower output of 370 bhp, and a maximum torque of 445 lbs-ft., which would prove to be the most powerful version offered, until the Ram Air option was dropped in 1971.

ram induction
Intake manifold containing passages of sufficient length to cause a resonant effect at a specific, predetermined engine speed, ramming a heavier charge at that speed. Note that there are similarities between ram induction and both *ram air* and *ram tubes*, but there's an extremely important difference; ram air scoops or ducts and ram tubes are placed ahead of the carburetor, while ram induction is applied after carburetion. See also *tuned exhaust, tuned headers.*

ram tubes
Short tubular stacks on top of carburetors. The length of the stacks are tuned to provide a resonant frequency that forces more air into the carb. Ram tubes are essentially the same as *velocity stacks*. See also *ram induction*, but note the difference.

ramp
Sloping section of a camshaft lobe which raises the lifter from the *base circle* to the actual lift area. See *lobe*.

ramp angle
On a car or truck, the angle formed by lines tangent to the static loaded radii of the front and rear wheels, converging at the point of lowest ground clearance under the middle of the vehicle. Also called *breakover angle*.

rake

R & D
Research and development.

R & R
Remove and replace or remove and repair, a common abbreviation used on vehicle repair orders.

rat, rat motor
Chevrolet big-block V-8, offered in 396-, 402-, 427- and 454-CID versions as regular production options. There were also special aluminum-block 427-, 430-, 465-, 495- and 510-CID rats, built expressly for race cars. As for the name, the Chevy big-block was an outsized companion to the small-block Chevy V-8, called the *mouse motor* because of its compact size and ability to "scare" the Chrysler Hemi or "elephant" motor. So, inevitably, the bigger engine became the rat.

ratchet
Short for ratchet wrench, which consists of a handle with a ratchet at one end, used to twist sockets on nuts and bolts. Also called a *socket wrench*.

reaction time
In drag racing, the amount of time elapsed from the moment the green light flashes on the Christmas tree, to when the car trips the starting line timing lights; in other words, how long it takes the driver to react to the light and apply the throttle. Many drag races are often won or lost by the difference in reaction time.

rear clip
1. In vehicle design, the area of a vehicle from the rear of the vehicle to the B-pillar.
2. In bodywork, to replace the severely damaged rear part of a vehicle, extending as far forward as the B-pillar, with another, undamaged rear section from a similar model.

rear drive
See *rear-wheel-drive*.

rear end
On a rear-wheel-drive vehicle, the differential and final drive assembly.

rear-engined
Automobile layout with the powerplant placed behind the rear wheels and driving them through a transaxle assembly. See also *front-engined* and *mid-engined*.

rear roll center
Center determined by rear suspension geometry around which the rearward part of a vehicle tends to roll. See also *front roll center* and *roll center*.

rear steer
Steering gear positioned behind the front wheel centerline.

rear-wheel-drive
Drivetrain layout which applies power through the rear wheels only. A rear-wheel-drive vehicle may be *front-engined, mid-engined* or *rear-engined*.

rebound
In a vehicle suspension system, the extension outward of the springs and shock absorbers in reaction to *jounce*.

recall
When a new car or truck proves to have a defect, the manufacturer may send out a notice to owners of that particular make and model, recalling the vehicle so that the defect can be corrected. Usually, this simply involves returning the car to the dealership for the repair and there is no charge to the owner. The recall may be initiated by the manufacturer, or it may be ordered by the Department of Transportation (DOT) as a result of consumer complaints about a defect to that agency.

reciprocating engine
Powerplant in which pistons move up and down, or back and forth, as the crankshaft rotates.

recirculating ball
Steering assembly with a worm gear at the end of the steering shaft, engaging a sector gear on the pitman arm shaft, with recirculating ball bearings between the worm and sector gears to reduce friction.

recon
Reconditioned; specifically, used auto part that has been reconditioned.

rectifier
Electrical device to convert an alternator's alternating current to direct current.

red flag
In road or track racing, a signal for all drivers to discontinue racing and come to a stop.

red light
In drag racing, to foul; that is to jump from the line before the starting signal is given. With an electronic starting system, an actual red light flashes when a driver fouls and he or she is disqualified.

red line
1. Maximum recommended engine speed, as indicated by an actual red line on the tachometer. Also referred to as *rev limit*.
2. In auto sales, the absolute minimum price a dealer will accept.

reducer
1. Adapter to allow use of a smaller tool with a larger one.
2. Compound which reduces the viscosity of paint, i.e., thinner.

regulator
See *voltage regulator*.

Reid vapor pressure
Measure of the volatility of liquid fuels, particularly gasoline, expressed in pounds per square inch at a standard temperature of 100 degrees F. or 37.8 degrees C. Oil companies alter the volatility of gasoline to suit seasonal conditions. For summer use, the RVP is down around 9.0 psi to help prevent vapor lock in hot weather; for winter, it's raised to about 12 psi for easier cold starting.

relative pressure
In a fuel injection system, the difference between intake manifold pressure and the system's output pressure.

relative wheel weights
The weight on each of a vehicle's wheels as measured by individual scales under each wheel. Determining and subsequently modifying the relative wheel weights is important in balancing a racing vehicle for specific track conditions.

relay
Electro-mechanical device consisting of an electromagnetic coil, a fixed core and a movable armature. The armature is generally connected to an electrical switch that moves according to whether the coil is energized. Like a switch, a relay is used to open and close circuits, but is usually activated by another switch in a remote location.

release bearing
See *throwout bearing*.

reliability run
Same as a *rally*, but with hot rods instead of sports cars.

relieved
In a high-performance engine, intake and exhaust passages which have been cleared of any ridges or obstructions. An engine which is relieved is usually *ported* at the

measuring relative wheel weight

R

same time. The object of both modifications is to increase airflow through the intake and exhaust systems.

reluctor
Magnetic switch used to fire the spark plugs in an electronic ignition system.

Renault
French automaker, established in 1898 by Louis Renault. In the 1980s, Renault gained control of American Motors Corporation and began replacing AMC's somewhat dated line of passenger cars with new Renault designs. In 1988, Chrysler bought out Renault's interest in AMC and soon dropped the Renault designs. That ended the last of several attempts by Renault to establish itself in the U.S. market.

REO
In 1904, Ransom E. Olds left Oldsmobile, a company he had started in 1896, to establish a new firm. He could not use his surname, which belonged to his first company, so this time he used his initials. REO Motor Car Company built both passenger cars and trucks until 1936, when it dropped the car line and began concentrating on heavy trucks. The company survived as an independent truck manufacturer until 1957, when it was bought out by another truck maker, Whit Motor Company.

replica process
Application of a special, softened plastic to a cylinder wall in order to replicate the wall's surface roughness for easier examination outside the engine.

replicar
Automobile built with modern mechanical components but with special bodywork, usually of fiberglass, designed to resemble one of the great cars of the past. Vehicles which have inspired replicars range from Auburn speedsters and Mercedes-Benz roadsters of the 1930s to Porsche speedsters and Shelby Cobra roadsters of the 1960s.

repo
Vehicle repossessed by a finance company when the buyer fails to make payments on time.

repro
Reproduction, such as repro parts for a car, as opposed to *NOS* or *OEM* components.

resin
Molten plastic part of *FRP*, or fiberglass reinforced plastic.

resistance welding
See *spot welding*.

resistor
Electrical device which reduces voltage flow.

resistor plugs
Spark plugs with built-in resistors which suppress the high-frequency portion of the ignition spark in order to reduce interference with radio or television reception.

resonator
In an exhaust system, a small auxiliary muffler that supplements the main muffler in reducing exhaust noise.

resto
Restoration of an older car.

restrictor plate
In stock car racing, a plate with holes of a specific diameter which must be installed between the carburetor and the intake manifold. It restricts airflow and, thus, reduces horsepower and speed.

restyle
To change the appearance of a vehicle in an effort to make it more distinctive; same as *customize*.

retarder
1. Chemical compound to reduce the rate at which paint dries.
2. On heavy-duty, diesel-powered trucks and buses, a mechanical, electrical or hydraulic device used to slow the vehicle, offsetting the fact the diesel engine doesn't have the manifold vacuum that helps a gasoline engine to slow down when the throttle is lifted. See also *compression braking* and *Jake Brake*.

retread
Used tire from which the old tread has been removed and to which a new tread has been applied.

retrocar
Modern automobile which has been styled to look like an older design. The retrocar differs from the *replicar* in that it isn't patterned after a specific make and model. It's a more generic representation of an earlier type of styling.

retrofit
To install improved vehicle parts in place of obsolete or defective ones. When a new car or truck is recalled by the manufacturer, the purpose is often to replace a defective part by retrofitting a corrected one.

rev
To increase engine speed noticeably. A drag racer will rev his or her engine when the green light is about to flash.

rev counter
Tachometer.

rev limit
Same as *red line*.

rev limiter
Electrical or mechanical device which restricts engine speed. Same as *governor*.

reveal molding
On an auto body, metal trim outlining an opening or depression.

reverse
In customizing, to increase wheel track or tread by installing the rims backwards.

reversed polarity
Condition when the cables are connected to the wrong poles on a battery.

reversion
See *stand off*.

revs
See *rpm*.

rheostat
Variable resistor, operated by knob or handle, used to alter the resistance in a circuit. An example is the dimmer control for instrument panel lighting. Sometimes referred to as a *potentiometer*.

rich mixture
Air/fuel mixture with a higher than normal proportion of fuel. See also *lean mixture*.

ride
1. In auto racing, an opportunity to drive in a particular event or series of events, such as a "ride at Indy" or a ride for the entire Indycar season.
2. One's personal car, a *beater* or *grocery getter*.

ride height

ride height
Vertical distance between the bottom of a vehicle's body-frame structure and the road surface.

ride shotgun
To occupy the right front seat in a car or truck. The term derives from the Old West stagecoach practice of a guard with a shotgun riding alongside the driver.

ridge
Condition in an engine with worn cylinders, caused by the rings wearing away the cylinder walls and leaving a ledge or ridge of metal just below the compression ring.

ridge reamer
Tool to remove cylinder *ridge*.

ridged hone
Cylinder hone that uses positive pressure against grinding stones to remove material from a hole.

right-hand thread
Thread pattern on a bolt or screw that requires that it be tightened by being twisted clockwise, or to the right at the top.

rigid axle
Same as *beam axle* or *solid axle*.

rigid motor mount, rigid transmission mount
Solid mount attaching the engine or transmission to the chassis without any provision for damping vibration.

rim
Outer edge of a bare wheel.

Rimac tester
Tool for measuring valve spring tension.

ring-and-pinion
Combination of the ring gear attached to the differential and the pinion at the end of the driveshaft. Divide the number of teeth on the ring by the number on the pinion and you'll have the *final drive ratio*. See also *ring gear*, below.

ring gear
Large diameter circular gear, such as the ring gear in the final drive assembly described for *ring-and-pinion*. The gearing around the edge of the flywheel engaged by the starter motor is an another example of a ring gear.

ring groove
Slot in a piston wall that holds a piston ring.

ring groove cleaner
Hand tool for cleaning carbon build-up from piston ring grooves.

ring groove spacer
Thin metal strip used to fill the gap between the piston and the ring groove after the groove has been machined.

ring land
Surface of the piston between ring grooves.

ring spacing
Distance of the ring land between grooves.

RO
Repair order.

roach coach
Catering truck.

road racing
Competition on an irregular course with a variety of straights and turns, simulating the variety of terrain found on public roads. Although road racing has traditionally been done on private, closed courses, there are an increasing number of road races, such as the annual Toyota Grand Prix of Long Beach in California, which are held on blocked-off city streets. The main reason for this is to provide exposure for sponsors in markets without closed course racing tracks, and to generate additional revenue for the host city. This trend, however, does not make road racing the same thing as *street racing*.

roadster
1. Two-passenger open car. The traditional roadster was a primitive, low-priced car with a skimpy folding top and removable side curtains rather than roll-up windows. Today, though, the term is applied to any two-passenger convertible, including such plush and costly ones as the Corvette and Mercedes SL.
2. Indycar of the late 1950s or early 1960s which had its front-mounted engine tipped sideways so that the driveshaft to the rear wheels ran alongside the driver's seat instead of underneath it. The result was a lower, wider body that, although a single-seater, looked like a two-passenger open car.

rocker arm
In an engine with overhead valves (but not overhead camshafts), a rocker arm is a pivoting lever in the valvetrain which applies motion originating at the camshaft to open an intake or exhaust valve. The camshaft lobe lifts the tappet or *lifter*, which lifts the

R

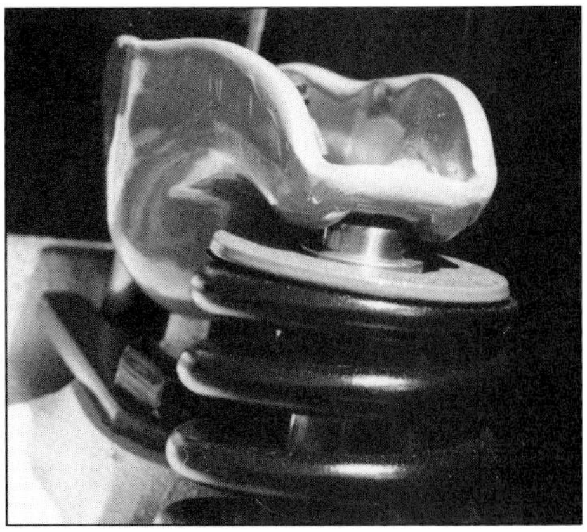

rocker arm

pushrod which, in turn, forces one end of the rocker arm up and the other end down on the valve stem, forcing the valve open. On some engines, the rocker arms in each cylinder head are arranged on a single shaft called, logically enough, a *rocker shaft* or *rocker arm shaft*. In an alternative layout, first used on the 1955 Chevrolet V-8, the rocker arms are simple stampings on individual, spherical pivots. This setup, called ball-type rockers, eliminates the rocker arm shaft; it's also simpler and lighter, and allows for higher engine rpm.

rocker arm ratio
The difference between the upward movement of the pushrod acting on one end of the rocker arm and the downward movement of the rocker arm acting on the valve stem. It is determined by dividing the length from the trunion centerline to the tip, by the length from the trunion to the pushrod seat.

rocker arm shaft
See *rocker arm*.

rocker panel
On an auto body, the sheet metal along the bottom of the body, beneath the doors and between the front and rear wheel openings.

Rocket
Oldsmobile's name for its original V-8 engine, introduced in 1949.

Rockwell test
Technique of testing the hardness of a metal. A small steel ball, 1/16 or 1/8 inch in diameter, or a sphero-conical diamond is pressed under a heavy load into the surface of the metal under test and the depth of its penetration is measured. The Rockwell hardness number is inverse to the depth of penetration, i.e., the shallower the penetration, the higher the number and the harder the metal. See also *Brinell test*.

rod
1. Engine connecting rod.
2. Steering or suspension arm or rod.
3. Abbreviated version of *hot rod*.
4. As a verb, to clean the piping in a radiator.

rod aligner
Tool for checking the alignment of a piston as assembled on a connecting rod.

rod bearing
In a connecting rod, the bearing at the crankshaft end, between the rod and the crankshaft journal. Also called *big-end bearing*, but should not be confused with *rod end bearing*.

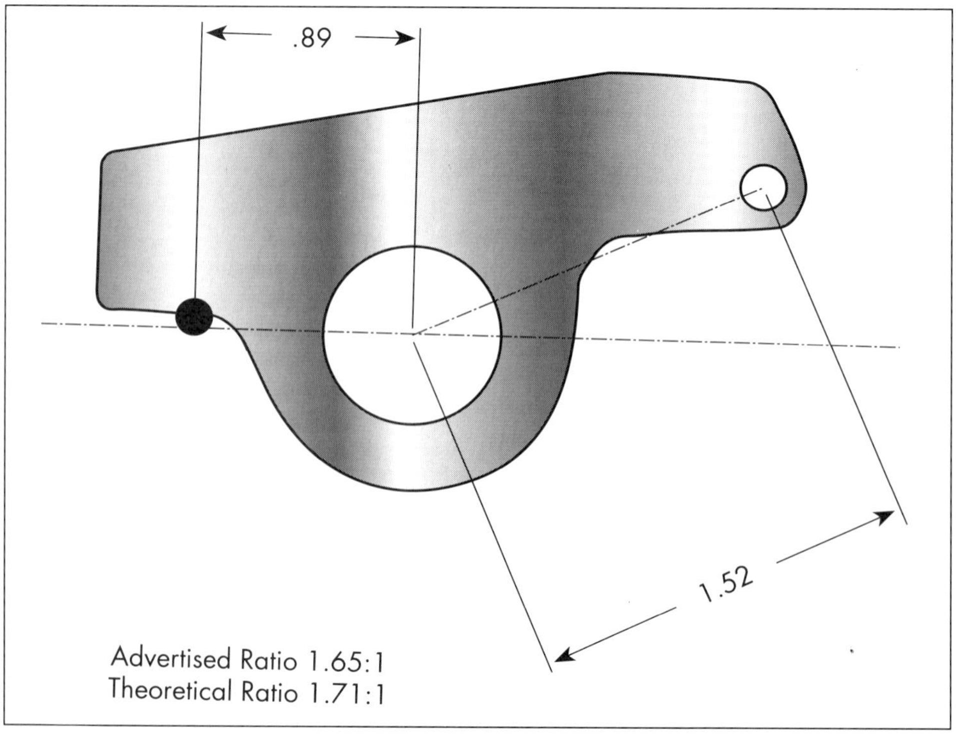

rocker arm ratio

rod end bearing
In a suspension system, spherical bearing used at the end of a suspension rod or arm.

rod boring machine
Device for boring the housing and pin bores of a connecting rod to proper size.

rod length ratio
See *rod ratio*.

rod ratio
Center-to-center length of a connecting rod, divided by piston stroke. Generally, at a given stroke, longer rods seem to provide more power than shorter ones. Also referred to as *rod length ratio* and *rod-to-stroke ratio*.

rod-to-stroke ratio
Same as *rod ratio*.

roll
Rotating motion of a vehicle's sprung mass about its longitudinal axis—or *X-axis*—compressing the springs on one side of the vehicle and extending those on the other side. In other words, the motion of a car's body toward the outside of a turn when cornering or changing direction suddenly.

rollaway
Large tool chest with several drawers, mounted on rollers so that it can be moved about a shop.

roll axis
Longitudinal axis—or *X-axis*—of a vehicle, as defined by an imaginary line passing through the front and rear *roll centers*. See illustration next page.

roll bar
Single tubular bar right behind the cockpit of a race car, usually projecting at least as high as the driver's head, to protect him or her during a rollover. Do not confuse roll bar with *anti-roll bar*. See photo next page.

roll cage
Tubular structure surrounding the cockpit in a race car, incorporating a roll bar at the rear and additional bars above the sides and front. The roll cage not only provides the driver with maximum protection during a rollover, it also adds to the vehicle's overall structural rigidity.

roll bar

roller bearing
Bearing using rollers within an outer ring or *race*.

roller cam, rolly
Camshaft which operates against a small roller at the base of each lifter, rather than directly against the lifter itself. The rollers are supposed to minimize friction and wear, especially at high rpm.

roller chain
Timing chain with rollers engaging the gear sprockets for reduced friction.

roller lifter
A hydraulic valve lifter with a roller at its base, used with a roller camshaft. See *roller cam* and *hydraulic valve lifter*.

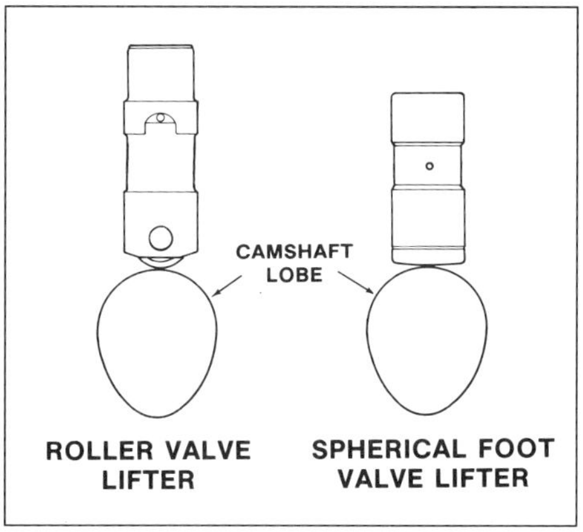

roller lifter

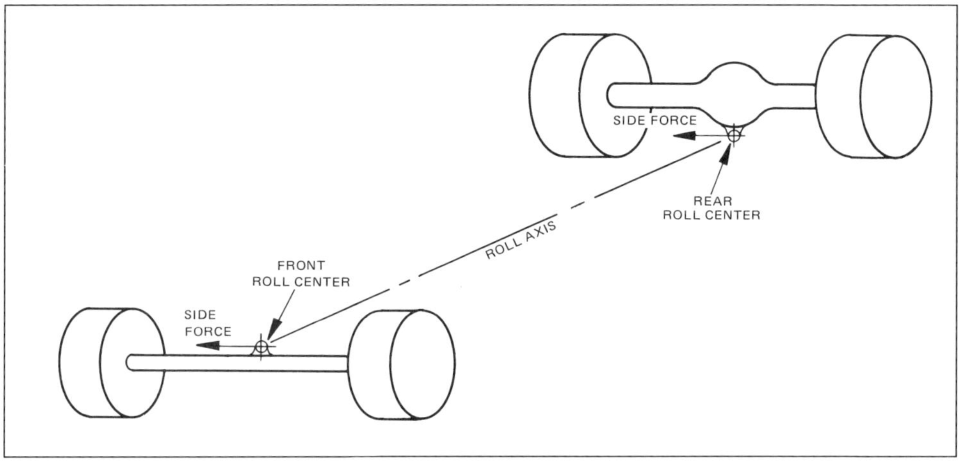

roll axis, roll center

rollout
In drag racing, the distance a race car travels at the beginning of a run before the front tires clear the stage beam and start the clock. There's an allowable margin of only a few inches within a legal staging position, and it varies with such factors as the height of the timing lights and the diameter of the car's front tires. *Shallow staging*, i.e., using maximum rollout, allows the car to gain momentum before the clock starts and can result in a quicker ET. *Deep staging*, on the other hand, using minimum rollout, can result in a higher ET and is sometimes used by a driver trying to avoid *breakout*.

rollover
Accident in which a vehicle rolls upside down.

roll centers
The points at the front and rear about which a vehicle's sprung mass will roll. The height of the roll centers is determined by the vehicle's suspension. In a rear-wheel-drive car with independent front suspension and a solid rear axle, the front roll center will be lower than the rear. Thus, the *roll axis*, the imaginary line connecting the front and rear roll centers, will slope downward toward the front.

roller
1. A race car offered for sale without the engine.
2. With a capital "R," *Rolls-Royce*.

rolling radius
Under the weight of a vehicle, the vertical distance between the center of a wheel and the contact point of the tire on the ground.

rolling resistance
Forces acting against the forward motion of a vehicle, consisting primarily of mechanical friction. Rolling resistance does not include *aerodynamic drag*.

rolling start
In closed-course racing, when the race cars are given the green flag by the starter as they complete the *pace lap*. If the starter determines that the field is not lined up correctly, or if someone is trying to *jump* the start, he will withhold the green flag and force the field into another pace lap.

Rolls-Royce
England's most famous luxury car was the result of a partnership between C.S. Rolls, a wealthy entrepreneur, and Henry Royce, an engineer, beginning in 1904. From the outset, the Rolls-Royce was a vehicle of the highest quality, advertised quite simply and unabashedly as "The Best Car in the World." From 1921 to 1931, Rolls-Royce built cars in the United States, at a plant in Springfield, Massachusetts. In 1931, Rolls-Royce bought out Bentley, developed its own new car to carry that nameplate, and introduced it in 1933 as "The Silent Sports Car." Today's Rolls-Royces and Bentleys have a great many parts in common but the company has tried to overcome an impression that the Bentley is merely a badge-engineered Rolls by presenting the Bentley as the ultimate in a high-performance sedan and the Rolls as the ultimate in a luxury vehicle. See also *Bentley*.

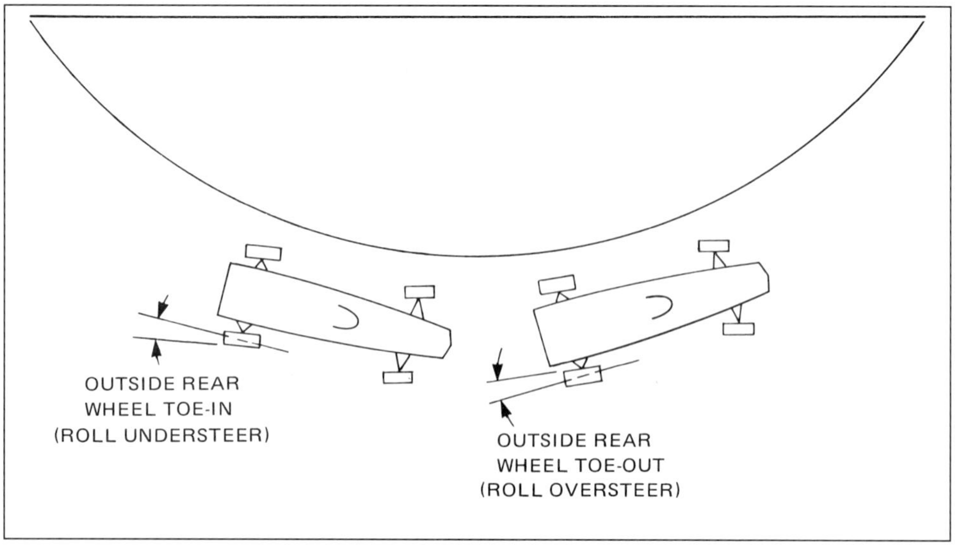

roll steer

roll steer
The amount and direction the rear axle might cause the car to steer as it moves through its travel when the body rolls during cornering. The preferred design characteristic is to have as little roll steer as possible, and if there is any, it should be in the understeer direction. *Roll understeer* makes the car turn less as the body rolls; *roll oversteer* makes the car turn more as the body rolls.

roll stiffness
Resistance of a vehicle's suspension to the rolling of the vehicle's mass, measured in pounds per inch of spring travel.

RON
Research octane number. See also *octane number*.

rookie
Racing driver competing in his or her first season in a particular event or series of events.

Roots supercharger
Positive-displacement, mechanically driven blower with hourglass-shaped rotors. The *GMC supercharger* long popular in drag racing is an example of a Roots unit. The blower evolved from a water pump invented in 1859 by Philander H. and Francis M. Roots of Indiana. It isn't connected in any way to British automaker Sir William Rootes, and should not be referred to with the spelling of his name.

rope seal
Engine seal made of a rope-like asbestos material.

rosette weld
See *plug weld*.

rosin
In drag racing, a sticky substance applied to the rear tires for better traction *off the line*.

rotary engine
1. In modern use, a powerplant with a three-sided rotor in a trochoidal or slightly hourglass-shaped oval chamber. Also called a "Wankel engine," after its inventor, Felix Wankel.
2. Historically, a form of radial engine used in early aircraft in which the crankcase and radially arranged cylinders rotated with the propeller around a stationary crankshaft. This type of rotary powerplant had become outmoded by the end of World War I.

rotary valve
In a two-stroke engine, a semi-circular, rotating disc in the cylinder wall which opens and closes the intake port.

rotator
In the cylinder head, a device which rotates a valve as it is actuated, in order to reduce carbon build-up on the valve.

rotor
1. Any mechanical device which rotates in operation, such as the rotors in the *Roots supercharger* and *Wankel engine*.
2. In a conventional auto ignition system, the rotating device in the distributor which momentarily connects the high voltage from the coil to each spark plug in turn.
3. On a disc brake, the disc itself which is connected to the wheel and rotates with it.

roundy-round racing
Oval track racing of any kind.

rotor, def. 3

Rover
Rover was founded in 1904 and, today, is the final survivor of a series of mergers and reorganizations that took place during the 1970s and 1980s that consolidated most of England's largest automakers into a single, government-owned conglomerate. Rover's most recent foray in the U.S. car market was with the Sterling, which featured a British-designed body on what was essentially the platform of Honda's Acura Legend. However, the Sterling proved unsuccessful and was withdrawn from the U.S. market in 1991.

rpm
Revolutions per minute. In an engine, the term means crankshaft revolutions per minute and is the standard measure of engine operating speed. It can be applied to any rotating part, however, such as the gearset, driveshaft, axle shafts and even the wheels and tires. Note that the term "rpms" is incorrect, because the "r" for "revolutions" already implies the plural.

running board

RPO
Regular production option, item of new car equipment available to any buyer. On lower-priced cars, an automatic transmission, power steering, power brakes and air conditioning would all be examples of RPOs. See also *LPO*.

RTV
Room temperature vulcanizing, i.e., curing an aerobic sealing compound made of silicone rubber.

rubberized cork
Mixture of rubber and cork sometimes used as a gasket material.

rumble seat
Folding external seat in the rear deck of some older 2-door coupes, convertibles and roadsters.

rumper
Big, high-performance engine that idles roughly and noisily due to an aggressive camshaft profile. Same as *loper*.

running board
On many older cars, a flat step stretching between the front and rear fenders to help passengers get in to and out of a vehicle. Today, they are no longer used on cars because the lower floors on most modern automobiles make them unnecessary. However, they are still available as an accessory on many light trucks and sport-utility vehicles, especially those built with high ride height for good ground clearance.

running gear
The undercarriage of a vehicle and all the mechanical components attached to it, including steering, suspension and drivetrain.

running on
Condition when a spark ignition engine continues to run after the ignition system has been switched off, usually as the result of hot spots such as carbon deposits in the combustion chambers. Same as *auto ignition* and *dieseling*.

runout
The amount any rotating device may *wobble* in or out of its plane of rotation.

run whacha' brung
Run what you bring to a racing event, especially a drag meet, open to all types of cars, including those which don't necessarily conform to specific class rules.

rust
See *oxidation*.

rust converter
A liquid sprayed on bare metal to eliminate light surface rust, and to chemically alter the steel to stop and/or slow down further rusting. Rust converters can be painted over.

rust inhibitor
Chemical added to the coolant in a vehicle's radiator to reduce the build-up of rust.

RV
Recreational vehicle, such as a camper, travel trailer or motorhome; same as *rec vee*.

RVP
See *Reid vapor pressure*.

RWD
See *rear-wheel-drive*.

RYY
Mandrel developed by Sunnen Products to hone pistons and rods, with a double-wide stone that allows it to skip over piston pin hole slots.

Rzeppa joint
Constant velocity U-joint with outer and inner races connected through balls in curved grooves and positioned by a cage between the two races.

R

S

SAAB
Swedish car. Svenska Aeroplan Aktiebolag, which is what SAAB stands for and which means Svenska Aircraft Company, began manufacturing automobiles in 1950. The SAAB has always been a front-drive car. Early models had two-stroke, two-cylinder engines of German DKW design, which were upgraded to three-cylinder units in 1955. In 1967, SAAB introduced its first car with a four-stroke engine, using a German Ford V-4. In 1968, the two-stroke engines were dropped and SAAB merged with Scania-Vabis to form SAAB-Scania. During the 1980s, control of the firm was acquired by General Motors.

SAE
Society of Automotive Engineers, 400 Commonwealth Drive, Warrendale, Pennsylvania 15096-0001; (412) 776-4841. Professional organization for automotive and aircraft engineers.

SAE horsepower
Corrected brake horsepower of an engine, as determined by dyno testing in accord with SAE standards, including an ambient temperature of 60 degrees F. (15.6 C.) and barometric pressure of 29.0 inches of mercury (98.2 kilopascals). See also *brake horsepower* and *corrected horsepower*.

SAE standards
Standards for automotive and aircraft engineering testing and measurement established by the Society of Automotive Engineers, such as *SAE horsepower*, above.

Safe-T-Trak
Pontiac limited-slip differential.

safety glass
Laminated glass used for vehicle windshields and windows. Safety glass consists of a layer of tough but transparent plastic between two layers of glass. It is designed to resist shattering on impact.

safety lap
Extra lap taken by the apparent winner of an oval track race, just to be sure of the victory in case an official lap scorer has miscounted.

safety rim
On a vehicle wheel, a groove around the outer edge to provide a lock for the tire bead. See also *J rim*.

safety valve
Valve which opens to relieve excessive pressure or heat.

safety wire
Wire which secures a specially drilled nut or bolt in place. Safety wire is usually made of a strong metal, such as stainless steel.

sail panel
On a closed, notchback body type, the roof rear-quarter panel, extending from the rearmost side window to the rear window.

saloon
1. In the United Kingdom, the same body type we call a sedan. In classified ads for used foreign cars, it is often misspelled "salon."
2. In this country, a place to avoid when you have to drive.

salt flats
Desert dry lake beds used by hot rodders for top speed runs. Bonneville, in Utah, is the most famous example in the United States.

salvage yard
Facility selling used parts for vehicles; same as *junkyard*.

Sam Sled
Drag race driver who is consistently slower than he or she should be.

sandbag
1. As a verb, to obtain equipment without paying for it. For example, a race driver running with factory support may be able to sandbag needed parts.
2. In drag racing, to hold back in the staging area in an effort to choose specific opponents during eliminations.
3. Also in drag racing, to hold speed down during class races in order to fall into a

favorable bracket during final eliminations.
4. In road or oval track racing, to run slower deliberately during qualifying or the race. A driver may sandbag to: conserve fuel and/or parts; psych his competitors out; or avoid dominating the race by a wide margin to prevent future rules changes designed to slow down the car and even out the competition.
5. As a noun, literally a bag, usually canvas, filled with sand, used by metal workers to help shape metal panels. See also *shot bag*.

sandblast
To clean or polish a surface by forcing an abrasive material against it with compressed air or steam.

sandblaster
Machine which or person who sandblasts.

sand cast
To form an object by pouring molten metal into an impression or mold made by a pattern in sand.

sand hole
Unwanted hole in a sand-cast part caused by an accidental shift of sand in the mold prior to pouring in the molten metal.

sandpaper
1. Heavy paper with an abrasive coating on one side, used to clean or polish a surface.
2. As a verb, to clean or polish with sandpaper.

sanding drums, sanding sleeves
Small shaft- or drum-mounted abrasive drum or sleeve for deburring parts.

sanitary, sano
Well engineered and constructed. The term refers to more than the superficial appearance of an engine or a complete vehicle; it means superior workmanship throughout, even where it cannot be seen.

Saturn
New division of General Motors which began building small, low-priced cars in the early 1990s. Although the "Saturn Project" took nearly a decade to realize, it has been successful, helping GM to recapture market share lost to imports during the 1980s.

sauce
Racing fuel.

SAW
See *submerged-arc welding*.

Saybolt viscosimeter
Device for determining the viscosity of liquids, especially petroleum lubricants, by measuring the time it takes for 60 milliliters of the fluid to flow through a capillary tube at specified temperatures between 70 and 210 degrees F. (21 to 99 C.).

SB
See *small block*.

SBEC
Single board engine controller, a single microprocessor used to control engine electrical functions.

Scarab
1. Remarkably advanced passenger car designed by William B. Stout and built in limited volume in Detroit from 1934 to 1939. Stout's Scarab had a Ford V-8 engine in the rear, and a bulbous body without a separate hood or rear deck. It was really a forerunner of the modern minivan.
2. Sports racing and Formula One cars financed and campaigned by American millionaire Lance Reventlow from 1958 to 1962.

scattershield
Reinforced housing around the flywheel and clutch assembly, to protect the driver from flying parts if the flywheel or clutch should come apart. A scattershield is absolutely essential in drag racing for any type of front-engined car other than a mild stock. See also *lover cover*.

scattered
Condition of an engine that has literally blown apart.

scavenge pump
Oil pump in a dry sump system which returns oil to the sump.

scavenger
Powerful car, hard to beat in a race.

scavenging
Forced removal of exhaust gasses from a cylinder during the overlap period, as incoming air/fuel mixture pushes the burned gasses out, or as resonance in the exhaust system draws them out.

SCCA
Sports Car Club of America, 9033 East Easter Place, Englewood, Colorado 80112; (303) 694-7222. Major road racing sanctioning body and a member of *ACCUS*.

schematic
Map-like chart that shows the placement of the wiring in a vehicle and the proper color of individual wires. Also called a *wiring diagram*. See illustration next page.

Schrader valve
Pneumatic valve with a central needle that can be depressed to admit or release air or to allow measurement of pressure. The most familiar example is a tire valve.

scoop
Opening in a body panel which takes in air for cooling or ventilation or, on the hood, which directs air to the engine induction system.

'scope
Short for *oscilloscope*.

score
Scratch or gouge on a finished surface.

SCORE
SCORE International, 31125 Via Colinas, Suite 908, Westlake Village, California 91362; (818) 889-9216; major promoter of desert races in Mexico and the southwestern U.S. SCORE was founded in the early 1970s to stage short-course, spectator-oriented races for off-road vehicles and the acronym originally stood for Short Course Off-Road Enterprises. However, the organization soon became involved with long-distance desert events, particularly in Mexico's rugged Baja California peninsula, and no longer has anything to do with short-course racing.

SCR
Silicon controlled rectifier, device which converts alternating current to direct current.

scrap yard
Facility selling used parts for vehicles; same as *junkyard*.

scraper
Tool to remove unwanted material from a surface.

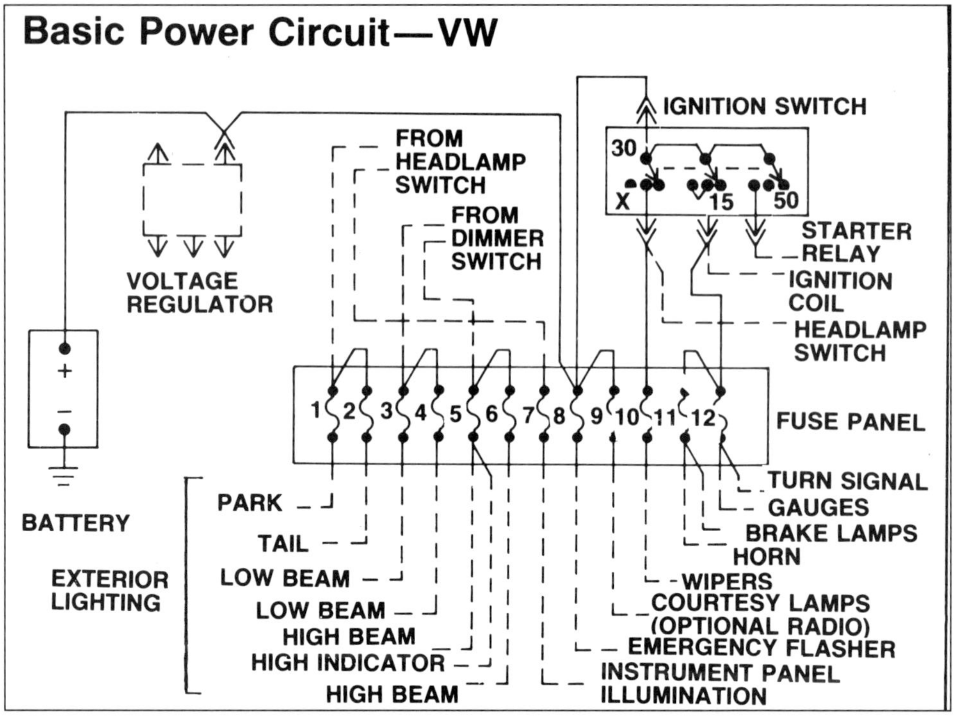

schematic

scraper ring
Second ring from the top on a piston, used to scrape excess oil from the cylinder wall.

scratch
1. As a noun, a mark on a surface, such as a body panel, made by scribing or scraping.
2. As a verb, to make such a mark.
3. Also as a verb, to spin a vehicle's drive wheels suddenly enough to leave tire marks on the pavement.

scratch-built
Vehicle of original design, built from the ground up, i.e., built from scratch.

screamer
Racing vehicle, especially a *dragster*, with spectacular performance.

screw
Final drive gear.

screw it on
To accelerate rapidly.

screw it on the meter
To install an engine on a dynamometer.

scrub
See *tire scrub.*

scrub radius
Distance between the point where the extended centerline of the steering axis would meet the ground and the centerline of the tire contact patch. Same as *steering offset.*

SCTA
Southern California Timing Association, a sanctioning body which originated in the 1930s, during the days of California dry lakes racing, but which now devotes most of its attention to the annual Bonneville speed trials.

scuff
To roughen a surface by scraping it.

screamer

scuff in, scuff off
To run a new set of racing tires enough to wear or "scuff" the manufacturer's protective coating off the tread and bring the tires up to temperature. This is done in drag racing with a *burnout* and in road or oval track racing by weaving the cars back and forth on the track.

scuffs
New racing tires that have been scuffed in. See *scuff in, scuff off,* above.

sea gull
Complainer at a drag race, someone who squawks all the time.

seasoned part
Part that has been *stress-relieved* by being exposed to repeated heating and cooling cycles before being machined.

seat back
Upright portion of a passenger seat.

seat, valve
See *valve seat.*

secondary brake shoe
On a drum brake, the rear or trailing shoe.

secondary circuit
1. Electrical circuit on the output side of an ignition coil, including the secondary windings, the high-tension lead and the spark plug.
2. Secondary fuel passage in a carburetor, fed by the main jet which, in turn, is fed by the primary fuel passage.

sectioned
Car or truck body which has been lowered by removing a horizontal section extending all the way around the vehicle.

section height, section width
Measurements of a tire; the *section height* is the straight distance from the rim to the tread, while the *section width* is the straight distance from the outside of one sidewall to the outside of the other. Dividing the section height by the section width provides the *aspect ratio*.

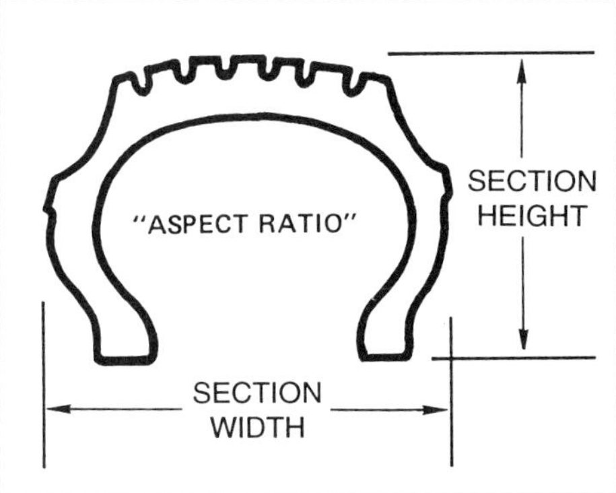

section height, section width

section repair
Body repair that is completed with a section of another vehicle. A *clip* is an extreme example of a section repair.

sector gear
In a *recirculating ball* or *worm and sector* steering gear, the sector gear converts the rotary motion of the worm to the straight-line motion of the pitman arm.

sedan
Two- or four-door closed car with front and rear seats accommodating a total of four to seven passengers, and with a separate trunk at the rear. A two-door sedan differs from a *coupe* in having more room for rear seat passengers.

sedan de ville
Formerly and formally, a chauffeur-driven, four-door sedan with an open cockpit and an enclosed passenger compartment. In this country, such a body was often called a *town car*. Cadillac has appropriated "sedan de ville" for an ordinary four-door sedan and Lincoln has done the same with "town car." See also *brougham* and *coupe de ville*.

Sedanet
Buick designation for a two-door fastback, five-passenger body type offered during the 1940s and early 1950s. Other GM divisions offered the same body type but with different names: Cadillac Club Coupe, Chevrolet Aerosedan, Oldsmobile Club Sedan, and Pontiac Coupe Sedan.

seize
To bind or weld together suddenly, such as a piston seizing to a cylinder wall, usually due to excessive heat caused by a lack of lubrication.

SEMA
Specialty Equipment Market Association, P.O. Box 4910, Diamond Bar, California 91765-0910; (714) 396-0289. Leading trade association for the automotive aftermarket industry. SEMA was founded in the early 1960s as the Speed Equipment Manufacturers Association but, over the years, the name evolved into its present form in order to broaden the organization's scope while retaining the original acronym.

semi
See *semi trailer*.

semi-elliptic spring
Leaf spring or a set of leaf springs of varying lengths stacked with the shorter ones at the bottom and the longer ones at the top, arched upward toward the ends so that they appear semi-elliptic in profile. The center of the spring or springs is attached to a beam axle, usually passing underneath the axle, and the ends of the spring or springs are attached to the chassis frame. There is usually a shackle at the trailing end to allow some spring movement under compression. See also *leaf spring*.

semi-floating axle
Drive axle in which the axle shafts support the vehicle weight as well as transmit power to the drive wheels. Each axle shaft rides in a single bearing within the axle housing and that bearing transfers vehicle weight from the housing to the shaft. See also *full-floating axle*.

semi-metallic brake linings
Brake linings made of steel fibers bonded with organic resins in an effort to combine characteristics of both metallic and organic materials. The result is a compromise that will resist fade at higher temperatures than organic linings but not at as high a temperature as full metallic linings. See also *metallic brake linings* and *organic brake linings*.

semi tractor
Large truck with a *fifth-wheel hitch* to tow a *semi trailer*; sometimes referred to as a *truck tractor* or simply as a *tractor*.

semi trailer
Large cargo trailer with an axle or axles only at the rear; the front of the unit is attached to and supported by a *fifth-wheel hitch* on a *truck tractor*.

sending unit
Electric or mechanical sensing device which measures some physical property, such as pressure or temperature, and transmits the result to a gauge. In an automobile, oil pressure and coolant temperature are examples of properties measured by sending units. Also referred to as a *sensor unit*.

sensor plate
Plate in the air intake path used to measure airflow in a continuous-flow fuel injection system.

sensor unit
See *sending unit*.

separator disc
Metal plate which separates the friction discs on a multi-plate clutch.

sequential port fuel injection
Fuel injection system where each fuel injector pulses in conjunction with the engine cylinder firing order, delivering fuel to the respective cylinder just prior to combustion. Opposite of *continuous flow injection*.

series circuit
Electric circuit in which two or more electric devices are wired in sequence, one to another, so that current must flow through each device to complete the circuit. If one device fails, the entire circuit is broken. Brake lights are often part of a series circuit. See also *parallel circuit*.

series-parallel circuit
Circuit where some devices are wired in series and others in parallel. An example is two loads wired in parallel with each other, but in series with the switch that controls them.

S

serpentine belt

serpentine belt
On the front of an engine, a flat drive belt which follows a complex path, snaking over several pulleys to drive various engine accessories.

serrated nut
Nut serrated on the contact side to reduce the possibility of loosening.

serrated rod cap
Connecting rod cap that has serrated parting edges to maintain alignment with the big end and cap.

setscrew
Type of screw used to secure a small pulley, gear or cam to a shaft; the setscrew usually has a point that fits into a matching recess in the shaft.

setup
Specific engine, drivetrain and chassis arrangement for improved performance.

sewing machine
Small foreign car.

shackle
Connector between the rear of a *semi-elliptic spring* and a mount on the vehicle's frame. The shackle can swing back and forth, allowing the spring assembly to lengthen as it is flattened.

shade tree mechanic
Amateur mechanic, usually with little or no formal training.

shadow graph
Scale for comparing weights of two parts, using a reflected shadow to indicate any difference in the weights.

shaft-mounted rocker arms
Rocker arms that are mounted in a row on a shaft, which provides extra rigidity to the assembly. See also *stud-mounted rocker arms*.

shaker
On some muscle cars, a hood scoop which ducts directly to the air cleaner and carburetor assembly. In some cases, the scoop is attached to the air cleaner through an opening in the hood, instead of to the hood itself, and vibrates when the engine is running; hence the name "shaker."

Shaky
Chevrolet, especially among Ford enthusiasts.

shaved
Bodywork with standard chrome trim removed. The mounting holes for the trim pieces are filled and smoothed over.

shear pin
On a powered device, such as a winch or the propeller on an outboard motor, a pin passing through two or more rotating parts that will break or shear at a predetermined level of force in order to prevent overloading the device.

Shelby
Shelby American, founded in southern California in 1962 by former race driver Carroll Shelby, produced two basic cars during its six years of existence: the Shelby Cobra, which was introduced in 1962 and used the chassis and body of the British AC roadster; and the Shelby GT, which

shaker

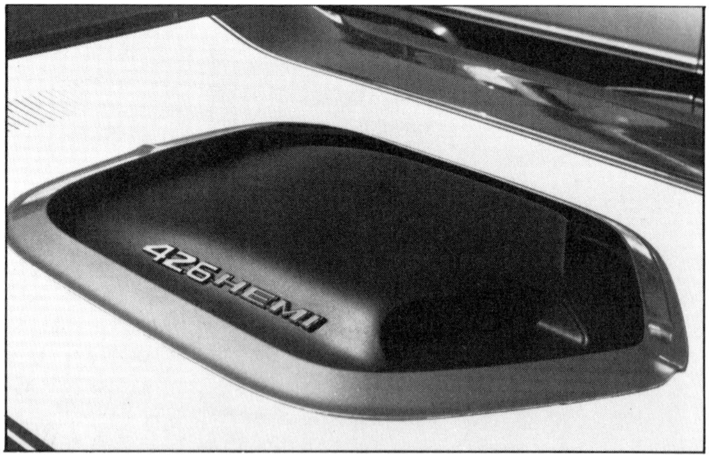

shaft-mounted rocker arms

debuted in 1965 and was based on the Ford Mustang. Early models of both had 4.7-liter Ford small-block V-8 engines but later they became available with 7.0-liter Ford big-block V-8s. Cobra production ended in 1968, effectively shutting down Shelby American. However, Ford took over manufacture of the GT and continued to build it for another two years. In recent years, Carroll Shelby has been associated with Chrysler and contributed to the development of the Cobra-like Dodge Viper. Despite that commitment, he has also produced on his own a limited number of expensive replicas of both the GT and the Cobra.

shell
Body structure, including sheet metal, of a car or truck.

shifter
In a motor vehicle, a control, usually a lever on the steering column, on the front floor, or on a console between the front seats, to change gears in the transmission, whether manual or automatic.

shifting forks
Pronged devices within a manual transmission which move the gears or, in the case of a synchromesh unit, the synchronizers.

shifting rods
Linkage in or on a manual transmission which connect the shifter to the shifting forks.

shift kit
Package of special parts for an automatic transmission to adapt it for high-performance use.

Shillelagh
Chevrolet engine, especially a hot V-8.

shim
1. Thin metal spacer used to adjust the alignment or clearance of a part, such as to adjust valve clearance.
2. As a verb, to install one or more shims.

shim stock
Sheet or roll of metal, of a specific thickness, used to adjust the alignment or clearance between two or more parts.

shimmy
Rapid, side-to-side vibration of steered wheels, usually because of imbalance.

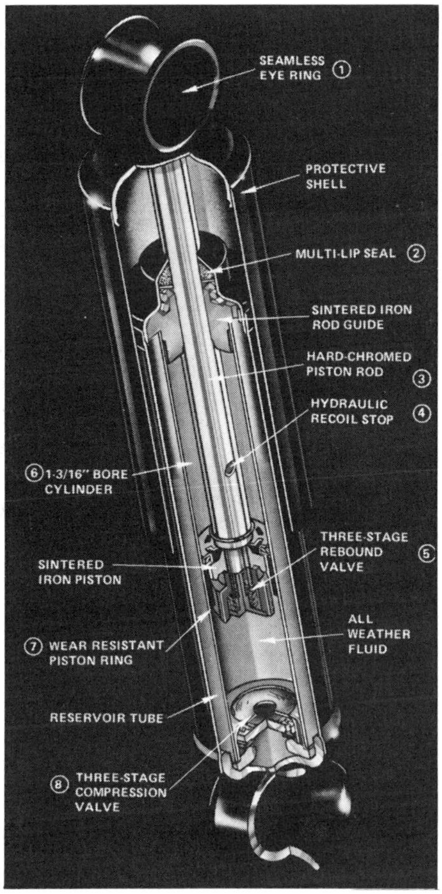

shock absorber

SHO
Super High Output, Ford's designation for a high-performance version of the Taurus, with a special DOHC, 24-valve V-6 supplied by Yamaha.

shock
See *shock absorber*, below.

shock absorber
In a vehicle's suspension system, a damping device used to control spring oscillation. Most shock absorbers on modern cars and trucks consisting of a piston that moves through hydraulic fluid or a combination of gas and hydraulic fluid. Often called *shock* for short.

shoe
Race driver, as in "He's a good shoe."

shoebox
1. Originally, the 1955-56-57 Chevrolet.
2. More broadly, any U.S.-made car with a boxy, non-aerodynamic shape, built from the late 1940s to the late 1950s.

shoot
To spray paint.

shortbed
Cargo box on a short-wheelbase pickup truck. A shortbed is usually only six feet in length, compared with seven or eight feet for a *longbed*.

short block
New engine block with all internal parts, such as the crankshaft, rods, pistons and appropriate bearings, but without parts external to the block, such as the heads and valves, and the intake and exhaust manifolds. The short block replaces the parts of an older engine that are most likely to be badly worn.

short circuit
Undesirable condition when current bypasses the load, returning to the source without doing any useful work. A *short*, as it is called for "short," is usually a result of a bare conductor wire accidentally touching a grounded metal part between the source and the load.

short course
In off-road racing, to take a short cut that bypasses a section of the official course. Searching for places where it might be possible to short course is one of the objectives of a prerun before a major off-road event. See *prerun*, def. 2.

short deck engine
When a basic engine design is available in two different block heights to accommodate crankshafts with significantly different strokes, the lower version is called a short deck and the higher one a tall deck. See also *tall deck engine*.

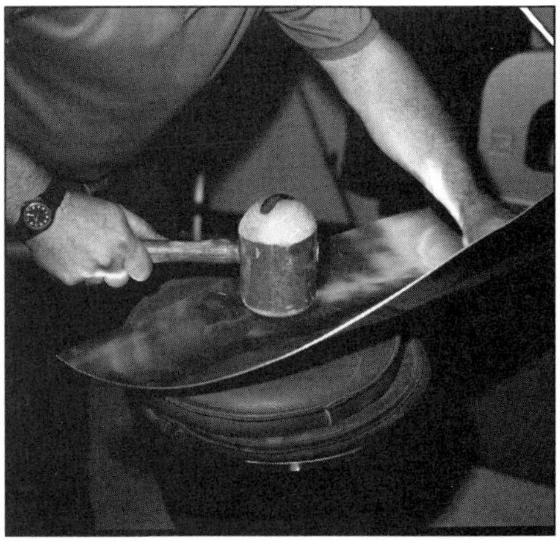

shot bag

shotgun motor

short gear
Final drive with *low gearing*, i.e., a numerically high ratio; opposite of *long gear* or *tall gear*.

short and long A-arms
See *unequal A-arms*.

short-side radius
Small radius in a port between the bottom of the port runner and the bowl area.

short track
Oval race track less than 5/8 mile in length.

shot bag
Leather bag filled with #9 birdshot used by metal workers to help shape metal panels. See also *sandbag*, def. 5. See photo previous page.

shotgun motor
Ford Boss 429 Hemi, a rare Ford big-block V-8 which had aluminum heads with hemispherical combustion chambers; offered in 1969 and 1970, toward the end of the muscle car era.

shot rodder
Individual who is a discredit to the sport of hot rodding, either because of personal behavior or because of running an unsafe or unsanitary car.

shot peen
To peen and, therefore, harden the surface of a metal part by using air pressure to bombard it with steel shot.

show car
Custom car built mainly for display purposes, one that is not necessarily practical for, legal or driveable on the street. Also used to describe a car of such immense value and rarity, that it should only be shown, but never driven. See also *putter*.

show 'n' shine
To display a custom or hot rod in a car show. Technically, the term is reversed, because one would most likely shine the vehicle before showing it.

show through
Appearance of sanding scratches on a surface after it has been painted.

shrink
In metal work, to reduce the area of a piece of metal by heating and hammering it. As the metal shrinks in area, it increases in thickness.

shrink fit
Tight fit achieved by shrinking a part with heat.

shrink wrap
In a vehicle's electrical system, an insulating material used to protect wire splices and junctions at terminals. When heat is applied, the wrap contracts to fit tightly on the wire or terminal.

show 'n' shine

shut the gate

shroud
Metal or plastic duct to direct airflow to the radiator cooling fan.

shrouding
In a combustion chamber, obstruction around a valve, such as from carbon buildup, that interferes with proper airflow.

shunt
1. In road or oval track racing, to bump or shove another car. See also *nerf.*
2. British term for a vehicle accident.

shunt winding
Bypass winding found on some alternators.

shut down
1. To defeat a competitor decisively, especially in drag racing.
2. To stop an engine.

shut-down valve
Valve which turns off the fuel supply to an engine. A shut-down valve is generally a safety requirement for most racing vehicles.

shut off
To release the accelerator and slow a vehicle down.

shut-off area
Portion of a drag strip or dry lakes course, beyond the measured distance for timing, where the vehicle is brought to a stop.

shut the gate
In closed-course racing, to pass an opponent and immediately cut in front, blocking the opponent from passing in turn; or, to *prevent* an opponent from passing on the inside of a turn by taking an early apex. Same as *close the door.*

SI
1. Système Internationale des Unités, or International System of Units, a system of measurement based largely on the metric system, but amplified with scientific units used in modern technology. The Système Internationale was adopted by 36 nations in 1960 and has since been accepted virtually worldwide. It is what most people really mean when they refer to the metric system, whether or not they realize it.
2. SI may also stand for *spark ignition*, just as *CI* stands for *compression ignition.*

siamesed
1. In an engine block, cylinders cast so closely together that there is no passage for coolant between their walls.
2. In an exhaust system, two exhaust pipes joined together.
3. In a cylinder head, two adjacent valves served by a single port.

side-bolt mains
Side-mounted bolts to help retain the main bearing caps in the block and increase the rigidity of the block's lower end.

side clearance
Clearance between a connecting rod and the cheeks of a crankshaft journal.

side-draft carburetor
Carburetor with a horizontal barrel or barrels. See photo next page.

side-guard door beam
Structural member in a vehicle side door designed to keep the door from being crushed inward when it is struck by another vehicle.

side load
Effect of centrifugal force on a vehicle as it goes around a turn.

side molding
Trim on the side of a vehicle to improve the appearance or to provide protection.

side-mount battery
Battery with terminals located on a side of the case, instead of on top.

side oiler
Ford big-block V-8 with the main oil gallery relocated low on the left side of the block, allowing a larger diameter passage, increased flow volume, and more direct routing to the main bearings.

side shift
Steering column-mounted gear shift lever.

side step
In drag racing, for a driver to slide his or her left foot off the clutch pedal suddenly while revving the engine, causing quicker engagement of the clutch than is normally possible by lifting the left foot upward.

side valve
Engine with intake and exhaust valves in the block, beside the cylinders and pistons,

rather than above them in the head. Same as *flathead* and *L-head.*

sidewall
Side of a tire, between the bead and tread.

sidewinder
Vehicle with its engine mounted transversely.

silencer
Device to reduce noise, such as the muffler in an exhaust system.

silencer band
On a disc brake or drum lathe, a rubber strap to cancel vibration and noise caused by inaccurate machining.

silent block
Rubber mount designed to reduce vibration and noise.

silhouette car
Modern 4- or 6-cylinder, front-drive passenger car converted to V-8 power and rear drive, combining a traditional standard in performance with a contemporary appearance or silhouette. The idea has become popular for drag cars such as *Pro Stock, NASCAR* stockers, the *IROC* series, and even *Pro Street.*

silicone
Silicone (with an "e") is a broad term for a group of organic compounds based on the non-metallic element silicon (without an "e"). Silicones are noted for their ability to resist extremes of heat and cold and, in liquid form, for their quality as lubricants.

silicone jackets
Silicone coverings for spark plug wires, used to resist high temperatures.

silicon-killed steel
Steel alloy which has been *killed* with silicon in the molten stage to refine its grain structure. Killing is a process of stopping molten steel from bubbling and combining with oxygen after it is poured into ingots. Generally, finer grain steels are tougher and more ductile than coarser grain steels. Commonly referred to as *SK steel.* See also *aluminum killed steel.*

silver tape
Same as *duct tape.*

side-draft carburetors

single-plane crankshaft
Crankshaft with throws 180 degrees apart, so that they are on opposite sides of the same plane.

single-plane manifold
Intake manifold with a single plenum between the carburetor and the intake ports.

sintered brake linings
See *metallic brake linings.*

6x4, 6x6
Six-wheeled trucks. A 6x4 drives through the rear four of its six wheels, while a 6x6 drives through all six of its wheels, front as well as rear.

six holer
Six-cylinder engine.

six pack
Carburetion system with a total of six barrels, such as a triple two-barrel setup.

six-stroke cycle
Cycle of operation on an experimental engine reportedly developed by Toyota, in which combustion occurs on every third revolution of the crankshaft. The six strokes are (1) intake or induction of air/fuel mixture; (2) compression; (3) combustion, power or expansion; (4) exhaust; (5) intake or induction of air only; and (6) exhaust again. The purpose of the fifth and sixth strokes is to scavenge as much exhaust residue left after the fourth stroke as possible, in order to reduce overall exhaust emissions.

sixty-foot time
In drag racing, the time in seconds it takes a vehicle to cover the first 60 feet from the starting line. It is in this initial stretch that drag races are often won or lost. In most cases, a time of more than 2.3 seconds indicates a sloppy launch, slow reaction time, spinning tires or improper gearing, and there is no way to make up for these deficiencies in the rest of the 1/4-mile—unless the car in the other lane breaks. To be competitive, a drag racing vehicle should cover the first 60 feet in less than 2.0 seconds.

SKD
Semi-knocked down, describing a vehicle shipped in partially assembled form to a final assembly plant. See also *CKD* for *completely knocked down.*

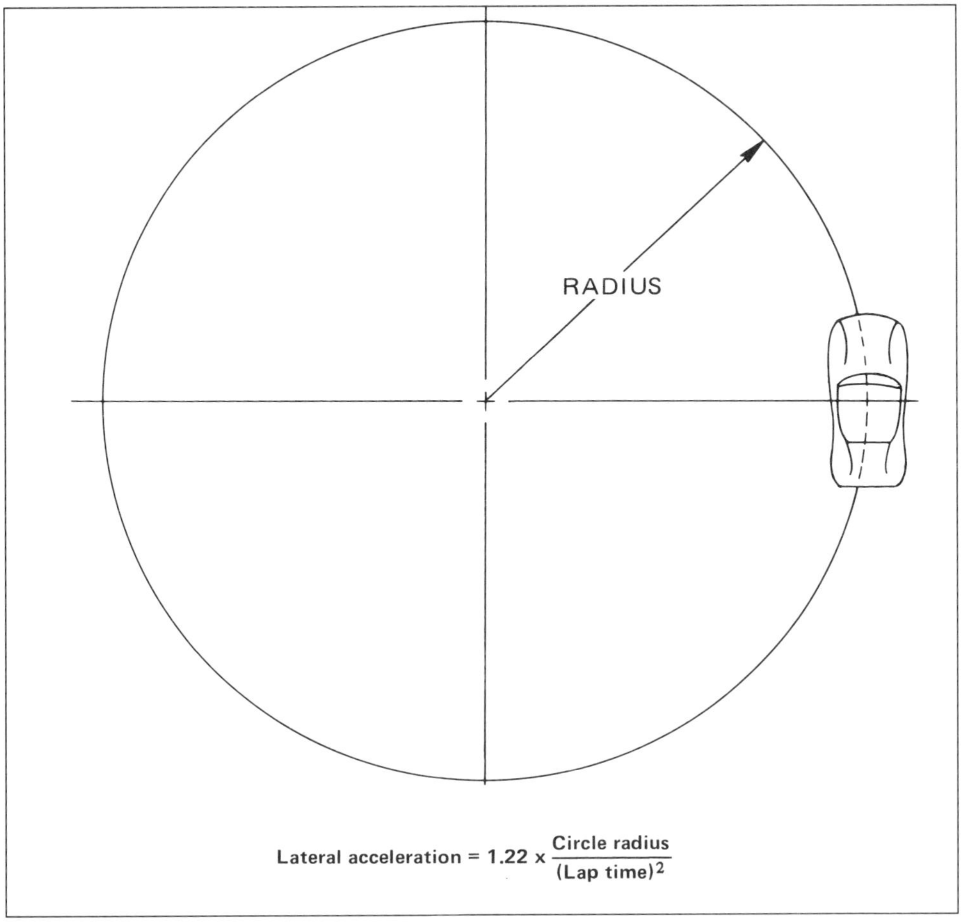

skid pad

skid plate

SK steel
See *silicon killed steel.*

skid pad
Flat area of pavement with a painted circle usually at least 200 to 300 feet in diameter, used to measure a vehicle's grip and *lateral acceleration*. The vehicle is driven around the circle as fast as possible without spinning out, the speed is measured, and the grip and lateral acceleration can be calculated from the speed and the size of the circle.

skid plate
On an off-highway vehicle, a shield under the powertrain to protect the engine and transmission from rocks or other terrain obstacles.

skin
1. Outer sheet metal on a vehicle body structure.
2. Early surface hardening of *RTV*.

skin effect
In a combustion chamber, a thin, unburned layer of air/fuel mixture next to the chamber surface.

skinnies
In drag racing, extremely narrow front wheels used to reduce weight and *rolling resistance*. Same as *pizza cutters*.

skins
Tires.

skirt
See *piston skirt*.

skunk works
In a large company, a small and usually secretive research and development group, working apart from the firm's regular R & D division and often focusing on more advanced or specialized projects. As an example, when Carroll Shelby was doing development work on Chrysler products in the 1980s, he referred to his operation as a "skunk works." The term appears to have originated at Lockheed Aircraft in Burbank, California, in the 1940s, when a group called the skunk works developed some of the firm's most significant and innovative products.

slalom
Contest of speed and maneuverability through an extremely tight, compact course, usually marked with pylons. The

competitors run through the course individually and one who scores the fastest time while knocking down the fewest pylons is the winner. There is usually a time penalty for each pylon knocked down. See also *gymkhana*.

slam
To lower a car or truck by modifying its suspension, i.e., to *slam it*.

slam the door
Yet another term for convincingly beating another vehicle in a race, or preventing one from passing.

slant six
Six-cylinder, inline engine offered by Dodge and Plymouth during the 1960s and 1970s, so called because it was mounted at an angle, rather than vertically, for more clearance under the hood.

slapper
Rectangular hand tool made of wood or metal, used with a slapping action to curve, smooth or flatten sheet metal. A wooden slapper is often covered with leather.

sled runner
Taper on the skirt of a piston from the oil control groove to the bottom of the skirt, usually more than 0.003 inch on each side, to compensate for heat expansion of the piston.

sleeper
Deceptive vehicle, one which looks ordinary but is actually a hot performer. See also *Q ship*.

sleeve
See *cylinder liner, cylinder sleeve*, as well as *dry liner, dry sleeve* and *wet liner, wet sleeve*.

sleeve bearing
Plain bearing.

slicks
Special tires for racing, designed for maximum traction during hard acceleration and cornering. Slicks have no tread for maximum tire contact and feature a broad, flat surface of extremely soft rubber (although compounds of varying hardness are available), which gets sticky when heated.

slider clutch
For drag racing, a special clutch which slips initially, allowing the engine to rev up fairly high before the clutch finally engages.

slinger
Metal disc attached to the crankshaft to keep oil away from the front seal.

slingshot
1. Passing technique, whereby a driver will quickly approach and *draft* another car to gain additional speed, and use the momentum to pull out quickly and pass, as if propelled by a slingshot.
2. Dragster with the cockpit behind the rear wheels, allowing a maximum percentage of the vehicle's overall weight to be placed toward the rear for the best possible traction. The slingshot was developed by the late Mickey Thompson and dominated dragster design until Don Garlits popularized the *mid-engined* dragster.

slip angle
Angle of difference between the direction a tire tread is pointing and the direction the tire is actually going. See also *oversteer* and *understeer*.

slip-in
Part that needs no modification or adjustment for installation.

slip rings
Electrical contact area for brushes on an alternator.

slipper skirt piston
Piston with a very short skirt to reduce weight, and to increase crankshaft clearance, allowing use of longer connecting rods in a block with a relatively *short deck*.

slippery
Streamlined, aerodynamically efficient.

slipstream
Partial vacuum created behind a car at high speeds, creating a pocket of low air pressure or *drag*. See *draft*.

sloper
Fastback body type.

sludge
In an older engine, a buildup of combustion byproducts, gum varnishes, and oil and water that can clog oil lines and interfere with lubrication.

slug
Piston.

slush pump
Automatic transmission.

small block
V-8 engine of no more than 400 cubic inches and usually less than that. The Chevrolet *mouse* and Ford *Cleveland* and *Windsor* powerplants are examples.

smog
1. Originally, a combination of smoke and fog, describing the atmospheric conditions often most prevalent in the Los Angeles, California area, although smog is rapidly becoming a major concern for most metropolitan areas around the world. Smog has evolved into a generic term for all types of air pollution.
2. As a verb, to *smog check* a vehicle.

smog check
Measure of the emissions levels in a vehicle's exhaust gasses to determine if they are within legal limits.

smog motor
Automobile engine with exhaust emissions controls. Generally, the term means any engine built since 1966, when the first such equipment was required by Federal law.

smog test
Same as *smog check*.

smoke
1. It is possible to judge some aspects of an engine's condition from the color of the vapor coming out the exhaust. If it is white, it is steam, not smoke, and indicates that water is getting into the combustion chambers, possibly because of a blown head gasket. If it is blue smoke, oil is getting into the combustion chambers, possibly because of worn piston rings. Finally, if it is black smoke, too much gasoline is getting into the combustion chambers; in other words, the air/fuel mixture is too rich.
2. As a verb, to defeat a racing competitor.

smoker
Vehicle with an engine that smokes excessively. See *smoke*, def. 1, above.

smoke it over
To analyze or discuss a problem, to give it careful consideration.

snap rings

smoke-off
In drag racing, to leave the starting line with the rear wheels spinning and smoking. In an extreme smoke-off, one driver will try to jump the other and create enough smoke that the other's view is blocked, forcing him or her to shut off and sacrifice the match.

smoothed
Vehicle body panels with trim removed and holes filled. Same as *shaved*.

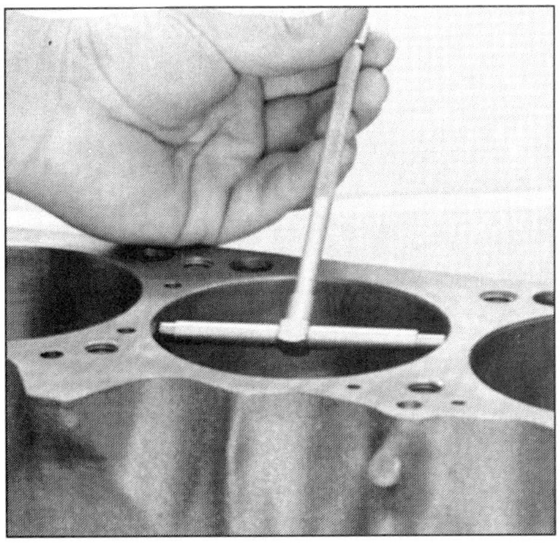

snap gauge

snap gauge
T-shaped instrument for finding the inside dimensions of cylinders and other holes in parts. The cross-bar of the T is a spring-loaded, telescoping arm, the ends of which snap into place against the inner walls of the cylinder. The gauge is then removed and the arm measured with a micrometer to find the *inside diameter* of the cylinder. Also called a *telescoping gauge*.

snap ring
Circular retaining clip used inside or outside cylindrical parts, such as shafts. Commonly used to retain floating *wrist pins*.

snap ring pliers
Tool with pointed tips that fit into the ends of snap rings in order to expand or contract them for installation or removal.

Snell Foundation
Organization which sets safety standards for racing helmets. Most race sanctioning bodies require that competitors wear Snell-approved helmets.

sniffer
Exhaust gas analyzer, placed in a vehicle's tailpipe to find the chemical composition of the exhaust gasses; used in making a *smog check*.

snipe
Pipe placed on a wrench handle to increase leverage.

snotty
Slippery surface. A drag strip which provides poor traction is considered *snotty*.

socket
1. Electrical outlet.
2. Hollow, cylindrical tool that attaches to the end of a ratchet wrench or handle and is used to twist nuts and bolts on or off.

socket extension
Steel rod that connects a socket and ratchet wrench, allowing the socket to be used on a nut or bolt inaccessible with just the socket and wrench.

socket wrench
Wrench consisting of a handle with a ratchet at one end, used to twist sockets on nuts and bolts. Also called a *ratchet*.

sodium-cooled valves
Exhaust valve with a hollow stem filled with sodium, which has a relatively low melting point (208 degrees F.) and consequently liquifies at engine operating temperature. The sodium sloshes up and down inside the valve stem, absorbing heat from the valve head and conducting it through the stem to the valve guide in the cylinder head. As a result, the exhaust valve runs cooler.

sodium bicarbonate
NaHCO, baking soda or bicarbonate of soda, powdery, white crystalline salt, whose most common auto shop use is for cleaning buildup of corrosion on battery terminals.

sodium hydroxide
NaOH, caustic soda, a white solid that is a strong, corrosive alkali which, when mixed with water, is a good parts cleaner.

sodium silicate
Any of several white, gray, or colorless compounds, also called *water glass*, with good adhesive properties which, when mixed with engine coolant, will seal small cracks or leaks in the cooling system.

soft top
Convertible top, or a vehicle with one.

SOHC
Single overhead camshaft. See *OHC*.

S

solar cell
Semiconductor which converts sunlight into electricity.

solar power
Electricity generated by solar cells.

solder
1. Alloy used to bond metals together. Soft solders are alloys of tin and lead that melt at relatively low temperatures, while hard or brazing solders are alloys of copper and zinc that melt only at higher temperatures.
2. As a verb, to use solder.

solenoid
Electromechanical device consisting of an electromagnetic coil surrounding a movable metal core. When the coil is energized, the magnetic field pulls the core until it is centered in the coil. Thus, a solenoid can convert electrical energy to mechanical energy. Usually, there is a return spring to pull the core back to its original position when the coil is shut off.

solid axle
Same as *beam axle* or *rigid axle.*

solid pushrod
Pushrod made from solid stock, as opposed to a *hollow pushrod* or *tubular pushrod.*

solid state ignition
Ignition system using non-moving, silicon devices such as transistors and diodes to control spark timing.

solids
1. Mechanical or solid valve lifters.
2. Type of paint pigment. Solid colors do not contain metallic or pearl particles to enhance or alter the appearance of the paint when viewed from different angles. See also *metallic paint* and *pearlescent paint.*

solid valve lifter
Same as *mechanical valve lifter.*

solo
Run by a single car during drag race eliminations. See also *bye run.*

soluble
Any substance—gas, liquid or solid—which will dissolve in a *solvent.* Oil and grease, for example, are both soluble in cleaning solvent.

solvent
1. In general, a substance, usually liquid, in which other substances can dissolve. Water is the most common solvent.
2. In auto shop use, solvent is usually taken to mean cleaning solvent, one of several petrochemical liquids which will dissolve oil and grease.
3. In paint, the solvent is the liquid part of the paint mixture that thins or reduces the paint so it can be atomized and transferred through the paint spray gun. The solvent evaporates during and after application, which has led to new environmental laws, and more environmentally safe equipment and paints.

sonic testing
Procedure to test engine blocks with sound waves for cylinder bore thickness, roundness and *core shift.* Sonic testing can indicate whether or not to overbore, and how much overbore would be safe.

SOP
1. Standard operating procedure.
2. Seat of the pants, as in a SOP rally, where instruments can't be used to check time or distance.

sorted out
Corrected. For example, when a driver recovers a car from a momentary loss of control, he has sorted it out. Or when the *teething troubles* in a new car have been resolved, they have been sorted out.

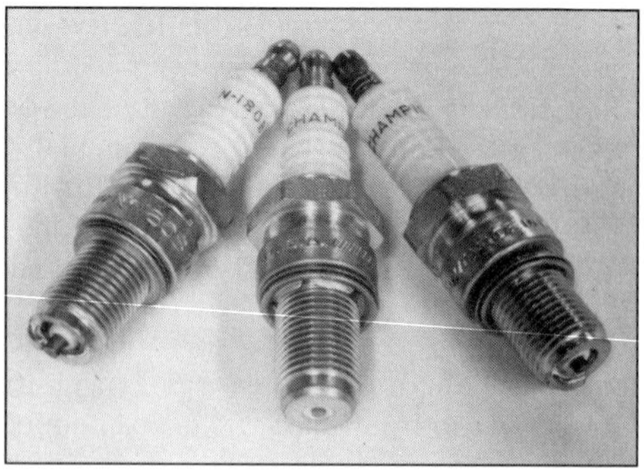

spark plugs

soup
1. To increase the output of an engine.
2. Special fuel mixture

space frame
Race car frame that consists of numerous, short, small-diameter metal tubes, welded together in a web-like structure that provides high rigidity with relatively low weight. See *birdcage.*

space-saver tire
A temporary spare tire which is either a much smaller, narrower tire than the original, or one that can be inflated with a can of compressed air. Both types are used to increase cargo space and reduce vehicle weight.

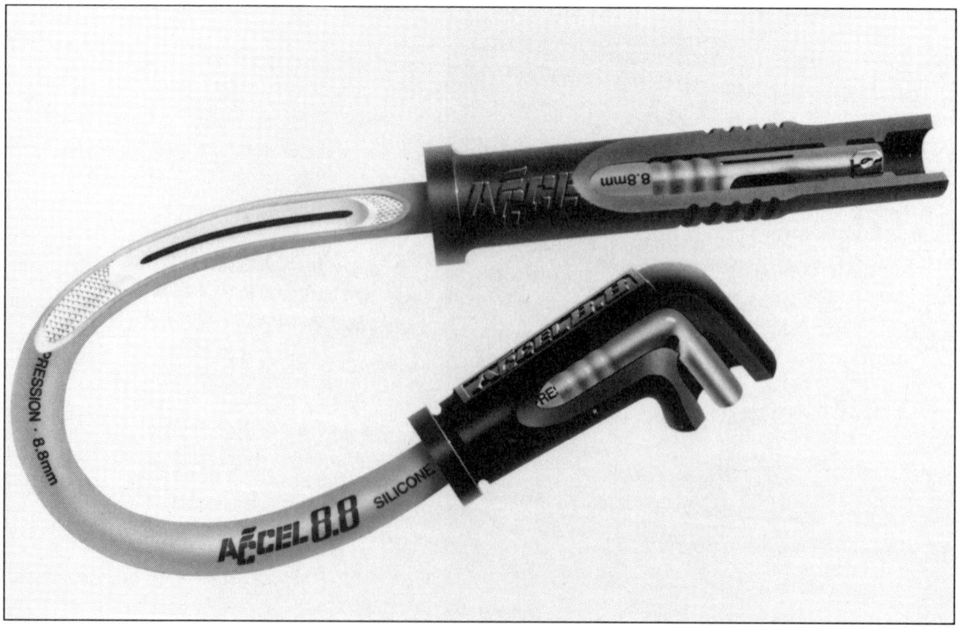

spark plug wire

spacer
Device, such as a thick washer, for increasing the distance between two parts.

span
Width of an air foil, as on a *spoiler.*

spanner
British term for wrench.

spark ignition
Operating system in which compressed air/fuel mixture is ignited by an electrical spark, as opposed to *CI* or *compression ignition.*

spark plug
Electrical device used to ignite compressed air/fuel mixture in a combustion chamber. See photo previous page.

spark plug well
Recess in the cylinder head for a spark plug.

spark plug wire
High tension lead from the ignition coil to the spark plug, capable of transmitting high voltage. See photo previous page.

spatter paint
Painting technique of applying two separate colors simultaneously to provide a speckled finish. Most spatter paints are available premixed in aerosol cans, and are usually applied in engine, trunk and interior compartments, and wheelwells. A grey base color with black and white speckles is a popular blend of spatter paint commonly used on race cars.

spec car
One of a group of identical cars that form their own racing category, such as *IROC* cars. Theoretically, the vehicles are built to the same specifications, eliminating any mechanical advantage in order to focus the competition on driving skill.

special
Individually built, high-performance car; the opposite of a *spec car*, above.

specifications, specs
Detailed description of a constructed object, such as a motor vehicle, including dimensions, weight, materials, settings and so forth.

specific fuel consumption
See *brake specific fuel consumption.*

speedbowl
Short, oval, dirt track.

speedometer
Instrument for measuring vehicle speed. The face of the speedometer usually also embodies the *odometer.*

speed shift
To upshift a manual gearbox as quickly as possible without releasing the accelerator. A skilled racing driver can speed shift without using the clutch.

speedster
Open, two-passenger roadster, such as the Auburn Speedster or the Porsche Speedster. See also *spyder.*

speedway
1. Generally, any large oval track racing facility, sometimes combined with a road race course in the infield, as at Daytona.
2. With a capital "S," the Indianapolis Motor Speedway and *only* the Indianapolis Motor Speedway.

SPFI
See *sequential port fuel injection.*

spider
1. Set of gears in the differential which allow each wheel to rotate at its own speed as the vehicle goes around a corner.
2. See also *spyder.*

spin
To slide out of control, with the rear end skidding around 180 degrees or more.

spindle
Shaft or stub-axle projecting from the steering knuckle upon which the wheel hub and bearings ride.

spinner
Same as *knock-off hub.*

spin-on filter
Oil filter with a threaded attachment for easy installation or removal.

spiral bevel gear
Differential *ring gear* with *helical gear* teeth.

splash lubrication
Non-pressurized lubrication system with which oil is literally splashed around the inside the engine by the movement of internal parts.

splash shield
Metal piece shaped to divert or reduce oil splash.

splines
Lengthways grooves on a gear or shaft, either external or internal. When two splined shafts are meshed, the splines enable one shaft to rotate the other, yet the two are free to move lengthways. Thus, splines allow a driveshaft or axle shaft to change in length as it rises or falls.

split ball gauge
Indirect measuring tool shaped like a ball, for finding inside diameters of small bores, such as worn valve guides.

split brake system
Hydraulic brake system with two separate master cylinders, each supplying pressure to a pair of wheels. The split may be simply between the front and rear wheels, or it may be diagonal, with the left front and right rear as one pair and the right front and left rear as the other.

split crankcase, split sump
Oil pan made with two or more pieces, split horizontally in the same plane as the crankshaft to simplify assembly.

split valve guide
Two-piece valve guide used with mushroom valves in some older flathead engines to facilitate installation and removal of the valves.

spoiler
Aerodynamic device attached to a car, usually below the front bumper or on the rear deck, either to reduce drag by deflecting air away from the vehicle or to provide downforce. As the term suggests, the device "spoils" the normal airflow over the car.

spoke
On a wire wheel, the wire bracing between the hub and wheel rim.

spokes
Wire wheels.

spook
To distract or unnerve an opponent at the start of a drag race, in hopes of pushing that opponent into making a poor start. See also *psych.*

spool
Final drive without any differential action; the axle shafts are permanently locked together and the drive wheels on either side always rotate at the same speed, whether they are going straight or around corners. The spool is a common feature of drag cars, which are driven around corners only at modest speeds when they are being maneuvered from trailer to pits to starting line and from finish line back to pits to trailer. The slight tire scrub that might occur under such conditions is of no consequence. See also *locked rear end* and *locker*.

sport utility vehicle
Truck-based vehicle with box-like bodywork, either open or closed, usually on a relatively short wheelbase and usually equipped with four-wheel drive. The Willys Jeep of World War II was the forerunner of the *SUV*, as it is called for short, and the modern Jeep Wrangler is its direct descendant. However, the category also includes enclosed two- and four-door wagons, such as the Chevrolet Blazer and Ford Bronco and Explorer. It is questionable, though, if the term can be extended to oversize wagons like the Chevrolet and GMC Suburban.

sport utility vehicle (Ford Explorer)

sports car
Automobile engineered for driving performance rather than passenger comfort. The sports car is an attempt to incorporate the performance and precise handling of a race car in a vehicle suitable for normal road use. It is often a two-seater, a roadster, and equipped with a manual gearbox, but it is not necessarily any one of those things.

sporty car
Same as *pony car*.

spot-on
Anything that is absolutely correct or accurate, such as a critical measurement.

spot putty
Type of *body filler* to fill slight body surface imperfections, such as sanding scratches or pinholes.

spot repair
In bodywork, a small localized repair, such as a minor dent.

spot welding
Production welding method to join panels of sheet metal. Electrical resistance heating and clamping are used to fuse the panels together with a series of small spots. Filler metal is not used. Also called *resistance welding*.

spray
Atomization of a liquid into a fine mist in order to apply it on a surface as smoothly and evenly as possible.

spray gun
Tool which uses compressed air to spray liquids, such as paint.

spread-bore carburetor
Four-barrel carburetor with small primary barrels and large secondaries. The small primaries improve fuel economy at steady cruising speeds, while the large secondaries increase performance under full throttle. General Motors introduced the idea with the Rochester Quadrajet carburetor. It was later adopted by two Rochester rivals, Carter and Holley.

spring
1. Elastic device, usually steel but sometimes composite material, which compresses as it absorbs energy, then releases that energy as it returns to its original position. In a vehicle suspension system, these characteristics of a spring are used to absorb irregularities on the surface the vehicle is traversing; the most common forms of springs in vehicle suspension are *coil springs*, *leaf springs* and *torsion bars*.
2. In an engine valvetrain, small coil springs are used to close the intake and exhaust valves when the cam lobe releases its pressure on the valve stem.

spring back
Tendency of metal to return to its original shape after being bent. In order to make a permanent bend, it may be necessary to overbend the metal, beyond the spring back point.

spring bind
See *coil bind*.

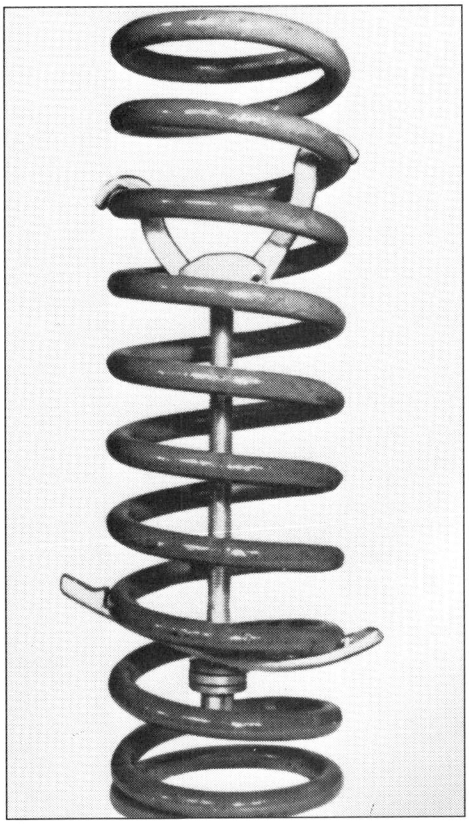

spring compressor (coil spring)

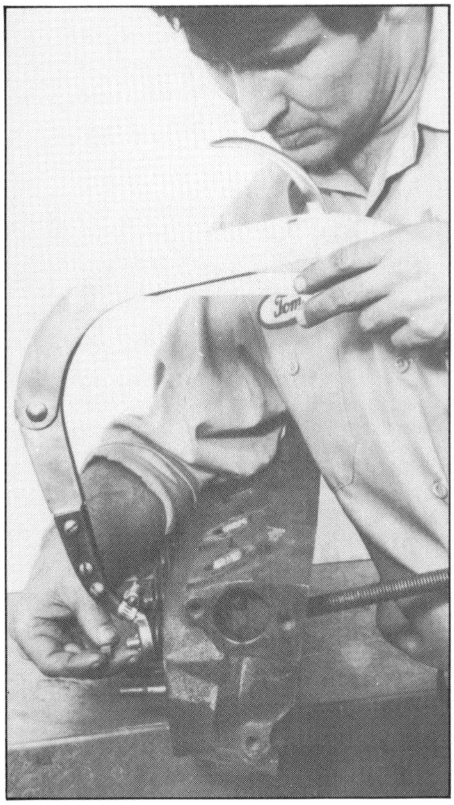

spring compressor (valve spring)

spring compressor
Tool to compress coil springs in order to install or remove them.

spring load
The measure, usually in pounds, of how much weight a spring can support at a given height, which is usually the *installed height*. If a spring has a free length of 15 inches, and an installed height of 10 inches, then its load at installation would be 5 inches times the *spring rate*. This would give you the pounds of load of the spring at the installed height. Unlike *spring rate*, the spring load can decrease during the course of the spring's life. See also *spring rate* and *spring sag*.

spring pin
Small piece of metal wound up in a tubular shape, used as a dowel in some small parts that may be disassembled and then reassembled occasionally. Spring pins may be used, for example, on some smaller pieces of carburetor linkage.

spring rate
In US units, the force in pounds needed to deflect a spring one inch, expressed in "pounds per inch" of travel. A 100 lb/in. spring requires 1000 lbs. to deflect it 10 inches. The higher the force, the stiffer the spring, and consequently the harsher the ride characteristics. Unlike *spring load*, spring rate will not change during the life of the spring, because the rate is determined by the size and shape of the metal, not the elasticity or "springiness." In SI units, spring rate is the force in newtons need to deflect a spring one millimeter, or "newtons per millimeter."

spring sag
Loss of *spring load*. This loss can be caused by poor metallurgy, over loading and fatigue due to high mileage. The problem should not be corrected by changing the *spring rate*, a common mistake. For *coil springs*, the solution is to place a rubber shim on top of the spring to increase load. For *leaf springs*, different *shackle* lengths can be used, or in extreme cases, the spring can be re-arched.

spring seat
Recess in a chassis frame where a coil spring is mounted.

spring shackle
See *shackle*.

spring walk
Tendency of a valve spring to bounce around in its seat, especially at higher rpm.

springy thingy
Dragster with a light, flexible structure to allow maximum weight transfer. Same as *flexible flyer*.

sprint car
Front engine, open wheel, open cockpit, single-seat race car designed expressly for short dirt and paved oval tracks, generally no more than 1/2 or 5/8 of a mile in length and sometimes as short as 1/5 of a mile. Sprint cars are the most powerful pure race cars competing on such tracks and, as a result, they are demanding to drive and exciting to watch.

sprint race
In oval track racing, a relatively short race, lasting only a few laps. Because of its brevity, a sprint race requires a maximum effort by a driver. There is no time to lay back in the field and not make a move toward the front until the last few minutes; the whole race *is* the last few minutes. A *trophy dash* is an example of a sprint race.

sprocket
Wheel with teeth around its circumference which mesh with a belt or chain drive.

sprung weight
The mass of a vehicle that is supported by the suspension system. The frame and body and everything they support are all part of the sprung weight, while the wheels and tires, outboard brakes, and axles are not. See also *unsprung weight*.

spun bearing
Rod or main bearing that has seized against the crankshaft journal and turned in the housing bore.

spur gear
Transmission or differential gear with straight-cut teeth, parallel to the gear's centerline. Spur gears are rarely used today because they are much noisier than helical gears and, in a differential, a spur gear requires a higher driveshaft. Also referred to as a *straight-cut gear*.

spurt hole
1. In an *OHV* engine, a hole in the side of a connecting rod, in the radial area between the rod beam and big end, which squirts oil

under pressure toward the camshaft to help lubricate it.
2. Oil hole on the pin end of the rod which squirts oil upward, to the underside of the piston crown in order to cool the piston.

spyder
Light, two-passenger sports car; generally, an open roadster, though Audi has exhibited a closed two-passenger sports model it calls the Spyder. Originally, a spyder was a light, two-passenger, horse-drawn carriage. See also *speedster.*

squat
During hard acceleration, the tendency of the rear part of a vehicle's structure to press down on the rear springs as a result of sudden weight transfer to the rear. See also *dive.*

squirrel
Poor driver, one who cannot handle a car properly.

squirrelly
Poor handling.

squirt racing
Drag racing.

squish area
See *quench area.*

SREA
See *SRMA*, below.

SRMA
Street Rod Market Association, formerly Street Rod Equipment Association or SREA; street rod-oriented subsidiary of the Specialty Equipment Market Association. See *SEMA.*

SRW
Single rear wheels, i.e., single wheels on either side of a rear drive axle, as opposed to *DRW* or dual rear wheels on either side of a rear drive axle, specifically on a Ford pickup.

SS
1. Super Stock, a drag racing category which is, according to NHRA rules, "Reserved for American factory-production automobiles and some foreign and domestic sports cars. Classified per NHRA performance rating as listed in the Official NHRA Stock Car Classification Guide. Only those cars listed in the Guide are eligible. All cars must be factory-production assembled, showroom available and in the hands of the general public."
2. Sports Sedan, under USAC stock car rules, but actually the same as *pony car.*
3. Showroom Stock, an SCCA racing class for factory-stock vehicles with minor modifications and safety equipment.
4. SS is also an abbreviation for *stainless steel.*

staging area, staging lanes

stabilizer bar
Same as *anti-roll bar.*

stacks
See *velocity stacks.*

stage
In drag racing, to place a vehicle in a proper starting position. A car is properly staged when both sets of *staging lights* are lit.

staged turbos
Two turbochargers in series, one feeding the other.

staggered timing camshaft
Camshaft with longer durations for the cylinders farthest away from the main intake tract, in order to equalize the amount of air/fuel mixture reaching all of the cylinders.

staging area
In drag racing, the area between the pits and the starting line, where cars are lined up. Usually, the staging area has several different lanes for cars grouped according to classes.

staging lane
See *staging area*, above.

staging lights
In drag racing, the pre-stage beam and stage beam used to guide the front wheels of a car into proper position before the start of a race.

stainless steel
Steel alloy highly resistant to rust or corrosion, consisting of 70 to 90 percent iron, 12 to 20 percent chromium, and 0.1 to 0.7 percent carbon.

staking
Exerting pressure on a part around an opening, such as a valve seat insert, in order to secure it in place.

standing kilometer, standing mile
International standards for acceleration records. A car attempting a record must start from a dead stop at the beginning of the measured kilometer or mile.

standing quarter-mile
Acceleration from a dead stop to the end of a measured 1/4 mile. The typical drag race is an example of a standing quarter.

stand off
During valve timing overlap, when both the intake and exhaust valves are open, pressure from within the combustion chamber may force a fine mist of air/fuel mixture back out through the carburetor. This is called stand off or *reversion.*

static balancing connecting rod

stand on it
1. To hold the accelerator to the floor.
2. *Stand On It By Stroker Ace* was a hilarious novel about a carousing but winning race driver, actually written by Bill Neely, a Goodyear publicist, and the late Bob Ottum, then an auto racing writer for *Sports Illustrated*. As far-fetched as the episodes in the book may seem, most of them actually happened, though not all to just one driver like Stroker Ace. The novel was later made into a motion picture called *Stroker Ace*, with Burt Reynolds in the title role. Unfortunately, the film was not nearly as entertaining as the book.

starter
Small electric motor, activated by turning the ignition key, to start a vehicle engine.

starter solenoid
Electrical device that transfers battery current to the starter when the ignition key is turned.

static balance
Process of checking and correcting the weight distribution and balance of interrelated parts while they are not in motion. Opposite of *dynamic balance*.

static timing
Setting ignition timing on an engine while it is not running.

station wagon
Enclosed two- or four-door passenger vehicle in which the interior compartment extends all the way to the rear bumper in order to carry cargo inside or, with an optional third seat, to carry additional passengers. While most station wagons are on passenger car platforms, the body type may also be truck-based, as is the case with the Chevrolet and GMC *Suburban*. The term is often abbreviated to simply *wagon*.

stator
1. In an alternator, three static windings that provide overlapping pulses to smooth the current flow.
2. In a torque converter, a bladed wheel which multiplies torque by redirecting oil from the turbine to the impeller.

steady rest
Journal support on crankshaft and camshaft grinders.

steam holes
In an engine cooling system, passages designed to expedite the flow of coolant near or around hot spots where steam pockets might otherwise form and obstruct the flow. For example, in an engine with *siamesed* cylinders, there are hot spots near where the cylinders are joined without coolant passages, and steam holes are used at those points to speed up the coolant flow, usually by diverting it into the cylinder head.

steam rollers
Huge drag racing slicks.

steelies
Ferrous wheels, as opposed to *mags*.

steel shim gasket
Basically the same as *corrugated metal gasket*.

steering axis
Vertical line through the centerlines of the upper and lower pivot points on a steered wheel. On older vehicles, particularly those with solid axles, the steering axis was simply a line through the centerline of the kingpin. With modern independent suspension, the steering axis is a line through the upper and lower ball joints.

steering brake
On an off-road vehicle, especially a racing buggy, a system with separate braking for the left and right rear wheels. Applying the left rear brake will cause the vehicle to veer sharply to the left, while applying the right rear brake will cause the vehicle to veer in that direction. The steering brake will usually bring the vehicle around more tightly than its usual turning circle.

steering column
Shaft which connects the steering wheel in the cockpit with the steering gear at the front of the vehicle.

steering gear
Gearset, usually either worm-and-sector or rack-and-pinion, which converts the rotary motion of the steering column to the straight-line motion of the pitman arm and the rest of the steering linkage.

steering geometry
Relationship of the *steering linkage* and wheels to the road, including but not limited to *camber*, *caster*, *scrub radius* or *steering offset*, and *toe-in, toe-out*.

steering knuckle
Part of the steering system at the end of the steering arms and supported by either the kingpin or ball joints. It is around the steering knuckle that each front wheel pivots as it is steered.

steering linkage
Rods and arms which are moved back and forth by the steering gear in order to point the front wheels in the desired direction.

steering offset
Distance between the point where the extended centerline of the steering axis would meet the ground and the centerline of the tire contact patch. Same as *scrub radius*.

steering ratio
Ratio of the steering gears, i.e., the ratio of the worm to the sector, or the rack to the pinion.

steering sector
See *sector gear.*

steering spindle
See *spindle.*

Stellite
Tradename for an alloy of cobalt, chromium, tungsten, molybdenum and iron, which is very hard and offers excellent resistance to corrosion and high temperatures. Probably the best known automotive use of Stellite is for valve seat inserts.

stemming
On a valve, condition when the radius section of the valve has corroded and become smaller in diameter than the stem.

straightaway

step
1. Ledge formed on one metal piece so that another can be joined to it. See also *stepped flywheel,* below.
2. To raise a portion of a chassis frame for added clearance over the axle. See also *C.*

stepped flywheel
Flywheel with a ledge to which the pressure plate attaches.

Stepside
Chevrolet tradename for a pickup truck with a narrow cargo bed between separate rear fenders; equivalent names for similar pickups of other makes are Dodge Utiline, Ford Flareside and GMC Fenderside.

stethoscope
Medical listening device used to detect and analyze noises within an engine while it is running.

stick
Camshaft.

stick shift
Manual transmission.

stinger
On some exhaust systems, particularly on Volkswagen Beetle engines modified for higher performance, a form of exhaust resonator consisting of a single, slightly conical pipe into which individual headers feed at the top of the engine. The term derives from the fact that the pipe sticks out toward the rear like a stinger on a bee.

stock car
Regular production vehicle. In actual practice, racing stock cars aren't really "stock" in a showroom sense. NASCAR stockers, particularly, are built from the ground up as racing vehicles and contain few if any stock parts. Even for milder forms of stock car racing, most racing associations allow some modifications to improve engine output or handling ability and, in fact, they insist on certain changes for safety. In drag racing, stock cars with manual transmissions are indicated by the letter "S" and with automatic transmissions, "SA."

stocker
Stock car, especially one built for racing.

stoichiometric ratio
The optimum ratio of air to fuel in terms of mass to achieve the most complete combustion possible, converting the carbon and hydrogen content of the fuel primarily into water and carbon dioxide. The stoichiometric ratio varies with the *heating value* of a particular fuel and is 15.1-to-1 for 100-octane gasoline, 14.6-to-1 for regular gasoline, 9.0-to-1 for ethanol, 6.45-to-1 for methanol, and 1.7-to-1 for nitromethane, according to the *Automotive Fuels Handbook* published by the *SAE.*

stoked
Enthused or excited. For example, drag racing fans were stoked when Kenny Bernstein turned the first, officially-clocked 300-mph run in the 1/4-mile.

stone
Poor performing engine or car.

storm
To perform extremely well. Often used to describe a competitor as he moves from the back of the pack to the front quickly.

stovebolt
Chevrolet. Originally, the term was applied to the Chevrolet six-cylinder engine introduced in 1929, which had connecting rod bolts which looked like ordinary stovebolts. By extension, it can mean any Chevrolet or any Chevy engine.

STP
In addition to being the brand name of a well-known line of oil and fuel additives, STP is an abbreviation for "standard temperature and pressure."

straight, straightaway
Any straight stretch on a closed race course, whether oval track or road race circuit, such as the front straight and back straight at *Indy.*

street rod

straightedge

straight-cut gear
See *spur gear.*

straightedge
Metal bar used with a feeler gauge to check an engine block deck or cylinder head for warp, and main bearing bores for alignment.

straight eight
Inline eight-cylinder engine, configuration once used by many makers of medium- and high-priced cars but which was eventually replaced by the more compact and efficient V-8.

straight four
Inline four-cylinder engine.

straight-in damage
1. Collision damage caused by one vehicle to another by hitting it directly, rather than by glancing off still another.
2. In closed course racing, crashing "straight-in" means to hit the wall nose first.

straight six
Inline six-cylinder engine.

stratified charge
Type of combustion involving a small amount of rich air/fuel mixture near the spark plug and leaner mixture throughout the rest of the combustion chamber. The rich mixture ignites easily and, in turn, ignites the leaner mixture more easily than could be done by direct spark. The result is lower combustion temperature, which can lead to reductions in exhaust emissions and fuel consumption. The best known practical application of the stratified charge principle was the Honda CVCC engine of the early 1970s. See *CVCC.*

streamliner
1. For dry lakes racing, a specific class of vehicle with aerodynamic bodywork fully enclosing the wheels.
2. In general, any racing car with aerodynamic, enclosed bodywork.

street legal
Vehicle which can be driven legally on public streets and highways.

street machine
Hot rod or custom built for street use, based on a US car or light truck manufactured after 1948. See also *street rod.*

street racing
Illegal racing, usually drag racing, done on public streets.

street roadster
1. In a broad sense, any hot rod with roadster bodywork built for normal street use.
2. In drag racing, a specific category of cars with stock, pre-1937 roadster bodywork, either original or fiberglass replica, and full legal street equipment. The engine may be set back up to 10 percent of the car's wheelbase. The street roadster is the open-bodied counterpart of the gas coupe or sedan and is designated by the letters "SR."

street rod
Hot rod built for street use and based on a US car or light truck manufactured before 1949. See also *street machine.*

streetside
On an RV, the left-hand side of the vehicle, i.e., the side normally next to the street, as opposed to the *curbside.*

stress-relieve
The condition of an engine block that has been relieved of the stress caused by casting and rough machining. A brand-new block will relieve itself of these stresses gradually, causing minute block movements that cause the cylinder bore to shift, so it will no longer be perfectly straight or round. Generally, 50 to 100 drag racing runs, 5 to 10 short-track races, or 5,000 to 10,000 street miles will stress-relieve a block. Top racing engine builders will stress-relieve a block on a dyno before building the final engine. A block that has been stress-relieved with any of these methods is said to be seasoned, and is the best type to begin building a race-only engine.

stress riser
Area or point on a part where damage from mishandling or misuse has increased the likelihood of the part cracking. An example would be a connecting rod which has

been indented in a vise with serrated teeth. The indentation could develop into a crack.

stretchout
Luxury sedan, such as a Cadillac Brougham or Lincoln Town Car, which has been lengthened and converted into a *limo*.

striping
Thin paint stripes applied to bodywork, usually contrasting with the main body color.

stripped
Vehicle from which parts and equipment have been removed for reuse or resale. Stolen cars, for example, are often stripped for their parts, rather than being resold as complete vehicles.

stripper
1. Lowest-priced car in an automaker's line, i.e., one "stripped" of all luxury equipment and special options.
2. Chemical compound used to remove paint from bodywork.

strobe
Short for *stroboscope*, an ignition timing light.

stroke
1. As a noun, the distance a piston travels up and down in a cylinder, or back and forth in an *opposed* engine.
2. As a verb, to increase the stroke in an engine. See *bored and stroked* and *stroker*.
3. Also as a verb, to drive carefully or treat gently. For example, if something goes wrong with a race car during an event, the driver is likely to "stroke" it back to the pits.

stroker
1. Engine which has been *stroked*.
2. Crankshaft for stroking a specific amount, such as a 1/4-inch stroker.

stub-axle
With independent suspension, front or rear, the short shaft upon which the wheel hub and bearings ride. At the front, specifically, the spindle projecting from the steering knuckle is a stub-axle.

stub frame
See *subframe*.

stud
Round metal fastener with threads at both ends.

Studebaker
Automaker which built cars and trucks in South Bend, Indiana, from 1902 to 1964, and in Hamilton, Ontario, Canada, from 1912 to 1966. The company's roots went back all the way to 1852, when brothers Henry and Clem Studebaker began building horse-drawn wagons in South Bend. The first Studebaker cars were electrics, built from 1902 to 1912. The first Studebaker with an internal combustion engine came in 1904. From 1931 to 1933, Studebaker also produced a car called the Rockne, after South Bend's most famous citizen at that time, Notre Dame University football coach Knute Rockne. In 1947, a year and a half after the end of World War II, Studebaker became the first US automaker to introduce a truly postwar car, at a time when other established car companies in the US were still building warmed-over prewar designs. Unfortunately, by the mid 1950s, Studebaker, like other independent US automakers, no longer had the resources to compete with the Big Three. A merger with Packard in 1954 only led to the latter's demise four years later. Studebaker shut down its South Bend operation in 1964 and its Canadian operation in 1966.

stud extractor
Tool used to remove studs.

stud-mounted rocker arms
Rocker arms that are mounted individually, each on a stud with a ball. The first widespread use of such as a setup was on the small-block V-8 Chevrolet introduced in late 1954 for its 1955 line.

stuffer
Supercharger.

Stutz
Harry C. Stutz founded the Ideal Motor Car Company in Indianapolis in 1911, but changed it to the Stutz Motor Car Company of America two years later. Stutz's most famous car was the *Bearcat*, an open two-seater introduced in 1914, that was a natural rival of the *Mercer* Raceabout. In late 1927, Stutz offered a speedster called the *Black Hawk* (two words), which was modified to compete in the 24 Hours Le Mans. In 1932, Stutz introduced the DV 32, with a straight-eight, DOHC, 32-valve engine. Short-wheelbase, speedster versions of the DV 32 continued the Bearcat name. The original Stutz company ended passenger car production in 1934, but lingered on another four years producing a rear-engined delivery van called the *Pak-Age Car*. In 1970, a new Stutz Motor Car Company of America was organized in New York, to market a *neoclassic* coupe called the *Stutz Blackhawk* (one word), which was actually built in Italy on a Pontiac chassis. In the years since, this firm has offered a variety of body types, all sharing the same basic styling and all on GM chassis'.

sub-arc welding
See *submerged arc welding*.

Subaru
Built in Tokyo by Fuji Heavy Industries, the Subaru carries the Japanese name of the six Pleiades of Greek mythology, daughters of Atlas, who became stars in the Taurus constellation. The Subaru emblem is a stylized version of the six stars, representing six companies which joined together to form what became Fuji Heavy Industries. Subaru entered the auto industry in 1958 with a two-cylinder, two-stroke, 16-hp mini car. The firm has specialized in smaller cars ever since. In the late 1970s, Subaru became a pioneering manufacturer of small, four-wheel-drive passenger cars.

subassembly
Self-contained group of mechanical or electrical components that form a part of an overall whole. On a car or truck, for example, an electronic fuel injection system is a subassembly relative to the engine, while the engine itself is a subassembly relative to the vehicle.

subframe
Partial front or rear chassis frame sometimes used in unibody vehicles to support engine or suspension subassemblies. With a subframe, road noise and vibration are usually less than they are when the engine or suspension are mounted directly to the unibody structure.

submerged-arc welding
Process in which the electric arc is submerged in powder flux, thus protecting the weld from atmospheric contamination. It is used where high accuracy and weld quality are wanted, such as when welding crankshaft journals. Also referred to as *SAW* and *sub-arc welding*.

suicide door

Suburban
Large, truck-based station wagon marketed by both the Chevrolet and GMC Divisions of GM. See also *Carryall.*

suicide doors
Car doors hinged from the rear and opening at the front; so called because, if the door opens while the vehicle is in motion, the wind can blow it wide open and expose a passenger sitting by it to danger.

suicide front axle, suicide front end
Special front spring and axle assembly for early Fords, attaching to a bracket ahead of the frame, rather than to the usual cross member, allowing a lower front end. The first attempts at this type of construction had a tendency to come apart at high speeds, hence the "suicide" part of the term.

sulfated battery
Battery that can no longer be recharged because a sulfate coating has built up on the plates.

sump
Reservoir for oil at the bottom of an engine, same as *crankcase* and *oil pan*—except, of course, when it is a *dry sump.*

sun gear
Central gear in a *planetary gearset.*

supe
Supercharger.

Super Car
Term originally used for a high-performance car with a big-block engine in a light-weight, mid-size chassis and two-door body, produced by most Detroit automakers from the mid 1960s to the early 1970s, until that type of vehicle became better known as a *muscle car.* Today, Super Car is more likely to be used for an ultra-powerful, ultra-expensive, and ultra-limited vehicle like the Ferrari F40, Porsche 959 and Jaguar XJ220.

supercharger
Compressor which pumps air into an engine's induction system at higher than atmospheric pressure. The supercharger thus increases the amount of air fed to the combustion chambers and, with it, the amount of fuel the engine can burn. The result is a substantial increase in engine output and, of course, in fuel consumption. Supercharger is sometimes interpreted to mean a mechanically driven compressor as opposed to an exhaust-driven *turbocharger*, but the turbocharger is really a form of supercharger.

super-duty parts
Heavy-duty or high-performance parts, whether *OEM* or *aftermarket.*

superspeedway
High-banked, paved oval track at least one mile long and usually longer. Superspeedways are identified with *NASCAR* racing and the first of them was a 1-3/8-mile track opened at Darlington, South Carolina, in 1950. The most famous of them is Daytona International Speedway, a 2-1/2-mile tri-oval which opened at Daytona Beach, Florida, in 1959.

Super Stock
1. According to *NHRA Drag Rules*, a group of 16 classes, "Reserved for American factory-production automobiles and some foreign and domestic sports cars. Classified per NHRA performance rating as listed in the *Official NHRA Stock Car Classification Guide.* Only those cars listed in the *Guide* are eligible."

Super Stock Eliminator
Under NHRA rules, an eliminator category for a total of 65 classes running under the NHRA's index/handicap system. The classes include not only Super Stock itself

S

but GT, Modified Compact, MX, Modified Stock, and Modified.

super tape
Yet another name for *duct tape.*

Sure-Grip
Chrysler, Dodge or Plymouth *limited slip differential.*

surface finish
Roughness or smoothness of a surface, as expressed in the measurement in micro inches of high and low points on the surface.

surface loading
Transferring pressure as one part acts on another, e.g., as a piston moves downward in a cylinder, the connecting rod applies surface loading to the crankshaft journal.

surfacing
Refinishing the surfaces of parts, such as engine blocks, heads and manifolds.

surge tank
In a cooling system, reservoir in which boiled coolant condenses before being returned to the radiator.

suspension
System of springs, shock absorbers and locating linkages used to support a vehicle's structure and powertrain on its wheels.

SUV
See *sport utility vehicle.*

Suzuki
Suzuki Motor Company of Hamamatsu, Japan, did not start producing motorcycles until 1952 nor cars until 1961. However, the company has roots that go back all the way to 1909, when Michio Suzuki established the Suzuki Loom Works to produce textile machinery. Suzuki actually built its first car, the *Suzulight,* in 1955, but only 43 of these were made during the next two years. It was not until the early 1960s that serious production began of a redesigned Suzulight. Today, Suzuki offers both small cars and four-wheel drive vehicles in this country under its own name, and also builds badge-engineered versions of both for the Chevrolet Division of GM, which markets them with the Geo *Metro* and *Tracker* labels.

swagged end
Technique of pressing together pieces of pipe or tube, such as exhaust tubing, when they are of the same diameter; the end of one is stretched open just enough to accept the end of the other.

swap
To replace one component with another considered better for a particular purpose, such as swapping a car's original engine for a bigger, more powerful one.

swap ends
To spin a vehicle around a full 180 degrees, so that it winds up facing opposite the direction it was originally heading.

sway bar
See *anti-sway bar.*

swept volume
See *displacement.*

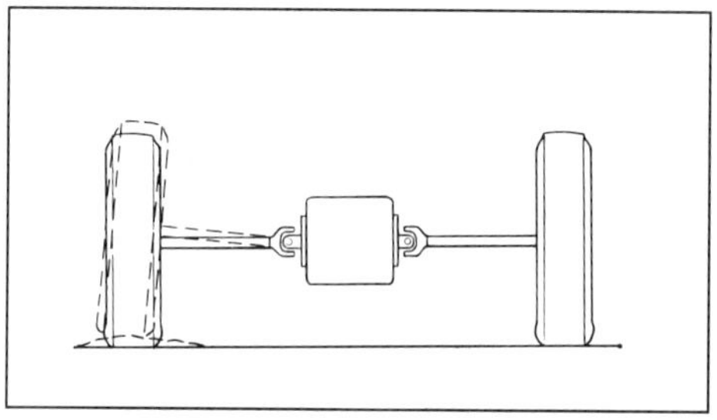

swing axle rear suspension

swing arm
Triangular arm or frame in an independent suspension system. See *A-arm, A-frame.*

swing axle
Drive system used with independent rear suspension, using axle half shafts attached by U-joints at their inboard ends to either side of the differential, but without U-joints at their outboard ends where they attach to the wheels. As the axles swing up and down, the wheels remain perpendicular to them and, relative to the road surface, the wheels undergo severe camber changes. The result can be unstable rear suspension behavior, particularly under hard driving conditions.

swing pedals
Clutch, brake and accelerator pedals which are suspended from beneath the *dash,* instead of applying pressure directly through the *floorboard.*

swirl
Cylinder head design that causes the incoming air/fuel mixture to swirl into the combustion chamber at a high rate of speed, increasing the atomization of the mixture and with it, combustion efficiency.

swivel foot
Valve adjusting screw with a ball that swivels when it contacts the valve stem.

symmetrical camshaft lobe
Cam lobe with identical opening and closing ramps.

Synchro
Tradename used by Volkswagen for an *all-wheel-drive* system.

synchromesh
Type of manual transmission in which a synchronizer, or synchro, is used to bring a selected gear up or down to the speed of the mainshaft. During a shift, it is the synchros which move back and forth, not the gears themselves; a shifting fork presses the synchro, which is rotating at mainshaft speed, against the gear, which is rotating freely on the mainshaft. As the two engage, the gear begins to rotate with the mainshaft.

synchronizer
See *synchromesh,* above.

synfuel
Synthetic fuel, i.e., gas or liquid or fuel made by liquefying coal, or by extracting oil from shale or tar sands.

synthetic oil
A type of engine lubricant consisting of highly polymerized chemicals. Synthetic engine oils do not leave behind carbon-like ash when burned during combustion, and generally have a higher viscosity and greater resistance to higher temperatures.

Système Internationale des Unités
See *SI.*

system pressure
Average pressure throughout a fuel injection system, from the fuel pump to the injectors.

T

T
Model T Ford, built from 1909 through 1927, or any hot rod based on either stock or repro Model T chassis and/or body components. T roadster bodies, especially those of 1923 and 1927 vintage, were popular for rodding when they could still be found in stock form in junkyards, and remain sought-after today as *repros*.

TAC
See *thermostatically controlled air cleaner*.

tach
See *tachometer*.

tach-dwell meter
Tune-up instrument for measuring both engine speed in rpm and ignition dwell in degrees.

tachometer
Mechanical or electrical instrument for measuring engine speed in crankshaft revolutions per minute or *rpm*.

tack cloth, tack rag
Varnish-coated cheesecloth with a tacky surface used to remove dirt and lint before painting.

tack welds
Series of small, temporary welds between two pieces of metal. Spaced about 1-1/2 inches apart, they align the two pieces, hold them together and help prevent warpage. When the final weld is made, the tack welds are remelted and become part of it. Most structures should be tack-welded before they are finish-welded. See photo next page.

tag axle
On a heavy truck, a second, non-powered rear axle which helps support the loaded vehicle's weight, mounted behind the drive axle.

tailgate
1. Rear opening on a station wagon or van.
2. As a verb, to follow another car extremely closely, a dangerous practice in highway driving. A similar technique is used in stock car racing, but there it is *drafting*, not tailgating. See *draft*.

tachometer

tall block
Engine assembly basically the same as a *short block*, but with the addition of the cylinder heads. See *short block*.

tall deck engine
When a basic engine design is available in two different block heights to accommodate crankshafts with significantly different strokes, the higher version is called a tall deck and the shorter one a short deck. The Chrysler B block V-8 announced in 1958 was an example. It first appeared that year in short deck form with a stroke of 3.38 inches. A few months later, a tall deck version was introduced with a stroke of 3.75 inches. The latter was known as the "RB" for raised block. See also *short deck engine*.

tall gear
Final drive with high gearing, i.e., a numerically low ratio; same as *long gear* and opposite of *short gear*.

tap
Tool for cutting internal threads, as for example, in an engine block.

tap drill
Tool for boring a hole that is to be tapped for threads.

taper
Condition of a cylindrical part, whether hollow or solid, which is larger in diameter at one end than at the other.

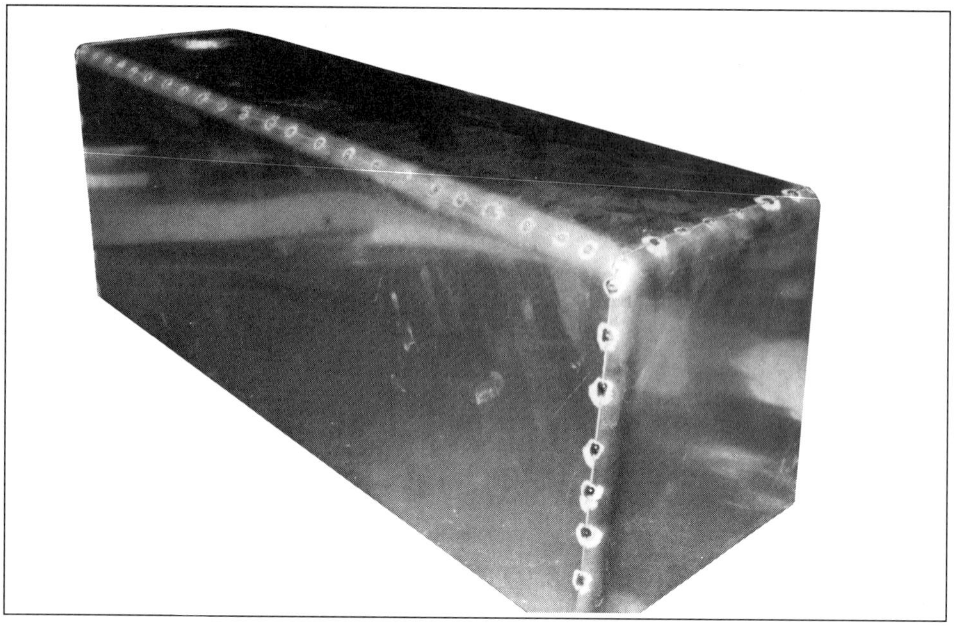

tack welds

taper adjustment
Machining procedure used to increase or decrease taper on a cylindrical part.

taper-bored piston pins
Piston pins with tapered bores for increased strength and reduced weight.

tappet
See *valve lifter.*

Targa
Two-passenger convertible with a fixed roll bar behind the seat, introduced by Porsche in 1965. According to a factory historical brochure, "As rumors spread that safety laws may prohibit convertibles in America, most manufacturers simply make plans to abandon them. Professor Porsche does not accept this. A sports car company must, in his opinion, offer an open-top car. Relying as so often on racing experience, an integrated roll bar is developed, and the world's first safety convertible is born. It is dubbed "Targa" after the Targa Florio race in Sicily, for two reasons: First, this is the site of repeated Porsche conquests. Second, and quite appropriately, the word "Targa" in Italian means "shield."

tarp
Short for *tarpaulin*, a flexible cover to protect the passenger compartment of an open car, such as a roadster, or the cargo bed of a pickup truck, when they are not in use. See also *tonneau cover.*

tar paper
Vinyl roof covering; same as a *landau top.*

taxicab
Race car with what looks like passenger car bodywork, but a pure racing vehicle underneath, such as a NASCAR *stocker* or an NHRA *Pro Stock.*

TBI
See *throttle body injection.*

T-bone
For one vehicle to strike another broadside, at a right angle; same as *center punch*, def. 1.

T-bucket, T-tub
Model T Ford roadster or phaeton.

TCS
Transmission-controlled spark, an ignition spark advance control device activated through the transmission. If there is an increase in load on the transmission, the TCS will advance the spark; if there is a decrease in load on the transmission, the TCS will retard the spark.

TDC
See *top dead center.* See also *BDC*

TE
See *top eliminator.*

tech
Technical inspection; examination of competing vehicles before a racing event to see that they conform with the rules of the sanctioning association.

teepee exhaust system
Exhaust system for the Volkswagen Beetle engine with primary pipes in a vertical position, resembling a Native American Indian teepee.

teething troubles
Difficulties with a new part or with a completely new vehicle. A radically different race car, for example, is likely to have teething troubles during its first few appearances in competition.

Teflon pin button
Piston pin retainer made from a solid piece of Teflon that fits between the pin and the cylinder wall.

TEL
See *tetraethyl lead.*

telescoping gauge
T-shaped instrument for finding the inside dimensions of cylinders and other holes. The cross-bar of the T is a spring-loaded, telescoping arm, the ends of which snap into place against the inner walls of the cylinder. The gauge is then removed and the arm measured with a micrometer to find the inside diameter of the cylinder. Also called a *snap gauge.* See photo page 155.

temp stick
Crayon-like stick designed to melt at a specific temperature when rubbed on a heated part. For example, a temp stick is used to tell when a pre-heated piece of metal is ready to be welded.

temper
1. Measure of a metal's hardness and elasticity.
2. As a verb, after hardening metal by heating it, to reheat it to a lower than critical temperature and then cool it, in order to reduce brittleness.

tensile strength
Maximum tension, pulling in opposite directions and measured in pounds per square inch, that a metal can withstand before breaking.

tenths
Measure of personal performance. For example, a racer who drives at the peak of his or her ability is running ten tenths, while one driving at a relaxed pace back in the pack may be running only six or seven tenths, or even less.

terminal speed
In drag racing, the maximum speed at which a vehicle passes through the traps at the end of a quarter-mile.

test lamp, test light
Light with two leads that can be used to test the continuity of a circuit. If the light illuminates when the leads are attached to two points on a circuit, there is continuity between those two points.

tetraethyl lead
$Pb(C_2H_5)_4$, a fuel additive which improved *octane* and, thus, reduced engine *knock*, and also provided upper cylinder lubrication, particularly around the valve seats. Gasoline containing tetraethyl lead was known as *leaded fuel*. The lead in tetraethyl lead has been judged to be toxic. Its use is now severely restricted and will eventually be prohibited. See also *Ethyl* and *leaded fuel*.

T-handle
T-shaped hand tool used to drive sockets.

T-head engine
Flathead engine with the intake valves on one side of the cylinders and the exhaust valves on the other, giving the cylinders and combustion chambers a T shape in cross section. The *Mercer Raceabout* was one of the most famous cars to use a T-head engine. See also *flathead*.

thermactor pump
Pump which injects fresh air into the exhaust system to promote secondary burning of the exhaust gasses in order to reduce harmful emissions.

thermal efficiency
Difference between the potential energy, in Btu's per pound or per gallon, of a fuel fed into an engine and the actual energy developed from that fuel by the engine.

thermal stability
Ability of a device to reach and maintain a specific temperature for long periods of time.

thermostat
Device which opens or closes a valve or switch in response to changes in temperature. One of the most important uses of a thermostat in a car or truck is in the cooling system, where such a device shuts off the flow of coolant from the engine back to the radiator in order to help a cold engine get up to proper operating temperature more quickly.

thermostatically controlled air cleaner
Device which regulates the temperature of air entering an engine's air cleaner in order to reduce emissions from too hot or too cool an air/fuel mixture.

thermostatic pressure valve
Valve that opens or closes in response to changes in temperature.

thermostatic vacuum switch
Vacuum switch that opens or closes in response to changes in temperature.

thermosyphon
Flow of coolant in a radiator made possible by the differences in density of coolant at higher and lower temperatures.

thin wall guide
Insert used to repair a worn or damaged valve guide; same as *false guide*.

thinner
Solvent used to reduce the viscosity of a liquid, such as paint.

thou
Short for thousandth or thousandths of an inch, the usual degree of precision in machining engine parts. For the sake of uniformity, thou is used even when the actual fraction is larger. For example, 0.030 is read as "thirty thou" rather than as "three one-hundredths," which it also is.

third member
Differential.

three on the tree
Three-speed manual transmission with a steering column-mounted shift lever.

three-piece valve
A valve manufactured from three different pieces of metal, often used in high performance racing engines. The valve head can be made of high temperature- and corrosion-resistant metal; the stem made of a softer material that reduces valve guide wear; and the tip made of a hard metal to resist the abuse of the rocker arm.

three-way catalyst
Catalytic converter with one section coated with platinum and palladium and the other with platinum and rhodium.

three-window coupe
Coupe body without rear quarter windows. Its three windows are the ones in each of the two doors and the one at the rear.

throat
1. Individual carburetor barrel.
2. Lower part of a connecting rod beam.

throttle
Accelerator pedal. In the early days of the automobile, the term referred to a hand control that governed engine speed.

throttle body
Housing that contains the throttle valve or valves in a *throttle body injection* system.

throttle body injection
System which injects fuel below a throttle valve in a carburetor-like barrel, rather than injecting it into individual ports or cylinders. Abbreviated *TBI*.

throttle plate
See *throttle valve*.

throttle position sensor
Device which detects the position of the throttle valve.

throttle valve
In either a carburetor or fuel injection system, a flap valve which controls the amount of air admitted to the induction system.

throw
Connecting rod journal on a crankshaft.

throwout bearing
In a clutch assembly, a shaft-mounted thrust bearing that reacts to pressure on the clutch pedal to disengage the clutch and, thus, disconnect the engine from the drivetrain.

thrust bearing
Bearing, usually part of a main bearing, which limits a crankshaft's end-to-end movement.

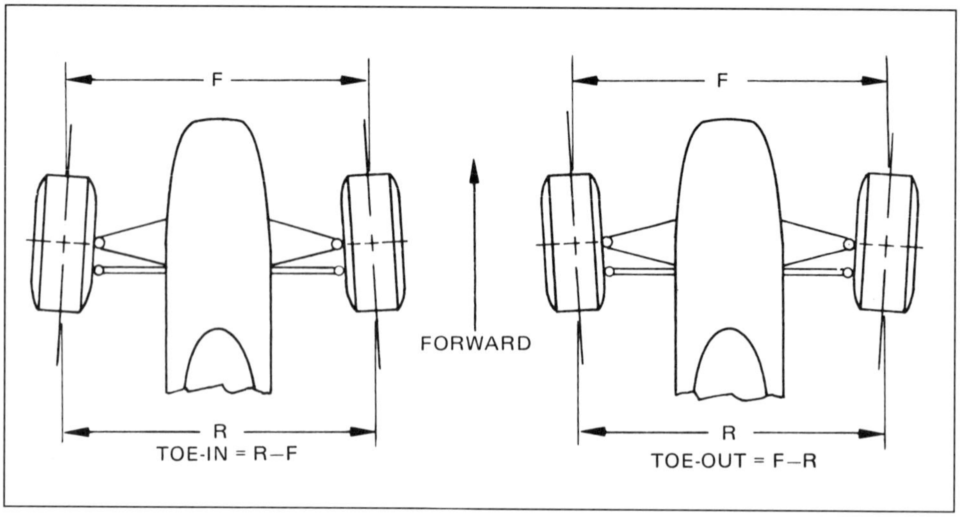

toe-in, toe-out

thrust plate
In an OHV engine, a retainer which positions the camshaft in the block, and also limits its end-to-end movement.

thrust surface
Area of a block or crank, at a right angle to the bearings, which absorbs end-to-end thrust pressure.

thrust washer
Bearing, usually separate from the main bearing, which limits a crankshaft's end-to-end movement.

thumbnail grooves
Thin grooves on a crankshaft thrust bearing which provide lubrication of the thrust surface.

tie rod
In a steering system, the linkage between a pitman or idler arm and a steering arm; the steering arm, in turn, turns the steering knuckle and, with it, the wheel.

tie rod ends
Bearing-like spherical joints at either end of a *tie rod*.

TIG welding
Tungsten inert gas welding. The electrode is tungsten because it doesn't melt at welding temperatures. The inert gas, usually argon, shields the weld from atmospheric impurities, providing a high-quality weld. TIG welding is also called *Heliarc*, a tradename of Linde Welding and Cutting Systems which developed the process, originally using helium as the inert gas. See *Heliarc welding* and *MIG welding*.

tie rod

Tijuana chrome
Silver spray paint.

time trials
Individual timed runs by race cars, often used to determine starting positions for a race. See also *qualify*.

timing belt, timing chain, timing gear
In an overhead valve or overhead cam engine, the belt, chain or gear through which the crankshaft drives the camshaft or camshafts.

timing light
Electronic instrument for checking ignition timing, i.e., the crankshaft angles at which the spark plugs fire.

timing valve
Valve in a fuel injection pump which times the delivery of fuel to the injectors.

tin
1. Although tin is a specific metallic element, the word is often used as a generic term for metal, as in *Tin Indian*, *tinny*, *tin snips*, *tin top* and *tinwork*.
2. Racing trophy.

Tin Indian
Pontiac.

tinny
Station wagon with an all-metal body, as opposed to a *woody*.

tin snips
Hand tool for cutting thin gauge sheet metal.

tin top
Car with an enclosed body. In some forms of racing, specifically, a two-door sedan or coupe.

tinwork
Auto bodywork.

tip the can
To increase the percentage of nitro in a racing fuel mixture.

tire black
Black liquid dressing used to freshen the appearance of tires.

tire iron
Thick bladed tool for removing a tire from a wheel.

tire pucker
Condition when a tire is installed on too narrow a wheel, causing the tread to pucker or pull up on the edges.

tire scrub
Sliding of a tire at an angle to the direction the tire is pointed. See *slip angle*.

tire stagger
On some oval track race cars, the difference in diameter between two tires on the same axle. The tires on the right side of the vehicle are larger than those on the left to provide more stable handling as the car goes around the track in what is essentially one long, left turn.

piston at top dead center

tire valve
See *Schrader valve*.

toe-in, toe-out
Vertical inclination of a pair of wheels slightly toward or slightly away from each other, as seen from the front of a vehicle. With rear-wheel drive, the leading edges of the front wheels tend to pull away from each other, so they are set with toe-in to counteract that tendency. With front-wheel drive, the opposite is true and the front wheels tend to push toward each other, so they are set with toe-out. See illustration previous page.

tolerance
Allowable variation from a standard specification.

toluene
$C_6H_5CH_3$, a colorless, flammable, liquid hydrocarbon, used as a cleaning solvent to dissolve gums and lacquers, and as a high-octane fuel. In fact, toluene was used as the reference fuel for a gasoline's anti-knock number until the auto and oil industries standardized on *iso-octane* for that purpose.

tongue weight
See *hitch weight*.

ton
Speed of 100 miles per hour.

tonneau cover
Flexible cover to protect the passenger compartment of an open car, such as a roadster, when it is not occupied. The tonneau cover usually has a zipper down the middle, so that the passenger's seat can be kept covered while the car is being driven. In recent years, the term has also been used to describe a variety of covers for the cargo beds of pickup trucks. See also *tarp*.

top dead center
The position of a piston at the end of an upward stroke.

top eliminator
In drag racing, the overall winner of a series of eliminations.

top end
1. High engine rpm, point at which horsepower is greatest.
2. In drag racing, the far end of the quarter-mile.

top-end power
Engine output at high rpm. See *top end*.

Top Fuel
Drag racing's hottest category. Top Fuel dragsters are the quickest accelerating automobiles in the world. They are powered by custom-built aluminum engines with supercharging and fuel injection, developing over 4000 horsepower. The best of them are capable of quarter-mile ETs of less than five seconds, and top speeds in excess of 300 mph. See photo next page.

top inch
First inch of the piston stroke downward from the deck; where the most wear is usually found in a cylinder.

top loader
Ford four-speed transmission introduced in the mid-1960s and produced in close-ratio, high-performance form through the early 1970s. The name top loader derived from the fact the access panel was on top of the gear case, instead of in its usual position on the side. The shift linkage connected through bosses on the side.

top-mount battery
Battery with terminals located on top of the case, rather than on a side.

top ring
Uppermost ring on a piston.

top time
In drag racing, same as *terminal speed*, the maximum speed at which a vehicle passes through the traps at the end of a quarter-mile. Top time is really a misnomer because it is speed, not just time, that is being measured.

Top Fuel

torque plate

torching
1. Flame cutting or burning of a valve face caused by excessive detonation. Torching will eventually destroy the valve.
2. To flame-cut metal, such as a rusted muffler, with an oxyacetylene welder.

torque
Measure of a force producing torsion and rotation around an axis. Torque is the product of the force, usually measured in pounds, and a radius perpendicular to the axis of the force extending to the point where the force is applied or where it originates, usually measured in feet. The result is expressed in *foot-pounds* or *pounds-feet*. Elsewhere in this book, those units of measure are defined for the sake of simplicity in terms of linear movement. To understand their application in rotational movement, as is the case in an engine, envision a unit of torque, or one pound-foot, as a force of one pound acting on a lever one foot long. Imagine such a lever attached at an angle of 90 degrees to one end of an engine's crankshaft. As the crank rotates, the free end of the lever will follow a circle with a radius of one foot. The force being applied at the free end of the lever during one revolution will be one pound over a distance equal to the circumference of a circle with a radius of one foot, which would be two times π (3.1416) times one, or 6.2832 feet. Note that, in an engine, the force originates at the axis, i.e., the crankshaft, and is applied at the outer end of the lever. When torque is used to tighten a nut or bolt, just the opposite is true. The force originates at the outer end of the lever, the torque wrench handle, and is applied at the axis, the nut or bolt. Some engineers prefer to acknowledge this distinction by limiting the term "pounds-feet" to the torque produced by an engine and "foot-pounds" to the torque applied by a wrench.

torque converter
Fluid coupling incorporating three basic elements, impeller, turbine and stator, used with an automatic transmission. The engine drives the impeller which, in turn, splashes oil to drive the turbine which is connected to the gearbox. The stator is a bladed wheel which multiplies torque by redirecting oil from the turbine back to the impeller.

torque plate
Thick metal plate bolted to the deck of a block during cylinder boring and honing to reproduce the stress caused when the heads are installed and the head bolts are properly torqued. Using a torque plate is a must for cast blocks with thin walls.

torque spec
Specified force in foot-pounds needed to tighten a particular nut or bolt.

torque steer
In a front-drive vehicle, especially one with a high-performance engine, torque steer is a tendency of the car to veer to one side when power is applied. The phenomenon is due to uneven steering forces generated by the axle half shafts. It is particularly a problem when the half shafts differ in length.

torque tube
Rear-wheel-drive system in which the driveshaft is enclosed in a tube extending from the transmission tailshaft to the rear axle. The torque tube prevents the axle housing from being twisted by engine power or braking force.

torque wrench
Wrench used to tighten nuts or bolts to specific torque figures. A torque wrench usually has a long handle for leverage and a digital or analog read out of the amount of torque in pounds-feet being applied, or some wrenches are spring-loaded in the handle. With the latter type, the handle is set to the desired torque, and as the nut or bolt is tightened, the ratchet head will click audibly to indicate that the torque setting has been reached. See photo next page.

torque wrench

torsion bar
Form of spring used in vehicle suspension, consisting of a long bar with one end attached to the chassis and the other to a lever or arm connected to a wheel. A torsion bar "springs" by twisting on its own lengthways axis; in a sense, it acts like a coil spring that has been unwound and straightened out. Torsion bars may be mounted either longitudinally or transversely.

torsional rigidity
Resistance of a structure, such as an auto body or chassis, to twisting or flexing.

totalled
Condition of a vehicle that has been damaged beyond repair. It would cost more to fix it than it would to replace it.

town car
Formerly and formally, a chauffeur-driven, four-door sedan with an open cockpit and an enclosed passenger compartment. In Europe, such a body was often called a *sedan de ville*. Note that Lincoln has appropriated "town car" for an ordinary sedan, and Cadillac has done the same with "sedan de ville." See also *brougham*.

tow vehicle
Car or truck set up to pull a trailer or another vehicle.

toy
1. Any vehicle driven for fun and not just for transportation.
2. Short for *Toyota*.

Toyota
"Toyota" is a variation of "Toyoda," the name of the family who established what became Japan's largest automaker and who remain active in its management to this day. Toyoda involvement in the motor industry began in 1933 with the formation of an Automotive Department within an established family enterprise, Toyoda Automatic Loom Works Company. Car and truck prototypes were completed by early 1935, both with an engine that was a duplicate of the Chevrolet six. By 1936, production of both was underway, with the emphasis on the truck. In 1937, the Automotive Department of the Loom Works was separated from the parent company and reorganized as the Toyota Motor Company. Production of Toyota cars never exceeded more than a few hundred units a year until after World War II, and it was not until the 1960s that the company began to grow to its current prominence.

TPI
See *tuned port injection*.

track
Distance between the center of the tread of a tire on one side of a vehicle and the center of the tread of the corresponding tire on the other side. Sometimes referred to as *tread*.

traction bar
Device to prevent axle twist and spring wind-up during hard acceleration in the rear suspension of a rear-wheel-drive race car, especially one with semi-elliptic springs; a traction bar on either side attaches to the axle housing at one end and to the chassis frame at the other. Traction bars are especially common on drag racing vehicles but are also found on oval track cars. See also *axle tramp, axle wind-up*.

Traction-Lok
Ford *limited-slip differential*.

tractor
See *truck tractor*.

traction bar

trail braking
Driving technique where the brakes are applied after the car is turned into a corner, and modulated almost to the apex. When properly applied, the combination of braking and cornering forces can help rotate the car, transferring weight more effectively, and theoretically make the car get through the corner quicker.

trailer
1. Non-powered vehicle, usually intended to haul cargo and designed to be towed with a car or truck. See also *travel trailer.*
2. As a verb, same as *put on the trailer.*

trailer tongue
Extension on the front of a trailer that attaches to a hitch ball on a tow vehicle.

trailing arm
Suspension arm that attaches to the chassis ahead of the wheel. Trailing arms on either side of a vehicle usually pivot on a common transverse axis. The most common use of transverse arms is for the rear wheels on front-wheel-drive cars.

tramp
See *axle tramp, axle wind-up.*

tranny, trans
Transmission.

Trans-Am
1. Trans-American Championship, annual SCCA road racing series for pony cars and small sedans. The first race was held at Sebring in 1966, and called "The Four-Hour Governor's Cup for Sedans." The race was won by Jochen Rindt in an Alfa Romeo 1600 GTA. During the late sixties and early seventies, the series became a veritable battleground between factory-sponsored teams, featuring the finest names in racing like Mark Donohue, Parnelli Jones, Dan Gurney and Roger Penske. However, from the early seventies through much of the eighties, the series declined in both the level of competition and popularity, as the U.S. manufacturer's curtailed their participation. But beginning in the early nineties, the series experienced a rebirth of sorts, as manufacturers again began sponsoring teams. It is the oldest road racing series in the United States.
2. Without a hyphen, Trans Am is the name of the performance version of the Pontiac Firebird. Pontiac pays a licensing fee to SCCA for every Trans Am sold.

transaxle
Contraction of transmission and axle, indicating a combined transmission and final drive assembly. Transaxles are common in front-engine, front-drive cars, and in both mid-engine and rear-engine, rear-drive cars. They have also been used occasionally in front-engine, rear-drive cars, because of a theoretical advantage in weight distribution such a setup provides.

transfer case
Gearing device in a four-wheel-drive vehicle which splits engine output between the front and rear wheels. A part-time transfer case is one which can be disengaged from one end of the powertrain, usually the front, allowing the vehicle to be used in two-wheel drive, usually at the rear, when four-wheel traction is not needed. A full-time transfer case is permanently engaged and incorporates a third differential to prevent bind between the front and rear drive systems. A two-speed transfer case has an extra low gear for particularly rugged driving conditions.

transistorized ignition
Ignition system with conventional mechanical breaker points, but using transistor regulation of voltage that is much more efficient at higher speeds.

transmission
Gearing device in the powertrain which allows variations in the relationship between engine speed or rpm and road speed or mph. At startup, for example, the vehicle needs power only available at higher rpm but has to apply it at low mph in order to get the vehicle underway; using a low transmission gear accomplishes exactly that. Conversely, it takes relatively little power to maintain highway cruising speed, at least over level terrain, so a higher transmission gear can be used for lower rpm at higher mph, providing smoother, quieter and more economical engine operation.

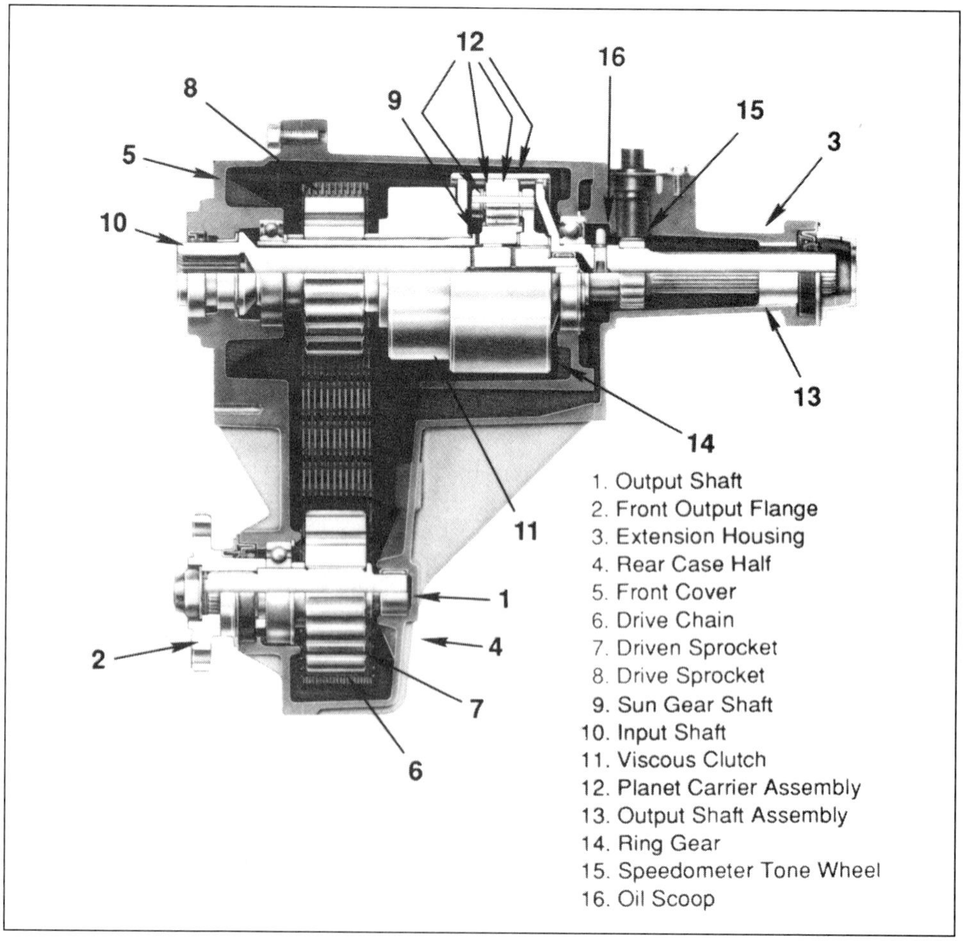

transfer case (GM)

transplant
1. Factory operated by an automaker in a country other than its own. The term was coined during the 1980s to describe the auto factories then being established in the United States by Japanese manufacturers. However, the practice is almost as old as the auto industry itself. To cite a couple of particularly significant examples, Ford established a transplant in England as early as 1911, while Rolls-Royce operated a transplant in Springfield, Massachusetts from 1921 through 1931. As for those Japanese transplants in this country, the two dominant automakers in Japan during the 1920s and 1930s were Ford and General Motors.
2. Transplant is also sometimes used to describe an *engine swap*.

transverse engine
Engine mounted sideways, or "east-west," in a vehicle chassis. Most modern front-drive cars have transverse engines.

transverse leaf spring
Leaf spring mounted sideways, perpendicular to a car's centerline instead of parallel to it. The idea is as old as the earliest Ford Model T and as new as the latest Chevrolet Corvette.

traps
1. In drag racing, the measured section at the end of a drag strip, usually beginning 66 feet before the actual quarter-mile mark and ending 66 feet beyond it for a total distance of 132 feet, where the maximum speed of a racing vehicle is measured.
2. In oval track or road racing, the fastest part of the course, usually near the end of a long straightaway, where radar guns are located to measure top speed.

trash box
Car or engine built up from junk parts.

travel trailer
Trailer with living accommodations for use as a recreational vehicle.

traverse handwheel
Wheel which moves a table on a grinding machine from one side to the other.

tread
1. Traction surface around the circumference of a tire.
2. Sometimes used as a synonym for *track*.

tree
See *Christmas tree*.

triangulation
Triangular arrangement of frame members for increased rigidity.

Tri-Chevy
1955, 1956 and 1957 Chevrolets.

tri-coat
Type of paint with three layers of top coat paint; the first coat is the color or base coat; the second coat is a clear paint with the pearl particles or flakes in it; and the third coat is the clear coat. Although tri-coats provide a glamorous, "wet" look, they are difficult to spot repair and color match.

tri-oval track
Closed course racing circuit with three sweeping, high-banked turns. Daytona International Speedway is the definitive example.

tri-power
Triple two-barrel carburetor setup. With capital letters, the term was used to describe Pontiac's triple 2-barrel Rochester setup in the 1960s, which was offered on a variety of Pontiac muscle cars.

tri-Y headers
Exhaust manifold that pairs cylinders according to their firing order, so that those which are at TDC or BDC at the same time merge into a single collector, and those collectors, in turn, merge into a single central collector. In a four-cylinder engine, specifically, this will result in a power pulse going into the header system every 180 degrees, which should provide better exhaust scavenging. See photo next page.

trophy dash
In oval track racing, a short match among the quickest qualifying cars at the start of the program.

trophy run
In drag racing, a match for an individual class trophy.

troubleshooting
Attempting to identify the source of a vehicle malfunction through the process of elimination.

truck tractor
Large truck with a fifth-wheel hitch to tow a *semi trailer*; often referred to simply as a *tractor*.

truing sleeve
Round metal device with a specific diameter hole, used to true a honing mandrel.

Tri-Power

tri-Y headers

tubbed

trunk
Separate storage compartment at the rear of most passenger cars.

TSB
Technical Service Bulletin, an official factory notice describing any problems on current model vehicles.

TSD
Time, speed and distance, a type or *rally* involving those three factors.

TT
See *top time.*

T-top
Partially removable car roof, consisting of a removable panel above each front door. However, a portion of the roof between the two panels remains fixed, helping the car to maintain structural integrity without special reinforcement.

tub
1. Phaeton body; See *phaeton.*
2. External structure of an auto body, the shell itself separate from any internal reinforcements.

tubbed
Standard passenger car body fitted with oversize rear wheel wells, or *tubs,* to accommodate drag racing slicks; a common modification for both *Pro Stock* and *Pro Street.*

tubing notcher
Tool which cuts a semicircle out of the end of a tube to facilitate welding completely around the tube.

tubular pushrod
Same as *hollow pushrod.*

tucked and rolled
Bold type of upholstery pleating sometimes used in customs.

Tucker
The Tucker Corporation was established by Preston Tucker in Chicago in 1946 to build a new and radically different passenger car. What eventually emerged was the Tucker '48, a relatively large sedan with such advanced features as an opposed six-cylinder engine mounted at the rear and fully independent suspension. Some 50 units were actually produced and most of them still exist. In fact, 22 of them were used in the 1988 film *Tucker.* Unfortunately, Tucker was charged by the Securities Exchange Commission with fraud and violation of its regulations in the way he handled his company's public stock offerings. Defending himself against the charges broke both Tucker and his company. Just how good a car the Tucker '48 really was remains a subject of controversy. Professional engineers who have had experience with the car feel it was not a fully developed design ready for mass production. But, as the film tried to show, Tucker does appear to have been sincere in his ambition to produce a truly advanced automobile.

Tudor
One-time Ford designation for a two-door sedan. See also *Fordor.*

Tuftride
Tradename of a liquid chemical process used to surface-harden metal parts, such as rods and crankshafts.

tules
Back country or boondocks. The term is the name of a cattail that grows in rural areas of California's San Joaquin Valley and, by extension, it has come to mean rural areas itself. Sometimes misspelled "Toolies." A racing driver who spins off course is said to be "off in the tules." See also *boonies.*

tulip valve
Intake or exhaust valve with a tulip shape on the backside of the valve head to increase air/fuel flow from the port into the combustion chamber.

tune-up
Routine maintenance procedure that, with an older point ignition system, includes

removal and replacement of the points, condensor, rotor and, if necessary, spark plugs, plus adjustment of the ignition timing. On a modern electronic ignition, the only items replaced are the rotor and spark plugs.

tuned exhaust, tuned headers
Exhaust system with equal length passages, long enough to cause a resonant effect at a specific, predetermined engine rpm, drawing burned gasses from the combustion chambers more rapidly and more efficiently at that rpm.

tuned intake
See *ram tuning*.

tuned port injection
Fuel injection system with equal length port runners to the cylinders. A familiar example is Chevy's TPI system used on 1985-1992 small-blocks. See photo next page.

tunes
Stereo system.

tunnel ram manifold
Intake manifold with a large plenum and long runners to the intake ports to improve output at high rpm.

turbo
See *turbocharger*.

turbocar
Automobile with a turbine engine.

turbocharger
Originally turbosupercharger, a turbine-type supercharger driven by the force of exhaust gasses rather than by mechanical means. See also *supercharger*.

Turbo Hydro
General Motors' Turbo Hydra-Matic automatic transmission.

turbo intercooler
See *intercooler*.

turbo lag
Delay in engine response when a driver hits the throttle in a turbocharged vehicle, as the turbo spools up to produce enough boost pressure to be effective.

turkey pan
Metal flange installed in an engine to reduce internal oil splash in the lifter area.

turn
In addition to its obvious meaning, to change direction, turn can also mean to reach a specific speed, such as to "turn 100 mph."

turning circle, turning diameter
Diameter of the circle a car would scribe if driven 360 degrees with the steering fully locked.

tunnel ram manifold

turret punch press
Machine tool used to cut various size holes in sheet metal.

TVS
See *thermostatic vacuum switch*.

TWC
See *three-way catalyst*.

twice pipes
On a hot rod, dual exhaust system.

twin
Two-cylinder engine.

twin cam
Dual overhead camshafts or *DOHC*.

Twin-Grip
AMC *limited-slip differential*.

twin I-beam
Front suspension system unique to Ford light trucks, using a coil spring and an individual, transverse I-beam at each wheel, with the I-beam attached to the chassis on the side opposite the wheel.

twin plug head
Cylinder head with two spark plugs per cylinder.

twin plug ignition system
Ignition system that not only has two spark plugs per cylinder, but two coils and two distributors as well.

twin torsion bar
Suspension system using two torsion bars, one placed above the other. Twin torsion bar setups are often used on sprint cars. See also *torsion bar*.

two-bolt main
Engine block with main caps held in place with two bolts. See also *four-bolt mains* and *main cap*.

two in the glue
Two-speed automatic transmission, such as the original Chevrolet Powerglide.

two-piece valve
Valve with a head and stem made from different materials. The head is usually made from very hard material for resistance to wear.

T

two-piece piston
Piston with a removable skirt assembly. The head is usually cast iron while the skirt is aluminum.

two-plane manifold
Intake manifold with two plenums between the carburetor and the intake ports. It is more commonly called a *dual-plane manifold.*

two-plus-two
Four/five-passenger, two-door body with limited rear seating space; see also *club coupe.*

two-stroke cycle
Cycle of engine operation in which combustion occurs in each cylinder on every revolution of the crankshaft. In other words, every downstroke is a power stroke. This is accomplished by having the piston perform some of the functions of valves, covering and uncovering ports in the cylinder walls, and by admitting fresh air/fuel mixture into a sealed crankcase, rather than directly into the combustion chamber.

2WD
Two-wheel-drive.

tuned port injection

U

U-bolt
U-shaped bolt with both ends threaded for nuts. A common use of U-bolts on motor vehicles is to attach an axle to leaf springs.

U-joint
See *universal joint.*

ultraviolet light
Portion of the light spectrum beyond violet; used in the Magnaglow and Zyglow processes of non-destructive testing for cracks in metal parts. See *Magnaglow* and *Zyglow*.

umbrella seal
Valve stem seal that rides through its center on the valve stem, formed in the shape of an umbrella to shed oil away from the stem and guide.

unburned hydrocarbons
Fuel which remains wholly or partly unburned after combustion. Along with carbon monoxide (CO) and oxides of nitrogen (NOx), unburned hydrocarbons (HC) are one of the three major pollutants in exhaust gasses.

undercarriage
The chassis or platform of a vehicle and all the running gear attached to it, including steering, suspension and drivetrain.

undersize
Condition of a part or any item that is smaller than the standard specification for it.

understaging
Placing a vehicle at the start of a drag race behind the usual staging position; the same as *backstaging* and the opposite of *deep staging* or *overstaging*.

understeer
Condition in cornering where the slip angles of the front tires are greater than the slip angles of the rear tires; the front end of the vehicle tends to break loose and slide, or *push* toward the outside of a turn. See illustration next page. See also *oversteer*.

unequal A-arms
Double A-arm suspension where one arm, usually the upper one, is smaller than the other.

unfair advantage
Extra edge enjoyed by a racing team which simply pays attention to every significant detail of vehicle construction, preparation and operation. The only thing unfair about it is that it forces other competing teams to work harder! Roger Penske's Indycar efforts provide an example of a consistently successful application of an unfair advantage.

unglued
Damaged or destroyed. An engine or transmission that has blown has come "unglued." The term can also be applied to a person who is very upset, such as the owner of an engine or transmission that has come unglued.

unibody
Short for *unit body*, a vehicle structure which combines the chassis frame and body in a single stressed unit.

unicast
Part or other item cast as a single, complete piece.

uniform pitch spring
Valve spring with equally spaced coils.

unit body
See *unibody*.

universal joint
Mechanical joint that can transmit rotary motion while swiveling in any direction. On a front-engine, rear-drive car, a *U-joint*, as it is known for short, is used to connect the driveshaft to the transmission and, in some cases, to connect the driveshaft to the differential. With independent suspension at the drive wheels, regardless of engine or drive location, U-joints are used to connect the drive axle half shafts to the differential or transaxle. Except in the case of swing axles, U-joints are also used to connect the half shafts to the wheels.

unleaded fuel
Gasoline which does not contain *tetraethyl lead.*

unobtainium
Mythical metal alloy which is both lighter and stronger than anything actually available.

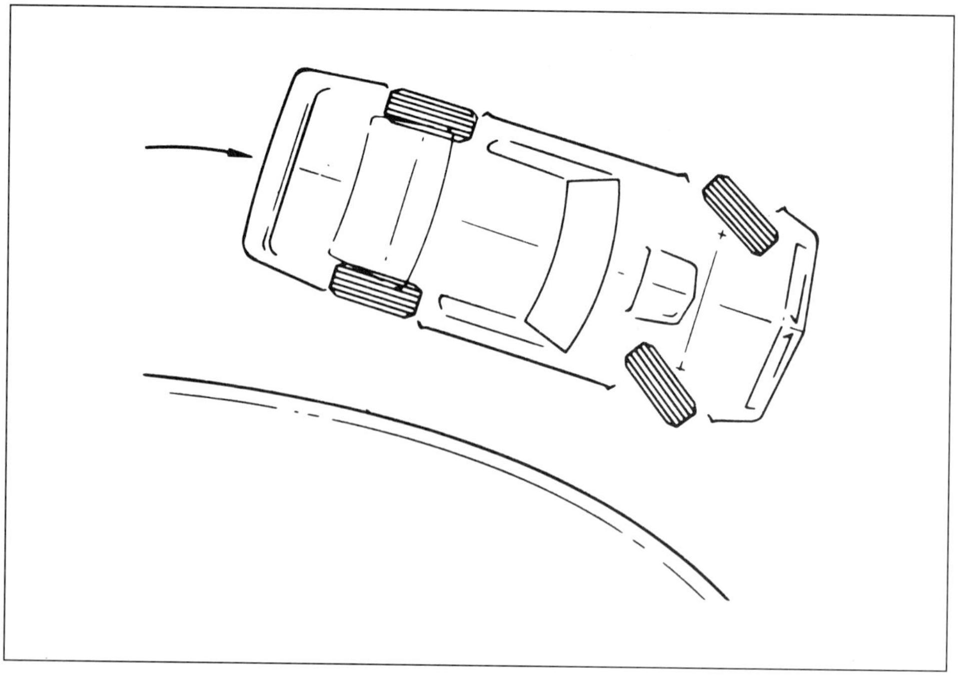

understeer

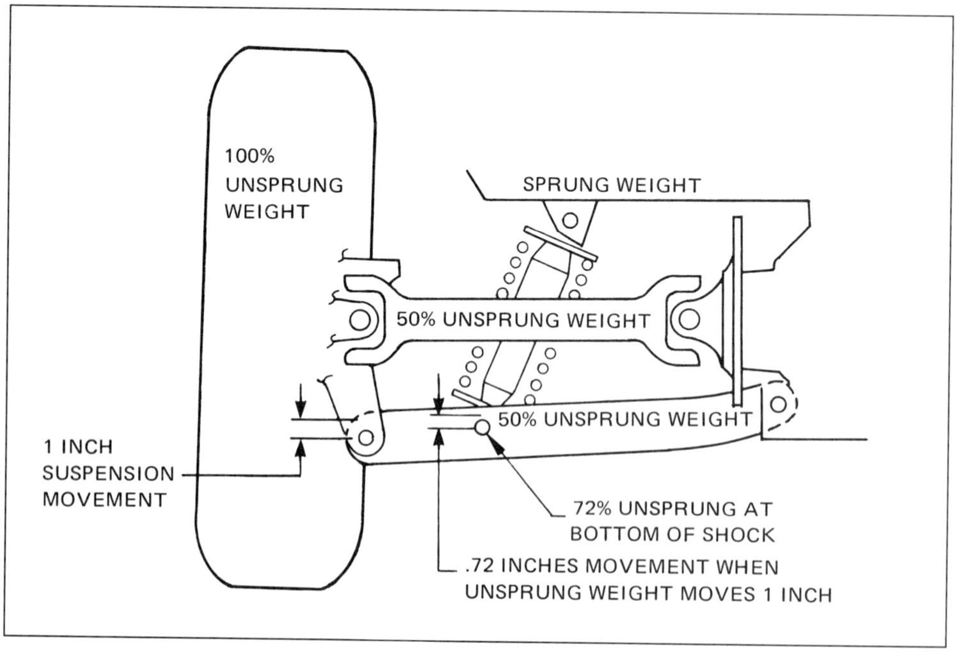

unsprung weight

unsprung weight
The mass of vehicle components not supported by the suspension system. Wheels, tires, outboard brakes and axles are all part of the unsprung weight. See also *sprung weight*.

updraft carburetor
Carburetor with upward airflow.

upper A-arm, upper control arm
Upper arm in a double *A-arm* suspension system. See *A-arm*.

upshift
To change from a lower gear to a higher one.

US
See *undersize*.

USAC
United States Auto Club, 4910 West 16th Street, Speedway, Indiana 46224; (317) 247-5151. Sanctioning body for the Indianapolis 500, as well as for various forms of oval track racing.

USCS
United States Customary System, the system of measurement traditionally used in the United States, as opposed to *SI*, the International System.

ute
Utility vehicle. The term originated in Australia, where it was applied to passenger car-based pickup trucks, similar to the Chevrolet El Camino and Ford Ranchero.

utility body
Replacement for the cargo bed on a pickup truck which resembles a cargo bed in general appearance, but has higher, thicker walls full of storage compartments of various shapes and sizes. The utility body is popular with craftsmen because of the space it provides for concealed, lockable storage of tools, equipment and supplies.

U tube
See *manometer*.

UV
Ultraviolet. See *ultraviolet light*.

V

vacuum
Enclosed space from which virtually all the air has been evacuated and which, consequently, has an atmospheric pressure near zero. A complete vacuum is impossible because the material used for the enclosure has definite vapor pressure, however slight it may be. Nonetheless, the difference between the very low pressure within the vacuum enclosure and the ambient pressure outside the enclosure is great enough that the vacuum can be put to work.

vacuum advance
Device which advances or retards ignition timing in accordance with the degree of vacuum in the intake manifold. When there is little or no vacuum, as is the case at either idle or wide-open throttle, there is no advance. When there is vacuum, as at part throttle, there is advance.

vacuum brake booster
Device which uses vacuum to amplify braking force.

vacuum canister, vacuum chamber
Vacuum enclosure which could serve the needs of vacuum-actuated accessories, eliminating reliance on vacuum within the engine, which could disturb proper air/fuel flow and cause misfiring.

vacuum motor
Small canister containing a diaphragm and rod actuated by vacuum and used to operate a part. The vacuum-operated windshield wipers on some older cars, for example, relied on such a motor.

vacuum pump
Device used to create vacuum.

vacuum secondaries
Secondary barrels on a four-barrel carburetor which are opened by vacuum.

vacuum tap
Point at which vacuum can be released from an enclosure, such as on an intake manifold.

vacuum test
Test to determine the presence of vacuum in an engine.

valve
Circular, stemmed device used in pairs, intake and exhaust, to control the flow of air/fuel mixture into an engine and burned gasses out of it. The intake valve opens to allow air/fuel mixture into a cylinder during the intake stroke and the exhaust valve opens to let burned gasses out during the exhaust stroke, while both close to seal the cylinder during the compression and combustion strokes.

valve angle
Angle at which the valve face is machined.

valve clearance
See *valve lash.*

valve face
Part of the valve which faces into the cylinder.

valve grinder
Machine used to grind the valve face and stem end.

valve guide
Passageway in the cylinder head through which the valve stem extends.

valve job
Disassembly and machining of all parts in the cylinder head, including grinding the valves, repairing or replacing valve guides, resurfacing the cylinder head, adjusting the spring tension, and adjusting stem end length.

valve keeper
Device to position the valve spring retainer correctly on the valve stem. See *keepers.*

valve lash
Specified clearance between a valve stem end and a rocker arm on an OHV engine, or between a valve stem end and the camshaft on an OHC engine, to allow for heat expansion. Also referred to as *valve lash.*

valve lift
Actual distance a valve opens. The *gross valve lift* includes the running clearance as specified by the engine manufacturer, while the *net valve lift* does not include the running clearance.

valve lifter
Cylindrically shaped part of the valvetrain that is directly lifted by the camshaft lobe and, in turn, lifts the valve off its seat. Also

called a cam follower or *tappet*. May be either hydraulic or mechanical in operation. See also *hydraulic valve lifter* and *mechanical valve lifter*.

valve pocket, valve relief
Area cut into the top of a piston for valve clearance at or near *TDC*.

valve retainer
Metal disc used to hold the valve spring at a specified distance on the valve stem.

valve rotator
Device which rotates a valve slightly while the engine is running; designed to even the wear of both the valve and valve seat.

valve seat
Ring of hard metal against which the back of a closed valve seals in the roof of the combustion chamber.

valve seat cutter
Cutter blade assembly used to counterbore a recess into a cylinder head for a replacement valve seat. The valve seat cutter is made with high speed steel or carbide cutter blades.

valve seat driver
Tool used to drive a valve seat insert into its counterbore.

valve seat insert
Replacement valve seat made of cast iron, steel, or Stellite.

valve spring
Spring, usually a small coil, which closes the valve when a camshaft lobe is not acting on the lifter and also keeps the lifter in contact with the lobe.

valve spring seat
Area in the cylinder head where the fixed end of the valve spring is attached.

valve stem
Long, slim, round part of a valve between the head and end.

valve stem groove
Part of the valve stem used to position the keepers and locate the valve retainer.

valve stud boss
Boss on a cylinder head which supports and holds a rocker arm stud.

valvetrain
In an OHV engine, the valves and the parts needed to actuate them, including valve lifters, pushrods, rocker arms and springs.

valve pockets

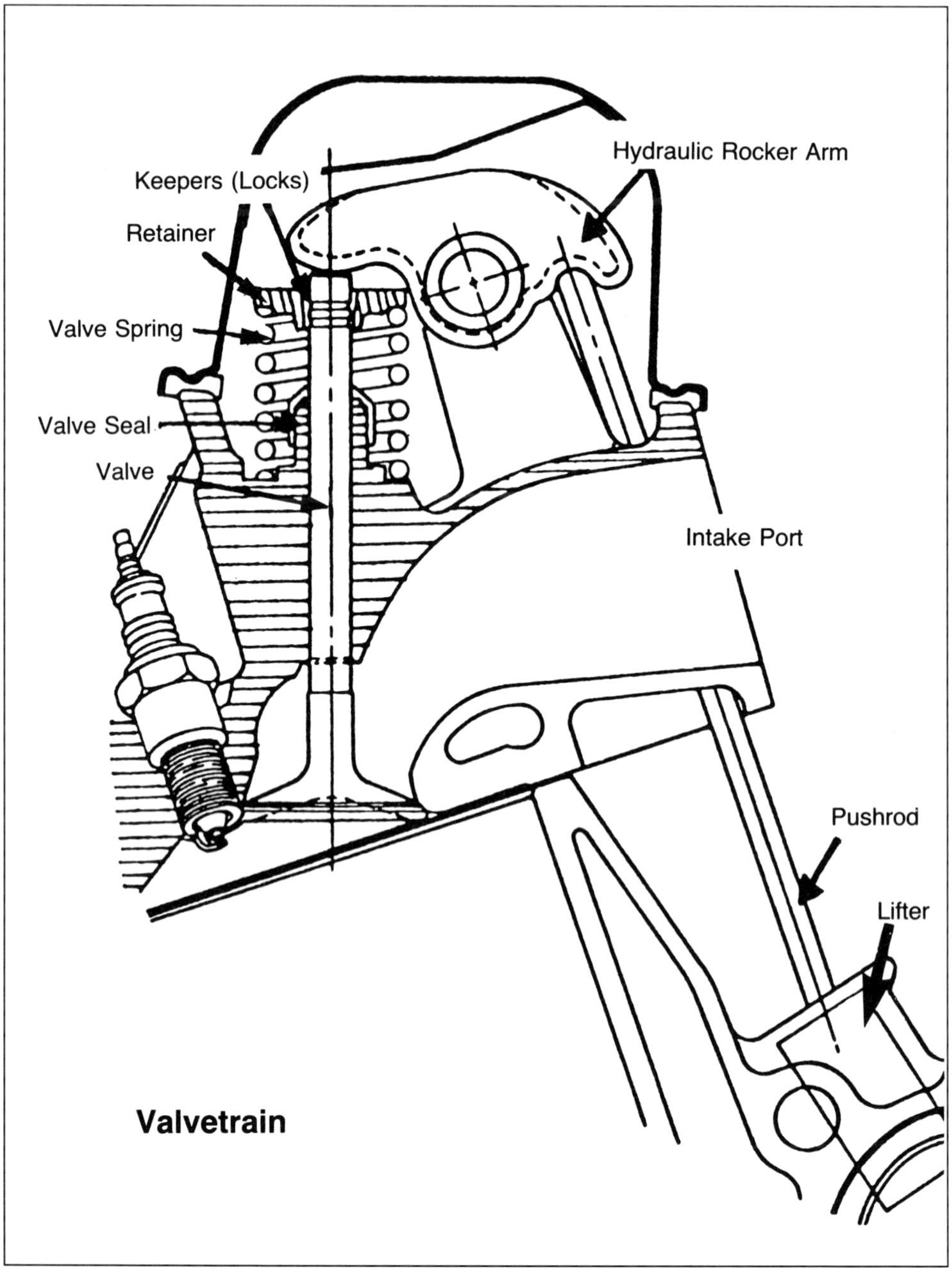

valvetrain (Chrysler)

van
Box-shaped light truck with a forward-positioned cab, providing a maximum amount of interior space for its overall size. A van can be used as an enclosed service or delivery truck or, with windows and seats, it can serve as a passenger vehicle—in effect, an oversize *station wagon.*

van conversion
Van that has been customized, either as a plush cruiser or as a camping vehicle.

vane pump
Hydraulic pump with small vanes in an elliptically shaped housing.

vapor
Gaseous form of a liquid or solid.

vapor lock
Condition when fuel boils in the fuel system, causing bubbles to form that interfere with the flow of fuel to the carburetor or, conversely, causing excess fuel to flood the carburetor. Either way, the engine will not run properly.

VARI
Vacuum Assisted Resin Injection, a body panel injection molding method developed by Lotus in England.

variable aperture carburetor
See *variable venturi carburetor.*

variable displacement engine
Engine which can be altered in working displacement by activating or deactivating cylinders, usually in pairs, by enabling or disabling their intake and exhaust valves. The object is to provide maximum displacement and horsepower for accelerating, passing and hill climbing, and minimum displacement for better fuel economy at steady cruising speeds. The Cadillac V-8-6-4 was an example of a variable displacement engine. As its name suggests, it could run on eight, six or four cylinders, depending on the load on the engine at any given moment.

variable pitch spring
Valve spring with unevenly spaced coils.

variable ratio steering
Power steering system which varies the steering ratio at different vehicle speeds. At low speeds, the steering is quicker to make it easier to maneuver the vehicle in and out of parking places. At higher speeds, the steering is slower so that the car does not dart around from small steering inputs by the driver.

variable resistor
Resistor which can be set at any level of resistance from zero ohms to the maximum capacity of the particular resistor. An everyday example is the volume control on a radio. A two-terminal variable resistor is a *rheostat*, while a three-terminal one is a *potentiometer* or *pot.*

variable venturi carburetor
Carburetor with an aperture or venturi usually square in shape, with one wall that moves in or out to vary the size of the aperture and, with it, the airflow capacity of the carburetor. The increase or decrease in aperture size is controlled by intake manifold vacuum. See also *venturi.*

varnish
Coating of oil and grease baked on parts.

VE
See *volumetric efficiency.*

Vee Dub
Volkswagen, from the pronunciation "vee double you" for "VW."

velocity stacks
Short tubes attached to carburetors. The length of the stacks is tuned to a resonant frequency that forces more air into the carb. See also *ram tuned*, but note the difference: Velocity stacks supply air to the carb, while ram tuning ducts air/fuel mixture from the carb to the combustion chambers.

Velvetouch
Specific brand of sintered steel brake linings.

ventilate the block
To throw a rod right through the block.

venturi
Slight hourglass shape in an air passage, as in a carburetor barrel or venturi. The narrowing of the passage at the "waist" of the venturi causes incoming air to speed up, creating a low-pressure area that draws in fuel through the jet from the float bowl. Named for G.B. Venturi, an 18th and 19th century Italian physicist.

vernier caliper
Precision instrument which can be used to measure either inside or outside dimensions of parts in inches and thousandths of inches. Invented by Pierre Vernier, a 17th century French mathematician.

'vert
Convertible.

vertical load
In chassis tuning, the amount of weight on a tire that serves as the input for a tire's performance. Vertical load changes continuously while the car is in motion, particularly during cornering, when weight from the inside tires is transferred to the outside tires. As vertical load is increased, the tire's cornering efficiency or traction, decreases.

velocity stacks

V

'Vette
Chevrolet Corvette.

vibration damper
See *harmonic balancer, harmonic damper.*

vicky
Victoria, a close-coupled two-door sedan body offered by Ford in the early 1930s, really a forerunner of the *club coupe*. Ford has since used Victoria inconsistently for a variety of two-door and four-door body styles, including most recently the Crown Victoria four-door sedan. The term originally meant a four-wheeled carriage with a passenger compartment seating two, a folding top for the passengers, and a separate high seat in front for the driver. It was first applied to such a carriage used to transport England's Queen Victoria.

victory lane
At an oval track or road course, an area usually opposite the grandstands on the main straightaway where the winner of a race is honored immediately after the event.

VIN
Vehicle identification number, the serial number identifying a specific car or truck and its basic equipment, such as engine, transmission and final drive ratio.

vintage car
Historic car, generally one built before 1925, which is considered the beginning of the classic car era.

viscosimeter
Device for measuring the viscosity of liquids. See *Saybolt viscosimeter.*

viscosity
Resistance of a liquid to flowing, i.e., the thickness of a liquid. The higher the viscosity, the thicker the liquid and the more resistant it is to flowing. For example, oil is generally more viscous than gasoline.

viscosity grade
Numerical rating of a liquid's viscosity as established by the American Petroleum Institute or *API.*

viscous coupling
Fluid coupling in which the input and output shafts are fitted with thin, alternating discs in a closed chamber. The chamber is filled with a highly viscous liquid which sticks to the alternating discs and tends to make them rotate at the same speed. At the same time, the fluid allows variations in speed due to mechanical force on either side of the coupling. A viscous coupling is sometimes used as an *interaxle differential* with *all-wheel drive* or *four-wheel drive.*

viscous damper
Type of crankshaft *harmonic balancer* that contains a high viscosity liquid to control engine vibrations. See *harmonic balancer.*

viscous fan
Cooling fan attached to a *viscous coupling.*

voiture omnibus
French for "carriage for all," source of the English word *bus.*

volatility
Measure of how readily a liquid evaporates. For example, gasoline has a greater volatility than diesel fuel.

Volksrod
Volkswagen modified for higher performance, i.e., a Volkswagen hot rod.

Volkswagen
In 1934, Ferdinand Porsche received a commission from the Nazi government of Germany to develop a small, inexpensive car. Within two years, he had produced the first prototypes of a small, beetle-shaped two-door sedan he called the VW or Volkswagen, German for "People's Car," literally, "Folks' Wagon." The car featured an air-cooled, opposed, four-cylinder engine mounted in the rear and fully independent suspension. Later, the government officially renamed the VW the KdF-Wagen, the initials standing for Kraft durch Freude, "Strength Though Joy," a slogan of the Nazi party. By 1939, a factory had been built in Wolfsburg to produce the KdF-Wagen, but only some 60 prototypes and pilot models had been built when the outbreak of World War II forced cancellation of the production of the little sedan. However, the KdF-Wagen chassis was used as the basis for an open, boxy-looking military vehicle called the Kübelwagen or "Tub Car." After the war, the partition of Germany put Wolfsburg in the British-occupied zone. British military authorities took over the KdF-Wagen factory in late 1945 and began limited production of the sedan under Porsche's original name for it, VW. By 1949, the factory had been returned to German administration, and serious production had begun of what would become known as the VW Beetle. It would eventually become the best selling car of all time. Volkswagen has gone on to build a number of more modern cars. But the Beetle, with its rugged construction, air-cooled engine and independent suspension, remains popular in developing countries. As of the early 1990s, for example, the Beetle was still being manufactured in Mexico and was still one of the best-selling cars in that country.

volt
Measure of electrical force. One volt will produce an electric current flow of one ampere through a resistance of one ohm. The volt is named for Alessandro Volta, an 18th and 19th century Italian physicist.

voltage
Specific quantity of electrical force, expressed in volts.

voltage drop
Any reduction in voltage in an electrical circuit. All wire, no matter how low its resistance, causes at least a trace of voltage drop.

voltage regulator
Electrical device which controls the voltage produced by a vehicle's alternator or generator. Its purpose is to provide enough current to operate the vehicle's electrical equipment but not so much that the battery is overcharged.

voltmeter
Instrument to measure voltage.

volumetric efficiency
The relationship between an engine's theoretical air capacity and its actual airflow; abbreviated *VE.*

Volvo
Swedish car with a Latin name meaning "I roll." The first Volvo rolled in 1927 and, in the years since, the company has developed a reputation for vehicles that are conservative in both appearance and engineering, but are also rugged and dependable.

VOR
Vehicle off road, an auto repair industry term for a vehicle which is out of service because of a lack of parts needed to fix it.

VW
See *Volkswagen.*

W

wagon
See *station wagon.*

wail
To perform at peak efficiency. If you started at the beginning of this book and read this far in a single sitting, you've wailed!

wander
Abnormal steering or tracking of a vehicle.

Wankel engine
Rotary engine developed in Germany in the 1950s by Felix Wankel. It has a three-sided rotor in a trochoidal or slightly hourglass-shaped oval chamber. NSU, a former German automaker, was the first of only two companies to offer production passenger cars with the Wankel rotary. In the 1960s, it introduced a small sports car called the Spider with the engine. In 1968, NSU also began building a medium-sized, Wankel-powered sedan, the Ro 80, which was produced for nine years, until NSU went out of business in 1977. The only other manufacturer to use the Wankel engine in production cars was—and is—Japan's Mazda, which introduced its first rotary-powered vehicles in 1968. Mazda uses a dual rotary engine in its highly successful RX-7 sports car. In 1991, Mazda became the first Japanese company to win the 24 Hours of Le Mans, with a rotary-powered sports racing car.

warm up
To allow an engine to reach its normal operating temperature from a cold start.

warm-up regulator
In a fuel injection system, a device used to adjust air/fuel mixture while the engine is warming up from a cold start.

warning light
Red light on a dashboard which illuminates when a specific malfunction has occurred, such as overheating or loss of oil pressure. The disadvantage of a warning light is that it does not come on until the malfunction has happened whereas, with an appropriate gauge, an attentive driver could see an incipient problem developing and take corrective action before the problem actually takes place. See also *idiot light.*

warp
Slight twist or curve in a surface which should be absolutely straight.

washboard
Corrugated surface on an unpaved road, caused by the repeated bouncing of vehicle wheels on the road.

washer
Round metal device with a hole in the middle for the shaft of a bolt; helps to secure a nut on a bolt tightly.

wastegate
Relief valve on a turbocharger which prevents the turbo from building up too much pressure. See also *turbocharger.*

water brake
Type of absorption unit found on some dynamometers. See also *dyno, dynamometer* and *prony brake.*

water burnout
See *burnout.*

water column
See *manometer.*

water diverter
Device to direct water flow in an engine block or head.

water filter
Replaceable filter to remove impurities from engine coolant.

water glass
See *sodium silicate.*

waterjacket
In an engine, a passage which conveys water through the block or head.

water-heated choke
Bi-metal spring on a carburetor that opens the throttle valve during warm up when the coolant reaches a specified temperature.

water pump
Pump which applies pressure to circulate coolant throughout an engine. See photo next page.

water soluble
Any material which will dissolve in water. Any oil that is able to mix with water.

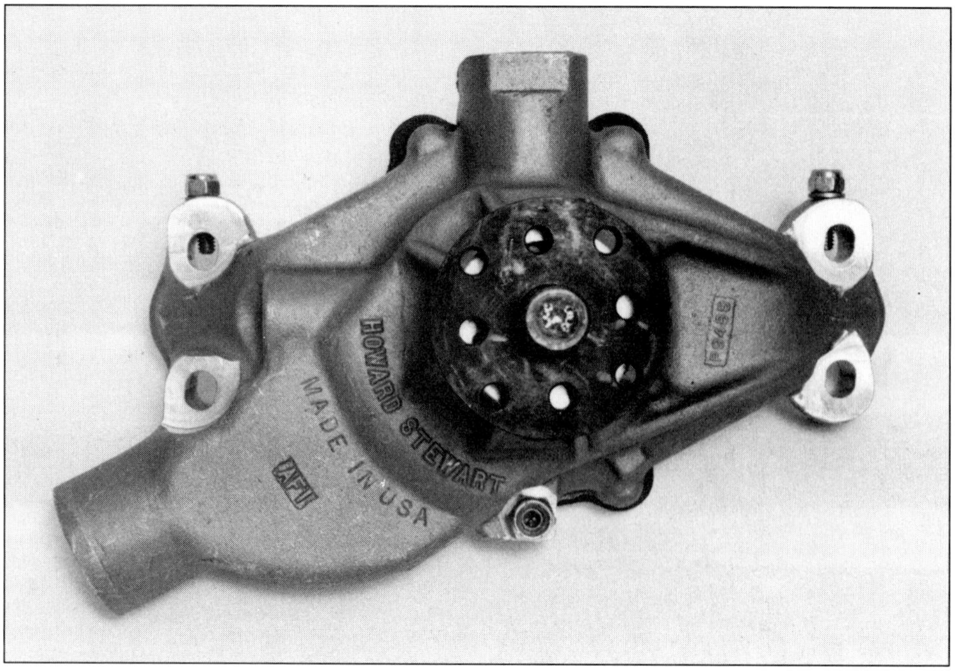

water pump

watt
Unit of measure of electrical power. One watt is equivalent to one ampere of electrical flow under one volt of pressure. The term is named for James Watt, an 18th and 19th century Scottish engineer and inventor best known for perfecting the steam engine.

wattage
Specific quantity of electrical power, measured in watts or kilowatts.

Watt's linkage
Three-bar arrangement to prevent lateral movement of a live rear axle or de Dion axle. Like the unit of electrical power, the watt, Watt's linkage was named for James Watt. Consequently, the spelling "Watts linkage," with an "s" but without an apostrophe, is wrong.

wave scavenging
Resonating within the exhaust system that increases the rate of extraction of exhaust gasses.

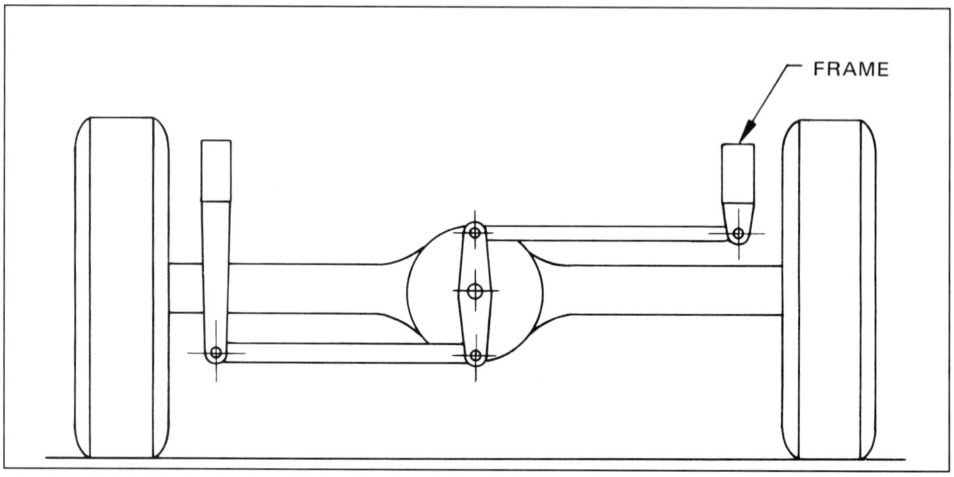

Watt's linkage

wax
1. A specially formulated compound designed to shine or improve a surface. Waxes are usually paraffinic or esters of long-chain fatty acids with long chain alcohols.
2. To beat another competitor decisively in a race.

wear limit
Manufacturer's recommendation as to how long a part should be serviceable.

wear-mated parts
Condition when parts rub or wear against each other.

wedge
In oval track racing, to raise or lower a car's springs with small blocks or wedges. The object is to shift weight distribution slightly in hopes of improving handling. See also *jacking*, def. 1.

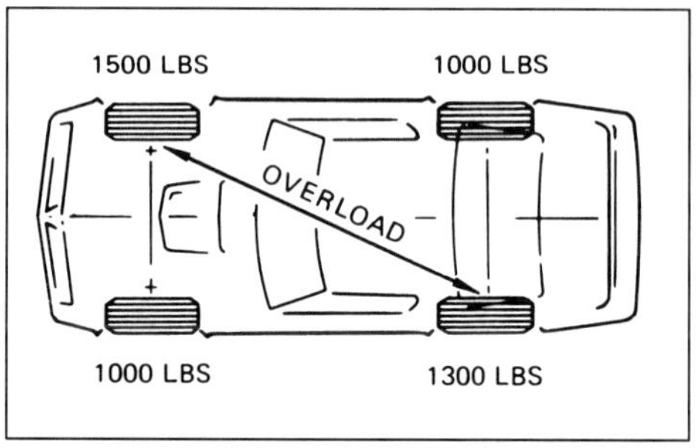

wedged car

wedge head
Cylinder head with wedge-shaped combustion chambers that provide a large *quench area*. In a wedge head, the intake and exhaust valves are usually, though not necessarily, in the same plane.

weedburners
On a drag car, exhaust headers which swoop down and to the rear, ending close to the ground.

weekend warrior
Racer who may compete on Saturday or Sunday but spends the rest of the week at a normal job, as opposed to a racer devoted to racing as a full-time occupation. Same as a *flyboy*.

weenie
See *wienie.*

weight distribution
In general, the percentage of a vehicle's overall weight on the front wheels and on the rear wheels. In oval track racing, the percentage of overall weight on each individual wheel.

weight-to-power ratio
Relationship of vehicle weight to horsepower; a 2000-pound car with 100 horsepower has 20 pounds per horsepower. Do not confuse with *power-to-weight ratio.*

weight transfer
Momentary shift of a vehicle's center of gravity forward or rearward as a result of sudden braking or acceleration. In drag racing, weight transfer at the instant a vehicle starts moving adds to the load on the rear wheels and thereby provides a momentary improvement in traction. See also *lateral weight transfer.*

wet liner, wet sleeve
Cylinder liner not contained by the existing cylinder wall and, therefore, in contact with the coolant.

whale tail
Large horizontal spoiler at the rear of a vehicle.

wheel adapter
Metal plate to allow the use of a wheel with one bolt pattern on a vehicle with another bolt pattern.

wheelbase
Distance from the center of the front wheel to the center of the rear wheel on the same side of the vehicle.

wheel cans
Wheelwells on a race car with a full-width body, such as a *stocker.* See also *wheel tubs.*

wheel cylinder
Same as *brake cylinder.*

wheel estate
Mobile home.

wheelie
Wheelstand. At the start of a drag race, power may be applied to the rear wheels so suddenly that the front wheels are lifted right off the ground. Wheelies look spectacular but most top dragster drivers try to avoid them because they waste power that is better applied to making the car move straight down the strip as quickly as possible. However, there have been some exhibition cars built to do wheelies intentionally for the sheer crowd-pleasing thrill of it.

wheelie bars
On some drag racing cars, a pair of long bars with wheels at the end which extend rearward from the vehicle and are intended to prevent front wheelstanding.

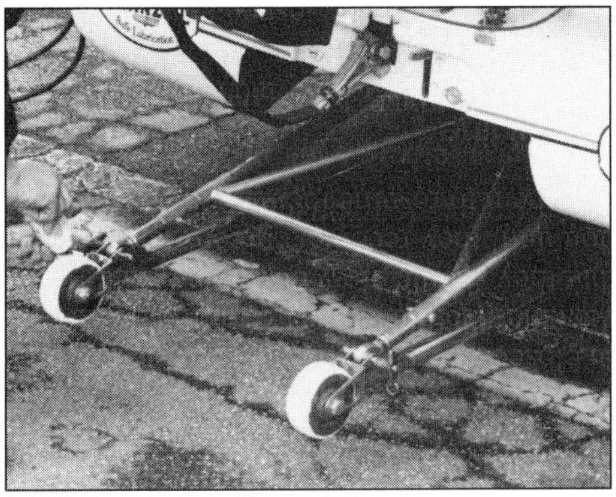

wheelie bars

wheel meter
Chassis dynamometer.

wheel offset
Wheel rim offset from the center of the mounting flange. If the rim is placed inward from the flange, it has *negative offset.* If it is placed outward from the flange, it has *positive offset.*

wheel shimmy
Rapid, side-to-side vibration of steered wheels, usually because of imbalance.

wheels
Car, especially one for everyday transportation.

wheel tubs
Replacement wheelwells installed to accommodate oversize tires. See *tubbed.*

white flag
In closed-course racing, a signal to a driver that he is about to start the last lap of an event.

whoop-dee-doo
In off-road racing, a bump or dip severe enough to get a speeding vehicle airborne.

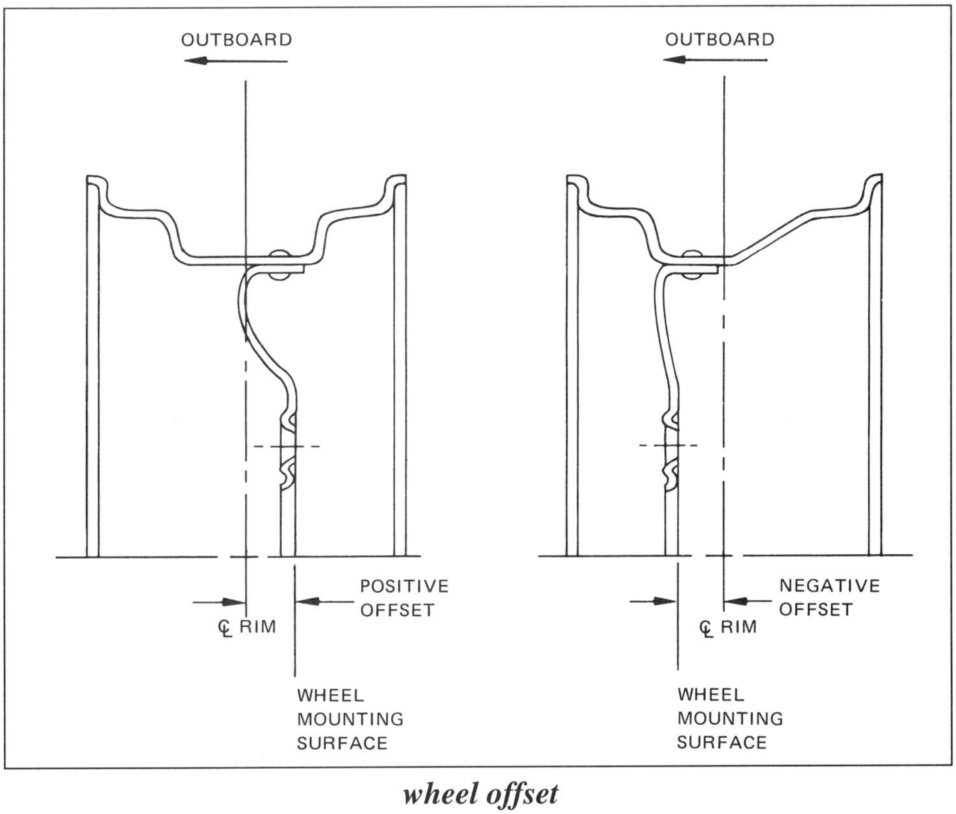

wheel offset

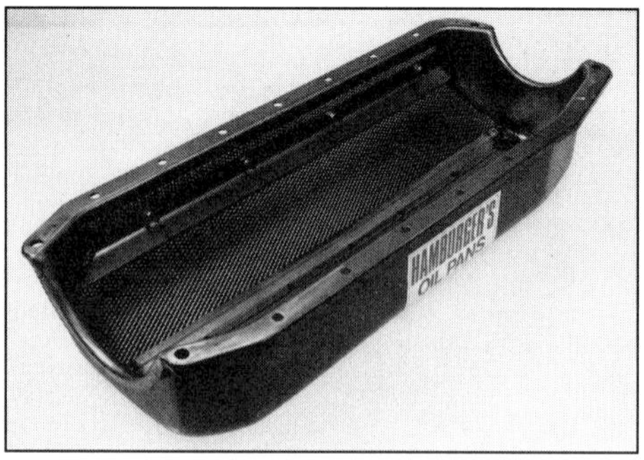

windage tray

wide ratios
Transmission setup with broad spreads between speeds in individual gears; wide ratios are important with small, low-powered engines because they allow a broader, more flexible range of road speeds. See also *close ratios*.

wienie
Tire, especially a drag racing slick.

wienie roaster
Jet-powered car for drag racing or lakes competition.

wild
Outstanding in appearance or performance.

Willys
The Willys-Overland Company of Toledo, Ohio, was founded in 1907 when New York auto dealer John North Willys bought the ailing Overland Company. Without question, the most famous product in Willys' long history was the military Jeep of World War II. Among hot rodders, Willys is also well remembered for its light-weight coupe bodies of the 1930s and early 1940s. Willys-Overland survived as an independent automaker until 1953, when it was absorbed by Kaiser. Ten years later, the company was renamed Kaiser Jeep Corporation. In 1970, Kaiser Jeep was bought out by American Motors Corporation. AMC, in turn, was taken over by Chrysler Corporation in 1988. See also *Jeep*.

winch
Power-driven spool with a wire cable, used for pulling or lifting. A winch is a popular accessory for a four-wheel-drive vehicle, because it can often be used to extricate the vehicle if it gets stuck.

wing

windage tray
In an engine crankcase, a metal meshed screen in the oil pan used to deflect oil away from the crankshaft as it rotates. That reduces the load on the crankshaft, thus providing an increase in horsepower, though admittedly a miniscule increase.

winded time
In drag racing, a 1/4-mile time recorded with the advantage of a tailwind.

windmill
Supercharger.

windscreen
British term for *windshield*, see below.

windshield
The forward-facing window on a motor vehicle, through which the driver views the road. The name derives from the fact that the first windshields were designed to

deflect wind from an open cockpit, or to prevent flying parts from striking a driver, in an accident.

window net
On some stock-bodied race cars, such as NASCAR stockers, a net in the window of the driver's door which serves as a restraining device to keep the driver's arm inside the cockpit.

Windsor V-8
Ford 351-W (for Windsor), a 351-CID V-8 built in Windsor, Ontario, Canada. See also *Cleveland V-8.*

wind-up
1. To rev an engine, particularly for maximum speed on a straightaway.
2. During hard acceleration in a car with rear-wheel-drive and rear leaf springs, tendency of the axle housing to rotate with the wheels, causing the springs to wind up slightly and then snap back. Once this action is underway, it may repeat several times until the driver releases the accelerator. See also *axle tramp, axle wind-up.*

wing
Spoiler, particularly one wing-like in shape; an open-wheeled race car, for example, may have a wing at the nose, or wings at either side of the nose, to apply aerodynamic force that will hold the front of the vehicle on the ground at high speeds. See photo previous page. See also *spoiler.*

wing nut
Small nut with wing-like flanges that make it easier to twist by hand.

wipe
To defeat another competitor in a race.

wiped out
Defeated or crashed.

wiring diagram
Map-like chart that shows the placement of wiring in a vehicle and the proper color of individual wires. Also called a *schematic.*

wiring harness, wiring loom
Major assembly of a vehicle's wiring system, with the wires properly color-coded and bundled together.

wishbone
Same as *A-arm, A-frame.*

witness lines
Lines scribed on the surface of adjacent parts during disassembly, so that they can be realigned properly when they are put back together.

wobble
Any unsteady movement off a normal axis.

WOO
World of Outlaws, 624 Krona Drive, Suite 150, Plano, Texas 75074; (214) 424-2202. Sprint car racing organization, an "outlaw" in relation to established race sanctioning associations such as USAC.

Woodruff key
Half moon-shaped key used to secure a pulley or gear to a shaft.

woody
Vehicle, particularly a station wagon, with wood-paneled bodywork. Originally, station wagon bodies were built of wood; today, though, the wood paneling is usually simulated.

work hardening
Brittleness of a metal part caused by stress from bending, hammering, rotating or rubbing against another part or other parts.

works team
Official, factory-supported racing team.

worm and sector
Steering assembly with a *worm gear* at the end of the steering column, engaging a *sector gear*, which converts the rotary motion of the worm to the straight-line motion of the pitman arm.

worm bearing preload
Adjustment of the worm gear bearing to control backlash.

worm gear
Gear at the end of the steering column in a worm and sector steering system. See *worm and sector*, above.

worm hole
Galvanic reaction in fast moving coolant that erodes metal away from the outer walls of wet cylinder sleeves.

WOT
Wide open throttle.

wraparound headers
Exhaust headers which fit closely to the engine block.

wraparound seat
Bucket seat which conforms to the body and provides good lateral support.

wrinkled paint
Type of paint that, when dry, has a wrinkled texture.

wrinkled walls
Sidewalls on drag racing slicks which wrinkle because of the very low inflation pressure used in such tires.

wrist pin
Pin which attaches the piston to the connecting rod. Also called a *piston pin.*

wrist pin bushing
Bronze bushing, sometimes steel-backed, which supports the wrist pin in a connecting rod.

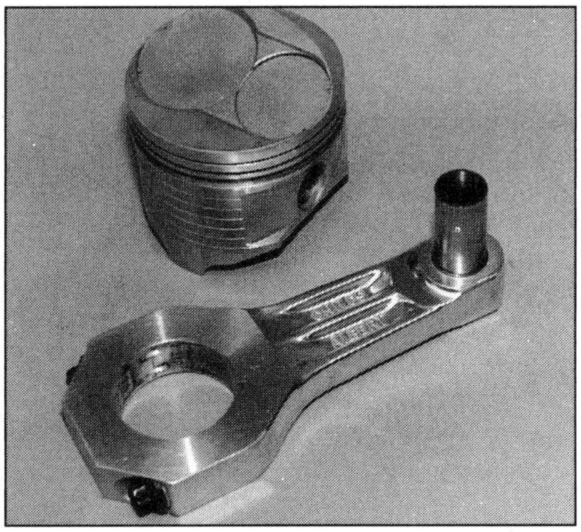

piston & connecting rod with wrist pin

XYZ

X axis
1. Longitudinal axis around which a vehicle structure rolls from side to side. See also *roll.*
2. Right to left movement on a milling machine.

X-drilled crank
See *cross-drilled crank.*

X-member
X-shaped structural reinforcement in a chassis frame.

xylene
C_8H_{11}, chemical solvent used to remove paint and grease.

yaw
Rotation of a vehicle structure around a vertical axis. See *Z axis.*

Y axis
1. Lateral axis around which a vehicle pitches fore and aft. See also *pitch.*
2. In and out movement on a milling machine.

Y block
V-type engine with a deep crankcase that, in cross section, looks more like a "Y" than a "V."

Y pipe
Y-shaped pipe which merges two passages into one.

yellow bumper
Freshman driver in NASCAR competition. During his first year on NASCAR tracks, a driver is required to have a yellow rear bumper on his car to let other drivers know he is a novice. As a result, the driver himself is called a yellow bumper or *yellowtail.*

yellow flag, yellow light
In closed-course racing, a signal to the drivers that there is a hazard on the track and that they should slow down and hold position until they receive a green flag permitting them to resume racing.

yellow line
1. Initial rev limit on a tachometer before reaching *red line.*
2. On an oval track, especially Indy, the line separating the *apron* from the racing track. At Indy, if a competitor crosses the yellow line when exiting the pit lane before the designated area, he or she is penalized.

yellowtail
See *yellow bumper.*

yield strength
Amount of force that can be applied to a material before it deforms or breaks.

Z
To lower a car by cutting Z-like notches in the chassis frame.

zap
1. To defeat an opponent.
2. As a verb, to overrev an engine enough to damage it. Zap in this sense usually means a deliberate overrev, as in a *banzai* effort. Drivers not in serious contention during a race have also been known to zap their engines intentionally in order to blame their withdrawal from the event on mechanical failure.

Z axis
1. Vertical axis around which a vehicle structure yaws, i.e., the front and rear ends swing back and forth. See also *yaw.*
2. Up and down movement on a milling machine.

zerk fitting
Nipple-like projection on vehicle parts, particularly on the chassis and suspension, through which a lubricant can be applied. Also called a grease fitting or *zirc fitting.*

zero emissions vehicle
Vehicle which discharges no exhaust pollutants. In practice, only an electric-powered car or truck would qualify as a zero emissions vehicle and even its claim is marred by the fact its ultimate source of electricity may be a fossil-fueled generating plant which discharges pollutants into the air.

zero gap ring
Piston ring without any clearance at the ends.

zero lash
Lack of clearance between a valve lifter and camshaft lobe.

zero toe
Setting of wheels so that they point straight ahead, without any *toe in* or *toe out*.

ZEV
See *zero emissions vehicle*.

ZF
Zahnradfabrik Friedrichshafen, a German manufacturer of transmissions and transaxles for high-performance cars.

zing
To overrev an engine unintentionally, as in an unexpected downshift.

zirc fitting
Grease fitting made of a zirconium alloy with the tradename *Zircaloy*. See *zerk fitting*.

zoomies
On an open-wheeled drag racing vehicle, exhaust headers which swoop back and upward toward the top of the rear tires. The blast of hot air they direct toward the top of the tires supposedly blows dirt off the rubber just before it contacts the strip on its next rotation. Also, the zoomies create a streamlining effect in the pattern of airflow by guiding it over the blunt tire area.

Zyglow
Type of non-destructive testing using a dye penetrant and ultraviolet light to check non-magnetic parts for faults or cracks.

zoomies

BIBLIOGRAPHY

Alexander, Don, and John Block. *The Racer's Dictionary*. Santa Ana, California: Steve Smith Autosports, 1980.

Ash, David. "Glossary of Terms," *Automobile Almanac*. New York: Simon and Schuster, 1967, pp. 169-183.

Atteberry, Pat H. "Glossary," *Power Mechanics*. South Holland, Illinois: Goodheat-Willcox Co., 1986, pp. 119-123.

An Automotive Styling Glossary. Dearborn, Michigan: Styling Office, Ford Motor Company, 1966.

Baskerville, Gray. "How to Talk Hot Rod," *Hot Rod Yearbook 1988*. Los Angeles: Petersen Publishing Co., 1988, pp. 143-144.

Berggren, Dr. Dick. "Glossary of Handling Terms," *Stock Car Racing*, March 1972, pp. 68-69.

Carley, Larry W. "Glossary," *Do-It-Yourself Car Care*. Blue Ridge Summit, Pennsylvania: Tab Books, 1984, pp. 173-215.

Christy, John, editor. "Understanding Hot Rod Language," *Building and Racing the Hot Rod*. New York: New American Library, 1966, pp. 49-74.

Csere, Csaba. "Technical Glossary," *Car and Driver*, Part I, October 1988, pp. 107-111; Part II, November 1988, pp. 131, 135, 138-139; Part III, December 1988, pp. 89-93.

Dickson, Paul. "Automotive Slang: How to Speak Car Talk," *Slang!: The Topic-by-Topic Dictionary of Contemporary American Lingoes*. New York: Pocket Books, 1990, pp. 22-36.

Diefendorf, Robert. "Light Truck Lexicon," *Pickup, Van & 4WD*, Part I, June 1992, pp. 39-46; Part II, July 1982, pp. 39-43, 45.

Dinkel, John. *The Road & Track Illustrated Auto Dictionary*. New York: W.W. Norton and Co., 1977.

[Fermoyle, Ken.] "How to Talk RV," *Wheels Afield*, December 1972, pp. 56, 58.

Finch, Richard. "Glossary of Terms," *Welder's Handbook*. Los Angeles: HPBooks, 1985, pp. 153-155.

Fitch, James William. "Glossary of Terms," *Motor Truck Engineering Handbook*, 3rd Edition. Anacortes, Washington: Published by the author, 1984, pp. 269-282.

Fournier, Ron and Sue. "Glossary," *Metal Fabricator's Handbook*. Los Angeles: HPBooks, 1990, pp. 172-173.

Fournier, Ron and Sue. "Glossary," *Sheet Metal Handbook*. Los Angeles: HPBooks, 1989, pp. 129-131.

Gilbert, Jim. "How to Talk Two-Wheeler," *Mini-Bike Guide*, October 1971, pp. 41-42.

Glasstone, Samuel, Ph.D. *Energy Deskbook*. New York: Van Nostrand Reinhold Co., 1983.

Glossary of Automotive Terms, SP 750. Warrendale, Pennsylvania: Society of Automotive Engineers, 1988.

Goodsell, Don. *Dictionary of Automotive Engineering*. Warrendale, Pennsylvania: Society of Automotive Engineers, 1989.

Harris, Bill and Hunter. *Automotive Answer Book*. Reston, Virginia: Reston Publishing Co., 1982.

Horner, Jim. "Glossary," *Automotive Electrical Handbook*. Los Angeles: HPBooks, 1986, pp. 154-156.

Horsley, Fred. "Hot Talk: A Glossary of Hot Rod Terms," *The Hot Rod Handbook*. New York: J. Lowell Pratt and Co., 1965, pp. 208-212.

"How to Talk Racing," *Mopar Performance News*, August 1990, pp. 18-19.

Lawlor, John. *Auto Math Handbook*. Los Angeles: HPBooks, 1991.

Lawlor, John. *How to Talk Car*. Chicago: Topaz-Felsen Books, 1965.

Leavell, Stuart, and Stanley Bungay. *Standard Aircraft Handbook*, 5th edition, edited by Larry Reithmaier. Blue Ridge Summit, Pennsylvania, 1990.

Lent, Henry B. "Glossary: Words and Terms Used in a Styling Studio," *The Look of Cars*. New York: E.P. Dutton and Co., 1966, pp. 152-153.

Lewin, Esther and Albert E. *The Random House Thesaurus of Slang*. New York: Random House, 1988.

MacDonald, Johnny. "Auto Racing Glossary," *Under the Green: A Complete Guide to Auto Racing*. New York: Peebles Press, 1979, pp. 217-219.

MacInnes, Hugh. "Glossary," *Turbochargers*. Los Angeles: HPBooks, 1984, p. 168.

McFarland, Jim. "Glossary of Terms," *The Great Manifold Bolt-On!* El Segundo, California: Edelbrock Corp., 1982, pp. 108-110.

Nagy, Bob. "CarWords: A Basic Glossary of Automotive Terminology," *Motor Trend*, Part I, October 1981, pp. 79-83; Part II, November 1981, pp. 35-36, 39-41.

Owen, Keith, and Trevor Coley. "Glossary of Terms," *Automotive Fuels Handbook*. Warrendale, Pennsylvania: Society of Automotive Engineers, 1990, pp. 481-508.

Puhn, Fred. *How to Make Your Car Handle*. Los Angeles, HPBooks, 1981.

Porter, John Paul, editor. "Glossary," *The Time-Life Book of the Family Car*. New York: Time-Life Books, 1973, pp. 342-347.

Radosta, John S. "Glossary," *The New York Times Complete Guide to Auto Racing*. Chicago: Quadrangle Books, 1971, pp. 205-220.

[Shedenhelm, W.R.C.] "Grand Prix Glossary," *Sports Car Graphic*, January 1966, pp. 69-70.

Stone, William S. "Glossary," *A Guide to American Sports Car Racing*. Garden City, New York: Doubleday and Co., 1963, pp. 204-208.

Tak, Montie. *Truck Talk*. Philadelphia: Chilton Book Co., 1971.

Truck & Bus Glossary, SP-732. Warrendale, Pennsylvania: Society of Automotive Engineers, 1988.